Human Rights and Charity Law

The 60 or so nations that subscribe to the common law tradition had for centuries broadly accepted the same legal definitions of what constitutes a charity. In recent years, however, a number of countries have embarked on charity law reform processes, designed to strengthen the regulatory framework and to review and encode common law concepts. A primary driver of reform was the need to modernise national charity law and ensure human rights compatibility. In light of these reforms, this book takes stock of how charity law is adapting to face the challenges presented by human rights.

The book identifies the key areas where human rights and charity law intersect and examines the importance of those areas, the principles involved and their political significance. It offers a comparative analysis of selected common law countries including England, Wales, Ireland, US, Canada, Australia and New Zealand, assessing the extent of national human rights and charity compatibility. Kerry O'Halloran also goes on to consider tensions arising from the intersection of human rights and charity law, including the significance of cultural values and heritage, the importance of proportionality and striking a balance between public and private interests in current society.

Kerry O'Halloran is Adjunct Professor at the Australian Centre for Philanthropy and Nonprofit Studies, QUT, Australia.

Human Rights and International Law
Series Editor: Professor Surya P. Subedi, O.B.E.

This series will explore human rights law's place within the international legal order, offering much-needed interdisciplinary and global perspectives on human rights' increasingly central role in the development and implementation of international law and policy.

Human Rights and International Law is committed to providing critical and contextual accounts of human rights' relationship with international law theory and practice. To achieve this, volumes in the series will take a thematic approach that focuses on major debates in the field, looking at how human rights impacts on areas as diverse and divisive as security, terrorism, climate change, refugee law, migration, bioethics, natural resources and international trade.

Exploring the interaction, interrelationship and potential conflicts between human rights and other branches of international law, books in the series will address both historical development and contemporary contexts, before outlining the most urgent questions facing scholars and policy makers today.

Available titles

Human Rights and Charity Law
International Perspectives
Kerry O'Halloran

Forthcoming titles

Human Rights and Development in International Law
Tahmina Karimova

Adoption Law and Human Rights
International Perspectives
Kerry O'Halloran

The Right to Truth in International Law
Victims' Rights in Human Rights and International Criminal Law
Melanie Klinkner and Howard Davis

About the series editor

Professor Surya P. Subedi, O.B.E. is Professor of International Law, University of Leeds, member of the Institut de Droit International and former UN Special Rapporteur for human rights in Cambodia.

Human Rights and Charity Law

International Perspectives

Kerry O'Halloran

Routledge
Taylor & Francis Group

LONDON AND NEW YORK

First published 2016 by Routledge

2 Park Square, Milton Park, Abingdon, Oxfordshire OX14 4RN
52 Vanderbilt Avenue, New York, NY 10017

Routledge is an imprint of the Taylor & Francis Group, an informa business

First issued in paperback 2020

British Library Cataloguing in Publication Data
A catalogue record for this book is available from the British Library

Library of Congress Cataloging-in-Publication Data
Names: O'Halloran, Kerry, author.
Title: Human rights and charity law / Kerry O'Halloran.
Description: New York: Routledge, 2016. | Series: Human rights and international law | Includes bibliographical references and index.
Identifiers: LCCN 2015040262 | ISBN 9781138956575 (hbk) | ISBN 9781315665696 (ebk)
Subjects: LCSH: Charity laws and legislation. | Human rights.
Classification: LCC K797 .O367 2016 | DDC 344.03/17—dc23
LC record available at http://lccn.loc.gov/2015040262

ISBN: 978-1-138-95657-5 (hbk)
ISBN: 978-0-367-59692-7 (pbk)

Typeset in Galliard
by Apex CoVantage, LLC

Contents

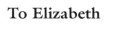
To Elizabeth

Acknowledgements

Sincere thanks are owed to Professor Myles McGregor-Lowndes[1] for his support and friendship and to the Australian Centre for Philanthropy and Nonprofit Studies for offering me an academic base to conduct the research for what is steadily growing to become a small shelf-full of charity law related books. This one necessarily overlaps to a slight degree with others completed during my tenure with the Centre and I am thankful to the publishers concerned, particularly to Elgar Publishing,[2] to Springer,[3] Oxford University Press[4] and to Cambridge University Press[5] for their understanding in respect of any material that may have first seen life under their imprint.

Thanks are also due to those who offered comment on draft chapters. In particular I much appreciated the helpful feedback received from Myles McGregor-Lowndes (Australia); Gerard Whyte[6] (Ireland); Terrance Carter[7] and Anna du Vent (Canada), Putnam Barber[8] (United States); and Dr Michael Gousmett[9] and Sue Barker[10] (New Zealand).

1   Director, the Australian Centre of Philanthropy and Nonprofit Studies, Queensland University of Technology, Brisbane, Australia.
2   McGregor-Lowndes, M. and O'Halloran, K. (eds.), *Modernising Charity Law: Recent Developments and Future Directions*, Elgar Publications, Cheltenham, October 2010.
3   O'Halloran, K., McGregor-Lowndes, M. and Simon, K., *Charity Law & Social Policy: National and International Perspectives on the Functions of the Law Relating to Charities*, Springer, The Netherlands, 2009.
4   O'Halloran, K., *The Profits of Charity*, OUP, New York, 2012.
5   O'Halloran, K., *Religion, Charity and Human Rights*, CUP, Cambridge, 2014.
6   Professor of Law, Trinity College Dublin, Ireland.
7   Carters Professional Corporation, Ontario, Canada.
8   Renowned Seattle-based writer and commentator on public policy issues affecting the work of nonprofits.
9   Founding Trustee, The New Zealand Third Sector Educational Trust and co-author of *The Law and Practice of Charities in New Zealand*, LexisNexis, Wellington, 2013.
10 Director of Sue Barker Charities Law, a boutique law firm in Wellington and co-author of *The Law and Practice of Charities in New Zealand*, LexisNexis, Wellington, 2013.

It is a privilege to make this contribution to the series *Human Rights and International Law*, edited by Professor Surya P. Subedi, and I am grateful to Routledge for the opportunity to do so. Despite the editorial diligence of Katie Carpenter[11] and Olivia Manley,[12] some mistakes, inconsistencies and other faults of omission or commission may have found their way into print, in which case, responsibility for same, as for all views expressed, must rest exclusively with me.

---

11 Commissioning Editor, Routledge, Law.
12 Editorial Assistant, Routledge, Law.

Introduction

Is charity simply the flip side of rights? Both address social disadvantage, but are they alternatives or complementary? Does it matter if charity does the work of rights?

The argument in this book is that charity law developed in ways at variance with or contrary to the principles now regarded as fundamental to human rights; the resulting lack of congruity is evident from the nature of concerns identified in recent Human Rights Council reports and from the case law which records that charity and human rights rarely intersect, but that contemporary social pressures – such as the 2015 European migrant crisis – now require a political context within which these two important strands of democracy in our developed common law nations can and should act in a complementary fashion. The book, therefore, explores the frames of reference for charity and rights: examining the respective bodies of law and noting the type of issues on which they intersect and also, equally importantly, those where they do not. It –

- Identifies concepts and boundaries and explores the differences between charity and rights.
- Explains the key areas where human rights and charity law intersect, giving particular attention to the case law.
- Examines and assesses the importance of those areas, the principles involved and their significance.
- Profiles and analyses the interface between charity law and human rights in selected common law countries (England and Wales, Ireland, the US, Canada, Australia and New Zealand).
- Drawing from the above, undertakes a comparative analysis of characteristic national differences in the balance struck between human rights and charity law.

The geographic scope is limited to the above jurisdictions both because charity law is essentially a common law phenomenon and because recent national law reform programmes in those countries illustrate the difficulties experienced by legislators in addressing the tensions between human rights and charity law principles.

Human Rights and Charity Law: International Perspectives consists of ten chapters. Part I begins with a background section of three chapters. The first deals with frames of reference for charity and human rights and considers certain significant parameters. The second two explain core concepts, principles, precepts and legal definitions, provide an historical overview of the developing relationship between charity and human rights in a common law context and identifies their respective key legal functions. Part II, which constitutes the bulk of the book, deals with contemporary international perspectives and in six chapters focuses in turn on England and Wales, Ireland, the US, Canada, Australia and New Zealand. These jurisdiction-specific chapters closely follow the same format: an introductory background history showing how charity law has developed in a way inimical to human rights, leading into an account of the public benefit contribution of both to civil society; a mid-section that outlines the relevant contemporary legislative and regulatory framework for the two bodies of law, noting government efforts to achieve congruity through charity law reform as contrasted with critical comments in recent reports from the Human Rights Council; then the substantive case law section that demonstrates, in relation to specific Universal Declaration of Human Rights articles, how and in what circumstances charity law and human rights continue to be mutually incompatible. Part III, the final section that consists of one chapter, concludes the book by drawing from Part II material to examine the nature of the tensions in the present relationship between these two bodies of law, to consider the significance of cultural context and reflect upon the relevance of contemporary politics.

Kerry O'Halloran
White Park Bay,
Autumn, 2015
k.ohalloran@qut.edu.au

Part I

Background

1 Frames of reference, boundaries and social context

Introduction

Arguably, 'charity' and 'human rights' are positioned at opposite ends of a legal spectrum of benign intervention in the affairs of citizens. The former is essentially discretionary, any assistance offered – relevant or otherwise – resting on the whim of a donor and, as legally defined, restricted to charitable purpose beneficiaries. The latter is available on demand as need requires and designed to assertively redress instances of social injustice. This view sees both as formally recognising that the normal functioning of society can leave individuals and groups exposed and vulnerable: they share a concern to set thresholds for intervention, protect the disadvantaged from abuse or exploitation and to prevent or offset the undermining of socially acceptable values and standards. It is a view that necessarily presupposes a democratic society in which policy places importance on maintaining the checks and balances necessary to promote pluralism, a sense of fairness and overall social coherence. This chapter explores the reality behind such a perception, examines the laws governing both frames of reference, considers other forms of mediation and establishes their respective boundaries.

The chapter, accordingly, falls into two halves. It begins by considering the primary modes of mediating on behalf of those in need. Starting with charity and the 'gift relationship' as conceived by Titmuss,[1] it briefly summarises other forms of mediation. It then focuses on the advantages offered by legal rights and examines more closely what might be seen as the two mutually exclusive approaches: charity and legal rights. It outlines and analyses the frames of reference provided by legal rights, justice and charity, drawing attention to the distinction between 'charity' as it is commonly understood and as legally defined. It leaves to Chapter 2, a more detailed examination of both the legal meaning of 'charity' and the extension of legal rights into fundamental human rights; and to Chapter 3, an analysis of the legal system as it relates to charity and human rights. It notes and reflects on areas of boundary permeability, identifying and evaluating themes common to rights and charity in a modern common law social context.

---

1 See, Titmuss, R., *The Gift Relationship: From Human Blood to Social Policy*, Allen and Unwin, London, 1970.

As the legal functions of charity and rights are dependent upon social context, the second half begins with an overview of social liberalism, as this is the
democratic model of society shared by the common law nations currently being
studied. It briefly identifies and considers the distinguishing characteristics of this
model compared with others, reflects broadly upon the significance of politics
and political ideology, before focusing on the current primary relevant social
policy concerns of government in those nations. It gives particular attention to
the key concepts of 'social capital' and 'civil society', the roles and expectations
prescribed to them in the post-9/11 era, and discusses the meaning, cause and
effects of the phenomenon known as the 'culture wars'. It considers the relationship between that phenomenon and the roles of charity and legal rights and
assesses any implications arising for building and consolidating civil society.

Charity as a mode of mediation on behalf of those in need

The Bible advises or admonishes that 'the poor you will always have with you',[2]
the corollary being that charity will similarly always be assured of a role in society. For some resigned to this symbiotic relationship there is consolation to be
found in the opportunities thus provided for demonstrating virtuous behaviour
which serves to alleviate hardship, develop altruistic methods of mediation and
generate the civic engagement that helps bond communities and promote social
cohesion. The 'gift relationship' as conceived by Titmuss and outlined below is
an exemplar of such a viewpoint.[3] For others, there is the view that charity has
always been the foil of capitalism: it being seen as politically expedient to leave
to charity the needs of those who fail and must pay the price for a society driven
by the competitive forces that constitute an 'open market' economy. A capitalist
society requires winners and losers, and charity is assured of a permanent role in
such a society in order to rescue the victims, salve the conscience of the successful and paper over the cracks sufficiently to allow capitalism to continue. Neither
view does justice to the more nuanced role of charity, as legally defined, in the
modern common law nations that are the subject of this study.

The 'gift relationship'

The moral and sociological intricacies that characterise the involvement of the
parties engaged in acts of charity have been explored by Titmuss in what he has
called 'the gift relationship' which he saw as epitomising the customary social
interpretation of that concept. He examined the act of 'giving', seeing it as the
voluntary and altruistic act of an individual, and compared it with a commercial
system in a study which focused on blood donors. The contrast, as he saw it, was
between ethically based behaviour and behaviour motivated by self-interest. In

2 See, Matthew 26:11.
3 See, Titmuss, R., op. cit.

the former instance, the National Blood Transfusion Service in the UK provided a service to which blood donors made anonymous contributions without financial or other reward and from which recipients took according to need, incurring no cost and without knowing the identity of the donor. In Titmuss's view, this free gift of blood left the relationship between giver and recipient uncompromised by any 'contract of custom; legal bond; functional determinism; situations of discriminatory power; . . . domination, constraint or compulsion'.[4] On the other hand, he considered that the alternative approach to the same service in the US reduced people's willingness to donate blood because the transaction had become tarnished by commercialism causing such adverse consequences as the repression of expressions of altruism and an erosion of a sense of community. This 'gift relationship', it has been argued, is something that can bond us as a society.[5]

Altruism

Titmuss considered that the reason why people donated blood without direct reward, at a cost of their own time and effort, to another with whom they have no direct contact, was altruism. A regard for the needs of others was the principle that motivated their action. Donors showed a high sense of awareness of belonging to a community and of social responsibility. It followed that it was important for the State to provide the opportunity for individuals to express their commitment to the community in which they lived; indeed, he developed this theme in his final chapter, 'The Right to Give'. This right was to be valued in a democracy both for its own sake, and, because it demonstrated altruism, it would thereby encourage others to become givers.

However, while this was true in relation to blood donation – which was within the gift of any citizen, was given anonymously, and in respect of which any citizen may need to be a recipient – the transaction was unrepresentative. An act of giving per se certainly modelled ethical conduct and generated a sense of shared morality and civic responsibility in communities, but the Titmuss example was exceptional, as such acts were generally not anonymous and were directed wholly at donor discretion. This was explicitly true in respect of charitable gifts as defined in law, which further constrained a donor's freedom of action by requiring the gift to be directed towards recipients with the group characteristics prescribed by a particular charitable purpose. The fact that the giving is done on the basis of selection – positively discriminating in favour of designated beneficiaries to the exclusion of all others – is an aspect of charity law that fundamentally questions its compatibility with contemporary human rights provisions.

4 Ibid.
5 It was de Tocqueville who perhaps first identified the 'moral tie' between giver and receiver as a means of the creating the bonds to build a more cohesive and caring society.

The gift relationship and the State

For the State to endorse the gift relationship is to affirm a value system that encourages altruism, reinforces a sense of obligation, stimulates social capital, provides a basis for community bonding and builds a more ethical society. The State can only gain from endorsing conduct that attracts the involvement of an army of volunteers, bolsters civic responsibility and thereby fosters the growth of social capital, strengthens the community's 'moral tie'[6] and consolidates civil society.[7] In addition to being a catalyst for a more civil and morally based society, the encouragement of altruistic conduct also has the happy consequence of reducing State expenditure.

The 'price' of the gift relationship

Undeniably there is baggage attached to the gift relationship: the price to be paid for 'the right to give' is costly.

The position of the recipient is compromised. The gift is always an acknowledgement of deficit. The fact that the recipient recognises and is comforted by the inherent virtue of the giver, who may have given anonymously, and values and uses the gift as intended, does not necessarily mean that they thereby become any better equipped to cope. For the recipient, the psychological dynamics of the gift relationship can all too often serve to single them out and isolate them within society, confirm personal or group inadequacy and induce long-term compliant dependency.[8]

The status of the donor, and/or that of the charitable organisation that gives effect to the gift, is elevated. Registration as a charity confirms the special status of an organisation dedicated to furthering the public benefit of the disadvantaged, and in the eyes of society confers upon it the stamp of virtue. This may well attract personal awards and privileges, granting political access and leverage to those whose particular charitable cause currently finds favour with government, with possible follow-on opportunities to bid for service provision contracts. As neither the charity nor its representatives are necessarily any better than others in their field, nor necessarily positioned where social need is most acute, their elevated status can result in distorted perceptions of social priorities, generate dissension and detract from effective interagency co-ordination.

For the State, endorsing the gift relationship comes at a price, as it has to forego both the considerable tax revenue to which it would otherwise be entitled

---

6 See, de Tocqueville, A., *Democracy in America*, University of Chicago, Chicago, 2000 (1835).

7 See, for example, Bothwell, J., 'Indicators of a Healthy Civil Society' in Burbridge, J. (ed.), *Beyond Prince and Merchant: Citizen Participation and the Rise of Civil Society*, Institute of Cultural Affairs International, Brussels, 1997.

8 A sentiment expressed in *Campden Charities* (1881) 18 Ch D 310 as: 'it tends to demoralise the poor and benefit no one', per Sir George Jessel MR at p. 327.

and with it the right to choose which areas of social need should benefit from that tax quotient. The latter, of course, also provides wealth redistribution opportunities which can allow the State to institutionalise altruism as a significant hallmark of social democracy. Determining the category of beneficiary to be singled out as particularly socially disadvantaged, together with the type of related gift qualifying for charitable status and thus for tax exemption are, after all, clearly social policy matters of importance to any government. In circumstances where health services are suffering from lack of government funding while charitable donations make animal refuges among the wealthiest charities in the State, this can be a very real dilemma.

The effects of social labelling, of overt, if positive, discrimination and possible substitution for entitlements – which to a varying extent are intrinsic to the process of charitable intervention – can inhibit the capacity for more strategic intervention and bring charity into conflict with fundamental human rights. Arguably, if charity as legally defined is to find a credible role in modern society, one that sits respectably alongside social justice, human rights and politics, this will have to involve the realignment of 'need' and 'gift'. These twin components of the gift relationship must be appropriately matched in keeping with standards of equity, equality and non-discrimination.

Other modes of mediation

The collapse of the customary buffers between citizen and State – the kith and kin support networks, the good neighbour relationships of settled communities and the slow erosion of religious belief – together with the dislocation caused by social mobility as the nuclear family unit relocates in response to employment opportunities etc, increased the vulnerability of families and individuals. By the mid-20th century, while some in difficulty could still turn to the traditional form of support offered by family, charity or Church, others looked to more assertive mediation offered by politics, trades unions, professions and other forms of intervention. These differed from their predecessors by being powerful negotiating bodies assured of access to relevant decision-making forums on which they exercised considerable leverage. They offered a different model – one that featured assertive action on behalf of members to address problems, set minimum standards and improve collective best interests – which contrasted sharply with the role of the sole supplicant as prescribed by Church and charity.

Religion

The mutual support that shared religious belief gave to the citizens of the more homogenous common law societies in earlier centuries has long since been dissipated. Partially this has been due to the relentless challenges presented by modern scientific discoveries into areas which for previous generations had been governed by religious belief: religions have shrunk as their adherents exchange inherited belief systems and spiritual and moral values for the new verities of

scientifically established knowledge. Partially it has been a consequence of a continuing process of religious fragmentation: the major religions experiencing a
number of subdivisions with, for example, more extreme Islamic organisations
and more evangelical Christian groups gaining adherents and prominence but
causing more moderate adherents to abandon a religious belief capable of generating such virulence, a process accompanied by a proliferation of emerging and
often transient belief systems in which a philosophical approach has replaced the
roles previously allocated to doctrines and God or gods. The outcome has been a
steady rise in the atheist proportion of the population of such societies.

The general retreat of religion and the diminishing power of the Church has
naturally led to a similar contraction in the latter's influence on the everyday
problems of its adherents. Throughout the 20th century, the increased secularisation of matters central to the traditional role of the Church in the community –
marriage, education, child care etc – inexorably redefined that role. More
importantly, perhaps, the fading role of the Church as mediator on behalf of
those in need has taken with it the traditional accompanying attitudes of suppli-
cation, deference and a resigned acceptance of God's will as a sufficient response
to difficult circumstances.

Mutual benefit organisations

Sometimes overlooked but of considerable importance in re-ordering the space
between Church, State and citizen was the emergence of organisations formed
to provide sustained economic security for its members, such as guilds, mutual
benefit associations and the Credit Union movement[9] which developed around
principles that required ownership, labour and profits to be shared among
their members. The Industrial and Provident Societies, the Friendly Societies,
co-operatives and community benefit societies, all with a mission to conduct
business for the benefit of their members or community, became established
in the 19th century. Many mutual benefit organisations were also self-help in
nature, often short-term with a single-issue focus and with governance arrangements heavily weighted in favour of user representation. These included housing
associations, community development organisations, and training for employment associations.

Together with other forms of associational activity dedicated to the pursuit of
social improvement, such organisations shifted the concept of citizenship away
from simple subservience to Church and State by laying the foundations for
what was to become the nonprofit sector and formed the basis of a new strategic
socio-economic counterbalance to the government and commerce sectors. They
initiated new models of collective action for the mutual benefit of members and

---

9 Organisations set up for the mutual benefit of members have consistently been refused charitable status: see, for example, *Nuffield (Lord) v Inland Revenue Commissioners* (1946) 175
LT 465.

provided opportunities for the latter to revise policy, set goals and hold others to account. In so doing they demonstrated the advantages of entities independent of Church and State that could control and direct the use of their own resources.

Politics

Politics as we now know it – collective movements, organised around an agreed agenda of policy and principles, intending to acquire the authority necessary to implement nationwide change and then organising to do so – is a relatively recent phenomenon. As a mode of mediation it has proven to be the best way to provide representation for and improve the circumstances of the socially disadvantaged. As Judt has noted:[10]

> Only a State can provide the services and conditions through which its citizens may aspire to lead a good or fulfilling life. These conditions vary across cultures. They may emphasize civic peace, solidarity with the less fortunate, public facilities of the infrastructural or even the high cultural sort, environmental amenities, free health care, good public education, and much else . . . only the State can adjudicate with reasonable impartiality between competing demands, interests, and goods. Most important, only the State can represent a shared consensus about which goods are positional and can be obtained only in prosperity, and which are basic and must be provided to everyone in all circumstances.

The party politics of modern social democracies have a tendency to dessicate rather than promote social cohesion – particularly as regards the agenda of contemporary social issues involving medical intervention on matters relating to life and death – e.g. abortion, birth control, euthanasia and genetic engineering – but by providing the means for balancing the competing claims of various interest groups, they also create the framework for pluralism. Given the alternatives, this has proven to be a better model (see, further, below). As centre-left politics have become the norm for modern western societies, with party politics locked into virtual stalemate, so politicians have sought to make progress through consensus on small issues of common interest rather than pursuing divisive 'big ideas'.

- THE 'WELFARE STATE'

This political experiment, by sketching the outer parameters of a State's responsibility for its citizens, had a profound impact upon the government/citizen relationship – with lasting consequences for the latter's perception of services that

---

10 Judt, T., *Reappraisals*, Vintage Books, London, 2008, at p. 423.

should be available as of right rather than as a charitable gift. Because it evolved most fully in the UK, it differentiated the development of the relationship in that jurisdiction from its equivalent in other common law nations.

The role politically assigned to charity in 1601 underwent a fundamental read-justment in the UK with the introduction in 1948 of the welfare state. This was intended to make health, social care, housing, education, welfare benefits etc as much the responsibility of government as the provision of such public utilities as roads, street lighting and tap water etc. By confering rights on citizens to such basic services, it removed the onus of provision from charities and consigned the latter to a role of filling in the gaps left by government. Arguably it was an approach that presaged that of human rights. By creating an interlocking floor comprised of different sets of services, it would prevent rather than ameliorate poverty; those in need would avail of non-stigmatising 'public' services as of right, in the same way as accessing a 'public' road, and not be left to submit to the 'deserving' criteria of charity (see, further, Chapter 10).

The UK was alone among the common law nations in fully experiencing the welfare state, and the model it represented of a politically defined government/citizen relationship built upon a radical rebalancing of charity and rights. Others shared in the experience, but to a lesser degree, and the jurisdictional variation in citizens' expectations of government differed accordingly. As will become apparent in Part II, the rolling up of this political experiment – as all common law governments reduce public service provision – has also had repercussions for the charity/rights balance and with a similar pattern of jurisdictional emphasis.

Trade unions

Following the abolition of serfdom and slavery, terms of employment had been established by an employer offering wages on conditions which a prospective employee was free to accept or reject. This traditional dynamic was altered by the emergence of bodies founded to represent the interests of their members, which negotiated with employers, government and other entities. To an extent these representative bodies were following in the footsteps of the guilds and confraternities that preceded them by several centuries.[11]

Trade unions made a positive contribution, not only to improving conditions for workers, but also in providing debating forums and social facilities that offered a supportive environment within which members could build a sense of collective solidarity and learn self-help strategies. The concepts of group representation, of bargaining and of contract that took hold over time have undoubtedly done much to erode certain attitudes – submissiveness, acceptance and compliance with authority – which contributed to sustaining the social roles of charity and religion.

---

11 See, Flack, T., 'Insights into the Origins of Organised Charity from the Catholic Tradition of Confraternities', Occasional Paper for Australian Centre of Philanthropy and Nonprofit Studies, Queensland University of Technology, Brisbane, 2008.

Throughout times when other nations were riven by totalitarian conflict and revolution, the trade unions in England seemed to stand on a middle ground demonstrating that collective bargaining could effect sufficient change in the lives of workers and their families to warrant rejecting alternative and more violent strategies.

Professions and professional bodies

One of the more significant 20th-century developments affecting relationships between citizen, family, and the State was the rise of the professional as the mediator of issues occurring within that context. This role did much to redress the power relationship between those in need and those with resources. By mediating in that space the professions have, perhaps, deskilled or demoted the family and further distanced the individual from traditional sources of support, but they also provided a tangible and accessible resource to which those with problems could turn and expect a response that respected their independence instead of inviting deference. The anonymity, confidentiality and problem-solving characteristics offered by a relationship with a chosen paid professional left authority and dignity with those in need of assistance and, when affordable, such a relationship was clearly more attractive than resorting as supplicant to the discretionary beneficence of Church or charity. The political leverage and negotiating power of profession-specific representative bodies, like their trade union counterparts, also did much to improve terms and conditions of employment on behalf of their members and to influence the shaping of related government policy.

Legal rights as a mode of mediation on behalf of those in need

It is customary to trace the earliest recognition of the more basic rights of citizens back to Magna Carta in 1215 when King John guaranteed his English subjects certain basic rights and freedoms including due legal process, with no one above the law, together with fair and impartial systems for administering justice and taxation. Principles that fell short of egalitarianism but permitted a broader interpretation of civil liberties were added following exposure to the French Revolution and the American Declaration of Independence, respectively.

The common law

The common law, which prevailed in England since the 12th century before being exported to its colonies, was grounded on the rights and duties of the individual.[12] There was no sense of collective legal interests, no provision was made

---

12 See, Sir William Blackstone, *Commentaries on the Laws of England*, Clarendon Press, Oxford, first published in 1765–1769.

for class or community actions, the law consisted merely of categories of causes actionable by or against individuals. The individual was left to apply to court and hope his or her needs would find legal recognition and redress. The changes introduced by concepts of legal rights and justice shifted the dynamic from the personal to the public domain. Only relatively recently, however, did this coalesce to become a sophisticated legal system governed by legislation and given effect through a complex web of legal functions (see, Chapter 3).

Unlike the civil law, which was adopted by the countries of mainland Europe and to a varying degree by many other countries, the common law was derived not from statute but from tradition, custom and judicial precedent as embodied in rules and interpreted and applied by the judiciary adopting an inquisitorial approach on a case-by-case basis. The common law, referred to as 'judge made law' and heavily reliant on case precedents, is readily distinguished from the prescriptive approach required by statutory law which relied mainly on an adjudication of the facts in accordance with relevant legislative provisions. The common law was distinguished by the following characteristics.

Judicial extension of law by analogy rather than principle

The common law approach of listing subjects for legal redress, permitting subsequent empirical extension by analogy, proved to be problematic. A grindingly logical approach led to the law being constrained by the rigidity of the specified where case law developments could only be accommodated by painstakingly distinguishing the facts of new cases from the old. Most importantly, at least until the Courts of Chancery gradually prevailed, the common law prevented the emergence of unifying principles which could have brought more cohesion. The result was evident in a reliance on endless lists and categorisation, with a consequent patchwork effect rather than a coherent body of law built around definitional statements and governed by clear principles.

Respect for social institutions

The common law would seem to be predicated on maintaining the status quo in society; most particularly it embodied a respect for social institutions and sources of authority by giving recognition to the government of the day, the place of religion, the role of the Church and the powers and duties of the judiciary. It was concerned less with matters of public policy and contemporary politics than with maintaining an almost feudal respect for king and country and for the institutions of the land.

Enforcement by financial penalties

The common law preoccupation with rules abstracted from precedents led to an intricate classification system that matched offences with penalties enforced by a tariff of fines. The business of levying and collecting fines required law enforcement to be concerned at least as much with administrative matters as with justice and adjudication.

Charity law and its common law context

The common law nations retained, to a varying degree, a shared legacy inherited by virtue of their participation in the British Empire. This provided the basis for subsequent similar jurisdictional developments in many areas, including charity law. Throughout the common law world, legislative inertia enabled charity law to survive into the 21st century relatively intact, shaped by the principles established through judicial precedent, as a pooled body of jurisprudence.

For most developed common law nations, the displacing of charity by rights was a phenomenon that only began to gather pace in the last half of the 20th century. International conventions and national legislation then began to assert basic entitlements, and in so doing they gradually eroded the traditional reliance upon charitable acts of gratuitous compassion. Litigation, or the threat of it, pushed aside the controls of price or grace and favour that had hitherto determined access to some of the more basic necessities of life.

The legal rights approach

This approach provides for assertive action in the courts by individuals for alleged breaches of entitlements provided for in legislation. Legal rights and corresponding legal duties, usually underpinned by statements of principle and enforced by legal powers, form the basis for a formal recognition of individual entitlement; objective adjudication on an alleged breach and appropriate recompense; and a process for enforcement.[13] A legal rights approach specifies entitlements, and the grounds under which they may be claimed, within a range of legislation that includes human rights, equity, equality and non-discrimination provisions. As such it should at least challenge the continuing moral and political relevance of charity. Where need can be met by established legal rights, charity has no role: need is then entitled to a legal remedy.

Moral principles

A very considerable body of academic work is now devoted to the existence or otherwise of a relationship between moral principles and legal rights. De Tocqueville, however, was unequivocal. His admonition to those in doubt still rings true nearly two centuries later:[14]

> How is it possible that society should escape destruction if the moral tie is not strengthened in proportion as the political tie is relaxed?

Essentially, this body of work can be grouped into two schools: 'legal positivism', with its focus on the technical and empirical aspects of law, seeks to explain

---

13 See, Hart, H.L.A., *The Concept of Law* (2nd ed.), Clarendon Law Series, Oxford University Press, Oxford, 1994.
14 See, de Tocqueville, A., *Democracy in America*, 1835.

law as essentially a body of inter-related rules,[15] enforced with penalties by designated agencies for the common good, which does not draw its authority from moral principles; and 'natural law', based on principles drawn from religious belief, that are held to inform and govern the law which is in turn enforced and adjusted by agencies and rules to ensure compliance with those principles. The former owes much to the political philosophy of Thomas Hobbes,[16] of which Jeremy Bentham[17] and John Austin[18] have been leading advocates. They argue that law in itself does not necessarily equate with morality or, as Simmonds comments, 'the concept of law, for positivists, is a concept with no intrinsic moral import'.[19] The latter is more ideological and based upon early Christian teachings with such eminent exponents as St Thomas Aquinas,[20] Aristotle,[21] John Locke[22] and Emile Durkheim.[23] Natural law scholars maintain that validity and authority originate in moral principles that transcend the confines of any set of social circumstances and cannot be subject to or explained by wholly temporal terms of reference.

In practical terms it is probably safe to assert that conceptually the more basic rights draw their authority from both law and morality. It is this double endorsement that vests them with greater weight than other considerations in play within an adjudicative process, and indeed any legal system is structured around the central need to establish and accord appropriate weight to legal rights. Underpinning principles guide the application of law and enable it to provide continuity and a degree of consistency in practice.

Types of legal rights

It was the transcending effect of certain legal rights that allowed 'causes' to be translated into categories of need that could be systematically addressed by statutory provisions. One of the earliest examples being the writ of *habeas corpus*

---

15 See, for example, Simmonds, N.E., *Central Issues in Jurisprudence: Justice, Law and Rights* (2nd ed.), Sweet & Maxwell, London, 2002, where he observes that 'law is viewed by many as basically an exercise in rule-application', at p. 2.

16 See, for example, Hobbes, T., *The Clarendon Edition of The Works of Thomas Hobbes, Vol III: Leviathan*, Malcolm, N. (ed.), Clarendon Press, Oxford, UK, 2012 (1668).

17 See, for example, Bentham, J., *Introduction to Principles of Morals and Legislation*, Macmillan, USA, 1970 (printed for publication 1780, published 1789).

18 See, for example, Austin, J., *The Province of Jurisprudence Determined*, Weidenfeld & Nicolson, London, UK, 1954 (1832).

19 Op. cit., at p. 5.

20 See, for example, St Thomas Aquinas, the *Summa Theologiae* (written 1265–1274).

21 See, for example, Aristotle, the *Corpus Aristotelicum*, 2nd century AD.

22 See, for example, Locke, J., *Two Treatises of Government*, Filiquarian, Minneapolis, 2007 (1689).

23 See, for example, Durkheim, E., *Rules of Sociological Method* (1895) The Free Press, New York, 1982.

which required those who had detained or unlawfully imprisoned a person to produce him or her before a court and justify the detention.[24] This in time came to represent, more generally, the legal right to individual liberty.

Many everyday aspects of life now taken for granted as governed by universally applied rights have only become so relatively recently, and then often in a 'welfare state' context. So, for example, rights to maternity leave, holiday pay, health and safety standards in the workplace etc – mostly the result of employer concessions agreed in the context of collective bargaining with a specific trade union – became generalised as legal rights when they subsequently acquired legislative endorsement. Similarly, the processes for asserting those rights through legal aid etc are also of recent origin.

Civil rights are perhaps best regarded as associated with entitlements due to persons by virtue of their citizenship status. These would include voting rights; equity, equality and non-discrimination rights; housing and welfare benefits rights; rights of free speech and to practice religion etc. This area of law is currently developing and rapidly diversifying to meet the demands generated by a widespread social policy of multiculturalism.

Holders of legal rights

Holders of legal rights are entities vested with special protection within the terms of and for the purposes defined by those rights. The holders may be persons, companies or corporations and are frequently entities such as trade unions, government departments, universities or certain types of partnerships and clubs. The rights vested travel with the holders and entitle the latter to rely on the legal protection provided, regardless of the circumstances, by courts or administrative bodies.[25]

It often occurs that two or more holders of legal rights find themselves in circumstances where their rights are in conflict. This may be the case, for example, when someone wishes to manifest their right to practise a religious belief – e.g. by prayer or the wearing of religious apparel – which conflicts with an employer's right to manage their business in accordance with agreed terms and conditions of employment. Where there is such a conflict of rights, then, in the absence of reasonable adjustments by the parties concerned, it will fall to the courts to establish which right in the particular circumstances should prevail. Not infrequently, the more fundamental legal rights will be embodied in national constitutions together with directions as to their relative prioritisation. It is a characteristic of any democratic society that its citizens should be both holders of legal rights and be prepared to manage situations where those rights are in conflict.

24 See, further, Sir William Blackstone, *Commentaries on the Laws of England in the 18th Century*, who recorded the first use of habeas corpus in 1305.
25 See, for example, Campbell, T., *Rights: A Critical Introduction*, Routledge, London, 2006.

Justice

In contrast to an approach based on the legal rights of the individual, social justice requires universal standards of equity, equality and non-discrimination to be entrenched in legislation, applied uniformly across society, largely through the procedures and practice of government agencies, with a right of recourse to the courts. All modern western societies have now put into place much the same legislative platform to ensure the provision of equal opportunities for citizens regardless of factors such as gender, age disability, race, religion or belief, sexual orientation, equal pay and fair employment etc. This requires more general social legislation to be proofed against such principles and provision for an independent overview by regulatory bodies, commissions or tribunals, coupled with power of referral to the court. This collective approach to justice is most apparent in national legislation dealing, for example, with civil liberties and freedom of information, but is also reinforced by international conventions.

Theories of justice

The contention between the schools of legal positivism and natural law as to whether or not there is, necessarily, a connection between law and morality is at its most heated in relation to the concept of 'justice'. For natural law theorists the concept is inexplicable without an acknowledgement that a set of moral imperatives lie at its core with the corollary, as encapsulated in the often-quoted dictum of Saint Augustine, *'lex iniusta non est lex'* (unjust law is not law). For legal positivists, as might be expected, justice is a more pragmatic affair often amounting to little more than adherence to the rule that like cases should be treated alike. This, of course, requires a common understanding of and agreement with the basis for making any such differentiation and a consensus that circumstantial factors should either play no part in mitigating the outcome or the part played will be strictly in accordance with accepted rules.

Arguably, both approaches depend on a common acceptance of the values employed to identify 'justice occasions' and measure the significance of a breach. To that extent justice functions as an attribute of its social context and is prone to variations from society to society and from time to time within the same society (e.g. acceptance of capital punishment). For present purposes it is the administration of justice with its focus on standards such as 'objectivity', 'impartiality', 'no one being above the law' etc that is of importance.

The charity/rights interface

Traditionally viewed as mutually exclusive, charity and legal rights have gradually developed roles that are assumed to be growing more complementary. This assumption may be incorrect. Indeed the point of this book is to examine the grounds for considering that charity law and human rights are now slowly achieving a congruity that they largely avoided for the past four centuries (see, further, Part II).

Charity and rights

Rights and charity once clearly functioned in an obverse relationship similar to justice and mercy. It was a relationship forever associated with corresponding stereotypical attitudes: the benefits won through adversarial assertion on the basis of merit, success accompanied by a sense of vindication, with honour and dignity restored; as opposed to the benefits conferred through discretionary patronage on a supplicant, accompanied by deference, gratitude and compliant dependency. Since the mid-20th century, however, an increasing social awareness of the boundary between charity and legal rights has seen, whether as cause or effect, a considerable displacement of charity in all modern nations by a raft of equity, equality and human rights legislation, leading to the emergence of a rights-conscious – if not an entitlement – culture.

Relating to social disadvantage

The developed common law nations are now struggling to cope with the additional stresses imposed by economic recession, international terrorism and large-scale population migration. In response to such stresses, the protection and entitlement afforded by legal rights will necessarily grow in importance, relative to the discretionary contributions of charity, as the socially disadvantaged seek access to basic social services and the means to acquire or preserve self-respect. It is this social context, exacerbated by effects of a shrinking welfare state and the growing tensions between those of different religious beliefs and between them and some increasingly strident secularists, that necessitates the further development and wider application of fundamental human rights.

Needs addressed by charity or by legal rights

It is a matter of some importance that a line be drawn between needs to be addressed by charity and needs addressed by legal rights. That line is one which traces and seeks, in profoundly different ways, to manage a power imbalance between: government and citizen; private and public interests and their related areas of law; and, essentially, between those in need and those controlling access to relevant resources. The approach of charity, as legally defined, focuses on specified 'charitable purposes': it deals with the effects not the causes of poverty; it constrains the use of advocacy to challenge political realities and institutional structures; it inhibits 'user involvement' in decision-making regarding resource distribution; and it settles for alleviating the adverse circumstances only of those designated as beneficiaries, all others similarly afflicted being excluded if construed as falling outside the ambit of donor intent and outside designated charitable purposes. Although, the redistributive effects of tax exemptions – most graphically in respect of high-value donors – must also be weighed in the balance. In contrast, legal rights empower and protect those in whom they are vested (see, further, Chapter 2).

Social context: the contemporary common law nations

'Society', in the developed common law nations, replicated the parliamentary democracy model established in the original jurisdiction. In the post-war period the nations currently under consideration, together with many others, developed in broad conformity with much the same policies of social liberalism: allowing for an emphasis on the 'open market' in the US and a welfare state legacy in the UK and to a lesser extent in Ireland. Charity law was also transposed from the progenitor jurisdiction – along with the English language and Church, social infrastructure, institutions, legal system and the processes and culture of civic administration – to develop in tandem with precedents forged in the English courts. In short, 'society' evolved remarkably similarly in the common law nations.

However, in recent decades 'society' in the same nations has undergone a considerable transformation as a consequence of exposure to much the same pressures. The relative cultural homogeneity they shared for many generations is rapidly fading. For reasons that will be explored in Part II, they are becoming not just culturally differentiated but are in increasing danger of cultural incoherence. It is therefore a matter of some importance that attention be given to the potential for charity law and human rights to contribute to safeguarding the interests of the socially marginalised, promoting social capital and consolidating the institutions and ethos of civil society.

Social cohesion

The law supports and sustains social cohesion by asserting and protecting a nation's culture and its associated emblems, icons, language and traditions; reinforcing its values and principles; policing its boundaries; and by setting the terms for negotiation with other societies. By legitimising the particular institutions, bodies, officials and processes that bind together the constituent elements of a society, it enables that society to function as a coherent entity. It can also do so by virtue of its integrative effect. The law facilitates pluralism by affording recognition and protection for the interests of minority groups through equality and non-discrimination legislation and the use of human rights provisions to accommodate diversity and achieve a balance in circumstances of competing rights.

In a common law context, the law is based on principles of social justice, is intimately linked to the democratic process and is increasingly governed by the provisions of fundamental human rights and other international conventions. It is a context that singularly provides opportunities for charity law to address issues of social inclusion[26] which, as the outcomes of the various national charity law reform processes reveal (see, further, Part II), have been strategically utilised by the governments concerned in order to improve general social cohesion.

---

26 See, further, O'Halloran, K., *Charity Law and Social Inclusion*, Routledge, UK, 2007.

The integrative effect of legal rights

Whether as cause or effect, the bonds that draw a society together are represented by its civil and criminal laws and mananged through the balancing of various sets of legal rights: the rights and reciprocal duties of each of the parties being statutorily delineated, moderated through related administrative bodies and enforced by the courts. On a wider scale, pluralism is facilitated by affording recognition and protection for the rights of minority groups through equality and non-discrimination legislation to accommodate diversity and achieve a balance between competing interests. To some degree, the integrative effect of legal rights is conterbalanced by a tendency for a rights-conscious approach towards complex problems to have a splintering effect on social cohesion, as evidenced in the manifestations of religious belief.

Charity law

Because contributing to the public benefit is its defining legal characteristic, charity might be thought to be innately programmed to further social cohesion, but in fact it may also have the opposite effect. While its role in alleviating poverty and establishing or maintaining public utilities – such as bridges, roads, harbours, universities, hospitals etc – undoubtedly contributes to the overall good of society, it has also been judicially interpreted to license a profusion of quixotic charitable causes and elitist aesthetic amentities which could be perceived as socially divisive. Overall, however, charity has, to a varying extent, served to ameliorate hardship, demonstrate altruism, generate engagement in community life, enrich the fabric of society and generally facilitate social cohesion.

Social capital

The concept of 'social capital' has been coined to describe the effect on a community of citizens constructively engaging in collective activity for altruistic purposes. There would appear to be general consensus that this is evidenced by the presence of a range of formal and informal networks; the willing engagement of a significant proportion of a community in civic activity of a reciprocal and mutually beneficial nature; together with a shared ethos of trust, values and responsible behaviour within that community. For the World Bank this concept, which became the subject of academic study in the closing decades of the 20th century,[27] refers to

---

27 See, in particular: Bourdieu, P. 'Forms of Capital' in Richards, J.C. (ed.), *Handbook of Theory and Research for the Sociology of Education*, Greenwood Press, New York, 1983; Coleman, J.C., 'Social Capital in the Creation of Human Capital', *American Journal of Sociology*, Vol 94, 1988, pp. 95–120 and *Foundations of Social Theory*, Harvard University Press, Cambridge, MA, 1990 and 1994; Putnam, R.D., *Making Democracy Work: Civic Traditions in Modern Italy*, Princeton University Press, Princeton, NJ, 1993 and 'Bowling Alone: America's Declining Social Capital', *Journal of Democracy*, Vol 6, No 1, 1995, pp. 65–78.

'the institutions, relationships, and norms that shape the quality and quantity of a society's social interactions'.[28] It argues that 'increasing evidence shows that social cohesion is critical for societies to prosper economically and for development to be sustainable'.

Charities and legal rights both have an undoubted capacity to generate social capital. Among the ways they do so are by reinforcing respect for the values and institutions of contemporary democratic society, raising social awareness as regards needs and entitlements, setting standards and improving coping capacity, and putting in place processes for positive social interaction. However, there is a distinction to be drawn between their respective contributions to 'bridging' as opposed to 'bonding' forms of social capital.

Social capital: bridging v. bonding

It has to be conceded that both legal rights and charity law make an ambivalent contribution to the bridging form of social capital. On the one hand, by singling out and formally recognising the vulnerability of specified social groups, they confer or reinforce a sense of group solidarity which is positively affirming for the identity and entitlements of group members. On the other, this may also have a contrary fragmenting effect by legitimising separate sets of interests and thereby encouraging a sense of competing entitlement.

The relationship between both areas of law and religion provides the most revealing example of the conflicting tensions between bridging and bonding forms of social capital. Religion, with its explicit doctrines and shared values and rituals, brings with it a capacity for social cohesion to which other groups can only aspire; indeed, scholars such as Schnabel[29] are strongly of the view that 'believers' have traditionally formed the cornerstone of civil society. Nevertheless, religion has proven to be challenging in the context of social capital because of its capacity to generate polarisation. Proselytism, together with the vast range of religious buildings, artefacts, activities and services etc accompanying such charities, raises questions as to how such an array of material that advertises the separateness, exclusiveness and competitiveness of organisations and their respective adherents could be conducive to promoting a collective sense of public good.

Being essentially a member-benefit activity, a religion is constrained by the exclusive committment of its adherents and the consequent rejection of those adhering to all other religious beliefs or to none. The 'benefit' quotient is restricted to personal and intangible rewards, and, indeed, it has been held that there can be no charity in attempting to save one's soul because charity, that is charity in law, is necessarily altruistic (for the benefit of others).[30] Nevertheless,

---

28 See, World Bank, *What Is Social Capital?*, 2000, at: www.worldbank.org/poverty.
29 See, Schnabel, P. and Giesen, P. (eds.), *What Everyone Should Know About the Humanities*, publisher unknown, Amsterdam, 2011, pp. 198–202.
30 *In re Delany: Conoley v Quick* [1902] 2 Ch 642 per Farwell J at p. 648.

for four centuries and in all common law nations the advancement of religion has carried a legal presumption that it is for the public benefit and entitled to charitable status. It is also singled out for preferential treatment by being exempted, for example, from the non-discrimination provisions of employment law and attracting specific protection under provisions protecting the freedom of religion.

However, experiences in many parts of the world including Northern Ireland and Iraq – and most recently in Paris – provide irrefutable evidence of religion's capacity to further the bonding form of social capital at the price of the bridging.[31] All common law nations are now riven with disputes between those who share conservative religious beliefs and those who do not, on much the same agenda of matters – including artificial insemination, abortion, homosexuality, gay marriage and adoption, and euthanasia – that constitute an ever-extending list of red-line issues for those of religious belief. Clearly, notwithstanding its preferential treatment in law, religion can serve to emphasise differences, accentuate the marginalisation of minority groups and exacerbate any tendencies towards polarisation. It therefore often presents a serious challenge to social cohesion.

Civil society

The concept of 'civil society' means different things to different people. Bothwell has usefully suggested that the literature on the subject reveals four distinctively different approaches:[32]

> First, scholars such as Robert Putnam, Larry Diamond and Francis Fukuyama focus on what they see as the results of a strong civil society – the behaviours they believe healthy civil society produces including trust, reciprocity, tolerance and inclusion (traits and networks that add to a society's social capital) . . . Second, other students of civil society, such as Rajesh Tandon, David Brown and John Clark focus on the preconditions that must be met before a healthy civil society can come about (e.g. freedom of speech, freedom of association, rule of law etc) . . . Third, many who have considered what is a healthy civil society have sought to define it as a desirable state of all society (e.g. free public education and health care available to all) . . . Fourth, most who write about civil society define it in terms of its composition (e.g. including religious organisations, social clubs and movements, community based organisations etc but excluding family, tribe, clan, political parties etc).

31 See, Puttnam, R., *Bowling Alone*, Simon and Schuster, New York, 2000. Also, see, Çelik, G., 'Breakpoint or Binder: Religious Engagement in Dutch Civil Society', *Journal of Civil Society*, Vol 9, No 3, 2013, pp. 248–267.
32 See, Bothwell, J., 'Indicators of a Healthy Civil Society'.

These are not discrete mutually exclusive categories, as it would be quite feasible to subscribe to some or all without losing much of the concept's egalitarian essence. As has been emphasised, 'the boundaries of the space in which civil society activities take place are permeable'.[33] In relation to charity law and legal rights, however, the concept is perhaps best seen as represented by the preconditions of the second approach leading to the goals of the first. Regardless of the approach adopted, the concept of civil society would seem to rest on the free association of people in the pursuit of aims that complement the public benefit efforts of the State and result in a more coherent and engaged body politic. Conceptually, this is clearly a context which would readily accommodate the principles underpinning charity law and human rights.

The nonprofit sector

The size of the nonprofit sector and the diversity of entities within it have greatly expanded in recent years, in keeping with the shrinking of the public sector. Particularly noticeable has been the flowering of what are best termed 'civil society organisations', i.e. those charities and other nonprofits that have as their *raison d'être* the building of a greater sense of civic responsibility and engagement of citizens in public benefit activity on a local, national and international basis. Of such organisations, charities are singular in that they are often the oldest, wealthiest, have the strongest association with disadvantaged groups and are custodians of the most relevant data archives. They are strategically positioned to act as a bridgehead between government and the community by representing a wide range of groups or causes, the concerns of some of which would otherwise remain unheard by government.

The common law has long provided a protective environment for charity, particularly in the UK and Irish jurisdictions where the trust has been the dominant legal form, enabling it to survive and flourish across the many nations sharing the same legal heritage. Charity law has accentuated this by treating charities as a discrete and relatively small subcategory of nonprofit, uniquely tax privileged, among the myriad forms of organisations that constitute the community and voluntary sector. More recently, however, as governments wind down their varied 'welfare state' commitment, there has been a growing demand for them to put in place (and encourage others to do so) the institutions and infrastructures necessary to establish or consolidate 'civil society'. This is seen as providing for a more structured relationship between government and the nonprofit sector; accommodating a diversity of religions, beliefs and cultures; and operating within a comprehensive legal framework, in which a more inclusive body of charity law and human rights law would embrace all public benefit entities.

---

33 See, Deakin, N., *In Search of Civil Society*, Palgrave, Hampshire, 2001.

Civic responsibility

A consequence of the gradual assimilation of principles associated with the altruistic activities of charity,[34] and the acceptance that all persons enjoy an equal entitlement to respect as holders of basic rights and freedoms, has been an overall leavening effect, diffusing a moral code throughout society, which has helped give citizens a shared sense of belonging and being valued. Both areas of law have raised the bar for standards of what constitutes socially acceptable treatment of citizens, clearly shifting norms of interpersonal relations from their traditional definition as matters of private law into the public arena, accompanied by public law processes of enforcement.

The role of legal rights

The law plays a crucial role in legitimising the particular institutions, bodies, officials and processes that constitute a legal system (see, further, Chapter 3). This in turn affirms and binds the component elements of a society, enabling it to function as a coherent entity. In particular, the fact that citizens and other entities are vested with legal rights has had the effect of requiring transparency and introducing processes of accountability into transactions that previously, being private to the parties concerned, were more vulnerable to abuse and could be subversive of collective best interests. The existence of a formal and uniform rule book, outlining the rights and corresponding duties of all legal entities, accompanied by clear arbitration mechanisms and related sanctions, generates citizen confidence in and commitment to a responsible and efficient civic life. Legal rights and frameworks also provide protection and allow individuals and various entities access to justice in relation to the actions of international organisations and other possible threats to their society.

The role of charities

Charities are viewed by government as having significant potential to strengthen citizenship and assist in the consolidation of civil society. They are distinctive among nonprofit organisations for characteristics that are uniquely relevant to this task: underpinning principles require charitable bodies to strive with a 'moral mission' to improve the circumstances of the socially disadvantaged,[35] to maintain independent governance[36] and to refrain from distributing any

---

34 Also known as the 'non-distribution constraint'. See further, Hansmann, H., 'The Rationale for Exempting Nonprofit Organisations from Corporate Income Taxation', *Yale Law Journal*, Vol 91, No 1, 1981, at pp. 54–100.

35 As specified in the Preamble and in the four *Pemsel* heads. See, further, Mitchell, C. and Moody, S. (eds.), *Foundations of Charity*, Hart Publishing, Oxford, 2000.

36 See, for example, Charity Commission, CC10 – 'The Hallmarks of an Effective Charity' (July 2008) where it states that a charity must ensure that it 'is independent and recognises that it exists to pursue its own purposes and not to carry out the policies or directions of any other body'. See, further, at: http://www.charitycommission.gov.uk/Publications/cc10.aspx#h3.

profits[37] for private gain in the process. Also their proven ability to attract volunteers and public donations enables them to provide services at a lower cost than for-profit or government bodies. Consequently, governments in all common law countries can be seen to be harnessing the selflessness, goodwill, manpower and resources of charities to achieve public benefit outcomes which provide opportunities for demonstrating the virtue and effectiveness of altruism, add to a shared sense of civic responsibility, and strengthen society as well as assisting the intended beneficiaries.

It would be hard to overstate the consolidating social function of the institutional range of charities – Churches, schools, universities, hospital complexes – that continue to provide the hard core of charitable activity and a repository for most charitable assets in all jurisdictions as they have done for generations. In centuries past they provided what was the only source of public benefit services, if often doing so as the outworkings of religion, and now continue to function as virtually part of the public sector. They have become such established components of social infrastructure, relatively impervious to political turmoil (at least in the common law countries) and yet accustomed to working alongside government, that their future seems safely assured. At the other extreme, the grassroots charities – welfare agencies for children, the aged, sick and disabled etc – which have long been closely enmeshed with their socially disadvantaged constituencies, also form a distinct group. This bedrock of charities and charitable activity has provided continuity, consolidation and consistency for the core public benefit functions of society in the common law nations. It prepared the ground for the 'welfare state', provided a model for the nationalisation of public utilities and laid the foundations for current State provision.

Given the incidences of increased social dysfunction – evidenced by the growth in prison populations, civil unrest, climbing rates of family breakdown, child abuse, suicides etc – governments in recent years have become alert to the possibility of using the good offices of organisations, with credibility in disadvantaged communities, to broker modes of intervention designed to effect positive and sustainable change. In that context, the proven capacity of charities to recruit armies of committed volunteers, reach the socially marginalised, and deliver value-for-money public benefit outcomes has undoubtedly been an attraction for contemporary governments in the developed common law nations.

The pressing need to share responsibility for public benefit service provision, reduce social alienation and promote harmony in the face of increasing cultural diversity has, in recent years, prompted a number of governments to reflect on the bridging role of charities and initiate processes of charity law reform in order to maximise the latter's potential.

---

37 See, *Commissioners of Inland Revenue v Oldham Training and Enterprise Council* (1996) 69 TC 231.

Engaging the electorate

Allied to government's wish to generate and harness a stronger sense of civic responsibility is its need to engage more directly with an increasingly apathetic electorate. Baroness Kennedy's observation that 'the public's disengagement from organized politics has gathered pace as they have lost faith in the more traditional forms of political engagement' holds true not just for the UK but for a number of leading common law nations.[38] In order to bridge this gap, ostensibly to revive and re-energise democracy but as much to win party political advantage, governments in the UK and elsewhere have been experimenting with opening direct lines of engagement to their constituencies.

Participative forms of political engagement

As politics in most modern commom law countries becomes more entrenched in competing struggles between centre-left and centre-right parties to win the 'middle ground', occupied by a majority of largely disinterested constituents, ways are being sought to broaden the traditional model of representative parliamentary democracy. The forging of formal strategic partnership arrangements between government and the nonprofit sector has been accompanied by the introduction of new government bodies to bridge sector divisions and by the creation of hybrid bodies to facilitate cross-sectoral exchanges.[39]

By the closing years of the 20th century it had become clear to government in a number of leading common law nations that if the promotion of civic engagement was to be maximised, so as to contribute towards consolidating civil society and towards bridging the gap between it and the electorate, then the nonprofit sector had to be strengthened and charities nudged towards developing in certain areas (e.g. generate more volunteering). There was a clear political need to extend charitable status eligibility to organisations with civil society purposes. The legislative outcomes of charity law reform recognised and facilitated this political objective by listing new charitable purposes which promoted and channelled such activities (see, further, Part II). Overall these developments can be seen as heralding a significant move towards a more participative form of democracy.

The 'culture wars'

As modern developed nations are stretched to accommodate evermore diversity, cultural homogeneity is replaced by pluralism, and 'community' is often more

---

38 See, Advisory Group, *Campaigning and the Voluntary Sector*, London, 2007, at p. 2: https://www.bond.org.uk/data/files/resources/302/campaigning.pdf.
39 See, for example, Giddens, A., *The Third Way and its Critics*, Polity Press, Cambridge, 2000.

virtual than locality based, there are clear indications that national solidarity is breaking up, giving way to clusters of membership-based groups that pursue their separate sets of interests. At best these groupings co-exist alongside each other with little reason to interact. At worst they are mutually atagonistic – as in the current competition between the religious and the secularists, between fundamentalists and mainstream adherents, between the traditional organised religions, and between them and a proliferating and mutating range of new forms of belief – which is undoubtedly contributing to an overall splintering of society. This reductionist tendency, responsible for proliferating 'islands of exclusivity',[40] as evidenced in many of the leading common law nations (and elsewhere), is now referred to as the culture wars.

Culture war issues

The modern phase of this phenomenon probably originates in the US, where it evolved from a number of morality-laden legal issues including the death penalty as a legitimate form of State punishment, war, female combatants in national armed forces, gun laws, abortion, surrogacy, homosexuality and euthanasia. These formative milestones in the evolution of contemporary culture wars, often linked to 'life' and/or sexuality,[41] proved to be deeply divisive in the US. As noted by Williams at the turn of the 20th century:[42]

> The major political cleavage in contemporary American politics is no longer class, race, region, or any of the many social-structural differences that divide the population. Rather, a major realignment of sensibilities and controversial issues means that the body politic is now rent by a cultural conflict in which values, moral codes, and lifestyles are the primary objects of contention.

Gay marriage, genetic engineering, DNA patenting, and stem cell research are now among the host of morally charged, contentious and socially disruptive issues that await a coherent policy response and leadership initiatives from government. Since joined by many other such issues, they have been exported to other countries and have grown to constitute the heartland of this phenomenon.

The challenge for charity law and legal rights

For legal rights and charity law, the challenge is to affirm and protect cultural identity, to balance minority interests against the collective good of society and

---

40 See, Esau, A.J., ' "Islands of Exclusivity": Religious Organisations and Employment Discrimination', *UBCLRev.*, Vol 33, 2000, p. 719.
41 See, for example, Sands, K.M. (ed.), *God Forbid: Religion and Sex in American Public Life*, Oxford University Press, New York, 2000.
42 See, Williams, R.H. (ed.), *Cultural Wars in American Politics: Critical Reviews of a Popular Myth*, Transaction Publishers, Rutgers University, New Jersey, 1997, at p.1. Also, see, Putnam, R.D. and Campbell, D.E., *American Grace: How Religion Divides and Unites Us*, Simon Schuster, New York, 2010.

to avoid further exacerbating existing social divisions. This will be difficult to achieve because many core culture war issues lie at the interface of morality and law (see, above) and are also central to the most integrative aspects of both legal rights and charity law.

This is perhaps most evident in relation to family law. The family is where many of the most contentious morality driven issues originate: medical intervention to commence or prevent birth (IVF, surrogacy, contraception and abortion); the legitimate status of the traditional marital family unit (heterosexual, monogamous, spouses for life with the children of their marriage) accompanied by the corollary that – for some – all other forms of union and their progeny are illegitimate; and medical intervention to end life (euthanasia). The extension to 'family' brings in issues relating to 'life' that are equally contentious such as research involving stem cells and human embryos, genetic engineering and DNA patents etc. This constellation of issues triggers a snake pit of conflicting legal rights with potential to dessicate the coherence that the body of family law and its associated network of principles once gave to our conceptualisation of family and its place in 'society'.

Similarly, the relationship between charity law and religion is now greatly challenged by culture war issues. The ever-expanding range of new religions, philosophies and moral or ethical belief systems – which exist alongside the institutional religions but without necessarily sharing their need for a theistic component or for any tenets or doctrines or, indeed, even for adherents who collectively share the same set of beliefs – has arguably deconstructed the meaning of religion and made risible the charity law presumption that it is per se conducive to the public benefit. The fact that for many 'believers' all conduct must conform to their beliefs has the effect of transferring private convictions into the public arena, which is perceived as threatening by atheists, who constitute an increasing proportion of the population in all modern common law countries, with divisive social and political consequences.[43] The rising tension generated by religious issues, when contrasted with the growing political importance of secularism[44] together with current government investment in policies of social inclusion and religious pluralism, is likely to make this a particularly contentious area for both charity law and legal rights.

'Society' and the significance of the culture wars

Devlin LJ warned, a half a century ago, that:[45]

> Societies disintegrate from within more frequently than they are broken up
> by external pressures. There is disintegration when no common morality is

---

43 Woltersorrf, N., 'The Role of Religion in Decision and Discussion of Political Issues' in Audi, R. and Woltersorrf, N. (ed.), *Religion in the Public Square: The Place of Religious Convictions in Political Debate*, Rowan and Littlefield, New York, 1997.

44 See, Taylor, C., 'Why We Need a Radical Redefinition of Secularism' in Mendieta, E. and Vanantwerpen, J. (eds.), *The Power of Religion in the Public Sphere*, Columbia University Press, New York, 2011.

45 See, Devlin, P., *The Enforcement of Morals*, Oxford University Press, Oxford, 1965, at p. 13.

observed and history shows that the loosening of moral bonds is often the first stage of disintegration.

This view was opposed by Hart, who responded that 'there is no evidence that the preservation of a society requires the enforcement of its morality "as such" '.[46] Unquestionably, social morality and cultural context have changed since this exchange of views. The Devlin concept of society is no longer tenable in the developed western nations. Pluralism has done away with the possibility of societies being integrated around, and voluntarily bound by, a set of principles and infused with a common morality. Even 50 years ago, neither Hart nor Devlin were living in such societies; indeed, this may not be unattainable outside a theocracy. Balance is now everything.

Society, in most contemporary developed nations, would seem to be increasingly composed largely of a patchwork of communities and scattered groups which have little in common with their neighbours other than geographic proximity. The varied cultural components are left to seek an affinity with parallel pockets within or outside the jurisdiction, which in turn introduces pan-national cultural stratification issues for 'civil society'. In conjunction with the cultural fracturing of society, the modern developed nations are subject to a range of socio-economic global pressures and to the moderating influence of international conventions and protocols. In many, the relevance of civil society rhetoric is fading as anti-terrorism legislation proliferates at the expense of civil liberties. Part II of this book will, therefore, explore the nature and effect of jurisdiction specific issues representative of the culture wars, consider the relative bearing upon them of charity law and legal rights, and assess the significance of jurisdictional similarity and difference for the future of civil society.

Conclusion

For Titmuss, 'the gift relationship', offering 'the moral choice of giving to strangers',[47] testified to the importance of 'altruism' as the key component for a conceptual interpretation of 'charity'. This was important because, as he then claimed, 'the social relations set up by gift-exchange are among the most powerful forces which bind a social group together'.[48] He viewed the gift-exchange transaction, underpinned by altruism, as a *sine qua non* for building trust relationships.

However, much has changed since 1970. A reliance on trust as sufficient for relationships – whether on a personal, institutional or international basis – is no longer deemed prudent. The gift relationship has given way to the contractual,

---

46 See, Hart, H.L.A., *Law, Liberty and Morality*, Oxford University Press, Oxford, 1963, at p. 82.
47 See, Titmuss, R., *The Gift Relationship: From Human Blood to Social Policy*, Allen and Unwin, London, 1970, at p. 12.
48 Ibid., at p. 73.

legal rights have largely displaced charity. The role of the latter has been steadily constrained by parameters in many different forms: displaced by Church and professionals; and restricted by legal rights, social justice and anti-terrorism measures. The welfare state embedded expectations in citizens that remain as government service provision is withdrawn. Legal rights rather than charity are now a binding force in society and are becoming increasingly important as their international reach extends and other forms of mediation lose potency. In response to the impact of various global forces, particularly in the aftermath of 9/11, regulatory mechanisms supported by sanctions are now preferred to trust as more likely to ensure a satisfactory outcome for any transaction. Nevertheless, as will become apparent in Part II, charity continues to have an important role to play in the contemporary domestic and international relationships of many leading common law nations.

2 Charity law and fundamental legal rights
Concepts and principles

Introduction

Beginning with the legal concept of 'charity', this chapter explains a 'charitable trust', identifies the related charitable purposes, analyses a range of matters held to constitute 'public benefit' and assesses the political significance of a charity's automatic entitlement to tax exemptions and other privileges. It briefly outlines the historical background of charity law and examines its primary characteristics and the main legal precedents which fixed the boundaries for construing what does and does not constitute charity, a charitable organisation, or a charitable gift to such, across the common law jurisdictions. It explores some basic charity law principles such as the 'public' and the 'benefit' arms of the public benefit test, before explaining the cause and effects of the ongoing rolling programme of charity law reform experienced by most leading common law nations.

It notes the ever-expanding range of relevant conventions from the Universal Declaration of Human Rights 1948 through to contemporary conventions and protocols and related international bodies. It explains the European Convention for the Protection of Human Rights and Fundamental Freedoms 1950[1] and the relevance of European Court of Human Rights (ECtHR)[2] doctrines such as 'the margin of appreciation' and the established caveats of 'necessity' and 'proportionality'. It considers whether a charity can be construed as a 'public body' for Convention purposes, noting that the Preamble declares its provisions to be binding upon 'every organ of society'. It specifically examines the freedoms of association and assembly, of expression, of non-discrimination, of religion, of access to justice, the right to family life, and discusses their implications for charity law.

In adopting this approach the chapter touches upon themes – such as whether charity is inherently discriminatory and, more broadly, the extent to which some

---

1 The European Convention on Fundamental Human Rights (ECHR), formally known as the Convention for the Protection of Human Rights and Fundamental Freedoms, was drafted in 1950 and took effect on 3 September 1953.
2 The European Court of Human Rights (ECtHR) was established by the Convention. It replaced the European Commission of Human Rights in 1998 and hears complaints that a contracting Member State has violated rights enshrined in the Convention and its protocols.

charity law principles have perhaps always been and may continue to be incompatible with human rights – that will be tracked and closely examined through the subsequent jurisdiction-specific chapters.

Charity: the concept

The concept of charity emanates from the altruism[3] of the individual. Within a common law context, it provides the means for discretionary gifts or activities to be directed towards purposes as defined under charity law, by individuals or organisations, for the public benefit.

The parties

Charity, as statutorily defined in all common law nations, is a transaction that involves the interests of donor, charitable organisation, recipient and the State.

The donor

The basis for exempting a charitable trust from certain tax and other financial impositions rests on the fact that, in deciding to make a gift, a donor has chosen not to confer a private benefit upon a selected recipient but to instead make an altruistic gift for the public good. The right to dispose of personal property, an important aspect of private law, has long been upheld as a key attribute of democracy. When that right is exercised so as to voluntarily redistribute private wealth for the public benefit, then that together with the ancillary need to protect the value of that gift and the associated entitlement to tax exemption transforms the transaction into one with a considerable public law dimension. This is reinforced by the fact that the right of donor choice, if it is to be exercised in the form of a charitable gift, is subject to certain constraints imposed by public law.

The charitable organisation

An organisation established and registered as dedicated to the pursuit of charitable purposes provides the conduit for channelling a donor's gift to the recipient. Such an organisation, by virtue of its charitable status as dedicated to public benefit activities and thereby supplementing or displacing the need for State service provision, will be eligible for tax exemption. Charities, being exempt from the rule against perpetuities,[4] may in theory exist forever. Many have existed for

---

3 Meaning an unselfish concern for the welfare of others: a private act for public benefit. It was Comte's *Philosophy of the Sciences* (translated by George Lewes, 1890) which first introduced the word 'altruism' (from the French '*alteri huic*') into the English language.
4 This rule, imposed by the Crown, sought to end the practice whereby testators made gifts of land to the Church 'in perpetuity' in exchange for masses being offered for the salvation of their souls.

centuries and in the process accumulated vast assets, databanks of irreplaceable worth and close bonds of mutual understanding with those socially disadvantaged whose interests they were established to serve.

The recipient

Being in need does not itself qualify a person to be a recipient of charity, nor is being wealthy necessarily a disqualification, and being discriminatory is a necessity, within the common law. The latter has long imposed limits on eligibility for charitable gifts: most obviously, potential beneficiaries are restricted to those designated by the definition of charitable purpose; but also, a recipient must be a stranger to the donor, and most usually there can be no legal or moral obligation or any form of personal nexus between them.

The State

The State's interest in charity is mainly to ensure that by facilitating the involvement of charitable organisations in public service provision, which it would otherwise be obliged to fund, it gets good value to compensate for lost taxes and prevent abuse. That regulatory aspect of its role has traditionally been entrusted principally to the tax collection agency (other government bodies such as Customs & Excise have also been involved) which has arbitrated on entitlement to charitable status and consequent tax exemption and has exercised ongoing supervision. In legal terms, the State's stake in charity involves: determining the rights and responsibilities of donor, recipient and charitable organisation; defining, or at least influencing, what constitutes a charitable gift and who is entitled to receive it; protecting the value of the gift; and supporting and regulating the proper and efficient functioning of charities. The jurisdictional variation in the State's role in charity and its management of the related interface with human rights requirements are of central importance to this book.

Charity and the law: historical background

Although charities and charitable activity have been in existence for at least the last millennium,[5] for common law purposes their essential elements were formed in pre-Reformation England, when Church and King were the twin institutions governing society. At that time, when English society was rigidly structured by feudalism, with wealth and power distributed accordingly, charity functioned to some extent to offset the gap between rich and poor, acting as a necessary solvent for maintaining social stability. Its capacity to contribute to

---

5 See, Picarda, H., *The Law and Practice Relating to Charities* (3rd ed.), Butterworths, London, 1999.

maintaining social order was still evident in the 18th century when, as has been observed:[6]

> Philanthropy and religion were ways of obviating the need for an interfering police force by providing other means of regulating the masses. Charity was a way of clearing a path for better reception of the word of God.

The common law origins of charity

The law relating to charities is of ancient origin.[7] Most probably, its origins lie in the 'pious use' employed to facilitate gifts made by landowners to religious bodies in return for masses being said for the salvation of their souls. In its initial religious context, as succinctly expressed in the *Report of the Committee on the Law and Practice relating to Charitable Trusts*, charity was 'more a means to the salvation of the soul of the benefactor than an endeavour to diagnose and alleviate the needs of the beneficiary'.[8] As a secular construct it can be traced to the *parens patriae*[9] responsibilities of the King of England (protecting the interests of charities, wards and lunatics). This common law phenomenon (see, further, Chapter 1), the judicial development of which was essentially untouched by legislation and remained governed by only the broad parameters of early 17th century legislation, is possibly unique in that it provided and continues largely to provide a shared platform of jurisprudence throughout the common law world.

A charitable trust

A charitable trust is a species of trust with the distinguishing feature that it is primarily intended to confer a public benefit; the fact that it is established for purposes rather than for persons sets it apart from other forms of trust. Its governing instrument is a deed of trust: property being vested by a donor in a trustee who holds it not for personal gain but merely as an administrator, duty-bound to give effect to the purpose of the charity as identified by the donor, for an indefinite period. For a trust to be properly constituted as a charitable trust, the law requires it to satisfy the 'three certainties test'.[10] In England and Wales (unlike

---

6 See, Wilson, B., *Decency and Disorder: The Age of Cant 1789–1837*, Faber & Faber, London, 2007, at p. 79.
7 See, for example, Westlake, *The Parish Gilds of Mediaeval England*, 1919, where mention is made of 'the gild of the Blessed Virgin Mary in the parish church of St Botolph at Boston founded in 1260 gave a yearly distribution of bread and herrings to the poor in alms for the souls of its benefactors'; cited in Brady, J., *Religion and the Law of Charities in Ireland*, Northern Ireland Legal Quarterly, Belfast, 1975, at p. 14.
8 HMSO, 1952, at para 36.
9 See, Seymour, J., '*Parens Patriae* and Wardship Powers: Their Nature and Origins', *Oxford Journal of Legal Studies*, Vol 14, No 2, 1994.
10 It was Lord Langdale MR in *Knight v Knight* (1840) who outlined the three certainties test: certainty of subject matter; certainty of intention; and certainty of objects.

the US, Canada and Australia), charities have traditionally taken the legal form of a charitable trust or, more simply, an unincorporated association.[11]

The common law found this interpretation of a 'trust' problematic: it failed to identify a named trustee who could, for the duration of the trust, enforce its terms and be held accountable for the property entrusted; and being indefinite, it ran counter to the principle that property should not be made inalienable. Therefore, at the beginning of the 17th century, legislation was introduced which recognised the singular validity of charitable trusts, assigned their enforcement to the Chancellor or Attorney General, and granted them exemption from the rules against inalienability and perpetuities.[12]

Reformation England

The contemporary social role of charity, however, can be traced back to the volatile Church/State relationship of pre-Reformation England. Parish-based relief systems for the poor were developed in many local English communities during the latter half of the 16th century in response to the collapse of the care facilities established and maintained by the Catholic Church until their removal by the Protestant Reformation. This system was extended by the Elizabethan legislation of 1597–1601 which secularised Church facilities, provided for the appointment of parish overseers to work with local churchwardens and raise the funds to assist all classes of destitute persons. This was a time when the hold of the Church on charity had been broken and the objects of charity became more secular as the majority of Englishmen 'reflected less on their souls and became more concerned with the worldly needs of their fellow men'[13] (see, further, Chapter 4).

The Statute of Charitable Uses 1601

The 1601 statute[14] legislatively established the respective responsibilities of charities and State for repairing social infrastructure and alleviating the suffering of the English poor following the ravages of war and the dissolution of monasteries. The statute, or at least its essential principles as applied by the courts, travelled with the armies of the Crown to lay the foundations for future charity law development throughout the common law world (see, further, Chapter 4). The Preamble to this Act set the legal parameters for the subsequent four centuries of 'charity', and continues to influence the reshaping of its role in response to

---

11   *Re Koeppler's Will Trusts* [1984] Ch 243, [1984] 2 All ER 111.

12   These rules date from the statute of *Quia Emptores* 1290 when the judiciary and legislature set limits on the discretion of persons to impose alienation constraints on their property to take effect after their death. Once vested, a charitable trust enjoys the considerable legal privilege that it may continue in perpetuity.

13   Jones, G., *History of the Law of Charity 1532–1827*, Wm. W. Gaunt & Sons, Inc., Holmes Beach, FL, 1986, at p. 10.

14   Also known as the Statute of Elizabeth, 43 Eliz 1, c 4.

the challenges of emerging social need. It declared the following purposes to be charitable:

> Releife of aged impotent and poore people, some for Maintenance of sicke and maymed Souldiers and Marriners, Schooles of Learninge, Free Schooles and Schollers in Universities, some for Repaire of Bridges Portes Havens Causwaies Churches Seabankes and Highwaies, some for Educacion and prefermente of Orphans, some for or towardes Reliefe Stocke or Maintenance of Howses of Correccion, some for Mariages of poore Maides, some for Supportacion Ayde and Helpe of younge tradesmen Handicraftesmen and persons decayed, and others for reliefe or redemption of Prisoners or Captives, and for aide or ease of any poore Inhabitantes concerninge paymente of Fifteenes, setting out of Souldiers and other Taxes.

Thereafter, the courts in England, duly followed by those in all common law countries, would not regard a purpose as charitable unless it was included in the above list or could be interpreted as coming within 'the spirit and intendment'[15] rule and was for the 'public benefit'. Having attained charitable status, the purpose – as given effect by a donor, organisation, gift or activity – became generally eligible for tax exemption.

Transfer to the colonies

The common law heritage bequeathed by England was neither wholly nor equally shared with its colonies. The 1601 Act did not necessarily apply and, unlike Ireland, no equivalent statute was ever passed in other jurisdictions to legislatively establish the same charitable purposes and regulatory regime.[16] Charitable trusts did not always transfer to become the preferred legal structure for charity and, therefore, neither did the considerable body of equity-based principles that governed trustees and did so much to shape the social role of charity in the UK and Ireland become as significant to charity law in distant colonies where company law was always more relevant.[17] However, judicial precedents established in the courts of England and deriving their authority from the provisions of the 1601 Act, or, more precisely, from the principles articulated in the Preamble, were assiduously followed throughout the colonies, and over the ensuing centuries this practice did much to build a common pool of jurisprudence.

---

15 This rule refers to the common law practice of extending by analogy a recognition of charitable purpose to those activities which, although not enumerated in the Preamble to the Statute of Charitable Uses 1601, are judicially viewed as being so close to those listed that they could be construed as coming within the intention of that legislation.
16 The Statute of Charitable Uses 1601 did not apply in Canada, though it did in Australia.
17 In New Zealand, however, the charitable trust did have an early and fairly enduring popularity, as is evident in its legislative history. In Canada there was little reliance on trusts, preference being given to the incorporation of charities, either as not-for-profit corporations or societies.

The ruling in Pemsel

During the next two centuries and more, as neither statute nor judiciary intervened to classify the charitable purposes listed in the Elizabethan statute, the Court of Chancery developed its own separate body of charitable trust jurisprudence. Eventually such classification was provided by Lord Macnaghten in *Commissioners for Special Purposes of Income Tax v Pemsel*,[18] who then classified all recognised charitable purposes under four heads and added that to be charitable, a gift must be 'beneficial to the community'. He ruled as follows:[19]

> 'Charity' in its legal sense comprises four principal divisions: trusts for the relief of poverty; trusts for the advancement of education; trusts for the advancement of religion; and trusts beneficial to the community not falling under any of the preceding heads. The trusts last referred to are not any the less charitable in the eye of the law, because incidentally they benefit the rich as well as the poor, as indeed, every charity that deserves the name must do directly or indirectly.

To be considered charitable in law, a trust had to fall into one of these four separate but not necessarily mutually exclusive categories. The Macnaghten ruling was subsequently adopted in all common law jurisdictions and defined the judicial approach to charities and to charitable activity thereafter (see, further, Chapter 3).

Interpretation

Within its common law definition, charity was never seen as having a broad application to human need and was not even intended to provide an answer to poverty. Indeed, while permitted to alleviate the latter's effects, charity has traditionally been debarred from addressing its causes.[20] Nor was it ever equipped to deal with the needs of those suffering from the many, often complex and interwoven, systemic forms of social disadvantage. The fact that charity was not broadly applicable to ameliorate human hardship, and often had no relationship to it, was ruefully acknowledged by Lord Sterndale MR:[21]

> I confess I find considerable difficulty in understanding the exact reason why a gift for the benefit of animals, and for the prevention of cruelty to

18　[1891] AC 531.
19　Ibid., at p. 583.
20　See, for example, Gurin, M.G. and Van Til, J., 'Philanthropy in Its Historical Context', *Critical Issues in American Philanthropy, Strengthening Theory and Practice*, Van Til, V. and Assocs. (eds.), 1990, where a distinction is drawn between charity (person-to-person alleviation of need) and philanthropy (strategic approach to social problems).
21　See, *Re Tetley* [1923] 1 Ch 258 at 266–267, as cited in Sheridan, L.A., Keeton and Sheridan's, *The Modern Law of Charities* (4th ed.), Barry Rose, Chichester, 1992 at pp. 4–5.

animals generally, should be a good charitable gift, while a gift for philanthropic purposes, which, I take it, is for the benefit of mankind generally, should be bad as a charitable gift. The gift for the benefit of animals, apparently, is held to be valid because it is educative of mankind, it being good for mankind that they should be taught not to be cruel but kind to animals, and one would quite agree with that. But if the benefit of mankind on that particular side makes that a good charitable gift it is a little difficult to see why any philanthropic purpose to benefit mankind on all sides is a bad one. But it is so.

Charity, as traditionally interpreted, was confined to channelling private acts of discretionary benevolence addressed not at 'poverty' but towards the donor's chosen class of beneficiaries, within those restricted areas of social need judicially recognised as constituting a valid charitable purpose. While the essence of this approach has been maintained, the interpretation of charity has long since evolved to accommodate an ever-growing range of organisations, activities and gifts that, in contemporary sophisticated western society, give effect to the broadening range of charitable purposes now held to satisfy the public benefit test. It nonetheless remains the case that for the past four centuries the core features of charity in a common law context have been that it is initiated and directed at donor discretion; recipient eligibility is conditional upon their needs fitting within a legally defined charitable purpose; and, with some variability, the public benefit test must be satisfied.

Charity law

It may seem anomalous that charitable activity should need to be subject to a specific body of law: the integrity and transparency of a personal altruistic gift for public benefit might be thought to be intrinsically irreproachable, hardly requiring the full enforcement powers provided by statute and court. In fact, however, and probably from its inception, charity has needed to be closely regulated for taxation purposes, to guard against abuse of process,[22] and to prevent or detect fraud and fiduciary irregularity. The current statutory legal framework that has evolved to govern charitable activity was heavily influenced by the common law legacy. This brought with it a reliance upon the trust as the preferred legal structure for charity,[23] a corresponding regulatory emphasis on charitable purpose, and a burgeoning sprawl of disparate case precedents.

---

22 See, for example, Dickens, C., *Bleak House* (1852), Trafalgar Square, London, 2008, for a parody of an abuse of process in the Chancery Courts which lasted for generations and totally depleted charity funds.

23 However, the trust was not uniformly accepted by all common law nations as the preferred legal vehicle for charity.

The legal hallmarks of charity

The core legal requirements for a charity to be recognised as such are that an entity must be confined exclusively to charitable purposes, be for the public benefit and be independent, nonprofit-distributing and non-political. There are some jurisdictional variations in the interpretation of these attributes, and donor intention can also be relevant, but throughout the common law world these have long been held to be the legal hallmarks of charity.

Charitable intent

Judicial support for those who choose to donate private wealth for the public benefit has a considerable history,[24] certainly pre-dating the 1601 statute, and gave rise to an assumption that the courts were obliged to give effect to a valid charitable gift in the terms as expressed by the donor,[25] an approach that applied particularly to testamentary dispositions (*voluntas testatoris servanda est*[26]). In most common law jurisdictions, but not in Ireland,[27] the test judicially applied to ascertain a donor's intention is an objective one, i.e. the fact that a donor believed when making the gift that it was charitable will not prevent the courts from ruling otherwise and vice versa because 'the court cannot inquire into the motives of the donor if the gift is in its nature a charity'.[28] In all jurisdictions and in all cases, however, charitable intent is in itself insufficient: no matter how charitable the donor's intention may be, this will not make charitable a gift which does not satisfy the common law definition of charity, has no intrinsic merit,[29] breaches the law[30] or is contrary to public policy.

Charitable purposes

Under the common law, the courts required that gifts be given exclusively for purposes recognised in law as charitable. The charitable purposes as classified in *Pemsel* and subsequently developed by the judiciary were for the relief of poverty; the advancement of education; the advancement of religion; and for other purposes for the benefit of the community not arising under the preceding heads. These were basically to do with those aspects of contemporary social infrastructure that government did not feel the need to exclusively

---

24 Some existing charities long pre-date 1601 (the oldest being, it is claimed, King Edwards School Canterbury, founded in 587).
25 See, *Philpott v St George's Hospital* (1859) 27 Beav 107, per Sir John Romilly MR at p. 111.
26 See, *Robertson v Robertson's Executors* 1914 AD 503, 507.
27 In Ireland the test is subjective, i.e. 'if he intended to advance a charitable object recognised as such by the law, his gift will be a charitable gift', as stated by Keane J in *Re the Worth Library* [1994] 1 ILRM 161 at p. 193.
28 See, *Hoare v Osborne* (1866) LR 1 Eq, 585 per Kindersley VC at p. 588.
29 *Re Pinion* [1965] Ch 85.
30 See, for example, *National Anti-Vivisection Society v IRC* [1948] AC 31.

control but which, in the absence of private contributions, might otherwise impose a drain on its tax revenues. The courts readily acknowledged that the test of what may or may not be lawful will 'vary from generation to generation as the law successively grows more tolerant.'[31] Therefore, the fact that a purpose was previously judicially found to be non-charitable will not prevent it from becoming charitable in the future and vice versa: as the meaning of charity is socially determined, it can be adjusted to ensure a better fit with the values of its contemporary social context, as illustrated, for example, in the jurisdictional differences in the charitable status of recreational sport, closed religious orders, rifle clubs and the prevention of poverty.[32] In recent years the common law approach to charitable purposes and its definition has, in some jurisdictions, been significantly affected by the outcomes of charity law reform processes.

In practice, the fact and nature of a charitable purpose is most often determined by reference to the objects stated in the charity's relevant governing instrument. However, in recent years there have been strong indications that in some jurisdictions the judiciary and/or charity regulators are becoming more willing to impose an 'activities test' to clarify the actual purposes of a charity. The rationale for this approach was succinctly expressed by Gummow J in the *Aid/ Watch* case:[33] 'It is one thing to have objectives. Another question is what you are actually doing'; or, as expressed by Kiefel J during the course of the appeal hearing in the High Court, 'whether an organisation has charitable purposes is determined by reference to the natural and probable consequences of its activities, as well as its stated purposes'.[34]

The public benefit principle

The moral and fiscal rationale for the State to exempt a charitable trust from certain tax and other financial impositions rests on the premise that a donor has chosen not to confer a private benefit upon a personally selected recipient but to instead make an altruistic gift for the public good. This has proven to be a critical component for the validity of a charity in a common law context. In the absence of legislative initiative, the public benefit principle provided the only means whereby new interpretations of charitable purposes could be introduced to develop the concept of charity, enabling it to accommodate newly emerging and local manifestations of social need.

To be charitable the gift must satisfy both arms of the 'public benefit test'; i.e. it must confer an objectively verifiable 'benefit' and it must do so in favour of

---

31 See, Lord Wright in *National Anti-Vivisection Society v Inland Revenue Commissioner*, ibid., at p. 42. Also see *Re Foveaux* [1895] 2 Ch 501.
32 Ibid.
33 *Commissioner of Taxation v Aid/Watch Incorporated* [2009] FCAFC 128 (September 2009).
34 *Commissioner of Taxation v Aid/Watch Incorporated* [2010] HCA 42, per Kiefel J, at para 67.

sufficient members of the 'public'. The test has been applied unevenly across the four *Pemsel* heads of charity,[35] falling most onerously upon the last.

• PUBLIC

While it is certain that a gift conferred on a very limited number of identifiable people is private and therefore not charitable, it is less certain what number of persons or other criteria would be sufficient to satisfy a definition of 'public' and justify charitable status. It will not be justified where the gift is to a closed class[36] (see, further, Chapter 4).

• BENEFIT

Traditionally, the benefit requirement was automatically satisfied if the entity conformed to a purpose recognisable as charitable within the *Pemsel* classification or could be found to be so on the grounds that it came within the 'spirit and intendment' of the Preamble. For all but the small minority of common law nations that have now substituted a legislative regime for the common law approach, as an outcome of their charity law reform process, this continues to be the case (only some within that minority have extended the *Pemsel* heads of charitable purposes).

The issue of public benefit has been particularly contentious in relation to gifts for religious purposes where the religious activity – private masses, 'closed' convents etc – was confined to a strictly defined membership that excluded any possibility of public involvement. Before, during and after the various charity law reform processes, this particular application of the public benefit test generated considerable controversy (see, for example, Chapters 4 and 5).

The public benefit test

Its essentially subjective quality has allowed this crucial test of charitable status to be applied in accordance with the eye of the judicial beholder. This has resulted in an accumulation of disparate case law and doubtful precedent, leaving the test exposed to accusations that it is not always serving the best interests of western society in the third millenium. For example, it has been argued that providing amenities for a privileged minority such as public school education, private hospital care, opera houses and concert halls etc is a doubtful interpretation of benefit for the public. Similarly, organisations which reinforce sectoral differences by ensuring affiliation to a particular religion arguably also provide only membership benefit to specified groups and are thereby discriminatory,

---

35 Generally presumed to be satisfied in respect of the first three heads but requiring proof in relation to the fourth.
36 See, *Re Hobourn Aero Components Ltd's Air Raid Distress Fund* [1946] Ch 194.

emphasise social divisions and possibly reinforce existing social inequity (see, further, Chapter 4).

Exclusively charitable

Case law in the common law jurisdictions has long established that for a trust to be charitable it must be confined exclusively to charitable purposes. The courts look for an exclusive charitable intent and have resolutely declined to save gifts as charitable where the donor had failed to unequivocally and unambiguously state such intent or had expressed mixed intentions, some charitable and some not. If a donor's gift included both charitable and non-charitable purposes, and allowed for the possibility of trustees using at their discretion some or all of the gift for non-charitable purposes, then the courts would refuse to recognise it as charitable.[37]

The cy-près *doctrine*

'*Cy-près*', a Norman French expression, has been generally interpreted by the courts as meaning 'as near as possible'[38] and signifies the judicial efforts across many centuries and common law countries to address problems and retrieve, where possible, the value of assets intended for charity. A *cy-près* scheme has traditionally provided the means of changing the objects of a viable charity, transferring the assets of one that is defunct and thereby giving effect to the charitable intentions of a donor. There is an equitable presumption[39] that such intentions should not be allowed to fail because of a difficulty, perhaps no more than a technical legality, which the donor may not have foreseen. It provides a means, restricted to charitable trusts, whereby assets intended for charity use may be so used and in a manner approximate to the initial intention.

Independent

Traditionally, under common law, a charity was required to be a free-standing, independent entity, founded by and bound to fulfil the terms of the donor's gift. The duty resting on trustees to honour the terms of their trust and ensure that the objects of the charity prevail has always been seen as the primary means whereby the integrity of the donor's gift could be protected.[40] Fulfilling this duty

---

37 See, for example, *Boyle v Boyle* (1877) I.R. 11 Eq 433 and *AG of the Cayman Islands v Wahr – Hansen* [2000] 3 All ER 642.

38 See, Keane, R., *Equity and the Law of Trusts in the Republic of Ireland*, Butterworths, Dublin, 1988, pp. 150–151.

39 See, *dicta* of Lord Hanworth MR in *Re Watt* [1932] 2 Ch 243, at p. 246. Also, see *Re Geary's Trusts* (1890) 25 LR Ir 171.

40 The essence of a trust is that the appointed trustee should exercise good stewardship in respect of the assets entrusted to him or her. See, for example, *Hallows v Lloyd* (1888) 39 Ch D 686.

has required trustees to be resolutely committed to the charity's objects and be free from any influence which may deflect from that focus.

Non-political

In England during the Victorian era, the protests against the conditions suffered by children employed in factories or as chimney sweeps were led by charities such as Dr Barnardo's and the NSPCC. However, it is now generally the case that charities must abide by certain constraints on political activity if they are to retain charitable status. The crucial issue is whether an organisation intends to pursue political activity as its principal objective or whether it is merely pursued ancillary to and in support of a main objective which is not itself political: the former has traditionally been held to be definitely incompatible with charitable status. Charities may engage in limited campaigning for political change but only as an incidental means to achieving a genuine charitable end.[41] The judicial dilemma, when faced with a charity that campaigns on policy issues arising from action or inaction by government or parliament, remains as stated by Parker LJ: 'a trust for the attainment of political objects has always been held invalid, not because it is illegal, for every one is at liberty to advocate or promote by any lawful means a change in the law, but because the Court has no means of judging whether a proposed change in the law will or will not be for the public benefit, and therefore cannot say that a gift to secure the change is a charitable gift'.[42] This has presented a considerable roadblock for charities wishing to engage in public advocacy or political campaigning, though in recent years some jurisdictions have moved beyond this constraint; in the UK it has proved more resilient (see, further, Chapter 4).

Nonprofit distributing

A charity does not compromise its legal status by making a profit. In general, the common law rule is that charities may make profits (or gains) or accumulate surpluses, provided these are not used for the profit or gain of its individual members or for distribution to its owners or members, or to any other person, either while operating or on winding up. Any commercial venture must remain incidental and ancillary to the pursuit of the organisation's overall charitable purpose.

Legal differentiation of 'charity' from other entities

While the common law has endowed 'charity' with sufficient elasticity to allow it to accommodate a disparate selection of entities – including soup kitchens,

---

41 See, for example, *Webb v O'Doherty* (1991), *The Times*, 11 February [1991] 3 Admin LR 731.
42 *Bowman v Secular Society Ltd* [1917] AC 406 at 442.

the Royal Opera House, hospitals, Churches and the saying of mass – it has also sought to prevent it from absorbing all manner of socially beneficial activity and to differentiate it from other nonprofits.

Benevolent causes

Gifts expressed for benevolent purposes have often been declared void, as they are open to being interpreted in ways that may go beyond what is exclusively charitable.[43] As Picarda has stated:[44]

> A gift simply to 'benevolent purposes' is objectionable:[45] a benevolent purpose may be (but is not necessarily) charitable. The same is true of gifts to philanthropic purposes,[46] utilitarian purposes,[47] emigration,[48] patriotic[49] and public purposes:[50] they all go further than legal charity. Likewise gifts for encouraging undertaking of general utility,[51] for hospitality,[52] for such societies as should be in the opinion of trustees 'most in need of help'[53] and for such purposes, civil or religious, as a class of persons should appoint,[54] are too wide . . . the permutations are endless.

As Sir William Grant, in *Morice v Bishop of Durham*, declared:[55]

> Do purposes of liberality and benevolence mean the same as charity? That word in its widest sense denotes all the good affections men ought to bear towards each other: in its most restricted and common sense, relief of the poor. In neither of these senses is it employed in this court.

43 *Houston v Burns* [1918] AC 337 (HL); *Re Jarman's Estate* (1878) 8 Ch D 584; *Re Rilands Estate* [1881] WN 173; *Chichester Diocesan Fund and Board of Finance Inc v Simpson* [1944] AC 341 (HL); *A-G for New Zealand v Brown* [1917] AC 393 (PC).
44 See, Picarda, H., *The Law and Practice Relating to Charities* (3rd ed.), Butterworths, London, 1999 at p. 221.
45 *James v Allen* (1817) 3 Mer 17; *Re Barnett* (1908) 24 TLR 788; and *Lawrence v Lawrence* (1913) 42 NBR 260.
46 *Re Macduff* [1986] 2 Ch 452; *Re Eades* [1920] 2 Ch 353.
47 *Re Woodgate* (1886) 2 TLR 674.
48 *Re Sidney* (1908) 1 Ch 488.
49 *A-G v National Provincial Bank* [1924] AC 262.
50 *Re Da Costa* [1912] 1 Ch 337; *Vezey v Jamson* (1822) 1 Sim & St 69; *Blair v Duncan* [1902] AC 37; *Houston v Burns* [1918] AC 337; and *Re Davis* [1923] 1 Ch 225.
51 *Kendall v Granger* (1842) 5 Beav 300; *Langham v Peterson* (1903) 87 LT 744.
52 *Re Hewitt* (1883) 53 LJ Ch 132; *A-G v Whorwood* (1750) 1 Ves Sen 534.
53 *Re Freeman* [1908] 1 Ch 720.
54 *Re Friends Free School* [1909] 2 Ch 675.
55 (1804) 32 ER 656, 9 Ves J 399.

Where the gift for benevolent purposes is expressed as being additional, rather than an alternative, to charitable purposes, then it will be construed as charitable.[56]

Philanthropic causes

Just as 'benevolent' fails the technical definition of charity in law, so too does 'philanthropic'. Where gifts are expressed as being for charitable or philanthropic purposes they invariably fail, as was the case with the following: 'to such religious charitable and philanthropic objects' as three named persons might select;[57] 'for charitable, religious educational or philanthropic purposes';[58] 'for such charitable, religious philanthropic educational or scientific institution or institutions';[59] and for 'charitable benevolent religious and educational institutions associations and objects'.[60] In recent years the law relating to charity in England and Wales has begun to relax its approach towards policing such distinctions.[61]

Other nonprofits

Charitable activity is now housed in a range of different structures. Government agencies, religious organisations and foundations as well as the more traditional trusts, incorporated and unincorporated associations, Royal charters, other bodies and eleemosynary corporations are now all likely to be claiming tax exemption on the grounds of their charitable activities. Industrial and Provident Societies, Friendly Societies and corporations may also, though infrequently, provide structures for charitable activity. However, charities remain differentiated from other types of nonprofit organisations by their adherence to the public benefit principle, the above-mentioned legal hallmarks, and by the legal form or structure chosen to give effect to their activities. The legal restrictions on trading and advocacy activities by charities quite often cause organisations to avoid charitable status and remain in the world of generic nonprofits.

56 *Re Best* [1904] 2 Ch 354; *Caldwell v Caldwell* [1921] 91 LJPC 95.
57 *Re Eades*, op. cit.
58 *Brewer v McCauley* [1955] 1 DLR 415. Also, *Re Young* (1907) 9 OWR 566 ('needful and worthy institution or institutions, or any needy and worthy individual or individuals'); *Re Street* (1926) 29 OWN 428 ('benevolent institutions'); and *Planta v Greenshields* [1931] 2 DLR 189 ('to aid and help any worthy cause or causes'). *Re Metcalfe* [1947] 1 DLR 567 ('religious, charitable and benevolent purposes').
59 *Re White* [1933] SASR 129 and also *A-G for New South Wales v Adams* (1908) 7 CLR 100; *Re Cole's Estate* (1980) 25 SASR 489.
60 *A.-G. for New Zealand v Brown* [1917] AC 393.
61 See, for example, the Charities Act 1992 where a 'charitable institution' is defined as 'a charity or an institution other than a charity which is established for charitable or philanthropic purposes'.

Charity law reform

By the early years of the 21st century, the governments of Barbados, Canada, Australia, New Zealand, the US, the UK, Singapore and Hong Kong had come to the realisation that the traditional common law approach, designed to address the social needs of Elizabethan England, no longer provided an appropriate or sufficient legal framework for charity in their respective jurisdictions.[62]

Reform drivers

Charity law and social need had fallen seriously out of synch. The functioning of the traditional approach was predicated on a steady flow of judicial judgments which was drying up as litigation became constrained by mounting costs, the protracted delays of court processes and charity concerns regarding unwelcome public exposure: in some jurisdictions, decades passed without any significant charity law cases being heard in the higher courts.[63] Until the closing decades of the 20th century there had been no real pressure to introduce legislation[64] to extend or adjust what had always been a benign regulatory framework. The disparate nature of traditional regulatory mechanisms was obstructive and accentuated an overall lack of coherence. Corporate corruption and mismanagement in the business world (Enron[65] etc) alerted governments to the potential for similar scandals in the charitable sector and stimulated awareness of the need to facilitate transparency, greater accountability and proper models of governance. Eventually, the impetus for regulatory reform was provided by the growing threat from international terrorism, accompanied by the suspicion that charities could unwittingly or otherwise become conduits for the illegal transfer of funds, unless they were subjected to a mandatory and specific registration system.

In part the rationale for charity law review was technical. The *Pemsel* classification no longer provided an appropriate and sufficient agenda of charitable purposes: new manifestations of social need were constantly emerging; the presumption that the benefit test was satisfied in relation to organisations and gifts that could fit within the first three *Pemsel* heads was controversial, particularly in respect of

---

62 See, further, McGregor-Lowndes, M. and O'Halloran, K. (eds.), *Modernising Charity Law: Recent Developments and Future Directions*, Elgar Publications, Cheltenham, 2010.

63 In Australia, for example, no charity law cases were heard by the High Court between *Commissioner of Land Tax (NSW) v Joyce* (1974) 132 CLR 22 and *Bathurst City Council v PWC Properties* (1998) 195 CLR 566.

64 Excepting the Recreational Charities Act 1958 in England and Wales, as subsequently replicated in many common law jurisdictions, which extended definitional boundaries to accommodate recreational sports.

65 The Enron scandal, revealed in October 2001, eventually led to the bankruptcy of the Enron Corporation, an American energy company based in Houston, Texas. This, the largest bankruptcy reorganisation in American history at that time, was attributed to audit failure.

religion; the requirement to prove public benefit for all organisations and gifts, under the fourth head, was arguably discriminatory; and there was uncertainty as to the thresholds of proof for both the 'public' and the 'benefit' components of the test. In the main, however, the rationale was cost driven: the burden of responsibility for present services had to be shifted to some extent towards the nonprofit sector as governments, embroiled in foreign wars and struggling with the revenue implications of unfavourable demographic trends,[66] lacked the spare capacity to meet the health, education and social care needs of their citizens. Moreover, the growing gap between government and the electorate was a matter of concern to the former in many jurisdictions. As had been observed:[67]

> There is a growing crisis at the heart of democratic accountability. The public's disengagement from organised politics has gathered pace as they have lost faith in the more traditional forms of political engagement.

Governments' need to generate a greater sense of civic responsibility had become pressing: in order to increase volunteer input and thereby ease the service delivery onus resting on government bodies; to generate the social capital necessary to build more cohesive and caring communities; and to bridge the gap with the electorate by demonstrating how government and citizens could work together and deliver tangible benefits to local communities.

Reform outcomes

While the particular outcomes achieved by individual countries are best considered in the context of the jurisdiction specific chapters, the following brief summary may be useful at this point.

Possibly the most significant reform outcome was the decision in Scotland, Northern Ireland, Ireland, Singapore and Hong Kong, temporarily in New Zealand and tentatively in Australia, to follow the lead given earlier by England and Wales and establish relatively independent, charity-specific, lead regulatory bodies statutorily responsible for the following: sector support; maintaining a register of charities; determining charitable status; providing advice and improving governance; monitoring through annual reports and financial statements; and conducting audits and investigations. In England and Wales, Scotland, Northern Ireland and Ireland the review processes concluded with – and in New Zealand, Australia, Canada and Singapore concluded without – changes to some core definitional matters. In all, the statutory definition of 'charity' simply restates the legal meaning given

---

66 See, Tanzi, V., *Government versus Markets: The Changing Economic Role of the State*, Cambridge University Press, Cambridge, 2011.

67 See, Advisory Group, Report on Campaigning and the Voluntary Sector (chaired by Baroness Helena Kennedy QC), London, 2007 at p. 1.

to it under the common law. In the UK and Irish jurisdictions, change has taken the form of a significant redefinition of 'public benefit' and a statutory restatement of all other common law concepts.[68] With the exception of Canada, all jurisdictions placed the key common law concepts onto the statute books, thereby giving their governments the future capacity to add, subtract from, or otherwise qualify, the list of charitable purposes, and amend or adjust the rules relating to matters such as public benefit, exclusiveness and independence. Additionally, although the UK and Irish jurisdictions reversed the public benefit presumption traditionally granted to the first three *Pemsel* heads (excepting religion in Ireland), this initiative has not been adopted elsewhere. Moreover, the precise criteria of such a test and the calibration and weighting to be given to it, in application to traditional institutional religions as opposed to emergent minority religious groups and to philosophical, moral or ethical belief systems, has yet to be determined. In this context, the warning given by the ECtHR in *Jehovah's Witnesses v Austria* must be borne in mind:[69]

> if a State sets up a framework for conferring legal personality on religious groups to which a specific status is linked, all religious groups which so wish must have a fair opportunity to apply for this status and the criteria established must be applied in a non-discriminatory manner.

The fact that all reforming jurisdictions chose to retain as charitable the set of purposes first identified and listed in the 1601 statute[70] and classified in *Pemsel* means that the currency of all related case law will maintain its value; all jurisdictions, whether or not engaged in law reform, will continue to share the basic common law platform; and they will keep the same associated public benefit service provision opportunities. However, of the handful of nations to embark on reform, a minority took an important further step. The UK jurisdictions and Ireland introduced legislation to give effect to government's plans for broadening charity's contribution by adding to the Preamble list of charitable purposes. This set of '*Pemsel* plus' charitable purposes, as has been explained,[71] identifies with remarkable consistency clusters of new purposes, cohering around clear social policy themes, that reveal matters central to government's intended partnership arrangement with charity. These are: the advancement of human rights,

---

68 Note that both s.8(2)(a) of the Charities and Trustee Investment (Scotland) Act 2005 and s.3(3)(a)(ii) of the Charities Act (Northern Ireland) 2008 insert a statutory requirement that when applying the public benefit test, regard must also be had to any possible negative side effects.
69 (2009) 48 EHRR 17, 445. This ruling has implications for countries with an 'established' religion.
70 Statute of Charitable Uses 1601 (43 Eliz. 1. Cap. 4).
71 See, McGregor-Lowndes, M. and O'Halloran, K. (eds.), *Modernising Charity Law*, Elgar Publishing, London, 2010 and also O'Halloran, K., *The Politics of Charity*, Routledge, London, 2011.

conflict resolution or reconciliation, and promotion of multiculturalism etc; the advancement of civil society; the advancement of health and related services; and promoting the welfare of specific socially disadvantaged groups. In addition, the reform processes in these jurisdictions concluded with statutory provisions allowing charitable purposes concerned with matters of poverty and health to accommodate a preventative dimension. Also, a statutory definition of religion now forms part of charity law in the UK jurisdictions and, to a lesser extent, in Ireland.

Human rights: the concept

Certain rights are held to be more important than others and to transcend all jurisdictions. Essentially these are defined as coming within the doctrine of human rights which declares that there are basic civil, political, economic, social and cultural rights that all human beings should enjoy – regardless of any differences in status due to citizenship, residency, ethnicity, gender, or other considerations – and in respect of which national and international mechanisms are available to provide for their protection, enforcement and to ensure accountability for any breach thereof. As Van Bueren explains, 'it is the universality of human rights, as fundamental to our sense of being human, which distinguishes human rights law from other areas of law'.[72]

The rights regarded as 'fundamental' include the freedoms of association and assembly, of expression and of religion. Being embodied in international conventions not only elevates their significance relative to all other civil rights, but it also serves to both reinforce the standing of corresponding charity law principles (e.g. to form unincorporated associations) while also clarifying the interface between charity and legal rights, the result being what Judt describes as 'rights bearing citizens with an unconditional claim upon the attention and support of the collectivity' leading to 'a more cohesive society, with no category of persons excluded or less "deserving"'.[73]

Fundamental human rights

The Preamble to the Universal Declaration of Human Rights, as adopted by the General Assembly of the United Nations on 10 December 1948, anticipates 'a world in which human beings shall enjoy freedom of speech and belief and freedom from fear and want'. Subsequently, under the auspices of the UN High Commissioner for Human Rights, a series of international human rights treaties have been concluded to which signatory nations have agreed to hold themselves accountable, reinforced by declarations, guidelines and principles that contribute to their implementation.

---

72 See, *The Human Dignity Trust v Charity Commission for England and Wales*, 6 July 2014, Appeal no CA/2013/0013 at para 94.
73 See, Judt, T., *When the Facts Change*, Penguin Press, New York, 2015 at p. 310.

Currently, although there are ten human rights treaties, each monitored by a committee of independent experts,[74] being unaccompanied by binding international enforcement mechanisms, they appear to be largely aspirational.

However, most signatory States have also adopted constitutional provisions or other overarching legislation (see, jurisdiction-specific chapters) to formally give effect to the provisions of some international human rights treaties. Ratification of any such treaty brings with it the obligation for the government concerned to put into place domestic measures and legislation compatible with their treaty obligations and duties. Where domestic legal proceedings fail to address human rights abuses, there are mechanisms and procedures for individual complaints, communications and appeals to be heard at an international level to reinforce specified human rights standards. But simply by becoming a signatory State a nation assumes obligations and duties under international law to respect, to protect and to fulfil human rights by refraining from interfering with or curtailing their enjoyment, by protecting individuals and groups against abuses, and by taking positive action to facilitate the enjoyment of those rights.

The international framework

The foundations of the contemporary international human rights framework were established by the above-mentioned United Nations Universal Declaration of Human Rights 1948, followed by various treaties, and the European Convention for the Protection of Human Rights and Fundamental Freedoms 1950. For present purposes the former is taken to be the basic yardstick applicable to all jurisdictions currently being considered, while the latter is of importance in relation to England and Wales and Ireland, particularly Articles 6, 9, 10, 11,14 and Article 2 of Protocol 1. Also important are the Convention on the Rights of the Child (UNCROC) and Article 18 of the International Covenant on Civil and Political Rights.

The twin European institutions applying this law are the Council of Europe and the European Union, while enforcement powers are vested in the European Court of Human Rights.

---

74 The ten international human rights treaties are: the International Convention on the Elimination of All Forms of Racial Discrimination (1965); the International Covenant on Civil and Political Rights (1966) and its optional protocols; the International Covenant on Economic, Social and Cultural Rights (1966); the Convention on the Elimination of All Forms of Discrimination against Women (1979) and its optional protocol (1999); the Convention against Torture and Other Cruel, Inhuman or Degrading Treatment (1984); the Convention on the Rights of the Child (1989) and its optional protocols (2000); the International Convention on the Protection of the Rights of All Migrant Workers and Members of Their Families (1990); the International Convention on the Rights of Persons with Disabilities (2006); the International Convention for the Protection of All Persons from Enforced Disappearance (2006); and the Optional Protocol of the Convention against Torture (2002). See, further, at: http://www.ohchr.org/EN/HRBodies/Pages/TreatyBodies.aspx.

- THE COUNCIL OF EUROPE

Founded in 1949, this body represents 47 States and is responsible for the European Court of Human Rights (ECtHR) as well as other treaties on specific issues, and seeks to develop common and democratic principles based on the European Convention on Human Rights. Its work includes promoting gender equality and, more recently, lesbian, gay, bisexual and transgender equality. It relates to charity matters, for example, in its formulation of a basic policy for NGOs as explained in *Fundamental Principles on the Status of Non-governmental Organisations in Europe.*[75] The resulting compliance pressure prompted the subsquent shaping of some aspects of UK case law to conform with those principles, and adjustments to legal structures (and pressure to accept a European foundation model) and in new processes for assuring the formal recognition of charities established outside the jurisdiction.

- THE EUROPEAN UNION

This includes 27 States and has responsibility for the European Court of Justice (ECJ), which enforces the Charter of Fundamental Rights that is binding on all EU institutions as well as member States when they are implementing EU law.

- THE ECtHR

This body, which was established by the European Convention and in 1998 replaced the European Commission of Human Rights, hears complaints that a contracting Member State has violated rights enshrined in the Convention and its protocols.

The human rights based approach

This approach is seen as represented by five legal principles:[76]

- Express application of the international human rights framework;
- Empowerment of rights-holders;
- Participation in one's own development (as of right and not just as best practice);
- Non-discrimination and prioritisation of vulnerable groups; and
- Accountability of duty-bearers to rights-holders (for process and impact).

The human rights recognised in international law are viewed as minimum agreed standards. States are expected and prompted to achieve higher standards and to constantly further develop their laws and practice.

75 See, the Secretariat Directorate General of Legal Affairs, Strasbourg, April 2002.
76 See, further, International Human Rights Network, at: http://www.ihrnetwork.org/what-are-hr-based-approaches_189.htm.

Human rights and civil society

As was explained in *The Human Dignity Trust v Charity Commission for England and Wales*, the purpose of international and constitutional human rights instruments is:[77]

> To withdraw certain subjects from the vicissitudes of political controversy, to place them beyond the reach of majorities and officials and to establish them as legal principles to be applied by the courts.

There can be little doubt that by requiring signatory States to establish and implement a basic platform of standards, the human rights approach is thereby reinforcing the institutions of civil society. This should strengthen the legitimacy, independence and self-reliance of such States. Arguably, however, it also detracts somewhat from that effect by instilling an awareness of a supervening source of authority – conventions, protocols and courts – lying outside national boundaries, to which entities may ultimately have recourse: citizens of common law nations within the EU may look to the ECtHR, rather than exclusively to their own national institutions, to rectify an issue of social inequality; this in turn could serve to weaken national civil society and, indeed, national sovereignity.

Moreover, there is a sense in which the solidarity necessary for civil society has also been weakened by the number and sometimes conflicting nature of new associational forms that have sprung up to assert the separate identity of minority groups. The social coherence that initially accompanied a fundamental human rights approach to social disadvantage is now endangered by the splintering effect of minority groups (e.g. gay, lesbian, disabled, faith based[78]) asserting their separate rights against the collective values of historically disadvantaged communities (e.g. poor, racially distinct). It is a sad irony that some of the more basic principles underpinning the Human Rights Convention – equality, non-discrimination – deployed to gain justifiable recognition for the singular identity of a group with shared interests would now seem to be licensing incremental social fragmentation.

Convention rights, freedoms and charity law

As has been pointed out, 'it is incumbent on domestic courts to construe domestic laws compatibly with Convention rights'[79] and, in particular, public authorities are required to act in accordance with such rights.[80] The practice, however,

---

77 Op. cit., at para 87.
78 See, for example, *Leyla Sahin v Turkey*, ECtHR, Strasbourg, Application No 44774/98.
79 See, *Eweida v British Airways plc* [2009] ICR 303, per Elias P, at para 27.
80 See, for example, the Office for Democratic Institutions and Human Rights, Organization for Security and Co-operation in Europe and European Commission for Democracy through Law, 'Guidelines for Review of Legislation Pertaining to Religion Or Belief', Venice, 2004.

varies: in some EU countries the European Convention on Human Rights, and decisions of the ECtHR, are incorporated into national law and override any national law inconsistent with them; in others, such as the UK, the courts are required, as far as possible, to interpret legislation in a Convention-compliant manner, but have no power to strike national legislative provisions even if they are found to be clearly inconsistent.

Convention rights with the most direct bearing on charity law are those relating to the following: establishing organisations; ensuring proper processes; safeguarding personal freedoms; asserting rights of expression, religion and advocacy; and prohibiting discrimination (see, further, Chapter 3). For charity, the Convention's importance in relation to these rights lies primarily in the fact that once acceded to by signatory States they then become firmly established as personal legal rights and not matters that may be left to the discretion of donor or government. In Europe, this is subject to the 'margin of appreciation' rule by which the ECtHR permits States a degree of latitude in their interpretation of human rights obligations.[81] Where human rights and charity converge, as in their fusion in the United Nations Children's Fund (UNICEF),[82] which is a registered charity in the UK, this can provide a powerful instrument for globally channelling public and private resources to raise awareness of rights and improve standards for the more vulnerable members of society.

On a broader front the Convention is important because the domestic law and procedures of signatory states are gradually being infused with Convention benchmarks and standards, while compliance requirements are serving to push legislatures and courts to recognise a broader definition of matters construed as being for the public benefit. Whether, following such recognition, charitable status can be awarded to organisations engaged in related activities (e.g. advocacy in respect of those seeking access to justice or challenging injustice) is subject to jurisdictional variation in accordance with the effects of recent national charity law reforms.

Convention benchmarks

Certain social justice benchmarks have emerged from Convention case law as key building blocks for international human rights jurisprudence. These are being absorbed into the practice and procedures of public bodies and are assuming a governing influence on the law relating to charity, as in relation to other matters, in all signatory States. In addition, the Convention gives permission not just to challenge State institutions but also to access and use those institutions in order to increase the effectiveness of that challenge.

---

81 See, for example, *Lautsi v Italy* App No 30814/06 (ECtHR Mar. 18, 2011). See, further, Legg, A., *The Margin of Appreciation in International Human Rights Law*, OUP, Oxford, 2012.
82 Founded in 1946 by the UN General Assembly to provide emergency food and healthcare to children in post-war countries, this organisation and its multimillion annual income is currently active in nearly 200 countries.

Convention benchmarks include the key standards of 'necessity', 'proportion-ality' and 'equality of arms' against which relevant national legislative provisions and decision-making processes of all democratic signatory States can be tested. They have potentially far-reaching implications for the socially disadvantaged and more broadly for social policy.

Necessity

The European Convention on Human Rights (ECHR) in *Olson v Sweden (No 1)*[83] explained that to be justifiable, State interference in family life must be: 'relevant and sufficient; it must meet a pressing social need; and it must be proportionate to the need'. Frequently the ECHR can be seen applying the test – is this form of state intervention necessary in a democratic society?[84]

Proportionality

The ECtHR looks at the interference complained of in the light of the case as a whole to determine whether it was 'proportionate to the legitimate aim pur-sued' and whether the reasons adduced by the national authorities to justify it are 'relevant and sufficient'. For example, an application of the proportionality test to the third of the four *Pemsel* heads, the advancement of religion, might conclude that it would be breached by any narrow common law interpretation of what constitutes a religion (e.g. by the exclusion of non-theistic religions such as Buddhism[85]).

Equality of arms

The principle that the State should ensure that those presenting or defend-ing a case are not disadvantaged, relative to the opposing party, by inadequate resources is clearly of considerable importance to the socially disadvantaged.[86]

Relevance for charity

The ECtHR responds to applicants alleging a breach of their basic human rights due to the actions or inactions of public bodies by protecting, asserting and balanc-ing those rights against the exercise of the statutory powers provided to the relevant public bodies. While for the UK and Irish jurisdictions (as with all other signatory

---

83   (1988) 11 EHRR 299.
84   See, *Olson v Sweden (No 1)* (1988) 11 EHRR 299, where it is explained that to be justifiable such interference must be 'relevant and sufficient; it must meet a pressing social need; and it must be proportionate to the need'.
85   *R v Registrar General ex p Segerdal* [1970] 2 QB 697.
86   See, for example, *Steel and Morris v the United Kingdom* (App No 68416/01) (2005).

States) those rights are to be found in the European Convention as assimilated by national statute law, broadly equivalent rights are located within the domestic legislation or constitutions of most other developed common law nations. For all concerned, the encoding of specific human rights imposes parameters on charity by demarcating between a rights entitlement and a discretionary gift.

The charity law/human rights interface

The Convention adds weight to corresponding charitable purposes: there is a degree of cumulative synergy in respect of certain common principles – most obviously via the recent inclusion of 'the promotion of human rights' as a charitable purpose in some charity legislation. For the UK and Irish jurisdictions, Convention rights together with the principles established by ECtHR rulings have broadened the role of charity, resulting in an extended list of purposes. That those such as the advancement of justice etc, previously denied charitable status,[87] have now been recognised as charitable (sometimes by legislative provision) is directly attributable to Convention influence. However, the unavoidable corollary is that where nations have not given such recognition, this must be assumed to be a political choice to avoid any human rights/charity law synthesis.

The above benchmarks inject standards to qualify the traditional roles of parties in the gift relationship and also serve to guide entitlement to public benefit services. By establishing a clear rights framework and processes for accessing justice, the option of relying upon rights rather than on charity becomes available for some as an appropriate route to secure a remedy for social need. The main impact of such a body of rights, however, remains largely undetected: by modifying the decision-making processes of national public bodies, particularly the courts, the rulings of the relevant court operate to embed conduct that is human rights compliant and obviate the need for it to hear further applications on that subject.

Public bodies and charities: convention requirements binding on charities

The Preamble to the European Convention declares its provisions to be binding upon 'every organ of society', but it has been a matter of some controversy as to whether or to what extent this applies to organisations such as charities. However, there can be little doubt that to the degree that they perform public functions, charities are subject to the Convention.[88] That such bodies come

---

87 See, *Mc Govern v Attorney General* [1982] Ch 321, per Slade J, who said that 'the elimination of injustice has not as such ever been held to be a trust purpose which qualifies for the privileges afforded to charities by English law'.
88 For a fuller discussion, see Warburton, J. and Cartwright, A., 'Human Rights, Public Authorities and Charities', *Charity Law Practice Review*, Vol 6, No 3, 2000.

within the jurisdiction of the European Court was clearly stated by it in *Foster v British Gas.*[89]

> A body, whatever its legal form, which has been made responsible pursuant to a measure adopted by the State, for providing a public service under control of the State and has for that purpose special powers beyond those which resulted from the normal rules applicable in relations between individuals is included among the bodies against which the provisions of a Directive capable of having direct effect may be relied upon.

Charities as agents of public bodies

The common law principle of 'agency', or *qui facit per alium, facit per se* (the one who acts through another, acts in his or her own interests), has been defined as 'the relationship between a principal and an agent whereby the principal, expressly or impliedly, authorises the agent to work under his control and on his behalf.'[90] Whether an agency relationship exists turns on the facts in each case: not all delegated authority necessarily constitutes agency; the span of control exercised is crucial. Where, as in a growing number of cases,[91] there is evidence that a charity has allowed itself to become subsumed into an agency/principal relationship with a government body, then, as noted in Tudor, 'the activities of the charity may be so enmeshed with those of a public authority as to be public functions'.[92] As the ECJ stated in *Calì & Figli v Servizi Ecologici Porto de Genova*, an entity acts a public body when it is performing 'a task in the public interest which forms part of the essential functions of the State and where the activity is connected by its nature, its aims and rules to which it is subject with the exercise of powers . . . which are typically those of a public authority'.[93] In that event, such a charity will then share the same level of accountability and on the same terms as a public body. Further, the extent to which a charity is dependent upon funding from a government department will also, to that extent, indicate that it is controlled by and is functioning as an arm of that public authority.[94]

---

89 [1990] 3 All ER 897.
90 See, e.g., Markesinis, B.S. and Munday, R.J.C., *An Outline of the Law of Agency* (4th ed.), LexisNexis, London, 1998.
91 See, for example: *National Union of Teachers v Governing Body of St Mary's Church of England (Aided) Junior School* [1997] 3 CMLR 630; *R (Weaver) v London & Quadrant Housing Trust* [2009] EWCA Civ 587; [2008] EWHC 1377 (Admin); [2008] WLR (D) 207; and *Poplar Housing and Regeneration Community Association Ltd v Donoghue* [2001] EWCA Civ 595, [2002] QB 48.
92 See, Warburton, J., *Tudor on Charities* (9th ed.), Sweet & Maxwell, London, 2003, at p. 393.
93 [1997] ECR I-1547 at para 23. Also, see, *Foster v British Gas* [1990] 3 All ER 897.
94 See, *National Union of Teachers v Governing Body of St Mary's Church of England (Aided) Junior School* [1997] 3 CMLR 630 and also see *R v Panel on Take-overs and Mergers, ex p Datafin plc* [1987] 1 QB 815.

In passing, it must be noted that as government draws closer to those chari-ties which have a direct service provision purpose (e.g. in health, social care and education) and increases their funding, so it is also inclined to distance itself from advocacy organisations (e.g. human rights) and at least reduce their funding or, in some cases, challenge their charitable status. While the first type of charity is treated as a proxy government service provider, the second is viewed as trouble-some because of the likelihood of their challenging government policy. Any cuts in government funding will disproportionately affect the latter (e.g. Amnesty International) as they have less chance than the former (e.g. Hospice Care) of making up the shortfall through public donations.

One objective of this book is to identify and explore any jurisdictional varia-tion in charity compliance with, or accountability for breaches of, human rights requirements, when acting as government agent in a service delivery capacity.

Conclusion

The Titmuss theory of the gift relationship is inadequate as an explanation for charity as defined by charity law, as it fails to address the constraints and negative aspects accompanying the transaction that legally constitutes an act of charity. There is less room for equivocation in respect of human rights, which comprise a clearly defined set of legal entitlements. While both charity and human rights represent ameliorative interventions in the affairs of those suffering from some form of injury, loss or disadvantage, their approaches are quite different: the for-mer is directed towards effects, alleviating the needs of a nexus of beneficiaries as defined by a charitable purpose; the latter deals with structural causes, correcting injustices to classes of persons as defined by breaches of specific fundamental legal rights. Their compatibility is at least open to question.

3 Legal functions

Introduction

Giving effect to legislative intent, accurately and effectively, requires the necessary authority to be operationalised through a coherent legal system, by appropriate bodies exercising legal functions that are fit for purpose. Difficulties arise when authority is not necessarily to be found wholly in legislative form, where the bodies vested with responsibility for exercising it are not best equipped to do so or where the legal functions are drawn from jurisprudence containing principles that are not always compatible. The marriage of charity law and human rights is flawed with such difficulties.

This chapter considers the interface between charity law and human rights in the developed common law countries. It proceeds by first examining in general the relationship between authority, social policy and legal systems before turning to address the specific charity law/human rights relationship. It then works towards designing a template that can be applied to focus a comparative analysis of that interaction in the sample of countries selected for study in Part II.

The chapter begins with an exploration of sources of authority. It examines the importance of a legal system, its component parts and operational methods: giving attention to the principles that inform charity law, the precedents that underpin it and the rules, institutions and agencies that give effect to it, while also noting the impact upon it of international human rights. This leads into the main section which deals with the legal system as it relates to the charity law/human rights interface: the relevant agencies, their respective roles, responsibilities and the intended outcomes are identified, introduced and explained as a precursor to the analysis that follows in Part II.

This chapter provides the material for a loose template the purpose of which is to identify matters congruent to both charity law and human rights, together with areas of conflict, thereby permitting a comparative evaluation of jurisdictional differences and their significance.

Sources of authority

Sources of domestic authority in the common law nations studied in Part II lie with government, the legislature and the judiciary, albeit in varying degrees and subject to formal checks and balances. It is then exercised by the courts, in accordance with principles of judicial independence and discretion and/or other bodies and institutions to which it has been duly delegated for purposes of administration and enforcement. International authority, emanating from outside the jurisdiction, only attains national currency if endorsed by the executive, or assimilated by domestic legislation, and is taken into account in judicial deliberations.

Government, politics and ideology

As Pol Pot followed the absolutist regimes of Maoism, Nazism and Communism into the ideological graveyard, the prevailing assumption was that liberal democracy would be left to safely consolidate its position as the only truly viable and enduring political model. A sentiment echoed by the assertion in the Preamble to the ECHR that peace and justice in the world 'are best maintained on the one hand by an effective political democracy and on the other by a common understanding and observance of the human rights upon which they depend'.

However, as the second decade of the 21st century advances, the indebted common law jurisdictions are still struggling to recover from the 2008 economic crisis. Their socio-economic fragility has been compounded by the need to become evermore embroiled in warfare in Islamic countries as stability in the Middle East and the domestic security of citizens in the west are threatened by a new brand of religious totalitarianism. Added to which there is the growing uncertainty regarding the future, as the EU prepares for the possible exit of one or more members and war in the Ukraine steadily increases the tension between NATO and Russia. These and myriad other pressures, including large-scale population migration, adds up to a defensive political climate that inclines government towards introducing tighter controls to guard against further destabilisation. This has had significant repercussions for the relationship between government and the nonprofit sector in the leading common law countries, as illustrated by a distinct change of emphasis in the policy driving charity law reform (see, further, below).

Politics and social policy

For government in the developed common law jurisdictions, as elsewhere, contemporary politics is largely concerned with consolidating civil society, firefighting the associated internal and external threats, and planning for the future. In recent years, for reasons that include the above mentioned, the resulting social policy has been very much focused on economic matters: funding public benefit services – particularly social welfare, unemployment benefits, education, health and social care – has become a pressing issue. This has been exacerbated by unfavourable demographic trends, featuring falling fertility rates and increasing numbers of frail elderly, that inescapably lead to an unfortunate combination of shrinking tax revenues combined with expanding social services costs.

Charity law

The policy agenda as first formulated by 'government' in the Preamble, and the role to be played by charity in addressing it, has endured and spread throughout the common law nations. That inaugural charity law statute represented a government statement of matters constituting the public benefit (charitable purposes) and the terms on which government proposed to engage with charity in addressing such matters (tax privileges, regulatory framework to prevent abuse etc). It was essentially a political blueprint and one that came up for re-evaluation in the context of recent charity law reform processes for reasons that were also clearly political.

The functioning of charity law shows where the emphasis lies in terms of government determined social policy priorities together with matching conditions or constraints, and discloses the gaps through which fall those sets of needs for which no provision has been made.

Human rights

On becoming signatory States of international treaties and conventions, the governments of the countries concerned are obliged to ensure not only that national social policies are human rights compliant but also that the embedding and further development of human rights becomes a social policy in itself. The results can be seen in the introduction of human rights legislation and in the inclusion of provisions in a range of supportive domestic legislation – including the post–charity law reform statutes.

Legislature and statute law

In all modern democratic common law nations, the 'will of parliament' as expressed by the government of the day and embodied in legislation – though subject in some to constitutional provisions – is usually prescriptive rather than enabling and intended to advance a particular social policy. However, that 'will' is being steadily circumscribed as an ever-extending raft of international treaties, conventions, protocols and other instruments form supervening sources of authority which are binding upon signatory nations, requiring compliance of domestic courts, administrative bodies and other decision-making forums.

Formative legislation

A statute is formative if it comprises a body of provisions which by consolidating existing law and comprehensively addressing both pressing and predicted issues, establishes a new baseline for the relationship between law and its subject matter. It may well include provisions that state governing principles.

Legislation and vesting authority

Legislation performs the important role of empowering the agencies designated to give effect to the law. It provides the source of relevant authority by defining and vesting the powers and duties of the courts, tribunals, officials and various other agencies charged with administering statutory provisions. The type and distribution of authority variously vested is crucial and clearly reflects the social policy priorities of government: as illustrated by the fact that in England and Wales the power to determine charitable status rests not with the Inland Revenue (HMRC) but with the Charity Commissioners, who in turn share jurisdiction with the High Court; this reflects government policy that the State should relate to the charitable sector primarily through a developmental role, and is quite different from the position elsewhere in the common law world where the revenue agency has traditionally borne that responsibility exclusively.

However, rendering legislative intent into appropriate and effective legal function can be problematic. New legislation has to operate in conjunction with a plethora of other statutes, becomes quickly outdated, is mediated through a legal system that may well re-interpret that intent and it can be operationally governed by authority drawn from other sources of law or become subject to ideology. The effectiveness of modern legislation very often depends not so much on its provisions, which can be brief and broadly stated, but on the accompanying bulky ancillary rules and regulations in which the intended legal function can be dissipated. Legislation, in whole or part, can be negated by rulings of a supervening authority such as the ECtHR, be simply ignored or, being unenforced, be allowed to lapse. The courts or other forum may – by responsible use of discretion, or by error or willfulness – subvert legislative intent in their interpretation of key provisions. Moreover, one legal function can be fatally undermined by the operational weighting given to another.

Judiciary and a body of jurisprudence

Statute law is for the judiciary to interpret, which they do by construing new provisions against established rulings, giving priority to the latter where uncertainty or ambiguity arises in discerning legislative intent. However, apart from provisions modelled in the Charity Act 1960, there had been virtually no other legislative initiative for several centuries, leaving charity law in all common law jurisdictions unusually heavily reliant upon the judiciary, largely the English judiciary, to adjust the law in accordance with contemporary patterns of social need. The nations studied in Part II have consequently all placed a high premium on authority derived from judicial rulings and from a shared body of established jurisprudence. Unfortunately, as Simonds LJ once noted, although 'a great body of law has thus grown up. Often it may appear illogical and even capricious'.[1]

Maintaining social cohesion requires the law to project its functions to some degree into the future. This it does by prescribing rules and procedures, to be given effect through its institutional infrastructure, accompanied by related

---

1 *Gilmour v Coats* [1949] AC 426, per Simonds LJ at p. 443.

penalties. Rules, drawn from established sources of authority, operate to give society clearly understood common parameters for present conduct and a basis for confidence that such conduct will continue into the future.

Precedents

Judicial precedents are an entrenched aspect of the common law with an extensive history. Indeed, their significance was noted by Richard Fitz-Nigel in the 12th century who reputedly said 'there are cases where the course of events, and the reasons for decisions are obscure; and in these it is enough to cite precedents'.[2] For all common law societies, the doctrine of precedent has been a crucially important and transferrable source of guidance for the exercise of authority. Except in those areas where a statute prescribes specific rules, the common law approach prevails requiring the statute to be strictly interpreted subject to existing established precedents (see, further, below).

Principles

The capacity of law to provide social continuity is greatly facilitated by the role of principles, whether elucidated and benchmarked by established precedent or prescribed by statute. This is particularly the case with 'grundnorms', or overarching norms which command wide acceptance and are powerful enough to govern other principles, as posited by Kelsen (e.g. the 'public benefit' principle in charity law or the freedom of speech principle in human rights law).[3] Principles inject an added dimension to the law, lifting it beyond being merely a technical response to a particular set of circumstances and setting standards for future conduct.

A legal system

A legal system[4] comprises a body of law drawn from different sources – including the common law, legislation, international treaties and conventions – together with the institutions authorised to implement that law, and the formal processes, procedures, forums and officials for applying it. The system as a whole has an integrative effect: ordering the relationships between government and the governed; validating and regulating the institutional framework and establishing a network of processes and procedures for accessing them; balancing and adjudicating between different sets of interests; and structuring that society's internal and external relationships for the present and foreseeable future.

---

2 Fitz-Nigel, R., *Dialogues de Scaccario*, 1177–1179; cited by Dias, ibid., at p. 56.
3 See, for example, Hans Kelsen, *Pure Theory of Law*, 1934 and *General Theory of Law and State*, 1946.
4 See, further, Hart, H.L.A., *The Concept of Law* (2nd ed.), Clarendon Law Series, Oxford University Press, Oxford, 1994, pp. 100–123.

Unsurprisingly, the common law nations have long adopted much the same legal system for regulating charity and its related organisations, activities, etc.

Blend of common law, statute and international law

Following the lead established by the progenitor nation, all common law jurisdictions assumed a similar conceptual format for interpreting charity together with the associated principles and legal definitions. On these foundations, each jurisdiction has in recent years added a not dissimilar layer of statutes and subscribed, with some significant exceptions, to much the same set of international conventions, protocols etc.

Common law

Centuries of legislative inertia, coupled with adherence to fixed definitional benchmarks, governing principles and analogous judicial precedents, for better or worse, served to keep the legal system as it relates to charity anchored largely on addressing the social policy agenda as initially stated in the Preamble. Until the recent series of national law reform programmes, any development continued to be almost entirely dependent upon a slowly evolving body of judicial precedents. Despite the subsequent widespread introduction of charity legislation, charity law issues will remain very largely governed by well-established jurisprudence. Consequently, the same legal hallmarks and governing principles that have for centuries characterised the legal definition of charity and differentiated it from other public, private, for-profit and nonprofit entities (see, further, Chapter 2) will continue to do so in much the same way throughout the common law nations.

Domestic legislation

In addition to relying on common law definitions, the jurisdictions considered in Part II have also mostly had in place basic charity specific legislation with a focus mainly on regulatory matters. While the national charity law reform processes generally tightened the regulatory regime, one further outcome has been the virtually unanimous statutory encoding of common law concepts, definitions and rules (see, further, Chapter 2). This has served to formally place the governments concerned on much the same charity law platform while also enabling each to introduce new charitable purposes by legislative amendment to address future changes in patterns of social need.

International law

Insofar as they are signatory States, the legal systems of the common law jurisdictions considered in Part II also give effect to the ever-expanding range of international conventions, protocols etc (see, further, Chapter 2). Although the absence of charity specific provisions is evident, nevertheless these instruments often have direct and significant implications for national legal systems, including their relationship to charity.

Regulatory framework

Charity law is largely administrative law. This requires the legal system to rely heavily on State agencies to establish and maintain a co-ordinated regulatory framework consisting of government agencies and the courts exercising clearly defined sets of responsibilities.

   The number of institutions with a level of responsibility for charity matters is considerable – with a degree of jurisdictional variation. However, as some jurisdictions make no distinction between charities and other nonprofit entities for regulatory purposes, this has consequences in terms of the role and responsibilities of certain agencies such as the tax authority.

   For the purposes of the common law nations surveyed in Part II, the network of institutions giving effect to the law relating to charity has always remained subject to the traditional oversight role provided by the High Court judiciary, the Attorney General, and the tax-driven supervision of the Revenue. Other bodies such as the Companies Office have a significant monitoring remit. In addition, the legal system also relies to a varying degree in different jurisdictions on the self-regulatory mechanisms of the charitable sector. In general, the number and range of agencies involved has not proven conducive to facilitating a co-ordinated national legal system for regulating charities.

Role of the High Court

In all common law jurisdictions, the High Court provides a mechanism for controlling the activities of charities and broadening the range of charitable purposes; and legal accountability for the proper management of a charity's affairs lies with it. Its potential capacity to broaden the purposes of charity to meet contemporary forms of need, thereby increasing the latter's usefulness to government, was never wholly fulfilled in any jurisdiction, as charity proceedings gradually acquired a reputation for being rare, excessively long and ruinously expensive.

Role of the Attorney General

The ancient *parens patriae* authority of the Crown in relation to charities, and the right to bring proceedings in respect of them, devolved from the Lord Chancellor to become vested in the Attorney General:[5]

> the King is to be considered as the *parens patriae*; that is he is the protector of every part of his subjects, and that, therefore, it is the duty of his officer, the Attorney General, to see that justice is done to every part of those subjects.

5 *Ludlow Corp. v Greenhove* (1827) 1 Bli. NS 17, at p. 48.

The traditional function of the Attorney General is to represent the public interest in litigation. The rule is that where proceedings involving a charity are commenced, then, if not already a party, the Attorney General should be joined. Whereas in England and Wales the Charity Commission has been statutorily assigned much of the responsibility previously vested in the Attorney General, the traditional powers of this office continue in theory to be largely available within a charity law context throughout the common law nations. Indeed, the fact that it is accompanied by the protection of the Attorney General – originally a distinguishing feature of charitable trusts – has extended to become a right associated with charitable status.

Role of the Revenue

Since the Income Tax Act 1799, charities in the UK have been stautorily exempt from most taxes. This exemption, endorsed a century later in *Pemsel*, was adopted in due course throughout the common law world. Consequently, the Revenue in all jurisdictions has, in the course of its duty to maximise the tax revenues payable to the State, been policing applications from organisations claiming tax exemption on grounds of charitable status. In the UK, as the Charity Commission has been steadily vested with increased statutory powers, so those of the Revenue have decreased. The latter, like equivalent bodies in other common law jurisdictions, applies established common law principles and precedents and issues practice guidance, but unlike those bodies it is now statutorily required to follow modern case law precedents set by the Commission, which marks an important point of departure between its role and that of any of its counterparts.[6]

The determining bodies

For most if not all organisations, the acquisition of charitable status has always been valued primarily as a means of gaining tax exemption. Accordingly, many common law jurisdictions simply relegated responsibility for determining both matters to the national Revenue authority. In England and Wales these two matters have always been treated separately: determination of the first being assigned to the Charity Commission and the second to HMRC. Because of the perceived added value of specialist support and inspection expertise derived from having a charity specific regulator, some jurisdictions, following charity law reform, have ended their traditional sole reliance on the tax authority, de-coupled the two sets of responsibilities and allocated the first to a newly established counterpart to the Charity Commission.

Other administrative agencies

It is now not unusual to find that in the leading common law jurisdictions a government department has oversight for developing and implementing policy as it

6 The priority role of the Commission was confirmed by the Finance Act 1986.

relates to the nonprofit sector, which includes a degree of management responsibility for the lead regulatory body. In England and Wales, the Office for Civil Society undertakes such a role. In addition a range of other agencies have some involvement in the affairs of charities, including Customs and Excise (now HMRC), the Office of Wills and Probate, the Rates Dept., the Companies Office and others.

Integrating concepts and processes

For its component parts to operate as an integrated legal system there has to be clarity and consistency of role in the institutions involved and a level of co-ordination, but in both respects there is considerable jurisdictional variation. The relative independence of the judiciary from both executive and legislative organs of the State is a characteristic of developed democratic nations. This in itself makes the legal system susceptible to a lack of cohesion, as the judiciary exercise discretionary powers of interpretation which in turn produces some jurisdictional variation in the law as it relates to charities. Where the responsibility for determining charitable status is vested in the tax authority, the consequent tension between its duty to maximise tax revenue and its obligation to facilitate a contemporary interpretation of charitable purpose can also be a source of uncertainty and jurisdictional inconsistency. For all common law nations, the fact that a fresh judicial precedent established outside the jurisdiction can have a capacity to influence the law within it introduces further potential for disruption.

However, institutional co-ordination is facilitated by the acceptance and uniform application of various doctrines, rules and constraints.

Doctrines, precedents and rules

The concept of altruism, the legal definition of 'public benefit' and 'charitable purpose', and the cross-jurisdictional acceptance of most judicial precedents and interpretations of the 'spirit and intendment' rule offer a doctrinal basis for achieving consistency in the application of charity law across all common law nations. As with the application of the legal system in any other subject area (e.g. family law), consistency is greatly enhanced by the manner in which law is mediated through the knowledge and experience of a specifically trained cohort of professionals. As regards the legal system as it relates to charities, however, there are relatively few professionals and fewer specialists available.

Constraints

Charity law is applied subject to much the same set of constraints in all common law jurisdictions. There are many such restrictions of variable weighting but perhaps the most significant are the following: the requirement that to be charitable an entity must fit within the legal definition of 'charitable purpose'; the necessity to prove that some charitable purposes satisfy the public benefit test (though all must); the exclusivity rule; and the prohibitions on private profit and political lobbying (see, also, Chapter 10). In addition to constraints specific to charity law, there are also those arising more generally as a consequence of public policy.

Balancing public and private interests

Any legal system must balance public and private interests. The history of 'charity' reflects a particularly long and complex struggle to achieve this within the common law nations. As Wigram VC expressed it more than 150 years ago, 'many things of public utility may be strictly matters of private right, although the public may indirectly receive a benefit from them'.[7] In a modern context, as these nations strive to attain the holy grail of 'civil society', the role played by charity law in defining public benefit and bridging the gap between government and the nonprofit sector has become particularly important.

Origins

Arguably the roots of current tensions between public and private interests in charity lie deep in the latter's religious origins. Ecclesiastic teachings, perhaps primarily the catechist instruction that only by doing good to another in this life could salvation of the soul of the giver be secured in the next, recognised and sought to disseminate the inherent public/private value of charity. This early interpretation saw private charitable acts as necessarily accompanied by very tangible benefits for the community. Religious leaders encouraged giving to needy people in their communities, to the poor in other lands, to the victims of natural disasters and for the support of their Church. Secular leaders were also quick to promote such activity and, indeed, even before the 1601 Act, many charitable gifts to the Church were diverted by religious leaders towards the maintainance of local community infrastructure – or 'public utilities' as they would now be called – such as roads and bridges. Those bound by the same set of beliefs then became further bound by such acts of mutual assistance, by a sense of group solidarity and by the shared values that fostered and were reinforced by civic participation. From at least feudal times, the advantages for leaders in encouraging private charitable gifts and activity as a means of contributing to the public good by generating responsible behaviour, maintaining order and social infrastructure and promoting social cohesion have been very evident.

Charitable purposes

Charity as legally defined primarily represents the public interest. This is clearly apparent from the classification of charitable purposes, long recognised in the common law as imposing restrictive parameters, and by the accompanying

---

7 *Nightingale v Goulburn* (1847) 5 Hare 484 at p. 490.

requirement that it be directed not to designated individuals but to a class of public beneficiaries. The Preamble was the initial government statement of matters constituting the public benefit (defined in terms of specified charitable purposes) and an acknowlegment that it would support (through tax-exemption privileges) those whose gifts or activities contributed to furthering it. Subsequently, the relief of poverty, the advancement of education and the provision of health and social care services and many similar activities have enabled private gifts to immeasurably improve public wellbeing (but, necessarily, also that of particular individual service recipients). The consistency and longevity of such purposes, across generations and jurisdictions, testifies to the importance of charity as a means of blending public and private interests.

The public benefit test

This test has three functions:

* it defines the weighting to be given to the benefit component when determining eligibility for charitable status;
* it establishes whether or not the nature of the benefit accrues to a sufficient quantum of the public to warrant charitable status registration; and, ultimately,
* it verifies that the purpose to be furthered by the organisation, gift or activity is charitable.

The differential weighting given to the public benefit component across the range of charitable purposes has always been a contentious matter. In particular, the presumption that Churches and religious bodies per se satisfy the test while the vast range of organisations established to provide health and social care services – e.g. hospitals, hospices, homes for the mentally ill, disabled or aged – must prove they do (unless established by a religious body), appeared increasingly inequitable in the secular societies that typify most developed common law nations.

A regulatory regime

Until recently, the regulatory regime – except in the UK and to a lesser extent the US – has lacked rigour. Charity law reform processes in some jurisdictions resulted in the legal functions of their regulatory regimes being strategically repositioned to more emphatically serve the public interest. This is perhaps particularly apparent as regards access to the registration process – eligibility criteria, prohibited applicants, identity profile data and requirements for remaining registered – comprise the acid test of an effective regulatory process. Statutorily imposed standards of accountability and transparency are also now more generally prevalent. The constraints have become such that, although satisfying eligibility criteria, some organisations opt to forego charitable status in order to retain independence.

The contemporary balance

The political reality framing the balance of public/private interests in charity law was clearly apparent in the terms of the Preamble, endured intact for 400 years, and has been restated and enlarged through the recent cycle of charity law reform programmes.

By playing a pivotal role in balancing public and private interests – addressing issues such as those relating to poverty, access to education, homosexuality, disability, racial and gender equality, not to mention enabling pathways for wealth redistribution etc – charity law continues to reflect and give effect to prevailing social policy themes in the developed common law nations. This is in keeping with the obverse of Article 14 of both the Universal Declaration of Human Rights and the European Convention of Human Rights, which prohibits discrimination. As has been judicially explained, the 'enjoyment of the rights guaranteed under the Convention is also violated when States without an objective and reasonable justification fail to treat differently persons whose situations are significantly different'.[8] In short, classifying the socially disadvantaged groups that merit charitable status is not only justifiable but necessary if government is to: differentiate between types of social need; recognise that the needs of some are more acute and urgent than others; give equal weighting to the claims of new categories relative to those already granted charitable status; and target resources effectively.

As in the Preamble, the purposes listed are those which governments view as matters both of pressing public importance and amenable to private funding: charitable status being a mechanism for channelling not just private donations but also the relatively cost-free activities of volunteers, subsidised by universal public taxes and donor tax incentives. This initiative has been adopted by some other jurisdictions for the same social policy reasons.

It is no coincidence that charity law reform has occurred against a background which, over the past few decades, has seen great changes in the public/private balance of responsibility for social service provision in the developed common law nations. In general there has been a marked shift from a position that the State should own and maintain its national resources, institutional infrastructure etc to one that it should, to some degree, settle for controlling access to services and ensuring standards by regulatory legislation and inspectoral bodies. The move towards privatisation of public utilities has given the State a one-off cash bonus and enabled it to leave the market to provide, at a price, services such as water, sanitation, transport, housing, electricity, gas, etc. It is demonstrating an increasing enthusiasm for similarly shedding responsibility for prisons, roads and transport, nursing home care, residential care of the elderly etc. This has led to charity being treated by government as a partner with which to share responsibility for public benefit service provision and has brought with it the need for

---

8 *Thlimmenos v Greece* (2000) 31 EHRR 411 at para 44.

charity law and practice to be compliant not just with human rights, equity, equality, freedom of information and other legally required benchmarks but also with standard indicators such as transparency, accountability and efficiency that are routinely applied to public services.

The new public/private balance being struck is resulting in much responsibility for safeguarding the interests of the vulnerable being devolved to charities. This politically generated fudging of the public/private divide in public benefit service provision is problematic for the latter's integrity and independence. For present purposes, it raises questions particularly regarding their legal status in the context of the ECHR, which requires the compliance of 'public bodies'. Where charities are acting as proxy government entities, being wholly funded to deliver services in accordance with government policy and specifications,[9] then to that extent they would seem to have chosen to suspend the singular characteristics of charity and voluntarily assume those of a public body. Having done so, they would appear to be accepting full accountability for implementation of human rights compliant standards of practice which, particularly but not solely for religious charities, carries implications in terms of their liability under tax, employment and equality laws. At the very least, this political elision of responsibility for public benefit service delivery serves to blur the distinction between public and private interests.

An obvious ancillary public dimension to charitable status, which should also be noted, is that the accompanying tax exemption necessarily shifts the tax burden to the general public: the shortfall in tax revenue, otherwise available from organisations and other entities engaged in purposes now designated as charitable, must be made up by increased taxes in other areas.

Applying the law

Maintaining order is the business of law. It does so through the enforcement of values-compliant conduct, by authorising judicial and other forums to arbitrate and mediate disputes and by establishing the related rules, processes and procedures. It is also an important, perhaps the most important, means of promoting social cohesion, order and continuity while also being a means for facilitating social change. The role of law and the mechanisms of the legal system for applying it have remained in place, conforming to much the same pattern, throughout the social democratic nations of the common law world.

Law and society

In a common law context, the law is based on principles of social justice, is intimately linked to the democratic political process and is increasingly governed by human rights provisions embodied in domestic legislation and a raft of international instruments.

---

9 See, for example, *Central Bayside Division of General Practice Ltd v Commissioner of State Revenue* [2005] VSCA 168.

Social change

There will always be a tension between the role of law to maintain the status quo through rules, processes and institutions that aid predictability and its role as independent guardian of principles of justice which require it to be open and responsive to the unpredictable. In the latter case, whether this occurs as a consequence of a shift in government policy or in circumstances, the law has a role in providing a bridge for social change, followed by legitimising that adjustment and then establishing the new rules, etc necessary for a new process of integration. Instead of being merely responsive, law may itself be the instrument for effecting social change, as when used to change attitudes towards racism and other forms of discrimination and inequality.[10]

Social change, charity law reform and the nonprofit sector

Charity law has, ever since the Preamble, continued to articulate the agenda for partnership between government and the nonprofit sector. Growing in sophistication, it became more deeply entwined in the workings of the democratic political system: charitable purposes were judicially broadened to address matters of general public benefit provision, strengthen citizenship and promote social cohesion; new statutory regulatory bodies for charity were introduced to bridge the gap between government and the nonprofit sector; umbrella groups with increasing political leverage, representing the sector and led by charities, were encouraged to develop a participative role with government. These developments varied considerably among the common law jurisdictions.

However, the core business of charity has always been its charitable purposes. These were and continue to be its *raison d'être* in the eyes of government: constituting a statement of the latter's social policy objectives in terms of specifying areas of public benefit for which it shares responsibility with charity. The need to broaden those purposes, partially to more appropriately address newly emerging patterns of social need but also to facilitate shifting the responsibility and expense of public benefit services from government to charity, was the primary trigger for government initiating the charity law reform processes.

From expanding charitable purposes to imposing tighter regulatory controls

As will be seen in Part II, the reform processes concluded with legislation that both expanded the range and interpretation of charitable purposes while also – for the first time – giving government the capacity to thereafter adjust those purposes whenever it considered it politically expedient to do so. However, as law

10 For example, the Race Relations Act 1976 in England and Wales.

reform proceeded, the above-mentioned global events began to impact causing governments to revisit their partnership policy with the nonprofit sector.

The 9/11 attack in 2001 brought home to government the urgent need for improved scrutiny of the domestic nonprofit sector: to develop a capacity to identify and engage with the socially marginalised and dissaffected; to track organisations and their funding streams; and to facilitate early State intervention when public interests were endangered. Then, as the 2007/8 banking crisis lurched into a global economic recession, government presumed that the financial irregularities in the public sector, which had triggered the crisis, must also be present in the less well regulated nonprofit sector, and its policy turned towards examining arrangements for good governance in the sector. This policy gained momentum when the global war against terrorism morphed into a strain of Islamic fundamentalism which not only saw Islamic State impose its merciless regime on large areas of territory in long unstable countries of the Middle East, Africa and Afghanistan but also saw atrocities being committed by its sympathisers in the cities of leading common law nations and elsewhere. Again, for government, this emphasised the need for tighter surveillance and regulatory controls in relation to the nonprofit sector. As will be seen later, the consequences became evident in the impact of government counter-terrorism policies on the sector and in its approach towards introducing new regulatory bodies modelled on the English Charity Commission.

Charity law and human rights: towards a template for comparative jurisdictional analysis

Singularly, the law relating to charities remained embedded in the common law for centuries, leaving litigation and court proceedings largely free from formative legislative intervention. Indeed, charity law continues to be primarily a common law phenomenon, and, therefore, more so than in other areas of law, any consideration of legal functions must focus primarily on the matters that may be litigated – the charitable purposes. Human rights on the other hand are freestanding legal functions. They cross-cut all civil and criminal law, generating principles and standards that have an equal bearing on both judicial and administrative forums. Some, clearly, are more relevant to charity law than others.

To focus the comparative jurisdictional analysis of Part II it is first necessary to identify the key points at which charity law and human rights intersect. This is most obvious in the presence or absence within the jurisdiction of legislation that specifically provides for charity law and human rights provisions and address crossover issues. Additional intersects can be located by identifying relevant regulatory bodies and the extent of their brief for matters arising within and between both bodies of law. More particularly, by sifting through the case law and cross-referencing judgments relating to key issues it becomes possible to build a profile of human rights/charity law complementarity on a jurisdiction specific basis, collate the data necessary for a comparative analysis of jurisdictions and identify related trends in practice and in any emerging governing principles. Such an exercise also needs to take account of areas where there is no intersect, no complementarity, and areas where charity law and human rights are in conflict.

The legislative and regulatory framework

Both charity law and human rights law are now generally to be found incorporated in domestic legislation.

Charity law

Traditionally, such legislation as existed in the common law nations was mainly concerned with regulating to prevent, detect and provide remedies for fiduciary abuse. The Charities Act 1960, a formative piece of legislation, reflected that emphasis in the law relating to charity not just in England and Wales but in many common law countries where it was taken as the model for similar domestic statutes. In the post–law reform era, while any new legislation retained such a focus, it also encoded common law concepts and rules, broadened the definition of charitable purposes and in some instances re-assigned regulatory responsibilities. For present purposes, an important consideration is to note that in some jurisdictions explicit legislative recognition has been given to the advancement of human rights as a charitable purpose.

• REGULATORY AGENCIES

Regulating charities in all common law jurisdictions, except England and Wales, has traditionally been a responsibility vested in the national tax authority. Post–charity law reform, all UK jurisdictions and some others have followed the example set in England and Wales and established bodies similar to the Charity Commission as the lead regulatory agency. Additionally, in all jurisdictions, the High Court exercises its customary adjudicative role while other offices such as the Attorney General, Probate and the Companies regulator also share their traditional administrative roles and responsibilities.

Human rights

The growing body of international human rights is mainly drawn from the Universal Declaration of Human Rights (UDHR). Over time other sources such as the ECHR and related treaties and protocols etc have gained prominence. These rights, or their equivalents, can also be found incorporated in domestic legislation or embodied in national constitutions. Across the ECHR signatory States and others governed by a similar supervening body of law, including many common law nations, practice is gradually conforming to the stratifying effect of human rights principles. Slowly and incrementally a level of international harmonisation in human rights law is being developed.

- REGULATORY AGENCIES

It has been customary for domestic human rights issues to be regulated by a designated Human Rights Commission, with a right of appeal to the High Court. Matters relating to inequality generally, but in the workplace particularly, have usually attracted separate adjudicative treatment in an administrative tribunal. As equality and non-discrimination legislation has grown, it is now not uncommon for all matters of inequity, inequality and discrimination to be assigned to the same merged administrative body.

In addition, the UN General Assembly introduced the Universal Periodic Review (UPR) procedure in 2006. This provides an opportunity for each State to periodically declare to the Human Rights Council the actions taken to improve the human rights situations in their countries in addressing their human rights obligations, to receive comment from their peer signatory States and to agree goals for the next review. The first cycle of reviews were completed by October 2011; the second commenced in 2012 and is due to be completed by 2016. In preparation, the appropriate body in each Member State may issue interim reports recording progress made towards addressing the concerns registered in the last review. This process operates in conjunction with the Principles relating to the Status of National Institutions (the Paris Principles), adopted by UN General Assembly in 1993,[11] which set out the minimum standards required by national human rights institutions to be considered credible and to operate effectively. In order to be effective and awarded 'A' status, national human rights institutions must be independent, adequately funded and have a broad human rights mandate.

Applying the law: the charitable purposes

Charitable purposes are the core business of charity and ultimately the functions of charity law are only important insofar as they give effect to them.

By the end of the 20th century, the *Pemsel* definition of charity had been judicially extended in the common law jurisdictions to include purposes such as the advancement of the following: human rights, conflict resolution or reconciliation; animal welfare and environmental protection; the arts, culture, heritage or science; and to a varying extent, the promotion of amateur sport. A decade later, this would be consolidated, legislatively in some jurisdictions, and further extended to accommodate such purposes as the promotion of multiculturalism,

---

11 See, *National Institutions for the Promotion and Protection of Human Rights*, UN Doc A/
   RES/48/134 (20 December 1993).

the advancement of civil society, health and social care services, together with other common law concepts and rules.

However, the net result of the charity law reform processes was a weakening of the shared platform. While the initial four purposes remained in place, their traditional flaws and anomalies, accompanied by a considerable weight of reinforcing case law, constrained functionality except in the few jurisdictions where law reform had resulted in this being legislatively rectified. The new set of '*Pemsel* plus' purposes was not uniformly defined and, being legislatively confined to a small minority of jurisdictions, served to distance the latter from all others. This will be examined on a jurisdiction-specfic basis in Part II, but for now it is necessary to identify the range of charitable purposes that broadly constitute the contemporary shared charity law platform and to consider the flaws that impair their general functioning.

The Pemsel *purposes*

The *Pemsel* ruling defines charity as comprising trusts for the relief of poverty, for the advancement of education, of religion and trusts beneficial to the community not falling under any of the preceding heads (see Chapter 2), and for centuries this provided the basic platform for charitable purposes in all common law jurisdictions.

- RELIEF OF POVERTY

Although, as was explained in *Pemsel*, 'the popular conception of a charitable purpose covers the relief of any form of necessity, destitution or helplessness',[12] charity law was never wholly focused on pursuing that purpose. Arguably, for example, whereas much judicial attention has been given to the poor and to parsing the eligibility of the various 'classes' of the poor, there has been a general failure to take into account the impact of the rise and fall in public funding for education, health and welfare services. Moreover, centuries of case law confirmed that it was the effects rather than the causes of poverty which must be the focus of this charitable's purpose and activity. Further, the law has interpreted the relative nature of poverty in a very flexible manner which extended eligibility, for example, to persons of professional standing. In practice, for the developed common law nations this charitable purpose is now usually associated less with domestic poverty and more with overseas aid: poverty relief has come to mean supporting the relief work of international humanitarian charities in the many impoverished, disaster struck or war-torn countries, constituting a very tangible and broadly spread civic contribution to the promotion of human rights in the less-developed parts of the world.

---

12 See, Macnaghten LJ in *Commissioners for Special Purposes of Income Tax v Pemsel* [1891] AC 531 at p. 572.

In some jurisdictions an outcome of charity law reform has been the inclusion of a preventative dimension to the definition of this purpose. Less success attended the attempts to correct the long-standing anomaly that permits a donor's 'poor relations' to be classed as meeting the public benefit test.

• ADVANCEMENT OF EDUCATION

An educational charity entails an 'improvement of a useful branch of human knowledge'.[13] The usefulness, or possible prospective usefulness, and to whom, of any particular knowledge can be difficult to determine. A gift intended for the general advancement of education in a general manner, such as a bequest for 'educational . . . purposes',[14] has usually been recognised as charitable. So also have gifts to schools,[15] colleges, to found a scholarship[16] or to advance or promote literature.[17] There has never been any doubt that a charitable trust would be for educational purposes if it provided for the study of subjects such as languages,[18] law,[19] medicine,[20] natural history,[21] archaeology,[22] economics,[23] theology,[24] religious instruction,[25] comparative religions,[26] agriculture,[27] mechanical sciences and engineering[28] or shorthand typewriting and bookkeeping.[29]

However, again this charitable purpose was functionally deficient in terms of giving effect to charity: it was never necessary to be poor to be a beneficiary under this *Pemsel* head. The fact that a large proportion of the educational institutional fabric – from schools to universities – in all common law jurisdictions resulted from charitable gifts, to the immeasurable benefit of the communities concerned, does not alter the fact that the benefit flowed as much if not more towards those who were not disadvantaged. That the benefit provided can be elitist in nature

---

13 See, *Incorporated Council for Law Reporting for England and Wales v Attorney General* [1972] 1 Ch 73 per Buckley LJ at p. 102.
14 *Re Ward* [1941] Ch 308.
15 *Incorporated Society v Richards* (1841) 4 Ir Eq R 177.
16 *R v Newman* (1684) 1 Lev 284.
17 *Re Hamilton-Grey* (1938) 38 SR (NSW) 262 and *Re Hopkins' Will Trusts* [1965] Ch 669.
18 *A-G v Flood* (1816) Hayes and Jo App xxi at xxxviii.
19 *Smith v Kerr* [1902] 1 Ch 774 (CA).
20 *Royal College of Surgeons of England v National Provincial Bank, Ltd.* [1952] AC 631.
21 *Re Mellody* [1918] 1 Ch 228.
22 *Yates v University College London* (1873) 8 Ch App 454; (1875) LR 7 HL 438; *Re British School of Egyptian Archaeology* [1954] 1 WLR 546.
23 *Re Berridge* (1890) 63 LT 470, CA; *Re Corbett* (1921) 17 Tas LR 139.
24 *Reagan* (1957) 8 DLR (2d) 541.
25 *A-G v Sepney* (1804) 10 Ves 22.
26 *Corrymeela Community v Commissioner of Valuation* VR/1/1967.
27 *Lylehill Young Farmers Club v Commissioner of Valuation* VR/7/1981, *Trustees of the Agricultural Research Institute v Commissioner of Valuation* VR/81+82/1967.
28 *Institution of Civil Engineers v IRC* [1932] 1 KB 149; *Re Lambert* [1967] SASR 19.
29 *Re Koettgen's Will Trusts* [1954] Ch 252.

has never been a contra-indicator for charitable status, and in all jurisdictions this aspect has largely survived the reform process (see, further, Chapter 4).

- ADVANCEMENT OF RELIGION

Religion, legally presumed in all jurisdictions to be of public benefit, has been defined as 'the promotion of spiritual teaching in a wide sense, and the mainte-nance of the doctrines on which it rests, and the observances that serve to pro-mote and manifest it'.[30] Moreover, it has been strongly asserted that 'any religion is at least likely to be better than none'.[31] Traditionally, an essential prerequisite has been a belief in the existence of a god: the 'two essential attributes of religion are faith and worship: faith in a god and worship of that god'.[32] Typically, gifts to ministers are charitable as being for the advancement of religion,[33] as also are gifts for building and maintaining churches, the maintenance of tombs and for missionary, proselytising and other 'outworking' purposes.

In the years imediately preceding charity law reform, the traditional theistic requirements were gradually judicially relaxed, if more so in some jurisdictions than in others. In *R v Registrar General ex p Segerdal*,[34] it was held that Bud-dhism was a religion despite a lack of belief in a supreme being. In line with a progressive and evolving approach to religion, faith healing in some jurisdic-tions was also deemed to be charitable when open to members of the public.[35] Following the reform process, many jurisdictions legislated or accepted judicial precedents to accommodate a non-theistic definition of religion or belief within this charitable purpose. Such a broadening of the definition – in some jurisdic-tions but not others – to include subjectively perceived belief systems, throws wide open the interpretation of this charitable purpose and, arguably, introduces the probability of such dissension as may wholly disrupt its traditional coherence and dissipate any 'public' benefit.

The varying salience of secularism in the common law jurisdictions and the legal balancing of the rights of those with and those without religious belief, accompanied by problems associated with equality and non-discrimination, have also emerged in recent years as an area of difficulty for charity law. This is fur-ther complicated by the nature of the Church/State relationship: varying from a constitutional separation of their interests to the blending of those interests in an 'established' Church relationship.

30 *Keren Kayemeth Le Jisroel v Inland Revenue Commissioners* (1931) 48 TLR 459 at p. 477. Also, see, *United Grand Lodge of Ancient Free and Accepted Masons of England v Holborn Borough Council* [1957] 1 WLR 1080.
31 *Neville Estates Ltd v Madden and others* [1962] 1 Ch 832, 853.
32 *Re South Place Ethical Society, Barralet v Attorney General* [1980] 3 All ER 918 at 924.
33 *Re Foster* [1939] 1 Ch 22.
34 [1970] 2 QB 697.
35 *Funnell v Stewart* [1996] 1 WLR 288.

- BENEFICIAL TO THE COMMUNITY AND NOT FALLING UNDER ANY
  OF THE PRECEDING HEADS

This fourth *Pemsel* head is a residual one, of charitable objects that cannot be conveniently fitted under the other three heads; even in England and Wales, where the number of heads have now been statutorily increased to 13, this default head has been retained (see, further, Chapter 4). Unlike the other three, all entities claiming charitable status under this head have always been required to prove compliance with the public benefit test (see, further, Chapter 2), and gifts to establish a wide range of public utilities including bridges, harbours and roads have been held to be charitable. The flexibility permitted by this *Pemsel* head allowed the judiciary across the common law world some room for manoeuvre in the struggle to align charity law with contemporary and local manifestations of social need.

A major consequence of charity law reform in all the jurisdictions concerned has been the removal of many clusters of purposes that had acquired charitable status on analogous grounds, from this heading, and their statutory recognition as distinct purposes in their own right.

Promotion of sport

Traditionally the promotion of sport and recreation has not been charitable. Where the intent was not so much to encourage sport as an end in itself but to provide the means for achieving a public benefit, then a gift could be awarded charitable status. As explained by Romer J, 'it is to be observed that the particular sports specified were all healthy outdoor sports, indulgence in which might reasonably be supposed to encourage physical efficiency'.[36] The same reasoning has been applied in awarding charitable status to gifts for the promotion of sports in schools,[37] a swimming pool in a private college[38] and athletic activities in a medical school.[39] Where the purpose of the activity was more to do with providing entertainment for spectators than improving the health of participants then it was generally viewed as non-charitable: an approach confirmed in England and Wales by the Recreational Charities Act 1958 and legislatively replicated in some other jurisdictions; it has largely remained so after the reform processes.

The Pemsel *plus purposes*

An outcome of the charity law reform has seen some jurisdictions legislate to establish much the same set of '*Pemsel* plus' charitable purposes. These variously list a number of activities that had gained judicial recognition over time, including

---

36 *Re Gray* [1925] Ch 363 at p. 365.
37 *Re Mariette* [1915] 2 Ch 284. Also, see, *IRC v McMullen* [1981] AC 1.
38 *Re Geere's Will Trusts (No 2)* [1954] CLY 388.
39 *London Hospital Medical College v IRC* [1976] 1 WLR 613.

the advancement of the following: human rights, conflict resolution or reconciliation, and the promotion of multiculturalism; civil society and the efficiency of
charities; health and social care services; animal welfare, environmental protection or its improvement; the arts, culture, heritage or science; and promoting
the welfare of specific socially disadvantaged groups. However, although much
the same set of additional charitable purposes have gained judicial or legislative
recognition in some countries, the fact that there is now jurisdictional variation
in the application of the public benefit test to those purposes can only lead to
further inconsistency and uncertainty in charity law.

Applying the law: human rights

The significance of the developing international harmonisation in human rights
law varies according to which rights are in play and where and how they impact
upon a domestic legal system: the fundamental human right to life being most
important; all such rights being more important in criminal than in civil law and
in an adjudicative rather than an administrative process; and their cumulative
effect in building a culture of human rights promising to be of greatest importance in the long term.

Human rights most relevant to charity law

For present purposes the focus is on those human rights with particular relevance
for charity law. From that perspective, as mentioned in the preceding chapter, the
following – as initially stated in the UDHR, subsequently enlarged in the ECHR
and continually judicially elucidated in the ECtHR and other forums – would
appear to be the most important: access to justice and ensuring proper processes;
rights of assembly and association; safeguarding personal freedoms; right of asylum;
asserting rights of expression and advocacy; the freedom of religion and belief; and
prohibiting discrimination. These rights are qualified by the general requirements
that their exercise is 'in accordance with law' and 'necessary in a democratic society'. They are reinforced by other international treaties, conventions and protocols
etc, but are also otherwise recognised in the domestic constitutions and legislation
of the common law jurisdictions currently being considered.

• ACCESS TO JUSTICE, LEGAL PROCESS AND PRINCIPLES

Article 10 of the Universal Declaration of Human Rights requires that proper
processes be available for accessing justice which is central to the rule of law and
a prerequisite for the recognition and enforcement of other rights. It addresses
such matters as the following: that relevant information is available and can be
readily understood; appropriate processes and proceedings exist and are accessible, before an independent and impartial tribunal; free legal aid and advice
being available where necessary, with adequate representation and without undue
delay; the proceedings are conducted independently, fairly, with a right of appeal;

and that the outcome is fully and fairly enforced. The role of the judiciary and Attorney General are also highly relevant.

For charities, this right implies that the legal functions of charity law must at least ensure that a proper formal procedure exists for determining charitable status by an appropriate independent body, that this relates relatively seamlessly with eligibility criteria for tax exemption, and that procedures are in place for the ongoing supervision necessary to monitor compliance with status requirements. Given that charity law has resolutely held the pursuit of matters of justice or injustice to be purposes that are incompatible with charitable status (viewed as the provence of the legislature, and charitable organisations could not seek to use the courts to effect change in laws set by parliament),[40] the Article 10 rights established a clear dividing line between the approaches of charity and human rights.

- RESPECT FOR 'PRIVATE LIFE'

Article 12 of the UDHR is directed towards the protection of individuals from arbitrary action by public authorities. It places obligations on the court: to ensure that the rights of an individual are properly secured and protected against infringements by other individuals;[41] to guard against individuals transgressing public policy such as, in Germany, by challenging the laws on assisted suicide;[42] and also requiring that public authorities exercise fairness in their procedures. The principles applied to the circumstances of those prevented from enjoying rights of privacy and family life extend to those unable to do so for reasons associated with, for example, disability, mental health, learning disability etc. By giving recognition to the special position of socially marginalised and cultural minorities, it resonates with those charitable purposes that channel resources towards such groups.

Article 12 is construed as imposing on a court not only a duty of watchful vigilance, to ensure that the rights enumerated are properly taken into account when determining proceedings, but also as imposing an obligation to be satisfied that any orders then made are given effect in a manner which continues to satisfy those rights.

- RIGHT TO ASYLUM

Article 14 of the UDHR confers the right for anyone suffering persecution to seek and be given asylum in another country. Grounded in Article 14, the Convention Relating to the Status of Refugees 1951, together with the 1967

---

40 *Mc Govern v Attorney General* [1982] Ch 321 per Slade J at p. 354. Also, see, *National Anti-Vivisection Society v Inland Revenue Commissioners* [1948] AC 31 and *A.Y.S.A. Amateur Youth Soccer Association v Canada* 2007 SCC 42.
41 *Airey v Ireland* (1979) Series A No 32, 2 EHRR 305.
42 *Koch v Germany* (App No 497/09) (19.06.2012).

Protocol, unequivocally requires asylum to be offered to anyone who – 'owing to a well founded fear of being prosecuted for reasons of race, religion, nationality, membership of a particular social group or political opinion' – presents in a foreign jurisdiction with such a request.[43] As the developed nations face the largest migration of people since World War II, the perceived necessity to differentiate asylum seekers from others, while responding appropriately and humanely to all, challenges the values and resources of both charity and government.

- FREEDOM OF RELIGION AND BELIEF

Article 18 of the UDHR provides for the right to freedom of thought, conscience and religion.[44] This right intersects primarily with the charitable purpose of advancing religion and in that context it includes the following freedoms: to change religion or belief; to exercise religion or belief publicly or privately, alone or with others; and to exercise religion or belief in worship, teaching, practice and observance. It also provides for the right to have no religion and to have non-religious beliefs protected. In this context, the nature of the Church/State relationship is of crucial importance.

The first time this Article was invoked to limit State action was in 1993,[45] and, except for two cases, until 1995 the European Commission on Human Rights had always denied applications from religions that could be called 'new', 'minority' or 'non-traditional'.[46] In recent years, however, the definition of 'religion' and 'belief' has become more elastic, allowing the protective reach of this right to extend to include Rastafarians, Zoroastrians and the Baha'i as well as those espousing such philosophical beliefs as vegans, pacifists and environmentalists.[47]

The above cases affirm the significance of freedom of religion for modern democratic states and indicate the nature and extent of its implications for future social policy. They need to be considered alongside two directives: the European Directive 2000/78/EC of 27 November 2000 (mentioned above) which prohibits discrimination on grounds that include religion or belief; and the European Directive on Race, also issued in 2000, which refers to beliefs as 'more than just mere opinions or deeply held feelings' but involve 'a holding of spiritual or philosophical convictions which have an identifiable formal content' and which have 'a

---

43 See, *A.C. and Others v Spain* (App No 6528/11) (24.04.2014).
44 See: *Universalles Lebene v Germany* [1996] (App No 29745/96); *Buscarini and Others v Sam Marino* [1999] ECHR 7; *Pichon and Sajous v France* [2001] ECHR 898; *Leyla Sahin v Turkey* [2004] ECHR 299; *Lautsi v Italy* [2011] ECHR 2412; and *S.A.S. v France* [2014] ECHR 695.
45 See, Gunn, T.J., 'Adjudicating Rights of Conscience Under the European Convention on Human Rights' in Van der Vyver, J.D., and Witte, J.D. (eds.), *Religious Human Rights in Global Perspective: Legal Perspectives*, Martinus Nijhoff, The Hague, 1996.
46 Ibid., at p. 311.
47 *Grainger plc v Nicholson* [2010] IRLR 4.

certain level of cogency, seriousness, cohesion and importance'.[48] Also relevant is Resolution 16/18, initially introduced in March 2011 at the UN Human Rights Council by the Organisation of Islamic Co-operation. This calls upon UN member states to combat 'intolerance, negative stereotyping and stigmatization of, and discrimination, incitement to violence and violence against, persons based on religion or belief'. Following that introduction, the Istanbul Process was created in July 2011 and continues in being; it last met in Geneva in June 2013.

The right to manifest religion or belief is subject to the rights of others. The threshold of such conduct required to justify intereference, often the subject of ECtHR rulings, would seem to have changed in recent years and now places a heavier onus upon those interfering to justify doing so. In *Jakobski v Poland*,[49] for example, the court ruled that it was unlawful for prison authorities to deny a Buddhist prisoner a vegetarian diet even though such a diet was not strictly required by Buddhism; it was sufficient and not unreasonable that the prisoner believed it necessary to manifest his beliefs in that way. The ECtHR in *Kokkinakis v Greece*[50] and *Manoussakis v Greece*[51] ruled, respectively, that the Greek anti-proselytism law impermissibly interfered with freedom of religion and 'the right to freedom of religion . . . excludes any discretion on the part of the State to determine whether religious beliefs or the means used to express such beliefs are legitimate'. As Justice Pettiti commented in *Kokkinakis*, 'religion is one of the foundations of a democratic society within the meaning of the Convention and the pluralism that cannot be disassociated from a democratic society depends on religious freedom'.

Article 2 of Protocol 1[52] also has a bearing on the exercise of Article 18 rights. This provides for the parental right to determine their child's religious education as follows:

No person shall be denied the right to education. In the exercise of any functions which it assumes in relation to education and to teaching, the State shall respect the right of parents to ensure such education and teaching in conformity with their own religious and philosophical convictions.

• FREEDOM OF EXPRESSION

Article 19 of the Universal Declaration of Human Rights guarantees the right to hold and express opinions, information and ideas (Articles 9 of the ECHR, 18 of the International Covenant on Civil and Political Rights (ICCPR) and

---

48 Both the European Directive on Race and the Employment Framework Council Directive were issued in 2000 and are known as 'the Article 13 Directives'.
49 [2010] 30 BHRC 417. Also, see, *Bayatyan v Armenia* [2011] 23459/03.
50 (A/260-A) (1994) 17 EHRR 397.
51 (18748/91) (1996) 21 EHRR CD3.
52 This Protocol was established on 20.3.1952. The leading case on Protocol 1 Article 2 is *Belgian Linguistic* (1968) 1 EHRR 252.

1 of Protocol 1 are also relevant). Again, this right is one of the hallmarks of a democratic society and is particularly important for charities: advocacy on behalf of the disadvantaged being a core activity. The traditional common law constraints on political activity by charities are therefore of considerable interest in the context of this right, particularly in view of the Council of Europe recommendation that non-governmental organisations, such as charities, should enjoy the right 'to undertake research, education and advocacy on issues of public debate, regardless of whether the position taken is in accord with government policy or requires a change in the law'.[53] As the promotion of human rights is now a charitable purpose in many countries, then, in the absence of evidence that such activity is incompatible with the values of a democratic society, the presumption may therefore be that advocacy on behalf of the socially disadvantaged for a change in law or social policy should be construed as a legitimate charitable purpose.

The ECtHR ruling in *Steel and Morris v the United Kingdom*[54] provided an important benchmark for the rights of individuals and small groups to actively campaign for peaceful change and to disseminate their views through the media. It shifted the issue from the accepted legal context of constraints imposed by charity law into a human rights framework. This is in keeping with a sentiment subsequently expressed in *Társaság a Szabadságjogokért v Hungary*[55] that 'the Court has repeatedly recognised civil society's important contribution to the discussion of public affairs'.

The right is one qualified by a requirement that any expressions are generally 'in accordance with law' and 'necessary in a democratic society' and also conform to a number of specific constraints such as public health/safety and morals.

- FREEDOM OF ASSEMBLY AND ASSOCIATION

Article 20 of the UDHR, which declares the right of citizens to form, join, or not to join associations, constitutes a hallmark of democracy;[56] indeed, the very existence of non-government organisations, including charities, is conditional upon this right. Its significance has been recognised by the legislatures of democratic states for centuries, and the constitutions of most countries in the world contain

---

53 See, Committee of Ministers, Council of Europe, *Recommendation on the Legal Status of Non-Governmental Organisations in Europe*, Recommendation CM/Rec (2007)14 (10 October 2007).
54 (App No 68416/01) (2005).
55 (2011) 53 EHRR 130.
56 The International Covenant on Civil and Political Rights (ICCPR) and the Universal Declaration of Human Rights both guarantee freedom of association internationally, as does the Helsinki Accords of the Organisation (former Conference) on Security and Cooperation in Europe (OSCE). Also, see, the Freedom of Association and Protection of the Right to Organise Convention, 1948 (No 87) and the Right to Organise and Collective Bargaining Convention, 1949 (No 98).

articles protecting freedoms of association and assembly. All laws and practice are required to be not only compliant with this right, which is a pre-condition for 'civil society', but governments must also ensure they positively promote it;[57] they must 'both permit and make possible'[58] opportunities for its enjoyment.

The ECtHR in *Sidiropoulos and Others v Greece*[59] held that the ability of citizens to form a legal entity in order to act collectively in a field of mutual interest is 'one of the most important aspects of the right to freedom of association, without which that right would be deprived of any meaning'.[60] The ruling of the court was important on an international basis because it emphasised that the existence of minorities and different cultures in a country was an historical fact that a 'democratic society' had to tolerate and even protect and support according to the principles of international law. When citizens organise for political purposes, they do not necessarily lose that protection. In *Zhechev v Bulgaria*[61] the ECtHR found a violation of Article 11 of the European Convention where an nonprofit organisation was refused registration because some of its aims were 'political goals'. However, in *Larmela v Finland*[62] the objectives of such an organisation in promoting the use of cannabis in Finland, where such use was at the time a crime, were held to go well beyond merely advocating for a change in the law.

This principle has clear application to indigenous minorities (e.g. the Aboriginal people of Australia), to ethnic or other culture specific communities (e.g. Muslims and newly arrived immigrants in the developed nations), and to the more prevalent socially disadvantaged groups requiring public benefit provision (e.g. the disabled, mentally ill etc) in all modern democratic countries.[63] For charities, the right of assembly is crucial for facilitating volunteering and advocacy by or on their behalf, while the right to form associations enables the forming of organisational structures to give effect to their activity.

- EQUALITY AND NON-DISCRIMINATION

Article 2 of the UDHR, which provides for the right not to be discriminated against, traditionally associated with religious differences, is a most important aspect of life in a democratic society. Its significance is demonstrated by its contiguous extension to afford protection from discrimination on the grounds of

---

57 *Wilson and Palmer v United Kingdom* (2002) 35 EHRR 20.
58 *National Union of Belgian Police v Belgium* (1975) 1 EHRR 578, at para 39.
59 *Sidiropoulos and Others v Greece* (26695/95) 27 EHRR, (1998).
60 Ibid., at para 40.
61 No 57045/00 (21 June 2007).
62 89 DR 64 (1997).
63 See, also: *Vogt v Germany* (1995); *The Socialist Party of Turkey and Others v Turkey* (1998) 27 EHRR 51; *RSPCA v Attorney General and Others* [2002] 1 WLR 448; *Refah Partisi v Turkey* App. Nos 41340/98 and 41342/98, 13 February 2003; *Yazar, Karat, Karatas, Aksoy and Hep v Turkey* (2003) 36 EHRR 59; and *Partidul Communistilor (Nepeceristi) and Ungureanu v Romania* (App No 46626/99), (2005).

gender, age and race and from differences arising from other such status designations.[64] The ECtHR has defined discrimination as 'treating differently, without an objective and reasonable justification, persons in analogous, or relevantly similar, situations'.[65] It must be shown that such different treatment cannot be objectively and reasonably justified, having regard to the concepts of legitimate aim, proportionality and margin of appreciation.[66] Discriminatory treatment may, therefore, be justified if it arises in pursuit of a legitimate aim or, as expressed in *Schmidt v Germany*,[67] where there is a 'reasonable relationship of proportionality between the means employed and the aim sought to be realised'. The more sensitive the issue, however, the heavier the onus to justify discrimination.

Article 2, as enlarged in Article 14 of the ECHR, is supported by the ICCPR,[68] of which Article 2 binds every signatory nation to 'respect and ensure all individuals within its territory and subject to its jurisdiction the rights recognised in the [ICCPR] without distinction of any kind'. Also relevant is the International Labour Organisation Discrimination (Employment and Occupation) Convention 1958 (ILOC)[69] and the Employment Framework Council Directive 2000/78/EC, issued by the Council of the European Union. The purpose of the latter, as stated in Article 1, is to 'lay down a general framework for combating discrimination on the further grounds of religion or belief, disability, age or sexual orientation, as regards employment and occupation'. It provides that 'persons who have been subject to discrimination based on religion or belief, disability, age or sexual orientation should have adequate means of legal protection'. So, for example, a refusal of full parental leave because the applicant was male was found to be discriminatory in *Konstantin v Russia*.[70]

The ECtHR in *Thlimmenos v Greece*[71] considered the effects of indirect discrimination where a blanket ban was imposed by a professional body on the employment of anyone with a criminal record, and ruled that it had a disproportionate effect on the applicant which could not be justified. For minority groups, this was an important decision, as it recognised that the right to non-discrimination also

---

64 See, further, the Human Rights Committee, General Comment 18 on Non-Discrimination. Also, see for example, *D.H. and Others v the Czech Republic* (App No 57325/00).
65 *Kiyutin v Russia* (App No 2700/10), March 2011.
66 See, for example, *Lithgow v United Kingdom* (1986) 8 EHRR 329, *Fredin v Sweden* (1991) 13 EHRR 784, *Abdulaziz, Cabales and Balkandali v United Kingdom* (1985) 7 EHRR 471.
67 [1994] 18 EHRR 513. Also, see, *EB v France* (2008) 47 EHRR 21, at para 91.
68 Opened for signature by General Assembly resolution 2200A (XXI) of 16 December 1966 and entered into force 23 March 1976. As of March 2012 the Covenant had 74 signatories and 167 parties.
69 Adopted by the General Conference of the International Labour Organisation on 25 June 1958 and came into effect on 15 June 1960. As of May 2011 the Convention had been ratified by 169 out of ILO 183 members.
70 (App No 30078/06) (22.03.2012).
71 (2001) 31 EHRR 411.

operates to afford protection from legal provisions that, although applied equally to all, have an adverse effect and discriminatory consequences for a few.

• PROHIBITION OF DISCRIMINATION; RELIGION

All rights and freedoms must be enjoyed without any discriminatory differential based upon the personal characteristics that distinguish people – such as sex, race, colour, language, religion, political or other opinion, national or social origin, association with a national minority, property, birth or other status.[72]

Within the common law tradition, the advancement of religion has long been a most important charitable purpose, carrying at least an implicit presumption (explicit in the statute law of some countries such as Ireland) that gifts to and the activities of religious organisations are for the public benefit and are therefore, *ipso facto*, charitable. The interpretation of 'religion' within this tradition has suffered from being construed in narrow terms, has often been applied inconsistently and has tended to exclude non-theistic religions. The ECtHR now requires that any interpretation of 'religion' be applied objectively, have reasonable justification[73] and be non-discriminatory; any differential treatment must comply with strict standards. This legal benchmark for non-discrimination in matters of religion is underpinned by Article 14 and supported by Article 9 of the ECHR (the right to freedom of thought, conscience and religion) and by Article 1 of the First Protocol (the right to peaceful enjoyment of property). It has the effect of requiring governments and other public bodies to give parity of recognition to Christian and non-Christian religions such as Buddhism and Hinduism and serves to reinforce the principle that 'religion', as known to charity law in a common law context, must accommodate at least non-Christian religions. Article 18 of the International Covenant on Civil and Political Rights is also relevant:[74] the right to manifest religion recognised by Article 18(1) is subject to restrictions in circumstances as specified by Article 18(3). In fact, all relevant major international declarations and conventions recognise the social reality that religious belief and its manifestation through practice are integrated, and extend protection to both.[75]

---

72 See, for example, the ongoing case of *D.H. and Others v the Czech Republic* (App No 57325/00).
73 See, for example, *Tsirlis and Kouloumpas v Greece* (1997) 25 EHRR 198. Also, see, the *Belgian Linguistic Case (No 2)* (1968) 1 EHRR 252.
74 Also, see, the United Nations Human Rights Committee 'General Comment 22' UN Doc CCPR/C/21/Rev.1/Add.4 [8].
75 See, for example: Article 18 of the Universal Declaration of Human Rights; Article 18(1) of the International Covenant on Civil and Political Rights; Article 9(1) of the European Convention for the Protection of Human Rights and Fundamental Freedoms; Article 12(1) of the American Convention on Human Rights; and Article 1 of the Declaration on the Elimination of all Forms of Intolerance and of Discrimination Based on Religion or Belief.

Trends in practice and emerging governing principles

Slowly and incrementally a level of international harmonisation in human rights law is being developed. Also, where human rights intersect with charity law, the indications are that a working relationship is gradually being achieved. However, as will become apparent in Part II, the long-established principles of charity law are essentially different from those underpinning human rights, and this is demonstrated by the infrequency with which both intersect; they largely operate on parallel lines. Where they intersect, charity law is in some areas becoming more human rights compliant, but there remain important points where these bodies of law are mutually estranged.

Conclusion

Since the ascendancy of Charles I to the throne in England, charity law has remained largely true to its common law origins. In the intervening centuries, layers of judicial precedent in that jurisdiction were shared with those that constituted the British Empire, thereby enabling all common law jurisdictions to retain a high degree of uniformity in the content and application of charity law's legal functions. By the closing decades of the 20th century, however, the lack of fit between *Pemsel* charitable purposes and patterns of contemporary social need had become so obviously inadequate as to trigger law reform processes in England and Wales and several other ex-colonial nations. The reform outcomes varied to some degree between those nations and served to distance them from their non-reforming counterparts. This has impacted on the legal functions of charity law, resulting in a jurisdictional differential in certain areas – mainly confined to differences in charitable purposes, the public benefit test and the presence of a charity specific regulator. The question is – to what extent has this been further compounded by the impact of international human rights to which all leading common law nations now subscribe?

The above material provides a flexible template of core legal functions and their indices, which will be employed to structure the Part II chapters, focus examination on the correlation between charity law and human rights and to undertake a comparative analysis of selected common law jurisdictions on that basis.

Part II

Contemporary law, policy and practice in a common law context

4 England and Wales

Introduction

This is the progenitor jurisdiction for charity law. The law which forms a small part of a common law heritage that over a period of several centuries has bequeathed a similar social infrastructure, political model and veneer of cultural conformity to many jurisdictions. With its origins in the Preamble,[1] as consolidated by the Macnaghten classification of charitable purposes[2] and subsequently enlarged under the 'spirit and intendment' rule,[3] it has long provided the basic legal framework for defining charities and regulating their activities throughout the countries that formerly comprised the British Empire (see, further, Chapter 2), including those presently being considered.

England and Wales retains its position as the leading jurisdiction in the UK while also continuing to hold its traditional lead role within the entire common law world as regards developments in the field of charity law. Because that unique standing resulted in much of the case law foundations established in this jurisdiction being transferred elsewhere, it is therefore necessary to now give close attention to formative principles and precedents – if only to avoid repeat references to the same material in subsequent chapters.

The chapter begins with a brief synopsis of early case law history, identifying some of the more basic flaws and anomalies of charity law that presaged difficulties of fit with a modern human rights framework. It then considers the charity law reform outcomes and their specific implications for human rights in this jurisdiction before moving on to outline the contemporary framework for both bodies of law, legislative and regulatory, identifying where they most often intersect. This leads in to the heart of the chapter which essentially undertakes a broad compliance audit of the extent to which the current law and practice relating to charity can be seen to be compatible or otherwise with human rights – as stated in the relevant articles of the UDHR, subsequently enlarged in the European Convention, and in the provisions of the Equality Act 2010.

1 The Preamble to the Statute of Charitable Uses 1601 (43 Eliz 1, c 4).
2 *Commissioners for Special Purposes of Income Tax v Pemsel* [1891] AC 531.
3 See, Sir William Grant MR in *Morice v The Bishop of Durham* (1804) 9 Ves 405.

Background: a history inimical to human rights

For four centuries the judicial leadership exercised in England and Wales further developed the definition of 'charity', thereby allowing it to attain a broadly similar political and socio-economic role in many nations.

Charity law and human rights: the early challenges

The early shaping of 'charity' in the courts of England and Wales imposed constraints that inhibited its growth but did so in ways that were also destined to infringe human rights.

Legal structures: charitable trusts

From at least the 15th century the law of trusts provided the vehicle for giving effect to charitable gifts. The public benefit purposes when eventually classified in *Pemsel* functioned thereafter as a straightjacket, inhibiting the ability of charity to respond to changing social circumstances, except insofar as judicial creativity employing the 'spirit and intendment' rule could establish precedents that widened its remit. Moreover, the charitable trust remained subject to normal trust rules (see, further, Chapter 2). The dominance of the trust as the preferred legal form for charities became a primary characteristic in the development of charity law in the UK, notwithstanding the introduction in 1862 of companies limited by guarantee and the resulting incorporation of some trusts. Charity and charitable gifts found further protection in archaic legal processes that imposed arcane obstructions, lengthy court hearings and immense expense on those who wished to query the terms of a charitable disposition.[4]

Exempt charities

Traditionally, many institutional charities were exempted from the obligation to register as such with the Charity Commission. They included national museums, the colleges and halls of Cambridge, Durham and Oxford Universities, the public schools of Eton and Winchester and Church Commissioners. Such exempted entities were wholly outside any exercise by the Commissioners of their statutory duties to supervise, inspect, and scrutinise annual accounts etc. The rationale for their exemption was attributable partly to the belief that their registration would impose a disproportionately onerous burden on the Charity Commission and partly to the fact that the institutions were accountable to other regulatory bodies – though the latter was often notional. This gave rise to queries as to the inequity of such institutions not being subject to the same statutory scheme as all other charities.

---

4 As parodied in *Jarndyce v Jarndyce*, by Dickens, C., *Bleak House*, Bradbury & Evans, London, 1853.

Political purposes

Over time a considerable body of case law accumulated to strengthen the view repeatedly expressed by the Charity Commission that an organisation with a primary political purpose could not acquire charitable status or retain that status if it embarked on such purposes. The rationale for this view was articulated a century ago by Parker LJ in *Bowman v Secular Society*[5] (see, further, Chapter 2). Consequently many organisations with laudable aims, which would now be regarded as very much in keeping with ECHR ethos and principles, were denied charitable status.

Charitable purposes: a tangential relationship with human rights

Judicial deference to donor charitable intent ensured from the outset that charity law would be distorted by the generous interpretation given to construing 'public benefit'. This led to it accommodating some matters that verged on the quixotic and others that seemed to defy a common sense understanding of what should be charitable. One such anomaly occurred in relation to a class of case where the public benefit test was (and continues to be) held to be satisfied even though the beneficiaries remain confined by a private nexus such as 'founder's kin', employer's dependants etc. By the closing decades of the 20th century, a wealth of case law had accumulated carrying telling portents of the difficulties that lay ahead in achieving compatability between charitable status and human rights.

The relief of poverty

Poverty, and the means for its relief, had steadily outgrown its definition, classification and administration as ascribed when the foundations of charity law were first laid down.[6]

For the purposes of charity, the definition of 'poor' carried with it connotations of 'deserving'.[7] The poor could be, and most often were, defined in an overtly discriminatory manner, for example by restricting gifts to adherents of a particular religion.[8] Gifts which were gender- or status-specific such as for the benefit of

5 [1917] AC 406 at p. 442 and endorsed in cases such as: *National Anti-vivisection Society v IRC* [1948] AC 31; *McGovern v Attorney-General* [1982] Ch 321; and *Southwood v AG* WLTR 1199, *The Times*, 26 October 1998.
6 See, Charity Commissioners, CC4, *The Public Character of Charities for the Relief of Financial Hardship*, London, 2003.
7 See, *Re Cohen* (1919) 36 TLR 16 (a bequest for deserving Jewish girls on their marriage) and *Re Lucas* [1922] 2 Ch 52 (the oldest respectable inhabitant of a named village).
8 *AG v Wansay* (1808) 15 Ves 231; *Dawson v Small* (1874) LR 18 Eq 114; *Re Wall* (1889) 42 Ch D 510.

spinsters,[9] widows,[10] working-men,[11] debtors[12] or 'for the purposes of helping edu-cated women and girls to become self-supporting'[13] were frequently upheld as char-itable trusts, as were gifts to recipients identified by reference to a personal nexus.[14]

The advent of the 'welfare state' saw the State assume responsibility for addres-sing the relief of poverty, but it also had a distorting effect on the relationship between charity and the poor. For example, following the nationalisation of health services, private insurance schemes were declared charitable as they relieved the burden on State facilities even though membership fees effectively excluded and continue to exclude the poor from their benefits.[15] By then, many charities had no relationship whatsoever with poverty, and, indeed, some of those associated with facilities accessed solely by the wealthy (fee-paying schools, clinics, hospitals, etc) served in part to exacerbate its effects. In *Re Courtauld-Thomson Trusts*,[16] the decision to grant charitable status to the gift of Dorneywood estate for use 'as an official residence for the Prime Minister or a Minister of the Crown nominated by him' was derided by one academic in that 'there is no public benefit in free housing for well-to-do-people or for one minister rather than another'.[17]

Most anomalous, however, was the continuation of case law confirming that it was the effects rather than the causes of poverty which must be the focus of a charity's purpose and activity. Alleviating the effects of poverty was charitable but to question its cause was possibly seditious.

The advancement of education

Educational charities gained their charitable status in an era when they provided the only means available for educating the poor. Over time, judicial interpretation of 'education' not only considerably broadened the range of activities that could be construed as charitable but also moved many away from any association with the poor. For example, in this jurisdiction, learned societies,[18] institutions and facilities established to promote and disseminate science (e.g. the Royal Literary Society, the Zoological Society and the British School of Egyptian Archaeology) have been deemed charitable as has the publication of law reports[19] (also in Aus-tralia and New Zealand).

---

9 *Re Dudgeon* (1896) 74 LT 613.
10 *Re Coulthurst* [1951] Ch 661.
11 *Guinness Trust (London Fund) v West Ham Borough Council* [1959] 1 WLR 233.
12 *A-G v Painter-Stainers' Co* (1788) 2 Cox Eq Cas 51.
13 *Re Central Employment Bureau for Women and Students' Careers Association Incorporated* [1942] 1 All ER 232.
14 *Dingle v Turner* [1972] AC 601.
15 *Re Resch's Will Trusts* [1969] AC 424.
16 *The Times*, 18 December 1954.
17 See, Keeton and Sheridan, *The Modern Law of Charities* (4th ed.) at p. 188.
18 *Beaumont v Oliveira* (1869) LR 4 Ch 309.
19 *Incorporated Council of Law Reporting for England and Wales v Attorney-General* [1972] Ch 73, [1971] 3 All ER 1029.

Providing aesthetic education has long been recognised as charitable because 'the education of artistic taste is one of the most important things in the development of a civilised human being',[20] even if limited to the education of the daughters of missionaries.[21] This permitted the extension of charitable status to activities and facilities that could be viewed as elitist, confined as they often are to a narrow group of privileged beneficiaries. So, establishing art galleries and museums has a considerable charitable history,[22] and gifts for theatres, a choral society[23] and music generally[24] came be viewed as valid educational charities.[25] Similarly, gifts to promote the training of singers of 'serious music' have been held charitable,[26] as has a gift to promote interest in a particular composer (Delius)[27] and to found annual chess tournaments specifically for males under the age of 21 and resident in Portsmouth.[28] Although the advent of State education for all led to the transformation of the existing patchwork of schools to exclusive fee-paying establishments, they nonetheless retained their charitable status.[29] In an ironic volte-face, while the State assumed responsibility for basic public benefit provision to the many, charities restricted access to the education provided by schools such as Eton and Harrow to the privileged few.

The advancement of religion

As the Charity Commission has explained, advancing religion is 'to promote or maintain or practise it and increase belief in the Supreme Being or entity that is the object or focus of the religion'.[30] The charitable status of religion, religious organisations, their activities and gifts to them had several distinctive and discriminatory characteristics that were established at an early stage in this jurisdiction.

Firstly, all such – with the exception of 'closed' religious orders – were presumed in law to be for the public benefit. This legal presumption was of long standing, as acknowledged in *In re White* when gifts for religious purposes were

20 *Royal Choral Society v Inland Revenue Commissioners* [1943] 2 All ER 101 at p. 104.
21 *German v Chapman* (1877) 7 Ch D 271 (CA).
22 *Re Holburne* (1885) 53 LT 212 and see *Re Town and Country Planning Act 1947, Crystal Palace Trustees v Minister of Town and Country Planning* [1951] Ch 132; and *Abbott v Fraser* (1874) LR 6 PC 96.
23 *Royal Choral Society v Inland Revenue Commissioners* [1943] 2 All ER 101.
24 *IRC v Glasgow Musical Festival Association* [1926] SC 920; *Shillington v Portadown Urban Council* [1911] 1 IR 247.
25 *Re Shakespeare Memorial Trust, Earl Lytton v A-G* [1923] 2 Ch 398, *Associated Artists v Inland Revenue Commissioners* [1956] 1 WLR 752.
26 *Re Levien* [1955] 3 All ER 35.
27 *Re Delius, Emmanuel v Rosen* [1957] Ch 299.
28 *Re Dupree's Deed Trusts* [1945] 1 Ch 16.
29 *The Abbey Malvern Wells Ltd v Ministry of Local Government and Planning* [1951] Ch 728.
30 See, Charity Commission, 'The Advancement of Religion for the Public Benefit', December 2008, at para C3 and *United Grand Lodge of Free and Accepted Masons of England and Wales v Holborn Borough Council* per Donovan J.

considered charitable unless shown otherwise,[31] even if that gift, such as a stained glass window dedicated to the memory of the donor,[32] was devoid of altruism, or, as to a trust to ring a peal of bells on the anniversary of the restoration of the monarchy,[33] was devoid of utility. However, and unlike many other common law jurisdictions, it was subject to the exception that gifts made to, or for the use of, a closed contemplative religious order,[34] for the saying of a private mass,[35] or for services in a private chapel[36] were held not to be charitable.[37] Secondly, English case law has traditionally confined charitable status to those entities with a central theistic component: indeed, for several centuries the Christian nature of the State was not to be questioned; no other religion would be granted equal legal status,[38] an approach commonly expressed by the judiciary[39] and rigorously enforced, as illustrated by the long history of blasphemy in which that offence was often treated as seditious. Thirdly, the Church of England continues to hold a unique constitutional position as the 'established' religion prevailing over all others, under arrangements which provide for the reigning monarch to be both its Supreme Governor and Head of State.[40] It also enjoys a stronger relationship with government: the hierarchy of Church officials hold their posts by government appointment rather than election; and all 26 Anglican bishops (the Lords Spiritual), and none of any other religion, sit as of right in the House of Lords on the government benches.[41]

It has always been judicially accepted that discrimination is an inherent characteristic of this charitable purpose: even if the gift deliberately discriminated against particular religions it could still be charitable.[42] Traditionally, the practice termed 'conditions in restraint of religion' by Lord Greene in *Re Samuel*[43] referred to a broad category of gifts and trusts, most usually created by testators

---

31 [1893] 2 Ch 41; followed in *In re Bain, Public Trustee v Ross* [1930] 1 Ch 224.

32 *Re King* [1923] 1 Ch 243.

33 *Re Pardue* [1906] 2 Ch 184.

34 See, for example, *Cocks v Manners* (1871) 12 Eq 574, where a contemplative order of nuns was found to be not charitable.

35 See, for example, *Kehoe v Wilson* (1880) 7 LR Ir 10. Also, see, *Re Hetherington's Will Trusts* [1990] Ch 1.

36 *Hoare v Hoare* (1886) 56 LT 147.

37 *Gilmour v Coates* [1949] AC 426. Also, see, *Trustees of the Congregation of Poor Clares of the Immaculate Conception v The Commissioner of Valuation* [1971] NI 114 at 169, per Lowry LJ.

38 *In re Masters & C. of the Bedford Charity* (1818) 2 Swans 470 at p. 527.

39 See, for example: Sumner LJ, 'Ours is, and always has been, a christian state. The english family is built on christian ideas' in *Bowman v Secular Society Limited* [1917] AC 406.

40 Under the Act of Union 1707, Article 2, the monarch is required to belong to the Church of England; the position is restricted exclusively to that religion.

41 From at least the time of King Edward's parliament in 1300, the Lords Spiritual have sat alongside the Lords Temporal in the House of Lords to consider matters of state.

42 See, *Re Lysaght; Hill v Royal College of Surgeons of England* [1966] Ch 191, [1965] 2 All ER 888, which concerned a trust to establish a medical scholarship unavailable to both Roman Catholics and Jews.

43 [1942] 1 Ch 1 at 30, CA.

but occasionally by donors, that required a prospective beneficiary to commit to or renounce a specified religion, often set in the context of marriage and/or the upbringing of children.[44] By the late 19th century the courts had become well accustomed to and accepting of such conditions.[45] This approach permitted many instances where donor-imposed religious constraints were respected,[46] and conditions that restrained religion (either requiring or prohibiting the practice of a particular religion) or marriage (either requiring or prohibiting marriage to a person of a particular religious persuasion, ethnicity or class) were almost always judicially endorsed.

Discrimination was also a prominent feature of missionary work, whether seeking to advance Christianity in general or the interests of a particular religion.[47] Proselytising or 'spreading the word' was invariably pursued in an overtly discriminatory manner – extolling the merits of one religion to the detriment of all others – and was an activity readily recognised as being for the public benefit and assured of charitable status. Indeed, it provided the grounds for charity law's most famous case,[48] which concerned the Moravian Church and its charitable purpose of 'maintaining, supporting and advancing the missionary establishments among heathen nations'. As it is now subject to the public benefit test, this, perhaps, raises questions as to what exactly is the benefit to an increasingly secular public of enducing those of no religious beliefs to acquire them or to exchange one set of beliefs for another.

Beneficial to the community, not falling under any of the preceding heads

By the mid-20th century this category held a massive and rapidly increasing range of charities, many competing, some overlapping or replicating, others with resources greater than the need to be addressed. In particular, there had been an exponential rate of growth in those associated with health and social care services, with specific localities and with sport and recreation. Also, the definition of 'charitable purpose' was broadened to include, for example, the promotion of agriculture (by the improvement of livestock etc)[49] and the promotion of industry and commerce.[50] Moreover, it was under this heading that considerable charitable funds were amassed for the protection and benefit of animals.[51]

44 See, further, Grattan, S. and Conway, H., 'Testamentary Conditions in Restraint of Religion in the Twenty-first Century: An Anglo-Canadian Perspective', *McGill Law Journal*, Vol 50, 2005, p. 511.
45 *Re Knox* (1889) 23 LR Ir 542 (Ch) and *Clayton v Ramsden* [1943] 1 AC 320.
46 *Re Lysaght* [1966] Ch 191 and *Re Dominion Students Trust* [1947] 1 Ch 183.
47 See, *United Grand Lodge of Free and Accepted Masons of England and Wales v Holborn Borough Council* [1957] 1 WLR 1080; 121 JP 595; 101 SJ 851; [1957] 3 All ER 281.
48 *Commissioners for Special Purposes of the Income Tax Act v Pemsel* [1891] AC 531 (HL).
49 *Inland Revenue Commissioners v Yorkshire Agricultural Society* [1928] 1 KB 611.
50 *Crystal Palace Trustees v Minister of Town and Country Planning* [1950] 2 All ER 857.
51 *Royal National Agricultural and Industrial Association v Chester* (1974) 48 ALJR 304 (a trust for improving the breeding and racing of homing pigeons).

In contrast, entities established for such purposes as educating the public on militarism and disarmament[52] or for the promotion of peace[53] were denied charitable status, while those with that status which sought to campaign against war[54] or for the supply of free milk to schoolchildren[55] were found to be in breach of it. However, and in keeping with human rights rationale, this *Pemsel* head did provide for recognition of public utilities as meriting charitable status. So, for example, conveying drinking water to a town was deemed charitable because 'the supplying of water is necessary as well as convenient for the poor and the rich',[56] as was the disposal of dead bodies by burying or cremation, as this was 'a matter of public necessity'.[57] A similar rationale, in an interesting contrast to current public policy, saw charitable status awarded to an organisation whose objects were 'to assist refugees, asylum seekers, migrants and others who recently arrived in the United Kingdom'.[58]

Unlike the other three *Pemsel* heads, satisfying the public benefit test in the context of the fourth was an essential prerequisite,[59] to be applied objectively, but it was unnecesary that a gift or other entity be directed solely towards relief of the poor; it sufficed that it was not directed exclusively for the benefit of the rich.[60] The use of explicit discriminatory criteria was no bar to charitable status, as illustrated by it being awarded to a gift made for the benefit of ten blind boys and ten blind girls resident in a specified area;[61] for best kept gardens and cottages;[62] and rest homes for nurses,[63] members of a religious community[64] and lady teachers.[65] Moreover, being thus subject to a mandatory application of the public benefit test, applicants under this head were inequitably disadvantaged relative to all other charitable status claimants.

It was this *Pemsel* head that, during the closing decades of the 20th century, witnessed a rapid growth in contracted service provision by charities acting as agents for government departments: a policy that gave rise to ongoing uncertainty as to the legal status of charities when so acting and the suspicion that they

---

52 *Southwood v Attorney General* (Unreported), *The Times*, 26 October 1998.

53 *Re Harwood* [1936] Ch 285.

54 *Webb v O'Doherty and Others* (1991) 3 Admin LR 731, *The Times*, 11 February 1991.

55 *Baldry v Feinbuck* [1972] 1 WLR 552; (1971) 115 SJ 965; [1972] 2 All ER 81.

56 *Jones v Williams* (1767) Amb 651.

57 *Scottish Burial Reform and Cremation Society Ltd v Glasgow Corporation* [1968] AC 138 per Upjohn LJ at p. 150.

58 *Ethnic Minority Training and Employment Project* Reg. No 1050917 (registered 22 November 1995).

59 See, *Trustees of the Londonderry Presbyterian Church House v Commissioners of Inland Revenue* [1946] NI 178, *Williams v IRC* [1947] AC 447 and *IRC v Baddeley* [1955] AC 572.

60 See, *Attorney General v National Provincial and Union Bank of England Ltd* [1925] AC 262, per Macnaghten LJ at p. 583.

61 *Re Lewis* [1955] Ch 104. Also, see, *Re Elliott* (1910) 102 LT 528.

62 *Re Pleasants* (1923) 39 TLR 675.

63 *Re White's Will Trusts* [1951] 1 All ER 528.

64 *Re James* [1932] 2 Ch 25.

65 *Re Estlin* (1903) 72 LJ Ch 687.

should then be regarded as 'public bodies.' It was a debate that would recur in the case law of this and other jurisdictions.

Public benefit: civil society, charity and the State

The 'welfare state' is the main factor differentiating the role of charity in England and Wales from all other common law jurisdictions, setting expectations regarding the respective responsibilities of government and charity for public benefit service provision. The demarcation between government and charity, as set out in the Preamble to the 1601 Act, had more or less endured until the introduction of the welfare state in 1948. Until then, provision by the Church and other charitable institutions had focused primarily on health and social care, education and housing, but extended to include public utilities (roads, harbours etc), social control facilities (asylums etc) and the use of volunteers to build a sense of coherent community solidarity.

The switch to government as public service provider brought with it not just the nationalisation, and extended range, of public utilities (water, electricity, sewage, street lighting etc) and of control (police force, prisons, detention centres etc) but also a new awareness of civic rights: the notion of public benefit provision as an entitlement, an incidence of citizenship rather than of the 'gift relationship', to be claimed as of right when needed, not left to altruism and bestowed at donor discretion (see, also, Chapter 10).

The integrity of this political experiment did not wholly survive the 20th century. In response to an ever-worsening financial crisis, the State embarked on a policy of shrinking the scale of public benefit provision. In addition to privatising much of what had been the public utility infrastructure – trains, water and power supply, mail delivery etc – government extended its policy of sub-contracting service delivery to charities from early beginnings in health and social care to include areas such as community development, prisons and probation. It then turned to the charity law reform process as an opportunity to redefine 'public benefit' and diversify responsibility for related service provision.

Partnership

Since the ending of the Thatcher era, and with it the power of the trade unions, a rapprochement had been steadily growing between government and the nonprofit sector as they negotiated their respective terms for sharing responsibility for future public benefit service provision. Aided by 'third way' and 'big society' political rhetoric, both main political parties pursued a policy of building a new institutional architecture to facilitate the closer engagement of government and citizen and to manage an evolving government/sector partnership. This was formalised in the Compact for England and Wales, launched in 1998 accompanied by Codes of Practice, duly replicated throughout the UK, which provided a set of principles to govern working relationships with application to all government departments and primary agencies. These introduced a nationwide framework for monitoring the government/sector relationship while 'local strategic partnerships' provided a framework for implementation of joint projects. By May 2010 a Minister for Civil Society had been appointed at Cabinet Office level to lead the new Office for Civil Society, and by 2012 the Charity Commission had formulated guidance for the charity delivery of public benefit services.[66]

Charity law reform and human rights: towards alignment

At the end of the 20th century, the UK embarked upon what was to be a protracted process of charity law reform. As explained earlier (see, Chapter 2), the reasons for doing so were in part due to the need to facilitate a closer harmonisation of charity law and human rights.

The charity law reform process

This reform process, including many of its aspects and intended outcomes, provided a model for other jurisdictions.

The process

The depth of engagement the process generated between government and nonprofit sector was perhaps unsurprising: charity law reform was seen by both as a welcome opportunity to negotiate their respective terms of engagement for sharing public benefit provision. Moreover, the nonprofit sector had grown more coherent and politically mature than its common law counterparts; bodies such as the National Council for Voluntary Organisations (NCVO) played a vital role in sector co-ordination, policy development and articulating sector interests.

Jurisdiction specific outcomes

The outcomes of the review process were more significant than those achieved elsewhere.

• INCREASED REGULATORY MEASURES

The extent of changes to the regulatory framework reflect government concerns to ensure tighter policing of charitable status, to prevent abuses and the consequent loss of tax revenue while also facilitating the tracking of funds to circumvent their use by terrorist organisations.

---

66 See, Charity Commission, 'Charities and Public Service Delivery' (March 2012).

- RECASTING OF PUBLIC BENEFIT

Of all jurisdictions to embark on charity law reform, only the UK concluded the process with a reversal of the public benefit presumption traditionally granted to the first three *Pemsel* heads. In so doing, the Charities Act 2006 seemingly gave the public benefit test an unequivocal mandatory application in respect of all charitable purposes, thereby achieving an even-handed approach to charitable status eligibility that is more human rights compliant than formerly, with potentially important implications for the charitable status of religious organisations and for facilities such as private schools, hospitals and other health and social care facilities with expensive admission fees. It was a change of central importance to charity law in this jurisdiction. Unfortunately, at this point and despite some interesting rulings,[67] it is not possible to state with any certainty the net legal effect of the recast test.

- POLITICAL PURPOSES

The reform process left untouched the established embargo on a charity having a political aim as its primary purpose. Any room for doubt on this matter was extinguished by the finding of Lewison J in *Hanchett-Stamford v Attorney-General*[68] that the 2006 Act did not change 'the fundamental principle that if one of the objects or purposes of an organisation is to change the law, it cannot be charitable'.

- *PEMSEL* PLUS CHARITABLE PURPOSES

This jurisdiction also introduced legislative provisions listing a set of charitable purposes additional to the existing *Pemsel* heads. While these largely give statutory recognition to those already judicially established as charitable, some of which are central to government's service delivery partnership with charity, there is clear evidence of political intent to accommodate human rights and equality, in particular, in s.2(2) of the 2006 Act: (a) the prevention of poverty; (d) the saving of lives; (e) the advancement of citizenship; (h) the advancement of human rights, conflict resolution or reconciliation or the promotion of religious or racial harmony or equality and diversity; and (j) the relief of those in need by reason of youth, age, ill-health, disability, financial hardship or other disadvantage. Further, a statutory definition of 'religion' was introduced, including an express reference to faiths that do not profess belief in a god as well as to polytheistic religions, a purpose made subject to the public benefit test.

---

67 See: *Charity Commission for England and Wales and others v Her Majesty's Attorney General (FTC/84/2011); Independent Schools Council v Attorney General* [2011] UKUT 421; and *The Human Dignity Trust: Charity Commission Decision* in October 2013 and 6 July 2014, Appeal no CA/2013/0013.
68 [2009] Ch 173 at pp. 181–182.

• STATUTORY ENCODING OF KEY COMMON LAW CONCEPTS

Finally, and of most significance, is the fact that all charitable purposes are now placed on the statute book, thereby enabling any future government to swiftly and directly delete, alter or add to those listed by simply amending the legislation.

Charity law and human rights purposes

In 2002, the Charities Commission began recognising the promotion of human rights as a charitable purpose, viewing it as analogous to the established purpose of promoting the moral and spiritual welfare and improvement of the community.[69] Statutory recognition came with encoding in the Charities Act 2006 and it is now firmly established in the 2011 Act, s.3(1).

Charity law and human rights: a contemporary framework for continuing dissonance

England and Wales has long had a charity-specific legislative framework and a lead regulatory body, which is now accompanied by domestic human rights and equality legislation with related adjudicative forums.

Constitution, public policy and human rights

While this jurisdiction does not have a written constitution, it does have particularly well-established, firm and clear constitutional arrangements which for centuries have orchestrated the balance of authority between monarchy, parliament, government, the established Church and the courts. It also has a claim to be the nation that founded the concept of human rights as a strategic civic contract binding the governed and governing in a formal document guaranteeing mutual respect for an agreed set of basic rights and obligations. Magna Carta of 1215, often regarded as the foundation stone of modern democracy, first gave recognition to such fundamental principles as the right to justice and a fair trial and paved the way for the birth of 'the mother of all parliaments'.

Public policy, charity law, overseas aid and anti-terrorism

In this common law jurisdiction – more so than in any other – the retraction in State services, combined with the redefinition of public benefit and the transfer of much responsibility for related services to charity, has created uncertainty regarding the boundaries of citizens' entitlement to public benefit services, an evermore acute awareness of the distinction between rights and charity, and an initially slow but now increasing willingness to look to a human rights framework for redress.

---

69 See, Charity Commission, *RR12 – The Promotion of Human Rights* (version January 2005).

However, while the main thrust of current public policy is to facilitate further diversification of responsibility for public benefit service provision, allowing a government retreat to the role of regulating service standards, it would seem that this is to be accompanied by use of the political purposes rule to continue policing the government/charity boundary. The 21st-century partnership, like its 17th-century precursor, is intended to function under firm government control.

- OVERSEAS AID

In 2011, overseas aid accounted for an estimated 0.56 per cent of the UK gross national income, reaching 0.7 per cent in 2013. This included spending on emergency aid and disaster relief, but also activities such as training police in Afghanistan, tackling corruption, Gift Aid for international development charities, defraying UK Border Agency costs, bilateral aid and multilateral aid (e.g. via the World Bank) as well as funding some of the work of selected charities and other nonprofits. There are a great many UK, or UK-affiliated, charities delivering overseas aid including Oxfam, ActionAid, the Red Cross and Save the Children. Statutory endorsement of the importance attached to their work was provided by inclusion of the following charitable purposes in s.2(2) of the 2006 Act: (a) the prevention of poverty; (d) the saving of lives; and (j) the relief of those in need. Arguably, initiatives such as awarding charitable status to the Fairtrade Foundation in 1995, thereby raising the competitive capacity of an organisation committed to exporting goods on behalf of producers in underdeveloped countries, and the work of disaster relief organisations, constitute clear examples of synergy between charity law and human rights.

- ANTI-TERRORISM

The effect of anti-terrorism provisions, such as those in the Terrorism Prevention and Investigation Measures Act 2011, are restricting the humanitarian work of many overseas charities, including Human Care Syria whose staff fear prosecution in the UK if payments are made to facilitate access, if proscribed groups become involved or if resources fall into the wrong hands. Interestingly, research into terrorism and the activities of terrorists has been deemed charitable in this jurisdiction.[70]

The legislative and regulatory framework

The separation of tax and charity regulatory systems, each governed by its own specific legislation, is an established and distinctive characteristic of the law relating to charity in England and Wales. As a signatory nation to the European Convention, the provisions of which are incorporated in the Human Rights Act

---

70 *The Institute for the Study of Terrorism* [1988] Ch Com Rep 7–8 [28–34].

1998, Schedule 1, its domestic courts are required under s.3 of that Act 'to construe domestic laws compatibly with Convention rights'.[71]

Charity law

The charity law framework is provided by the provisions of the Charities Act 2011 and the Charities Act 1992 (insofar as not repealed by the 1993 and 2006 Acts). Specific statutory recognition is now given to the advancement of human rights by the Charities Act 2011, s.3(1):

> (h) the advancement of human rights, conflict resolution or reconciliation or the promotion of religious or racial harmony or equality and diversity

However, as has been recently noted, 'the advancement of human rights is a description of a charitable purpose for which there is as yet no legal authority'.[72] It may also be accommodated within the 'any other purposes' of s.3(1):

> (m)(i) that are not within paragraphs(a) to (l) but are recognised as charitable purposes . . . under old law

This purpose is not statutorily defined[73] and, like all others, is required to be for the public benefit but is not in any particular instance presumed to be so.

- THE CHARITIES REGULATOR: CHARITY COMMISSION FOR ENGLAND AND WALES

The above provisions are implemented by the Charity Commission which is vested with the statutory authority to determine charitable status. It maintains a register of all charities which provides the basis for supervising and holding to account all organisations so registered. The rulings it makes on charitable status may be appealed to the First-tier Tribunal and thence to the Upper Tribunal of the Tax and Chancery Chamber.

- ATTORNEY GENERAL

In this jurisdiction the Charities Act 2011, s.318, details the circumstances in which the Attorney General 'may' be made a party to proceedings. In practice, however, the role of this officer is now largely restricted to cases where criminal

---

71 See, *Eweida v British Airways plc* [2009] ICR 303, per Elias P, at para 27.
72 *The Human Dignity Trust v Charity Commission for England and Wales* 6 July 2014, Appeal No CA/2013/0013 at para 108.
73 See, however, the Charity Commission for England and Wales, Guidance RR12, 2005.

prosecutions are being brought on charity-related matters and where *cy-près* schemes are being presented before the judiciary.

Human rights

The legislative framework for human rights is comprised of the following: those rights guaranteed by the UDHR, enlarged by the European Convention on Human Rights,[74] as applied by the Human Rights Act 1998,[75] which allows a court to make a 'declaration of incompatibility' where it finds that legislation or a rule of law is incompatible with the ECHR; and the Equality Act 2010.[76] Also relevant are the ICCPR, which the government ratified in 1976 with certain reservations and declarations; the UN Convention on the Elimination of All Forms of Discrimination Against Women (CEDAW) and its Optional Protocol, and the non-binding Beijing Declaration and Platform for Action for Women; the Convention on Action against Trafficking in Human Beings, ratified in 2008; and the Convention on the Rights of Persons with Disabilities, ratified in 2009. In addition, a Commission was established in 2012 to investigate the creation of a United Kingdom Bill of Rights.

As the First-tier Tribunal has pointed out, 'human rights is to be given its ordinary natural meaning and that there is no authority for the Charity Commission's view that it is to be understood only as referring to those human rights accepted by the law of England and Wales'.[77]

• THE EQUALITY AND HUMAN RIGHTS COMMISSION

This office acts as the regulator in respect of matters arising under the Equality Act 2010.[78]

• THE EMPLOYMENT APPEAL TRIBUNAL

Alleged discriminatory practices in the workplace are heard by the Tribunal and on appeal to the High Court.

---

74 Including Article 2 of Protocol 1. Also relevant are the Race Equality Directive 2000/43/EC; the Employment Equality Directive 2000/78/EC; the Gender Directive 2004/43/EC; and the Recast Gender Equality Directive 2006/54/EC.
75 Note that as set out in the 1998 Act, s.1: 'Convention rights' mean the rights and fundamental freedoms set out in – (a) Articles 2 to 12 and 14 of the Convention, (b) Articles 1 to 3 of the First Protocol, and (c) Article 1 of the Thirteenth Protocol – as read with Articles 16 to 18 of the Convention.
76 In conjunction with the Equality Act 2010 (Specific Duties) Regulations 2011, SI 2011/2260.
77 See, *The Human Dignity Trust v Charity Commission for England and Wales*, op. cit., at para 43.
78 See, EHRC, 'Equality Act 2010 Code of Practice – Services, Public Functions and Associations', 2011.

• THE UN REPORTS

The 2012 CRC UPR,[79] which considered a composite report on the four UK nations, expressed concerns on such matters as use of police 'stop and search' powers, pre-charge detention, terrorism prevention and investigation measures and the policy of deportation of terrorist suspects; complicity in rendition flights, secret detention centres and torture overseas; the low age (10) for criminal responsibility of children, the use of corporal punishment and the level of child poverty; the gender pay gap; prison overcrowding and the absence of a comprehensive policy for the management of women in prison; poor implementation of laws prohibiting female genital mutilation (FGM); the impact of inadequate water and poor sanitation; human trafficking, indefinite detention of migrants and asylum seekers, protection for migrant and domestic workers; and the need to promote multiculturalism.

The contemporary charity law/human rights interface: a compliance audit

This section collates jurisdiction-specific case law illustrating the nature and extent of tensions currently involving charities as they interface with human rights. It is not wholly confined to relevant rights as defined and listed in the UDHR and developed in the European Convention and by the ECtHR, though this is mostly what happens. Judgments arising in other legislative contexts are also examined, litigation initiated under the 2010 Act being a particularly important source.

Access to justice, legal process and principles

Article 10 of the Universal Declaration of Human Rights (ECHR, Article 6), as supplemented by ss. 6–10 of the 1998 Act, safeguards this composite right.[80] Only a few relevant UK cases have arisen from a charity law context.

Access to justice

An essential element of a 'fair hearing' is the provision of appropriate legal representation which may include access to legal aid. In *Steel and Morris v the United Kingdom*[81] the ECtHR ruled that two environmental activists had been denied a fair trial in violation of Article 6(1) of the ECHR. The court found that the refusal of legal aid to the applicant members of Greenpeace had deprived them of the opportunity to present their case effectively before the court and contributed

---

79 See, further, at: http://www.uprinfo.org/sites/default/files/document/united_kingdom/session_13_-_may_2012/ahrcwg.613l.7unitedkingdom.pdf.
80 A similar provision exists in Article 14 of the International Covenant on Civil and Political Rights (ICCPR).
81 (App No 68416/01) (2005).

to an unacceptable inequality of arms with the multinational McDonald's conglomerate. This ruling serves as a firm warning to the UK legal system that charities, almost by definition, may not have the resources necessary to advocate their cause but must not be left disadvantaged as a consequence (see, also, Chapter 2).

An important case in this context is the *Human Dignity Trust v Charity Commission for England and Wales*.[82] The First-tier Tribunal then ruled that the appellant Trust's purposes – (i) promoting and protecting human rights, by means of supporting and conducting litigation to protect individuals in other countries from criminalisation processes for homosexual activity in private and (ii) promoting the sound administration of the law – both meet the public benefit test and are charitable under the Charities Act 2011, s.3(1)(h) and s.3(1)(m)(i), respectively. Although this decision is carefully confined to the facts of the case, it does offer a clear way forward for other organisations seeking charitable status for human rights activities of a parallel nature and can thereby only strengthen the legal rights of, and improve the opportunities to access justice for, very many potential victims of human rights abuse in other countries.

Due process

Following on from the Tribunal's ruling relating to public benefit and fee-charging charities in *Independent Schools*,[83] the Charity Commission issued its long-awaited new guidance in 2013.[84] The most significant aspect of this is that it gives much greater freedom to fee-charging charities to decide how they meet their public benefit requirements: advising trustees of charities that charge fees or offer services that 'the level of provision that trustees make for the poor must be more than minimal or token'; but that it is for trustees, not the Commission or the courts, to decide how to do this.

The shift is one which reflects the Commission's new approach, adopted in the light of the Tribunal ruling, indicating that in future it will apply a less prescriptive, more nuanced interpretation of public benefit when analysing charitable status. This move represents a significant change of tack and one which reveals that it has taken on board the charge of inappropriately assuming a judicial role in making rather than administering law.

Proportionality

In the torturous case of *Catholic Care (Diocese of Leeds) v the Charity Commission for England and Wales and the Equality and Human Rights Commission*,[85] an

82 6 July 2014, Appeal No CA/2013/0013.
83 *R (Independent Schools Council) v Charity Commission for England and Wales* [2012] Ch 214.
84 See, further, at: http://www.charitycommission.gov.uk/detailed-guidance/charitable-purposes-and-public-benefit/.
85 [2010] EWHC 520 (Ch).

issue of proportionality arose for the High Court. Following the Charity Commission's rejection of charitable status, on the basis that their refusal to allow adoption placements with homosexuals constituted a breach of the statutory prohibition on discrimination on grounds of sexual orientation in the provision of services to the public, the charity appealed to the High Court. Briggs J then remitted the case back to the Commission to reconsider the issues in the light of certain principles he set out in his judgment. These included that, although applicable human rights law allowed charities to restrict services on the basis of sexual orientation, this was only possible if the restriction amounted to a proportionate means of achieving a legitimate aim. The Commission concluded that this test was not made out, reasoning that religious conviction was insufficient to justify the discrimination by the charity because of the public nature of the charity's activities. The ruling by Briggs J stands as an important reminder to the Commission – and to other bodies – that the Convention benchmark of 'proportionality' must now be a guiding principle in any UK adjudicative process.

Respect for 'private life'

This right is protected under Article 12 of the UDHR (ECHR, Article 8) and carries an inherent requirement that States ensure their public authorities have and implement procedures that provide citizens with a fair hearing on matters concerning them. For example, such rights will be breached where a public authority has failed sufficiently to involve the subject in a decision-making process affecting his or her interests. Although it has generated or otherwise influenced a huge volume of case law, little has directly involved charities.

In *Human Dignity Trust* the Tribunal took the view that Article 8 was a composite right which included 'rights to human dignity, to be free from cruel, inhuman or degrading treatment or punishment, the right to privacy and to personal and social development'.[86] The Tribunal then found that the appellants' purpose of providing support to and assisting in litigation, on behalf of those in other countries at risk of criminal prosecutions for private homosexual activity, met the public benefit test because the criminalisation of such activity represented 'a serious contravention of international human rights law' and as such it was therefore of benefit to the public in England and Wales that the issue be addressed.[87] Accordingly, the Trust was held to be charitable.

Where charities are found to be acting as 'public bodies' they may find themselves drawn into Article 8 issues. *Weaver v London and Quadrant Housing Trust*,[88] for example, concerned Mrs Weaver, a housing association tenant who

---

86 See, *The Human Dignity Trust v Charity Commission for England and Wales*, op. cit., at para 53.

87 Ibid., at para 78.

88 [2009] EWCA Civ 587; [2008] EWHC 1377 (Admin); [2008] WLR (D) 207. See, also: *Poplar Housing and Regeneration Community Association Ltd v Donoghue* [2001] EWCA Civ 595 [2002] QB 48 and *Bath Festivals Trust Ltd v Revenue and Customs* [2008] UKVA V20840.

having repeatedly defaulted on her rent payments became liable to the mandatory statutory penalty of eviction. During the course of the ensuing court proceedings, it was sucessfully asserted that, because of the particularly close nature of the association's ties with the local authority, its legal status was effectively that of a public body which therefore brought its functions within the scope of the ECHR.[89] This in turn engaged Article 8 and the association found itself having to defend its actions within that frame of reference. The number and variety of charities potentially subject to ECHR requirements, perhaps particularly Article 8, is extensive. In this context it is also worth noting that the ECtHR case law relating to Article 8 has determined that the definition of 'family' is not to be restricted to one based on marriage: it may include unmarried couples, non-marital children and lesbian or homosexual relationships, depending as a matter of fact on the existence of actual close family ties.[90] This approach is certain to attract the future involvement of charities representing such parties.

Freedom of religion and belief

This right (to freedom of thought, conscience and religion), guaranteed by Article 18 of the UDHR (ECHR, Article 9) in conjunction with Article 18 of the ICCPR, tends to involve charities largely in relation to religion. To that extent the right includes the freedom to change religion or belief; to exercise religion or belief publicly or privately, alone or with others; and to exercise religion or belief in worship, teaching, practice and observance. It also provides for the right to have no religion and to have non-religious beliefs protected. The right to manifest religion or belief is declared to be subject to the rights of others.

Church and State

That a distinction should be drawn and maintained between the interests of Church and State has attracted academic[91] and judicial[92] support in this jurisdiction and was recently and directly raised in *McFarlane v Relate Avon Ltd*,[93] a religious discrimination case concerning the Relate charity. Lord Carey, the former Archbishop of Canterbury, had sought to intervene by making suggestions as to the desired composition of the court (deemed by Laws LJ to be 'deeply

---

89 See, *Calle e Figili* [1997] ECR I-1547, at para 23, where it was held that an entity acts a public body when it is performing 'a task in the public interest which forms part of the essential functions of the state and where the activity is connected by its nature, its aims and rules to which it is subject with the exercise of powers . . . which are typically those of a public authority'.

90 See, for example, *Smith and Grady v United Kingdom* (2000) 29 EHRR 548 and *Goodwin v United Kingdom* (2002) 35 EHRR 447.

91 See, for example, Habermas, J., 'Religion in the Public Sphere', *European Journal of Philosophy*, Vol 14, No 1, 2006, p. 10.

92 See, for example, Munby J in *X v X* [2002] 1 FLR 508 at para 112.

93 [2010] IRLR 872; 29 BHRC 249.

inimical to the public interest'[94]) and the need to address what he perceived to be an alleged 'lack of sensitivity to religious belief'[95] by the judiciary when dealing with such cases. In response, while acknowledging that 'the liturgy and practice of the established Church are to some extent prescribed by law', Laws LJ added, 'but the conferment of any legal protection or preference upon a particular substantive moral position on the ground only that it is espoused by the adherents of a particular faith, however long its tradition, however rich its culture, is deeply unprincipled'.[96]

While the right of a church to choose its own clergy is well established,[97] in practice issues can arise in regard to the following: the appointment of chaplains in the armed forces, prisons, universities etc when such posts may be restricted to, or give preference to, Church of England clergy; government grants and service provision contracts which again may favour the established Church and mainstream organised religions rather than new minority religions and belief systems.

Definition of 'religion': theism

The Charities Act 2011, s.3(2), states that 'religion' includes 'a religion which involves a belief in more than one god, and; a religion which does not involve a belief in a god'. This wording ended the requirement for a supreme being and overruled centuries of theistic case law that reached its apotheosis with the decision in *Bowman*.[98] Then, in December 2013, the Supreme Court in a landmark ruling[99] revisited the decision in *Segerdal*[100] and reversed its effect to determine that Scientology was indeed a religion. In coming to this conclusion the court made the finding that:[101]

> religion should not be confined to religions which recognise a supreme deity. First and foremost, to do so would be a form of religious discrimination unacceptable in today's society.

Interestingly, nearly two years later the Charity Commission has still not followed suit and reversed its equally long rejection of Scientology's eligibility for charitable status. Given Toulson LJ's opinion, at the close of the Supreme Court

---

94 Ibid., at para 26.
95 Ibid., at para 20.
96 Ibid., at para 23.
97 See, for example, *R v Chief Rabbi of the United Hebrew Congregations of Great Britain and the Commonwealth, ex parte Wachmann* [1993] 2 All ER 249 (QB) at 255.
98 [1917] AC 406.
99 *R (on the application of Hodkin and another) v Registrar General of Births, Deaths and Marriages* [2013] UKSC 77.
100 *R v Registrar General, ex parte Segerdal* [1970] 2 QB 697.
101 *R (on the application of Hodkin and another) v Registrar General of Births, Deaths and Marriages*, op. cit., per Toulson LJ at para 51.

hearing, that to treat adherents of Scientology differently to those of other religions would be 'illogical, discriminatory and unjust', and that other jurisdictions have conceded legal recognition to the organisation as both a religion and a charity, it is difficult to see how it can be denied charitable status in the UK.

Definition of 'religion': belief system

While the above interpretation of religion has broadened the entitlement to charitable status, this effect has been greatly increased by a further broadening to accommodate 'belief systems' as being equally eligible. Such 'beliefs' must amount to 'more than just mere opinions or deeply held feelings', they must involve 'a holding of spiritual or philosophical convictions which have an identifiable formal content'.[102] The long-term consequences of this development for charity law, and for the social roles of the traditional religions, are at best uncertain.

The Commission gave effect to the new interpretation when it examined the standing of spiritualism and registered the Sacred Hands Spiritual Centre as a charity.[103] Again, in September 2010, it recognised the activities of the Druid Network[104] as meeting the requirements for registration as a charity for the advancement of religion, followed in October 2011 when it registered the British Humanist Association as a charity, thereby recognising as charitable the Association's aim to pursue the 'advancement of humanism, namely a non-religious ethical life stance, the essential elements of which are a commitment to human wellbeing and a reliance on reason, experience and a naturalistic view of the world'.[105] In 2013, the Employment Tribunal found that Wiccas and their beliefs were entitled to recognition and legal protection in the workplace.[106] However, a judicial warning has been given regarding the inherent contradictions and dangers for legal objectivity in attaching undue weight to subjectively perceived 'truths'.[107]

Equality of religions

In this jurisdiction the principle that the law must treat all religions equally has been firmly established since at least *Re Pinion (deceased)*[108] when it was held that

102 See, for example the judicial endorsement in *Campbell and Cosans v United Kingdom* [1982] 4 EHRR 293 that corporal punishment in Scottish state schools offended the plaintiffs' philosophical convictions and in *H v UK* (1993) 16 EHRR CD 44 that veganism constituted a belief system.
103 See, Charity Commission, 'Decision to register Sacred Hands Spiritual Centre as a Charity', 5 September 2003.
104 See, the Charity Commission decision 21 September 2010.
105 See, further, at: https://humanism.org.uk/humanism/.
106 *Holland v Angel Supermarket Ltd & Anor* [2013] Employment Tribunal 3301005–2013.
107 *McFarlane v Relate Avon Ltd* [2010] EWCA Civ 880; [2010] IRLR 872, per Laws LJ at paras 23–24.
108 [1965] Ch 85. Also, see, *Nelan v Downes* (1917) 23 CLR 546.

'the court cannot discriminate between religions.' It was reiterated more recently by Laws LJ, in the charity case *McFarlane*, above, when continuing his peroration against religious preferencing he advised that:[109]

> The precepts of any one religion – any belief system – cannot, by force of their religious origins, sound any louder in the general law than the precepts of any other. If they did, those out in the cold would be less than citizens; and our constitution would be on the way to a theocracy.

• SECULARISM

Again in *McFarlane*, Laws LJ drew attention to two principles generally considered to be central to liberal democracy: that the State should remain neutral in relation to religion, and that public policy should be rigorously secular. There are those, however, who believe that the need for the State to be resolutely non-partisan has now evolved into 'a militant secularism'.[110] In a recent UK case, the Human Rights Commission contended that the applicant charity's religious beliefs concerning homosexuality did not satisfy the threshold requirements for protection under Article 9 because the belief was not consistent with the basic standards of human dignity and integrity, a position described by counsel for the applicants as 'fundamental secularism'.[111]

The right to manifest religion or belief

The right to manifest religion is subject to restrictions in certain circumstances and is reinforced by other articles in relation to discrimination on the basis of religion. Also important (see, further below) is the International Labour Organisation Discrimination (Employment and Occupation) Convention 1958 (ILOC) and Article 18 of the International Covenant on Civil and Political Rights.

In the leading case of *Gallagher v Church of Jesus Christ of Latter-day Saints*,[112] it was asserted that the exclusion of the public from the Temple (their place of worship) was a manifestation by the Mormons of their religion and to deny them a rates exemption would be to discriminate against them on the grounds of religion, contrary to Articles 9 and 14 of the Convention. Lords Hoffmann and Hope held that the rating legislation did not prevent the group manifesting its religion. In a more recent and not dissimilar case, the Charity Commission

---

109 *McFarlane v Relate Avon Ltd* [2010] EWCA Civ 880; [2010] IRLR 872, per Laws LJ at para 24.
110 A term used by Baronness Warsi, Britain's first Muslim cabinet minister and then chair of the Conservative Party.
111 *Christian Institute and Others v Office of First Minister and Deputy First Minister*, Neutral Citation no. [2007] NIQB 66.
112 *Gallagher v Church of Jesus Christ of Latter-Day Saints* [2008] 1 WLR 1852, 1867 [51].

refused to accept an application by the Preston Down Trust to be registered as a charity, as it was unconvinced that the Trust was established for the advancement of religion for public benefit.[113] However, in the above-mentioned *R (on the application of Hodkin and another) v Registrar General of Births, Deaths and Marriages*[114] the Supreme Court, in a finding that will have significant future consequences for the law relating to religion and to religious charities, held that a 'place of meeting for religious worship . . . has to be interpreted in accordance with contemporary understanding of religion and not by reference to the culture of 1855'.[115]

Parental right regarding religious education of their children

The leading English case on such matters has long been *Mandla (Sewa Singh) and another v Dowell Lee and others*[116] which concerned a Sikh boy, Gurinder Singh, who was denied admittance to Park Grove School, a private school with charitable status, because he refused to comply with a school uniform requirement to cut his hair and remove his turban. The House of Lords held that it was unlawful indirect discrimination for a headmaster of an independent school to insist on a uniform requirement of short hair and caps for boys, thus excluding Sikhs who wear turbans with long hair.

This jurisdiction accommodates a high level of faith-based schools, which almost always have charitable status. Many see their mission as the transference of religious belief and culture from one generation to another, and have closed admission procedures with all or the majority of places allocated to those from their own faith community. They permit an extensive range of discriminatory practice: preferential treatment in terms of funding to become established; permission to discriminate in pupil admissions and staffing; a teaching curriculum skewed in favour of a particular religious belief; and a corresponding alignment of taught social values in regard to issues such as gay marriage, abortion etc. Possibly, as the religious context generates more social divisions, it may become open to question whether such facilities continue to meet the public benefit test and should be entitled to charitable status.

Freedom of expression

This qualified right as stated in Article 19 of the Universal Declaration of Human Rights (ECHR, Article 10), read in conjunction with s.12 of the 1998 Act, includes the freedom to hold opinions and to receive and impart information and ideas without interference by public authority (see, also, Chapter 2). It has

113 *Preston Down Trust (Exclusive Plymouth Brethren) v Charity Commission for England & Wales*, June 2012.
114 [2013] UKSC 77.
115 Ibid., per Toulson LJ at para 34.
116 [1983] 2 AC 548.

a particular significance for charity because it incorporates advocacy rights which have always been held to be an important aspect of their role in addressing the needs of the socially disadvantaged – but advocating to change or retain laws or policy has long been viewed as incompatible with charitable status.

However, there are signs that the resolute stand taken on this issue in the UK is beginning to weaken. Quite probably the above-mentioned case of *Steel and Morris v the United Kingdom*[117] may have been the turning point. The court then expressed the view that a strong public interest existed in enabling such groups and individuals outside the mainstream to contribute to the public debate by disseminating information and ideas on matters of general public interest such as health and the environment. The free circulation of information and ideas about the activities of powerful commercial entities, and the possible 'chilling' effect on others, were also important factors to be considered in this context.

This may help explain the difference in the approach taken by the Commission in the pre–*Steel and Morris* case of *Internet Content Rating Association*[118] and its subsequent decisions in *Concordis* and *PEN*. In relation to the first, although the Commission did decide to register the Association, it denied the applicant's claim that its secondary aim 'to protect free speech on the internet' could be a charitable purpose. The argument that it conformed to the freedom of expression was rejected on the grounds that government could decide to restrict activities under that aim, which would then transform the Association's aim into a political object which could not be charitable. It was agreed that the Association would delete its secondary aim. In contrast, the Commission accepted, rather surprisingly, that the aims of Concordis International Trust[119] and PEN[120] were both charitable despite finding that a high level of political activity was entailed in carrying out their human rights work. The aims of the former were concerned with national and international conflict resolution and reconciliation while those of the latter were to promote literature and defend freedom of expression. Both were held to be for the public benefit and deemed to be charitable, the Commission deciding that any political activities carried out by PEN would be ancillary to its charitable purpose.

Of considerable importance in this context is the most recent decision in the *Human Dignity Trust* case[121] that the promotion of human rights by establishing whether particular laws (within or outside the jurisdiction) are valid – through a process of analysing those laws relative to the bearing of a supervening source

---

117   (App No 68416/01) (2005).
118   Charity Commission decision, 12 September 2002.
119   See, Charity Commission decision, 23 July 2004.
120   See, Charity Commission decision, 21 July 2008.
121   *The Human Dignity Trust v Charity Commission for England and Wales* 6 July 2014, Appeal no CA/2013/0013 at paras 95–101. Note also, *Cage Advocacy UK Ltd v Charity Commission* (Judicial Review, High Court, 22 October 2015) when, in response to the Commission's directive that charities should not fund the plaintiff advocacy organisation, the court held that 'trustees must be free to exercise their fiduciary powers and duties in light of the circumstances that exist at the time, if acting properly within their objects and powers and in the best interests of the charity'.

of authority (such as the provisions of a domestic constitution or international treaty, convention or protocol to which the country concerned is subject) – does not fall within the five categories of political activity which Slade J in *McGovern*[122] had ruled could not constitute a valid charitable purpose. The Tribunal declared itself satisfied that:[123]

> The promotion and protection of human rights (a) by means which include the support or conduct of litigation which is (b) aimed at securing the interpretation and/or enforcement of superior constitutionsl rights (c) in a foreign country which has given effect to the relevant treaty obligation so as to enable that process – is not a political process and neither is it in our view a political activity.

Bearing in mind that 'the promotion of human rights through the conduct of such litigation has not previously been considered by the courts', the Tribunal endorsed Van Bueren's 'living instrument' approach to human rights, and took the view that a human rights instrument may only evolve if it is tested from time to time in such a manner.[124]

Freedom of assembly and association

The right of citizens under Article 20 of the UDHR (ECHR, Article 11) underpins the modus operandi of charities. Only convincing and compelling reasons can justify restrictions on the freedom of association,[125] although this will not prevent a charity constituted as an unincorporated association from imposing membership restrictions – e.g. on a particular ethnic group – provided it can still satisfy the public benefit test.[126] The requirement that all laws and practice are not only human rights compliant but that the UK government also positively promotes this right has been judicially reinforced by the ECtHR.[127]

Clearly, anything that inhibits a charity from organising itself so as to give effect to its charitable purpose would be at risk of breaching this requirement, and in practice the limited legal structures available have been a constraint. Among the outcomes of the charity law reform process has been the gradual introduction of Community Interest Companies (CICs) and Charitable Incorporated Organisations (CIOs), but they have not proven to provide the flexibility that many charities need to cope in the contemporary fast-moving fiscal environment. Moreover, added complications have arisen with the proposal to introduce a European

---

122 *McGovern v AG* [1982] Ch 321.
123 *The Human Dignity Trust v Charity Commission for England and Wales*, op cit., at para 101.
124 Ibid.
125 See, for example, *Young, James and Webster v the United Kingdom* (1982) 4 EHRR 38, where the court stressed the importance of ensuring 'the fair and proper treatment of minorities' and held that the 'closed shop' was a violation of Article 11. In contrast, see *Neville Estates v Madden* [1962] 1 Ch 832 (Ch) 853.
126 The Equality Act 2010, s.107, and Schedule 16.
127 *Wilson and Palmer v United Kingdom* (2002) 35 EHRR 20.

foundation that will offer a common legal structure for all charities and other nonprofit public benefit entities operating throughout Europe.

Equality and non-discrimination

Article 2 of the UDHR (ECHR, Article 14) broadly prohibits discrimination and has been incorporated into UK domestic law by the corresponding Article 14 of the 1998 Act.

The Charities Act 2006, s.2(2)(h), first gave statutory recognition to the promotion of religious or racial harmony or equality and diversity as charitable purposes. This was reinforced by the Equality Act 2010, which prohibits discrimination against an individual on any of nine 'protected grounds' whether occurring in the workplace, when providing goods, facilities and services, when exercising public functions, in the disposal and management of premises, or in education and by associations (such as private clubs) and whether the discrimination takes the form of direct, indirect, harassment or victimisation. The nine grounds are the previously established six (sex, race, disability, sexual orientation, religion or belief and age) together with an additional three (marriage and civil partnership, gender reassignment and pregnancy and maternity) transferred from the Sex Discrimination Act. An applicant will have established direct discrimination if he or she can show that other persons in a similar or analogous situation, as evidenced by the set of facts governing each situation, are being treated differently to the applicant, and there is no justification for the difference in treatment.[128]

The Equality Act 2010, s.193, provides charity-specific exemptions. Unequal treatment is permissible in respect of persons who share one or more of the protected characteristics, and is provided in order to tackle a particular disadvantage or need linked to that protected characteristic; the restriction must be justified as being a fair, balanced and proportionate way of carrying out a legitimate aim, taking into account the discrimination involved. According to the Charity Commission, a legitimate aim is one that has a reasonable social policy objective; is consistent with the lawful carrying out of the charity's stated purpose for the public benefit, though not necessarily identical with that purpose; and is not itself discriminatory.[129] Numerous carve-outs are specified, such as exempting those who provide single-sex services:[130] if it can be demonstrated that this is a proportionate means of achieving a legitimate aim under s.193(2)(a), or to prevent or compensate for disadvantage under s.193(2)(b). The point of the 'positive action' provisions – as with the 'margin of appreciation' rule – is explicitly to permit discrimination in order to allow compensatory measures that may redress existing inequalities.

---

128 See, for example, *Abdulaziz, Cabales and Balkandali v United Kingdom* (1985) 7 EHRR 471.
129 See, Charity Commission, 'Equality Act guidance for charities: Restricting who can benefit from charities', 2012, at para C4.
130 See, for example, the Equality Act 2010, ss.114 and 120.

Religious discrimination

The Equality Act 2010 identifies four types of religious discrimination: direct, indirect, harassment or victimisation. The first takes the form of unequal treatment whereby some are directly treated less favourably than others because of their religious beliefs. The second incidentally disadvantages a certain religious group as when a service provider's provision, criterion or practice imposes restrictions that affect their ability to access services available to others. The third results from 'whistleblower' circumstances involving a complaint about religious discrimination, while the fourth is behaviour that may range from physical attack, verbal abuse, to causing discomfort because of a religious or racial difference.

The religious exemption

A religious charity is permitted to give preference to employing staff that share its religious ethos where to do so enables the charity to give effect to its purpose.[131] Such a body may restrict employment opportunities on religious or sexual grounds where such criteria constitute a genuine occupational requirement of the post to be filled. A restriction can only be made (i) on the grounds of religion or belief, where necessary because of the organisation's purpose, or to avoid causing offence to adherents, or (ii) in relation to sexual orientation, if this is necessary to comply with the organisation's doctrine or to avoid conflict with the religious or belief-based convictions of many adherents.[132]

The exemption privilege must be exercised reasonably. For example, in *Reaney v Hereford Diocesan Board of Finance*,[133] the Employment Tribunal held that where a homosexual was committed to working for the Church of England, he could expect to discuss the perceptions of homosexuality within the Church during a job interview and, as the questions put to the job applicant (about his sexuality and future intentions about relationships) had been reasonable and had been expected by him, he had not been subjected to harassment. However, as he had been the preferred candidate after competitive interview, the failure to offer him the job was an act of direct sexual orientation discrimination. The defence of a genuine occupational requirement was not available to the Church.

Exemption is directly linked to the religious functions of the charity and is not to be interpreted as carte blanche for operating a 'closed shop' employment policy exclusively favouring persons of a designated religion or belief. This was clearly illustrated in *Hinder & Sheridan v Prospects for People with Learning Disabilities*[134] which concerned Prospects, a Christian charity that provided housing

---

131 See, for example, the 'organised religion' exception and the Equality Act 2010, Sched 9. Also, see the School Standards Framework Act 1998, s.60.
132 Ibid., at para F5.
133 1602844/2006 (April 2007).
134 *Hender & Sheridan v Prospects for People with Learning Disabilities* [2008] Employment Tribunal (nos 2902090/2006 & 2901366) (2008).

and day care for people with learning disabilities. Prospects introduced a policy whereby it would recruit only practising Christians for the vast majority of roles and told existing non-Christian employees that they were no longer eligible for promotion. The Tribunal found that it was insufficient to assume that, as a matter of principle, every job in a Christian organisation should be done by Christians. In a decision that sent a clear message to faith-based organisations regarding blanket policies which discriminate on this protected characteristic, the Tribunal held that the charity had unlawfully discriminated against one of its managers by requiring him to only employ Christians and not to promote its existing non-Christian employees.

The Marriage (Same Sex Couples) Act 2013 is inevitably going to raise human rights issues – particularly for the Church of England, as its canons clearly restrict marriage to heterosexual relationships. The fact that under the new legislation, accompanied by amendments to the Equalities Act 2010, the Church is relieved of any duty to conduct gay marriages is going to be problematic. It is thereby statutorily handicapped relative to other religions, its functional capacity diminished by the State. Moreover, it also compromises the equality principle and may give rise to a charge that the law operates in a discriminatory fashion to the clear detriment of Anglican same-gender couples. There is, of course, also the fact that the permission not to officiate at same-sex marriages is restricted exclusively to the Church: all other religious institutions, wishing for similar exemption, may well protest that this provision discriminates against them.

Discrimination (and exemptions) on other grounds

The 2010 Act permits a charity to restrict itself to beneficiaries identified by a protected characteristic if this is in accordance with its terms of registration and is a 'proportionate means of achieving a legitimate aim', or if doing so prevents or compensates for a disadvantage linked to the protected characteristic.[135]

In recent years the courts have tended to adopt a more rigorous approach to policing unequal treatment that disadvantages those with personal characteristics (including sex, race and sexual orientation) which they cannot change and in regard to which discrimination could be particularly demeaning,[136] as also has the government with the launch of its Hate Crime Action Plan.[137] In deciding whether unequal treatment is justified, it will be relevant to take into account whether the aim could have been achieved through other means or, effectively, whether 'reasonable adjustments' could have been made.[138]

---

135 See, for example, the Women's Resource Centre charity at: www.wrc.org.uk.
136 See, for example, *R (Carson) v Work and Pensions Secretary* [2006] 1 AC 173, per Walker LJ at p. 192E.
137 See, 'Challenge It, Report It, Stop It – The Government's Plan to Tackle Hate Crime' at: https://www.gov.uk/government/uploads/system/uploads/attachment_data/file/97849/action-plan.pdf.
138 See, for example, *Glor v Switzerland* (App No 13444/04), April 2009.

- GENDER DISCRIMINATION

Although there has been an Equal Pay Act in force in the UK since 1975, women still earn an average of 19.8 per cent less than men.[139] This pay gap has been attributed, at least in part, to the so-called motherhood penalty. Specific charities have been established to promote gender equality and women's rights at work, at home and in public life.[140]

- RACIAL DISCRIMINATION

In *Board of Governors of St Matthias Church of England School v Crizzle*[141] the complaint of an unsuccessful Asian applicant for the post of headteacher that the criterion of being 'a committed communicant Christian' constituted discrimination was treated as indirect discrimination on the grounds of race and therefore justifiable, as the charity had the legitimate aim of seeking to protect the religious ethos of the school; seemingly, the religious exemption trumps racism.

However, more recently in *R (on the application of E) v Governing Body of JFS and the Admissions Appeal Panel of JFS*[142] judicial attention was focused on the rules of admission to a Jewish school with charitable status that had, for 52 years, required a child to have a mother who was born Jewish. The issue for the court was whether the school could claim an exemption against a charge of racial discrimination on the grounds of their religious commitments. The High Court ruled that a school which accepts State funding must not discriminate in its admission policy on the basis of ethnicity. Subsequently, the UK Supreme Court, in a majority ruling, held that such a matrilineal religious condition was in fact direct racial discrimination, a ruling compliant with Lord Steyn's earlier views on 'the legal right of equality with the correlative right of non-discrimination on the grounds of race'.[143]

It should be noted that the above-mentioned 2012 CRC UPR report expressed concern regarding the fact that the Equality Act 2010 permits public officials to discriminate on the basis of nationality, ethnic and national origins.

- SEXUAL DISCRIMINATION

Although not specifically referred to, sexual orientation discrimination is plainly within the ambit of Article 2.[144] Indeed, as Briggs J has warned, 'a charity which

---

139 See, Office for National Statistics at: http://www.ons.gov.uk/ons/index.html.

140 See, the Fawcett Society at: http://www.fawcettsociety.org.uk/about/what-we-do/.

141 [1995] ICR 401.

142 *R (E) v Governing Body of JFS* [2010] IRLR 136; [2009] UKSC 15 on appeal from [2009] EWCA Civ 626.

143 *R (European Roma Rights Centre) v Immigration Officer at Prague Airport* [2004] UKHL 55; [2005] 2 AC 1, 46 [46].

144 As noted in *Catholic Care (Diocese of Leeds) v the Charity Commission for England and Wales and the Equality and Human Rights Commission* [2010] EWHC 520 (Ch), per Briggs J at para 57, citing *Salgueiro Da Silva Mouta v Portugal* (2001) 31 EHRR 47.

proposed to apply differential treatment on grounds of sexual orientation otherwise than as a proportionate means of achieving a legitimate aim might thereby fail to achieve charitable status (or lose it, if it sought to pursue such activities by amendment of its objects)'.[145]

• EMPLOYMENT DISCRIMINATION

The 'Framework Directive' (or 'Employment Equality Directive') requires the provisions of the 2010 Act to be interpreted and applied in accordance with its stipulations for equal treatment in employment and occupation.[146] So, for example, in *Amnesty International v Ahmed*[147] the charity was found guilty of direct discrimination, as it had chosen not to promote the respondent to a post, for which she was qualified and would otherwise have attained, because of her racial affiliation which it believed would place her at risk in the particular environment where the post was to be located. As became clear in *R (Age Concern England) v Secretary of State for Business Enterprise and Regulatory Reform*,[148] any regulations permitting derogation from the requirements of the Directive must be justified by and limited to clear and precise 'social policy' aims: under Article 6 of the Directive, the aims that can be regarded as legitimate in this context include 'legitimate employment policy, labour market and vocational training objectives'.

A number of cases have considered the question whether clergy are 'employed' by their Church. These were reviewed in the important ruling given by Underhill J in *Moore v President of the Methodist Conference*[149] when he concluded that the plaintiff, who had been appointed for a five-year term as minister to a group of congregations in Cornwall, had been employed in a contract of service and was accordingly entitled to bring a claim of unfair dismissal. He considered that there were sufficient incidences of a contractual relationship – including, an offer and acceptance, a fixed term of appointment and a stipend – to bring the plaintiff within the definition of employee and within the protection of Article 18 (ECHR, Article 9).

The above reasoning is, arguably, not irrelevant to the finding in *X v Mid-Sussex Citizens Advice Bureau*[150] that volunteers are not employees and that the Framework Directive[151] does not impose an obligation to outlaw discrimination against volunteers. This decision does seem a bit prescriptive. In practice the

145 *Catholic Care*, op. cit.
146 See, the Council Directive 2000/78/EC of 27 November 2000.
147 [2009] IRLR 884 (EAT).
148 [2009] ICR 1080. Also, see *R (on the application of Incorporated Trustees of the National Council on Ageing (Age Concern England)) v Secretary of State for Business, Enterprise and Regulatory Reform* (C-388/07) [2009] All ER (EC) 619.
149 [2010] UKEAT 1219 10 1503 (15 March 2011).
150 [2012] UKSC 59, [2013] IRLR 146. Also, see, *South East Sheffield CAB v Grayson* [2004] IRLR 353 EAT.
151 Council Directive 2000/78, Article 3.

term volunteer is open to a considerable spectrum of interpretation. The appointments of most would share similar contractual characteristics with those of clergy, most often including a formal interview, requirements such as a driving licence, an offer and acceptance, a fixed term of appointment, obligations to perform a service to a required standard, mandatory training (e.g. in child protection), and re-imbursement for travel and meals. Many in fact receive actual remuneration. In the 21st century, the concept of employment is much more diffuse than its traditional definition and it is questionable whether the legal treatment of volunteers, as illustrated by the *Mid-Sussex* case, is wholly human rights compliant.

- SERVICE PROVISION DISCRIMINATION

Any restriction on the provision of services to people defined by a protected characteristic must be in accordance with the Equality Act 2010. This was stressed by the Charity Commission in *JNF Charitable Trust, JNF Educational Trust and KKL Charity Accounts*.[152] The probability of difficulties arising in relation to same-sex issues had been demonstrated in the earlier case of *McFarlane v Relate Avon Ltd*[153] which concerned a charity that provided relationship support services including counselling for couples, families, young people and individuals, sex therapy, mediation and training courses. Mr M, a relationship counsellor, had been dismissed when he indicated to his employer that he did not approve of same-sex relationships on biblical grounds and did not wish to be involved in counselling such couples. The court ruled that Mr M had not suffered religious discrimination. The ECtHR endorsed the approach of the English judiciary and regulators that an individual's right to manifest religious beliefs in the workplace is subject to the employers right not to accommodate them in circumstances where to do so may conflict with their obligation to protect the rights of others.

At much the same time, Catholic Care, a charity based in Leeds, took the position that it was outside the tenets of the Roman Catholic Church to provide adoption services to same-sex cohabiting couples or civil partners, and, in fact, it provided adoption services only to married couples. However, ultimately the First-tier Tribunal (Charity)[154] ruled that the charity had failed to meet the statutory test imposed by s.193 of the Equality Act 2010 requiring it to demonstrate that the less favourable treatment it proposed to offer same-sex couples would constitute a proportionate means of achieving its legitimate aim of providing suitable adoptive parents for a significant number of 'hard to place' children. Because adoption is a public service, funded (in part) by local authorities, Catholic Care could not avail of exemptions under the 2010 Act.

---

152 See, Charity Commission Decision, 31 January 2014, at: https://www.gov.uk/government/uploads/system/uploads/attachment_data/file/324179/jnf-decision.pdf.
153 [2010] EWCA Civ B1 (29 April 2010). Also, see, *R (Johns) v Derb City Council* [2011] EWHC 375 (Admin); [2011] 1 FLR 2094.
154 *Catholic Care (Diocese of Leeds) v The Charity Commission for England and Wales* [2011] Eq LR 597.

• *'POSITIVE ACTION'*

This type of intervention became law as part of the Equality Act 2010 and provides specific opportunities for charities to take action in circumstances that would otherwise constitute unlawful discrimination. Positive action is permitted if it is a proportionate means of addressing the disadvantages of a group with shared protected characteristics[155] and if it serves to encourage a more proportionate take-up in activities or services by members of such a protected group. This was illustrated by the ruling in *R (Kaur and Shah) v Ealing LBC*[156] when Southall Black Sisters[157] appealed the decision of Ealing Council to withdraw its funding because the charity's focus on black and Asian minority communities was considered contrary to the Council's perceived obligation to sponsor a non-discriminatory service. As Moses J explained:[158]

> There is no dichotomy between the promotion of equality and cohesion and the provision of specialist services to an ethnic minority . . . [I]n certain circumstances the purposes of [the Public Sector Equality Duty] may only be met by specialist services from a specialist source.

The general positive action provisions allow employers to target measures such as training towards groups such as ethnic minorities, which are under-represented or disadvantaged in the workplace, or to in other ways address their particular needs.

• CHARITIES AS PUBLIC BODIES

Any charity when acting in an agency capacity on behalf of a government body is bound by the laws governing discrimination; the services offered by the above-mentioned *Catholic Care* society came within this category. A case in point was that of *National Union of Teachers v Governing Body of St Mary's Church of England (Aided) Junior School*,[159] where the Court of Appeal found that the Church of England school was in the State system, the governors were a body charged by the State with the running of the school and were exercising their functions with a view to securing provision by the school of the national curriculum. In these circumstances the governors were to be regarded as an emanation of the State for the purposes of the doctrine of direct effect.

Also relevant in this context is the 'Public Sector Equality Duty'. Established by the Equality Act 2010, this duty falls mainly on public authorities but is also applied by s.149(2) to charities carrying out 'public functions'. It requires

155 The 'protected characteristics' are age, disability, gender reassignment, marriage and civil partnership, pregnancy and maternity, race, religion or belief, sex and sexual orientation.
156 [2008] EWHC 2062 (Admin).
157 This nonprofit was established in 1979 to address the needs of black (Asian and African-Caribbean) women experiencing domestic violence.
158 [2008] EWHC 2062 (Admin) at paras 55–56.
159 [1997] 3 CMLR 630.

removing or minimising disadvantages suffered by people due to their protected characteristics, taking steps to meet the needs of people from protected groups where these are different from the needs of other people, and encouraging people from protected groups to participate in public life or in other activities where their participation is disproportionately low. It has given rise to a number of cases where charities have challenged government action that has had a disproportionate adverse effect upon them or on their client group. For example, in *R (Hajrula) v London Councils*[160] users of the charity Roma Support Group successfully challenged London Councils regarding the latter's £10 million cut in funding for voluntary organisations, without having first undertaken an equality impact assessment, which had resulted in their organisation being treated as a low priority.

Conclusion

This jurisdiction laid the foundations for the development of charity law in the many nations that constitute the common law world. Over the centuries, the case law precedents forged here have enabled it to maintain its customary leadership role. A cornerstone of that role has been a regard for the concept of altruism – as epitomised in the Titmuss iteration of 'the gift relationship'. This, together with a reputation for championing equality, suffered a setback in 2015 with revelations of what were commonly perceived to be excessive salaries being paid to charity executives. Many have found it hard to square the morality of altruism with the levels of self-remuneration by charity executives that often exceed the Prime Minister's salary.[161]

It is possible, however, that the outcome of charity law reform, as implemented by the Charities Act 2006 and further consolidated under the Charities Act 2011, will for the first time set England and Wales on a somewhat different trajectory from other common law jurisdictions. It remains to be seen just how enduring these changes prove to be. As matters stand, the recalibration of the public benefit test, the radical re-interpretation of 'religion' and the use of charity law to further the strategic bridging of the business of government and the nonprofit sector will alter the role traditionally allocated to charity in this jurisdiction and may also trigger repercussions elsewhere in the common law world.

In addition to its leadership in charity law development, this jurisdiction has also sought to ensure that such development takes fully into account modern human rights requirements. Some of the consequences resulting from the forced marriage of these two bodies of law are illustrated in the above case law.

---

160 [2011] EWHC 448 (Admin). Also see: *R (Fawcett Society) v Chancellor of the Exchequer* [2010] EWHC 3522 (Admin); *R (Rahman) v Birmingham City Council* [2011] EWHC 944 (Admin), [2011] Eq Lr 705; and *R (Barrett) v Lambeth LBC* [2012] EWHC 4557 (Admin), [2012] BLGR 299.
161 See further, Hope. C., '32 charity chiefs paid over £200,000 last year', The Telegraph, (26 Feb 2015) at: http://www.telegraph.co.uk/news/politics/10224104/30-charity-chiefs-paid-more-than-100000.html.

5 Ireland

Introduction

Charity law in Ireland, uniquely among the common law jurisdictions, does not trace its legislative roots to the Statute of Charitable Uses 1601.[1] Instead they lie in the Statute of Pious Uses 1634.[2] The difference is one which, on the face of it, reflects an association with religion that arguably has grown in the intervening centuries to become the dominant characteristic of charity law in this jurisdiction.

This chapter begins with a brief background history of charity law and the social role of charities in Ireland. It identifies early indications of areas in which charity law and human rights were not wholly compatible. It considers the changes brought about by the charity law reform process and reviews the resulting implications for human rights. This leads into the main section which deals with the contemporary framework for charity law and human rights and an assessment of the areas of tension between them as illustrated by recent case law. The chapter concludes with a summary of the main difficulties that currently obstruct the synchronising of both bodies of law in Ireland.

Background: a history inimical to human rights

Although very closely resembling the 1601 Act, the purposes listed in the 1634 statute differ from those in its English counterpart by their pointed reference to 'pious uses' in the title. Otherwise, the Irish statute was held by Sugden LC, in *Incorporated Society in Dublin for Promoting English Protestant Schools in Ireland v Richards*,[3] to fulfil essentially the same functions. The Preambles to both the 1634 and the 1601 Acts were never judicially regarded as definitive; a 'public benefit' element was vital and a gift could still be judged charitable if it could be found to be within the 'spirit or intendment' of either statute.

---

1 43 Eliz. 1, Cap. 4.
2 10 Car. 1, Sess. 3, Cap. 1. Entitled 'An Act for the Maintenance and Execution of Pious Uses', it was repealed by the Statute Law Revision Act (Ireland) 1878.
3 (1841) 1 Dr & War 258.

Charity law and human rights: the early challenges

Following the foundations laid by the 1634 Act, the ruling of Macnaghten LJ in *Commissioners for Special Purposes of Income Tax v Pemsel*,[4] outlining four categories of charitable trust, was wholly accepted in Ireland. Thereafter, although Irish case law closely followed precedents established in England and Wales, with equal respect for common law definitional matters (see, further, Chapter 4), it did so subject to certain singular and important differences. One of these was, and remains, the judicial view that the donor's intent is all important, and any question as to whether the intention meets the public benefit test should be interpreted subjectively. As Fitzgibbon LJ explained in *In re Cranston, Webb v Oldfield*,[5] 'the benefit must be one which the founder believes to be of public advantage, and his belief must be at least rational and not contrary either to the general law of the land or to the principles of morality', an approach reiterated more recently by Keane J in *Re the Worth Library*.[6]

> In every case, the intention of the testator is of paramount importance. If he intended to advance a charitable object recognised as such by the law, his gift will be a charitable gift.

Another difference, as the same judge noted in *Campaign to Separate Church and State v Minister for Education*,[7] has been the centrality of religious belief and activity to Irish culture and society which, as he then reasoned, explained the presumption of public benefit in relation to religious charities.

Legal structures: charitable trusts

The Statute of Uses (Ireland) 1634 extended to Ireland the provisions enacted a century earlier in England in the Statute of Uses 1535[8] hastening the evolution of the feudal concept of the 'use'[9] into its modern manifestation as a 'trust'. As in England, a trust must meet the 'three certainties test' (see, further, Chapter 2).[10]

The constitution

The Irish Constitution provided an authoritative source for religious values that continues to colour Irish law, including charity law. While Article 44 prohibited

---

4 [1891] AC 531.
5 [1898] 1 IR 431 at p. 447.
6 [1994] 1 ILRM 161.
7 [1998] 3 IR 321, per Keane J at pp. 330–331.
8 See, Keeton and Sheridan, 'The Development of the Law of Trusts' in *The Law of Trusts*, op. cit. at pp. 21–35.
9 It was Maitland who first remarked that 'the modern trust developed from the ancient use'. See, further, Keane, R., *Equity and the Law of Trusts in the Republic of Ireland*, Bloomsbury Professional, London, 2011, at pp. 69–77.
10 See, *Chambers v Fahy* [1931] IR 17, per O'Byrne J at p. 21.

any State establishment or endowment of religion,[11] or any State discrimination on the basis of religious belief, the Constitution nonetheless gave clear precedence to theism, to Christianity and to Catholicism, in that order.[12]

Exempt charities

The distinctive approach to religious institutions in Ireland is reinforced by an additional privilege granted to them in the definition of 'charitable organisation' in s.2 of the 2009 Act which provides an exception to the general rule that to satisfy the definition such an organisation 'under its constitution, is required to apply all of its property (both real and personal) in furtherance of that purpose'. The provision goes on to provide an exemption from the restrictions solely in favour of 'a religious organisation or community, on accommodation and care of members of the organisation or community'. In addition, one of the four main exemptions from the requirement to register, under s.48(6) of the 2009 Act, is in relation to an 'education body'. As many of these are owned and/or managed by religious organisations, this has the effect of enabling them to avoid the levels of fiscal monitoring, regulatory accountability and public transparency now expected of all other charities.

Political purposes

As in England and Wales, charitable status and political purposes were held to be incompatible. Initially, in this jurisdiction, the rule was applied with some equivocation. A gift to the Society for the Abolition of Vivisection was found to be charitable,[13] as was a gift to promote temperance among the poor and labouring classes[14] – rulings that seemed to breach the prohibition.

Charitable purposes: a tangential relationship with human rights

As Irish case law closely followed corresponding English decisions, it also replicated some doubtful precedents established in that jurisdiction.

However, aspects of Irish charity law remain quite distinctive. A particularly influential factor was, and continues to be, the fact that (as mentioned above) in Ireland the subjective view of the donor is decisive. Judicial application of the subjective test has in the past allowed gifts to acquire charitable status and be directed towards such marginal if not questionable areas of need as 'the Dublin Home for Starving and Forsaken Cats'.[15] There were early warnings of the difficulties that lay ahead on the charity law/human rights interface.

---

11 The Irish Church Act 1869 dis-established the Church of Ireland.
12 *Re Tilson Infants* [1951] IR 1 (SC) and *Re McNally (an Infant)* (1949) 84 ILTR 7 (HC).
13 *Clancy v Commissioner of Valuation* (1890) 25 LR Ir 325.
14 *Armstrong v Reeves* [1911] 2 IR 173.
15 *Swifte v Att-Gen for Ireland (No 2)* [1912] 1 IR 133.

The relief of poverty

This charitable purpose has traditionally attracted a lax application of the public benefit test: if a trust was in danger of not qualifying under the other *Pemsel* headings, then it would be saved for charity as being for the relief of poverty. In Ireland, as in England and Wales, gender- or status-specific gifts and gifts to the poor of specific localities and facilities have equally been upheld as valid charities. Moreover, 'poverty' has been generously interpreted, with charitable status being awarded in respect of 'houses for poor decayed gentlemen and gentlewomen'[16] and 'old Presbyterian persons'.[17]

However, as the conservative approach of the court in *Re Cole*[18] demonstrated, the Irish judiciary also had a capacity to construe public benefit in a blinkered manner. This case concerned a gift of funds from the sale of houses which were to be used for the general benefit and welfare of the residents in a local authority home for deprived children. Harman J ruled that the gift was not a charitable trust, as the eligible children might use it to purchase luxury items such as a television and record player, and this would be incompatible with the objects as listed in the Preamble to the Elizabethan statute. This decision was upheld by the Court of Appeal.

A further constraint upon the equitable application of Irish charity law, following precedents forged in England and Wales, resulted from the creative judicial interpretation of public benefit which was responsible for broadening the precedent established by the 'poor relations' trusts, thereby seriously undermining the cardinal public benefit principle of charity law.[19] The poor relations exception was in time extended to trusts for 'poor members' and to 'poor employees', all of which constituted an anomalous travesty of the public benefit test.

Finally, charities in this jurisdiction, as elsewhere, have always been restricted by the traditional common law limitation that the charitable activity be directed towards the effects and not the cause of poverty.

The advancement of education

In Ireland, religion and education are closely linked. Unlike the position in the UK, a very large proportion of the buildings and teachers comprising the educational system were and continue to be provided by religious bodies. The significance of the second *Pemsel* head was illustrated by *The Governors of Erasmus Smith's Schools v The Attorney-General of Saorstat Eireann*[20] when Meredith J considered whether an endowment to establish schools of a certain ethos was

---

16 *R v Guardians of the Poor of the Mitchelstown Union* (1855) 4 ICLR 590.
17 *Re Dunlop* [1984] NI 408.
18 [1958] Ch 877.
19 See, the judgment of Gavan Duffy J in *In re McEnery* [1941] IR 323.
20 (1932) 66 ILTR 57. Also, see, *Governors of Wesley College and the Trustees of the Methodist Church in Ireland v The Commissioner of Valuation* [1984] ILRM 117 and *Maynooth College v Commissioner of Valuation* [1958] IR 189; (1957) 91 ILTR 132.

essentially religious or educational in nature and held in favour of the latter, and again in *Crowley v Ireland*[21] which established that the State could support denominationally controlled education in discharging its obligation to provide for free primary education.

As in the neighbouring jurisdiction, educational charities in Ireland were often somewhat elitist: gifts to schools 'for the sons of gentlemen' have long been recognised as charitable.[22] In *A-G v Bagot*,[23] for example, a testator left a sum of money to be used to provide a perpetual endowment for the encouragement of fine arts in Ireland. In *Re Shaw's Wills Trusts, National Provincial Bank Ltd v National City Bank Ltd*[24] Mrs Bernard Shaw established a trust for, among other things:

> the teaching, promotion and encouragement in Ireland of self-control, elocution, oratory, deportment, the arts of personal contact, of social intercourse and the other arts of public, private, professional and social life.

Vaisey J upheld this as a valid charitable trust reasoning that 'education' included 'not only teaching, but the promotion and encouragement of those arts and graces of life which are after all, perhaps the finest and best part of the human character'.

Educational charities in Ireland have also shared with England and Wales the interpretation of the public benefit test that permitted a degree of nepotism by allowing donors to give preference to their relatives. If the donor's primary intention was to achieve a bona fide educational purpose, then a subsidiary condition favouring relatives could be attached without prejudice to the trust's charitable status. For example, O'Connor MR in *Re Lavelle*[25] upheld a bequest to a college which was subject to a condition that the income be used to educate those students who were relatives of the testator.

The advancement of religion

Unusually for a modern western society, in Ireland the national experience of religion and the associated charity law cases were, for many years, almost exclusively concerned with issues relating to the Roman Catholic Church which enjoyed singular constitutional recognition.[26] By specifying certain religions and not others, the Constitution intended and achieved preferential discrimination in favour of

---

21 [1980] IR 102.
22 *Attorney-General v Lord Lonsdale* (1827) 1 Sim 105.
23 (1861) 13 ICLR 48.
24 [1952] Ch 163.
25 [1941] 1 IR 194.
26 Bunreacht na hÉireann, Article 44. 2: 'The State recognises the special position of the Holy Catholic Apostolic and Roman Church as the guardian of the Faith professed by the great majority of the citizens.' Deleted by the Fifth Amendment of the Constitution Act 1972.

those mentioned. Not until the turn of the century did adjustment creep in:[27] as Barrington J said in *Campaign to Separate Church and State*,[28] 'the recognition of the "special position" of the Roman Catholic Church was merely a recognition of a fact and implied no privileged position in law'; a similar view was later expressed by Geoghegan J in *Ó Beoláin v Fahy*.[29] This bias towards Catholicism in particular was reinforced by one that favoured religion in general: the public benefit test has never had any application to trusts for the advancement of religion; religious bodies and gifts to them have been, and continue to be, assumed to benefit the public and thus automatically entitled to charitable status,[30] a presumption that for many years has been given statutory recognition.[31]

The traditional definition of 'religion' has dominated case law in Ireland: a religion would be denied judicial recognition as such unless its adherents at least professed a belief in a 'supreme being'; elements of faith and worship were also required. The continued leaning towards a theistic rather than a secular State can be seen in the enduring constitutional and statutory ban on blasphemy,[32] itself at variance with ECHR principles of equality. However, it has never been sufficient in charity law that a body adheres to religious purposes; it must also actively promote or advance the spiritual teachings or doctrines of that religion, which has generated a wide range of gifts, including for the celebration of masses, to religious orders, for the benefit of churches and their fixtures, for the upkeep of graves, for the support of clergy and gifts for missionary purposes; many of such gifts have been denied charitable status in England and Wales. In *O'Hanlon v Logue*,[33] for example, Palles CB established that a gift for the saying of masses, whether in public or private, satisfied the public benefit test and could be charitable in Ireland even if not in the neighbouring jurisdiction. Gavan Duffy J in *Maguire v Attorney General*[34] set the law in Ireland on a different course from that taken in England and Wales in respect of closed and contemplative religious orders when he commented that:

> it is a shock to one's sense of propriety and a grave discredit to the law that there should, in this Catholic country, be any doubt about the validity of a trust to expend money in founding a convent for the perpetual adoration of the Blessed Sacrament.

27 Author acknowledges advice of Gerard Whyte on this matter (note to author, 22 July 2015).
28 [1998] 3 IR 321 at p. 355.
29 [2001] 2 IR 279 at p. 356.
30 See: *Powerscourt v Powerscourt* 1 Moll 616; *Arnott v Arnott* [1906] [1911] 1 IR 289; and *Rickerby v Nicholson* [1912] 1 IR 343.
31 See, the Charities Act 1961, s.45(1) and now, albeit qualified, the Charities Act 2009, s.3(4).
32 See, Article 40.6.1 of Bunreacht na hÉireann and the Defamation Act 2009.
33 [1906] IR 247. In *Gilmour v Coats* [1949] AC 426, the House of Lords took the opposite view.
34 [1943] IR 238. See, also, *Re Howley* [1940] IR 109, where Gavan Duffy J stated:

> The assumption that the Irish public finds no edification in cloistered lives, devoted purely to spiritual ends, postulates a close assimilation of the Irish outlook to the English, not obviously warranted by the traditions and mores of the Irish people.

Dixon J in *Bank of Ireland Co. Ltd v Attorney General*[35] held that a gift to the convent of a closed order of nuns for building repair work was charitable. Again, unlike in England and Wales, gifts for the upkeep of graves have always been assured of charitable status.[36] Gifts for the support of clergy have usually been upheld as charitable. Moreover, religious organisations which send their members overseas to spread their religious beliefs, on an overtly discriminatory basis, have never had any difficulty in acquiring charitable status: gifts to 'the Christian Brethren'[37], to 'foreign missions'[38], to enable Church of Ireland missionaries to convert Roman Catholic Irishmen[39] and to 'Presbyterian missions and orphans'[40] have all been upheld as charitable.

Finally, as regards discriminatory testamentary dispositions, Parachin[41] has pointed out that the courts in Ireland followed the precedents established in English courts. For example, in *Duggan v Kelly*,[42] a condition against marrying a Papist was upheld, and so, in *Re McKenna*,[43] was a condition against marrying a Roman Catholic, while in *Re Knox*[44] the court upheld a condition restricting marriage to a Protestant wife with Protestant parents. Only when the right to make such a conditional testamentary disposition was trumped by a greater duty, such as the educational obligation of parents under Article 42 of the Constitution, did the courts rule discriminatory dispositions invalid.[45]

Beneficial to the community, not falling under any of the preceding heads

As in the neighbouring jurisdiction, gifts and organisations etc seeking charitable status under this head attract the most rigorous application of the public benefit test.[46] Its contents, which have similarly grown in profusion and complexity, have been found to consist mainly of charities for illness and disability,

---

35 [1957] IR 257.
36 *Re Rigley's Trusts* (1866) 36 LJ Ch 147; *Toole v Hamilton* [1901] 1 IR 383; and *Re McIntyre* (1930) 64 ILTR 179.
37 *Re Browne* [1898] 1 IR 423.
38 *Dunne v Duignan* [1908] 1 IR 228.
39 *Attorney-General v Becher* [1910] 2 IR 251.
40 *Jackson v Attorney General* [1917] 1 IR 332.
41 See, Parachin, A., 'The Definition of Charity and Public Law Equality Norms' Paper Presented at Conference Private and Public Law – Intersections in Law and Method, the T C Beirne Law School at the University of Queensland, Brisbane, July 2011.
42 (1847) 10 Ir Eq R 295.
43 [1947] IR 277.
44 (1889) 23 LR Ir 542 (Ch).
45 *Burke v Burke* [1951] IR 216 and *Re Blake, deceased* [1955] IR 89.
46 See, comments of Babington LJ in *Trustees of the Londonderry Presbyterian Church House v Commissioners of Inland Revenue* [1946] NI 178, 196; Lord Simonds in *Williams v IRC* [1947] AC 447 and *IRC v Baddeley* [1955] AC 572, 615 and of Lord Somervell in *IRC v Baddeley* [1955] AC 572, 592 (although note the quite different conclusion reached by Lord Reid in *Baddeley* at pp. 612–613).

welfare services, the advancement of knowledge, public utility and for sport and recreation.[47]

In this jurisdiction, as in England and Wales, gifts expressed to be for the purpose of promoting peace were regarded as political in nature and thus not charitable. Though this was not the approach adopted by Farwell J in *Re Harwood*[48] who found that gifts which the testatrix had left to 'the Peace Society of Belfast' and to the 'Dublin Peace Society' (neither of which were in existence at the time of hearing) were charitable. Again, in both jurisdictions the promotion of sport and recreation were not per se charitable activities, and the same approach was taken in both towards animal charities, though with more judicial latitude being given to the subjective intent of the Irish donor.[49]

The discriminatory targeting of specific groups, exclusively and without any need for their members to be poor, is particularly evident in gifts for 'elderly or infirm' nurses;[50] the donor's dwelling house to the Young Men's Christian Association in Cork for use as a rest and holiday home for Protestant men;[51] 'to Presbyterian missions and orphans';[52] to a community of nuns for the purpose of maintaining a 'home of rescue for prostitutes';[53] and in a home for 'Old Presbyterian Persons'.[54] The latter ruling was duly reinforced by Keane J in *Re Worth Library*[55] when he found the public benefit test to be satisfied and the trust to be charitable under this *Pemsel* head because the library itself 'in its beautiful setting would have provided a haven of quiet intellectual relaxation for the beneficiaries'. The necessary 'benefit' quotient was supplied by the intrinsic quality of the library environment, even though the 'public' quotient was restricted by the terms of the trust to the physician, surgeon and chaplain. This approach was markedly different to the more rigorously objective stance adopted by the English judiciary.

Public benefit: civil society, charity and the State

By the end of the 20th century, Ireland's fairly unique position among developed western nations of rapid socio-economic growth had collapsed: the 'Celtic Tiger' boom of 1997–2005 had given way to an equally dramatic 'bust' which left the nation bankrupt and facing an uncertain financial future. The resulting

---

47 See, Ruddle, H. and O'Connor, J., *Reaching Out: Charitable Giving and Volunteering in the Republic of Ireland*, Policy Research Centre, Dublin, 1993.
48 [1936] Ch 285.
49 *Swifte v Attorney General* [1912] 1 IR 133.
50 *Re McCarthy's Will Trusts* [1958] IR 311.
51 *In re Mcnamara; Coe v Beale* [1943] IR.
52 *Jackson v A-G* [1917] 1 IR 332.
53 *Mahony v Duggan* (1883) 11 LR Ir 260.
54 *Re Dunlop* [1984] NI 408. See, also, Dawson, 'Old Presbyterian Persons' – A Sufficient Section of the Public? [1987] Conv. 114.
55 [1994] 1LRM 161, at p. 193.

fiscal stringency, coupled with high levels of emigration and unfavourable demographic trends, triggered a review of how government proposed to manage its public benefit service provision. This hinged to some extent on charities and other entities in the nonprofit sector developing a capacity to shoulder the burden for public benefit provision that government was seeking to shed.

Partnership

In Ireland, the government has since 1987 cultivated a model of social partnership with certain groups designated as 'pillars' of contemporary Irish society (employers, the trades unions and the farming organisations). The nonprofit sector was seen as the fourth pillar in this partnership arrangement with government.[56] This 'four pillars' approach to public policy planning demonstrated government commitment to sharing responsibility and accountability for the management of national socio-economic matters. Although it never developed a UK level of institutional infrastructure, the social partnership model has served a similar strategic function as a means for consolidating civil society. It prepared the ground in much the same way to facilitate a new sharing of public benefit provision between government and the nonprofit sector following the financial crash of 2008 and subsequent prolonged economic crisis. One aspect of that partnership has been an increased devolving of responsibility for public benefit provision from government to charity, usually by way of service contracts mostly in health and social services, education and social housing.

Charity law reform and human rights: towards alignment

Until October 2014, charity law in Ireland had remained more facilitative than regulatory and was dependent upon an outdated statutory framework closely modelled on the provisions of the English Charities Act 1960.

The charity law reform process

In partnership with the nonprofit sector,[57] the government formally launched the charity review process in 2002, declaring that 'a comprehensive reform of the law relating to charities will be enacted to ensure accountability and to protect against abuse of charitable status and fraud'.[58] It included a consultation

---

56 See, the national agreement *Towards 2016: The Ten-Year Framework Social Partnership Agreement 2006–2015* and *Towards 2016: Review and Transitional Agreement 2008–2009*, Government Publications, Stationery Office, Molesworth St., Dublin, 2006 and 2008.

57 See Ministry for Social, Community and Family Affairs, *Supporting Voluntary Activity: A White Paper on a Framework for Supporting Voluntary Activity and for Developing the Relationship between the State and the Community and Voluntary Sector*, Department of Social Welfare, Stationery Office, Dublin, 2000.

58 See, the 'Agreed Programme for Government' (2002) and 'Establishing a Modern Statutory Framework for Charities' (2003).

process and the issue of two Bills,[59] and concluded in February 2009 with the 2009 Act being signed into law,[60] although its implementation was delayed until October 2014.

The process

As the reform process continued, its prospective outcomes shrank. Some important matters, expected to be among the new legislative provisions but were not, included new legal structures for charities; the role and responsibilities of trustees; advocacy rights of charities; and the promotion of human rights as a charitable purpose. An incidental but significant outcome of this process, however, would seem to have been a further consolidation of the relationship between government and the sector within the social partnership model.

Jurisdiction-specific outcomes

The Charities Act 2009 provided for certain regulatory changes but, despite the very considerable cultural changes experienced over recent decades – particularly as regards the traditional congruity between citizenship and Catholicism – there was nothing in the 2009 Act to reflect the religious pluralism characteristic of Irish society in the early years of the 21st century.

- INCREASED REGULATORY MEASURES

The long-standing deficiencies of this regulatory regime – the absence of both a mandatory register of charities and a lead regulatory body with charity specific supervisory duties – ended with the introduction of the Charities Regulatory Authority (CRA)[61] in October 2014. This body, replacing the Commissioners of Charitable Donations and Bequests for Ireland which had existed since 1845, is now responsible for establishing and managing the mandatory Register of Charities pursuant to s.39 of that Act and for supervising and supporting those registered.

- RECASTING PUBLIC BENEFIT

Under s.3 of the 2009 Act, '(2) a purpose shall not be a charitable purpose unless it is of public benefit', but under s.3, '(4) It shall be presumed, unless the contrary is proved, that a gift for the advancement of religion is of public benefit.' The latter discriminates in favour of religion as the only exception to the test and changes the law to the limited extent that it substitutes a rebuttable presumption for the previous prescriptive approach. In total, this revised test removes the previous presumption of public benefit under the first two *Pemsel* heads and requires

---

59 The Irish Charities General Scheme of Bill 2006 and Irish Charities Bill 2007.
60 The 2009 Act was signed into law by President Mary McAleese on 28 February 2009.
61 An tÚdarás Rialála Carthanas.

all gifts made in respect of the new charitable purposes to prove compliance. As no specific reference is made to the judicially established characteristics of the test (subjective interpretation and generous interpretation of what constitutes 'public' and 'benefit') it must be assumed that these jurisdictionally distinctive features are retained.

- POLITICAL PURPOSES

The reform process left untouched the established prohibition on a charity having a primary political purpose.[62] Under s.2(b) of the 2009 Act, only organisations that advocate in favour of a political cause, directly related to the advancement of their charitable purpose will be able to register as charities. This leaves the law in as an unsatisfactory state after as before the 2009 Act: an organisation intending to campaign for a change in the law, as its sole or main objective, will still have to forego charitable status.

- *PEMSEL* PLUS CHARITABLE PURPOSES

The 2009 Act defines a purpose as charitable if it is of public benefit and if its aim is the prevention or relief of poverty or economic hardship, the advancement of education, the advancement of religion, or any other purpose that is of benefit to the community. In addition to enlarging the first head to allow for the prevention as well as the relief of poverty, s.(3)(1)(d) restates the fourth head but adds, under s.3(11), that this is to include 12 specific new charitable purposes.

For present purposes, the most distinctive aspects of the *Pemsel* plus list embodied in the Charities Act 2009 are an absence of any reference to human rights or of equality and diversity, and the inclusion of the advancement of conflict resolution or reconciliation as supplemented by the promotion of religious or racial harmony and harmonious community relations.

- STATUTORY ENCODING OF KEY COMMON LAW CONCEPTS

Finally, and of even greater significance, is the fact that all charitable purposes are now statutorily encoded, thereby making them amenable to government amendment as and when deemed expedient.

Charity law and human rights purposes

There are no charities registered with the purpose of promoting human rights, as this is not a statutorily recognised charitable purpose: no mention is made

---

62 See, *Re Ni Brudair*, Unreported, High Court, Gannon J, 5 February 1979 and *Colgan v Independent Radio and Television Commission* [2000] 2 IR 490, HC. Also, see *Gurhy v Goff* [1980] ILRM 103 (SC).

in the 2009 Act of human rights nor of equality and diversity. However, it must be acknowledged that the inclusion of 'the promotion of religious or racial harmony and harmonious community relations' does give explicit statutory recognition to an area of pressing human rights concern in contemporary Irish society.

Charity law and human rights: a modern framework for continuing dissonance

Charity in Ireland is now governed by a modern legislative framework and a new charity specific lead regulatory body. Charity law is required to be administered in compliance with the provisions of the European Convention on Human Rights Act 2003,[63] while the latter in turn is subject to the provisions of the Constitution, particularly the personal rights provisions enumerated under Article 40.3.

Constitution, public policy and human rights

Article 29.4.6 of the Constitution makes express provision for European Union law to prevail over Irish domestic law, where the two are in conflict, but only to the extent that such EU law is 'necessitated' by Ireland's membership. Moreover, Articles 40–44 of the Constitution specifically provide protection for fundamental rights. Article 40.1. declares that:

> All citizens shall, as human persons, be held equal before the law. This shall not be held to mean that the State shall not in its enactments have due regard to differences of capacity, physical and moral, and of social function.

Public policy, charity law, overseas aid and anti-terrorism

The 2009 Act, s.2(1), denies charitable status to bodies that are (i) unlawful, (ii) contrary to public morality, or (iii) contrary to public policy.

There is a dearth of charity law cases illustrating Irish public policy. However, it could be argued that traditionally (and presently, if to a lesser degree) government has demonstrated such a strong preference for supporting Catholicism and its associated values and charitable emanations that this has amounted to an implicit public policy. The consequences can be seen in the long absence of government initiatives in respect of matters that would challenge the authority of the Catholic Church, specifically as regards access to contraception and abortion.

---

63 European Convention on Human Rights Act 2003 (Commencement) Order, 2003 (SI No. 483/2003).

• OVERSEAS AID

Irish Aid is the government agency responsible for delivering on the programme outlined in 'One World One Future: Ireland's Policy for International Development'.[64] The agency's website explains that its focus is on 'reducing hunger and improving resilience; inclusive and sustainable economic growth; better governance, human rights and accountability'. Ireland has a long and well-established reputation for providing overseas aid, traditionally linked with missionary work and the Catholic Church, but now largely channelled mainly through the charities Trocaire and Concern, but also such others as Gorta, Sightsavers, GOAL and Oxfam. In this context, the synergy between charity law and human rights has been reinforced and facilitated by inclusion in the Charities Act 2009, s.3(11), of such charitable purposes as the advancement of community development, including rural or urban regeneration, and the promotion of health, including the prevention or relief of sickness, disease or human suffering.

• ANTI-TERRORISM

In 2004 the UN Security Council's Counter Terrorism Committee formally requested that Ireland review and update its charity law, specifically to regulate more rigorously the flow of charitable funds. Consequently, the 2009 Act, s.2(1), now specifically excludes the following bodies from having charitable status:[65] a body that promotes purposes that are (iv) in support of terrorism or terrorist activities, whether in the State or outside the State, or (v) for the benefit of an organisation, membership of which is unlawful.

The legislative and regulatory framework

The contemporary legislative framework for charity and human rights is of very recent origins: the Charities Act 2009, as operationalised in October 2014, and the Irish Human Rights and Equality Commission Act 2014.

Charity law

Since staged implementation of the 2009 Act commenced in October 2014, the new processes are taking shape under CRA management.

• THE CHARITIES REGULATOR: CHARITIES REGULATORY AUTHORITY (CRA)

An tÚdarás Rialála Carthanas or the Charities Regulation Authority (CRA) was finally established on 16 October 2014 under the terms of the Charities Act 2009.

---

64 See, further, at: https://www.irishaid.ie/what-we-do/.
65 2009 Act, s.2(1).

• ATTORNEY GENERAL

The Charities Act 2009 specifically extinguishes the Attorney General's brief for charities. This rather surprising statutory development is probably unique to Ireland.

Human rights

The Human Rights Act 2003 partially incorporates the European Convention, together with several of its Protocols, into domestic law. Irish courts are consequently instructed, in s.2, that 'in interpreting and applying any statutory provision or rule of law, a court shall, insofar as is possible, subject to the rules of law relating to such interpretation and application, do so in a manner compatible with the State's obligations under the Convention provisions';[66] in s.4, that 'judicial notice' be taken of the Convention provisions and of judgments of the ECtHR or any decision of the Committee of Ministers established under the Statute of the Council of Europe on any question in respect of which it has jurisdiction; and they must also, when interpreting and applying the Convention provisions, take due account of the principles laid down in such judgments or decisions. Under s.5, a court may make a 'declaration of incompatibility' where it finds that legislation or a rule of law is incompatible with the State's obligations under the ECHR, in which case the matter must be referred to parliament.

The primary body of legislative provisions governing matters of equality and diversity is comprised of the Employment Equality Acts 1998–2011 and the Equal Status Acts 2000–2012.

• THE IRISH HUMAN RIGHTS AND EQUALITY COMMISSION (IHREC)

The Equality Authority, established in October 1999, was responsible for regulating equality matters arising under the above Employment Equality and Equal Status legislation. The Human Rights Commission Act 2000 provided for the setting up of the Irish Human Rights and Commission later that year. On 1 November 2014 the agencies merged to become the IHREC, which assumed responsibility for matters arising under both sets of statutes.

• THE WORKPLACE RELATIONS COMMISSION

Established under the Workplace Relations Act 2015, the Commission replaces the Employment Appeals Tribunal and consolidates the functions of many other bodies including the Labour Relations Commission, Rights Commissioner Service, Equality Tribunal and the National Employment Rights Authority.

---

66 See, *Foy v An t-Ard Chlaraitheoir & Others* [2007] IEHC 470, when a declaration of incompatibility was made concerning the lack of legal recognition for transgender people under Irish law.

The UN has repeatedly criticised Ireland's record on human rights and government inaction on several fronts, including the rights of disabled people and victims of symphysiotomy, the treatment of survivors of the Magdalene laundries, the absence of safe and lawful abortion, the rights of transgender people and the recognition of Travellers as an ethnic group.

In July 2014, following its fourth 'universal periodic review' of Ireland's compliance with the ICCPR, the report of the UN's Human Rights Committee called for two referendums to be held: on abortion and on the place of women in society. It reported that both the new abortion legislation and the Constitution must be revised to ensure women who are pregnant as a result of rape, incest or who have a diagnosis of fatal foetal anomaly have access to abortion if they so choose, and called for access to abortion where a woman's health is at risk. It reiterated its 'previous concern regarding the highly restrictive circumstances under which women can lawfully have an abortion owing to article 40.3.3 of the Constitution and its strict interpretation by the State party'.

The committee also considered Article 41.2 which declares that 'by her life within the home a woman gives to the State a support without which the common good cannot be achieved' and guarantees to protect mothers from having to work outside the home 'to the neglect of her duties within the home'. It recommended that 'the State party should take concrete steps . . . to facilitate the amendment of Article 41.2 of the Constitution to render it gender neutral and further encourage greater participation of women in both public and private sectors'.

The committee raised concerns about domestic and sexual violence against women, the institutional abuse of women and children and called for corporal punishment to be banned 'in all settings'. It referred to 'the lack of prompt, independent, thorough and effective investigations into all allegations of abuse, mistreatment or neglect of women and children in the Magdalene Laundries, children's institutions, and mother-and-baby homes'.

In relation to Travellers, the committee called upon the State to 'take concrete steps to recognise' their ethnicity and address their housing needs. Concerns were also raised about such other matters as accommodating asylum seekers,[67] the lack of non-denominational schools, the lack of appropriate assistance to victims of human trafficking and prison conditions.

The contemporary charity law/human rights interface: a compliance audit

The following largely relies on benchmarks initially laid down in the UDHR, and subsequently enlarged in the ECHR, to identify and weigh charity law/human rights interface issues.

---

67 Doras Luimni, a national charity established in 2000 to assist migrant integration into Irish society, has suffered repeated cuts to its government funding. By 2015, the paid employment of its CEO had been reduced to one day per week.

Access to justice, legal process and principles

Article 10 of the Declaration (ECHR, Article 6), as incorporated into the European Convention of Human Rights Act 2003, provides for this composite right.

Access to justice

There have been cases in which Irish court processes were found by the ECtHR to be non–Convention compliant and, although not directly related to charity,[68] some decisions concerning undue delay have implications for the future conduct of all judicial and administrative processes.

Undue delay, inadequate redress for victims and insufficient accountability of perpetrators have also been conspicuous features of official enquiries into systemic child abuse by religious organisations. In this jurisdiction, where Catholicism had such a pervasive influence, religion and charitable status provided a double indemnity for Catholic clergy, obscuring the extent and duration of child abuse, allowing perpetrators and institutions to delay if not avoid culpability, and obstructing access to justice for victims.[69]

Due process

Arguably, the five-year suspension of the 2009 Act – thereby delaying the introduction of a mandatory registration process and the regulatory supervision of the CRA – infringed the requirements of Article 10 of the UDHR. This point is brought home by the fact that it was only in the immediate aftermath of the public scandal affecting the Central Remedial Clinic[70] – the nation's largest and most prestigious charity – that provisions were activated to establish the CRA and accompanying regulatory processes.

Proportionality

When, as for example in *Temple Street v D. & Anor*,[71] a blood transfusion urgently required by a three-month-old baby was refused by his Jehovah's Witness parents on grounds of their religious belief, the court then had little difficulty in finding the parental veto disproportionate.

---

68 See, *McFarlane v Ireland* (App No 31333/06) Grand Chamber Judgment, 10 September 2010 (delay of over ten years) and *C v Ireland* (1 March 2012) (App No 24643/08) Committee Judgment, 1 March 2012 (delay of over 11 years). Also, see, *In re Haughey* [1971] IR 217.
69 See, for example, the Department of Justice and Equality, 'Report of the Irish Commission Inquiry into Child Abuse' (The 'Murphy Report'), May 2009.
70 This concerned the use of public donations to top up the salaries of executives and strongly resembles the entitlement culture among some British charity executives that triggered a similar media outcry. See, further, at: http://www.breakingnews.ie/ireland/central-remedial-clinic-ceo-quits-after-wage-top-ups-scandal-616613.html.
71 [2011] IEHC 1.

Respect for 'private life'

Article 12 of the UDHR (ECHR, Article 8) places an obligation on the court to ensure that the rights of an individual are properly secured and protected against infringements by other individuals;[72] it is at variance with the concept of 'family' as defined in the Constitution. Articles 41 and 42 of the latter strongly imply that 'family' refers to a marital family unit: Article 41.1.1 'recognises the Family as the natural primary and fundamental unit group of Society, and as a moral institution possessing inalienable and imprescriptible rights, antecedent and superior to all positive law', and guarantees its protection by the State; Article 41.3 avows that 'the State pledges itself to guard with special care the institution of marriage, on which the Family is founded, and to protect it against attack'. The inescapable corollary is that non-marital families, one-parent families and other families such as those where the parents are of the same gender are all relatively disadvantaged in the eyes of the Constitution, contrary to Convention expectations.

The fact that in Ireland the non-marital family has always attracted less protection in law than the family based on marriage[73] has implications for many charities working with those in non-traditional relationships. For Transgender Equality Network Ireland (TENI), for example, a charity committed to supporting transgendered and transsexual people in Ireland, the case of *Foy v An t-Ard Chlaraitheoir & Others*[74] was of great significance. In what was then the nation's first declaration of incompatibility between domestic legislative provisions and human rights requirements, McKechnie J ruled that Irish law was deficient and in breach of such rights, as it failed to provide legal recognition for transgender people. He commented that:

> Everyone as a member of society has the right to human dignity, and with individual personalities, has the right to develop his being as he sees fit; subject only to the most minimal of State interference being essential for the convergence of the common good. Together with human freedom, a person, subject to the acquired rights of others, should be free to shape his personality in the way best suited to his person and to his life.

Following the judgment, the Irish Human Rights Commission (IHRC) made a submission to the government on the need to protect the rights of transgender people and urged it to undertake appropriate law reform.

---

72 See *Airey v Ireland* (1979) Series A No 32, 2 EHRR 305.
73 See, for example, *The State (Nicolaou) v An Bord Uchtála* [1966] IR 567. Walsh J for the Supreme Court then stated that, 'the family referred to in [Art.41 was] the family which is founded on the institution of marriage'. See, also, *G v An Bord Uchtála* [1980] IR 32; and *WO'R v EH (Guardianship)* [1996] 2 IR 248.
74 [2007] IEHC 470.

Freedom of religion and belief

Article 18 of the UDHR (ECHR, Article 9), in conjunction with Article 18 of the ICCPR, guarantees this freedom. It is also provided for by Article 44.2.1° of the Constitution under which a citizen's freedom of religious conscience, practice and worship is assured, 'subject to public order and morality'.

Church and State

While the Constitution declares that the State may not 'endow' any religion (Article 44.2.2°), nor discriminate on religious grounds (Article 44.2.3°), it also asserts the Christian values of the State – derived specifically from Catholic teachings – in the Preamble and elsewhere in various Articles.[75] This legacy of an earlier era, when Ireland had the highest rate of church attendance in Europe, continues to pervade much of the law and institutions of the State. Indeed, this is apparent from remarks made relatively recently by the then head of the Irish government:[76]

> There are those who would argue that religious belief should be confined to the private domain, as a matter of purely personal choice and practice . . . That is not my position, nor that of my Government. Neither is it one of privileging religion and religious organisations . . . The State must acknowledge and recognise the spiritual dimension of its citizens. It must see as legitimate . . . the importance of their religious faith for so many of our citizens.

Concern has been expressed regarding the authenticity of a State commitment to secularity by a former President who refers to 'the dubious relationship between the State and the Catholic Church, the constitutional prohibition on divorce, the ban on the use of contraception, the criminalisation of homosexuality'[77] and is evident also in the lack of information and advice to women about abortion, and in an enduring culture that permits inequality of rights and status for women in the workplace and in the family.

As Whyte has pointed out,[78] the constitutional constraints in Article 4 – prohibiting State endowment of religion and State discrimination on grounds of religious profession, belief or status – have been considered in a series of cases. The earlier cases were concerned with religious practices[79] and decisions of

75 In *Norris v Attorney General* [1984] IR 36.
76 See, address by Taoiseach Berti Ahern (04.02.008) at: http://www.taoiseach.gov.ie/eng/index.asp?locID=582&docID=3747.
77 See, Robinson, M., *Everybody Matters: A Memoir*, Hodder and Stoughton, 2012.
78 See, Whyte, G., 'Religion and education – The Irish constitution' Paper Presented at the TCD/IHRC Conference on Religion and Education: A Human Rights Perspective, Dublin, 27 November 2010.
79 *Quinn's Supermarket Ltd v Attorney General* [1972] IR 1.

ecclesiastical authorities,[80] but, more recently, they have embraced the promotion of social conditions which are conducive to, though not strictly necessary for, the fostering of religious beliefs.[81] The record also provides evidence of judicial diligence in policing the Church/State interface and ensuring that the former is free of interference from the latter.[82]

Definition of 'religion': theism

Article 44.1 of the Constitution declares that:

> The State acknowledges that the homage of public worship is due to Almighty God. It shall hold His Name in reverence, and shall respect and honour religion.

In charity law, in keeping with the Constitution, religion will not gain recognition as such unless its adherents at least profess belief in a 'supreme being'. The view that a legal definition of religion could be satisfied by a system of belief not involving faith in a god has been consistently rejected, and the legislators have clearly chosen not to avail of the opportunity to break with tradition by extending recognition to either non-theistic faiths or philosophical beliefs in the 2009 Act.[83] However, while Irish statutory law retains the traditional requirement of a belief in god, the case law explicitly extends the constitutional guarantee of freedom of religion beyond monotheistic Christian religions.[84]

Definition of 'religion': belief system

There is no specific provision in the Irish statutory definition of charitable purposes for recognition of philosophical beliefs. Attempts to introduce recognition

80 *McGrath and Ó Ruairc v Trustees of Maynooth College* [1979] ILRM 166.
81 See: *Re Article 26 and the Employment Equality Bill 1996* [1997] 2 IR 321; *Greally v Minister for Education (No 2)* [1999] 1 IR 1, [1999] 2 ILRM 296; and *Campaign to Separate Church and State Ltd v Minister for Education* [1998] 2 ILRM 81.
82 See, for example, *Re Article 26 and the Employment Equality Bill 1996*, op. cit. at p. 359. See, also, *Corway v Independent Newspapers (Ireland) Ltd*, Barrington J when considering the standing of the Muslim, Hindu and Jewish religions under Art. 44 of the Constitution, commented that it:

> is an express recognition of the separate co-existence of the religious denominations, named and unnamed. It does not prefer one to the other and it does not confer any privilege or impose any disability or diminution of status upon any religious denomination, and it does not permit the State to do so.

83 See comments of Minister Curran, Report Stage Debates of the Charities Bill, Vol 192, No 16, 2007, *Seanad Debates* 1059.
84 See, Breen, O., 'Neighbouring Perspectives: Legal and Practical Implications of Charity Regulatory Reform in Ireland and Northern Ireland', *Northern Ireland Legal Quarterly*, Vol 59, No 2, 2008, p. 223, at p. 230.

for humanism as charitable under the advancement of religion heading failed, and instead it is registered under education. After implementation of the 2009 Act, any recognition for a philosophical or other value system, as charitable under any heading other than as a religious purpose, now requires it to first satisfy the public benefit test: an additional and discriminatory burden, in human rights terms, which now differentiates religion from other belief systems.

Equality of religions

Article 14 of the Convention, as supported by Article 9 (the right to freedom of thought, conscience and religion) and by Article 1 of the First Protocol (the right to peaceful enjoyment of property), requires the government and other public bodies to give parity of recognition to Christian and non-Christian religions. This approach finds constitutional support. As Hogan J explained in *Temple Street v D. & Anor*:[85]

> Article 44.2.1 protects not only the traditional and popular religions and religious denominations – such as, for example, Roman Catholicism, the Church of Ireland and the Presbyterian Church – but perhaps just as importantly, it provides a vital safeguard for minority religions and religious denominations whose tenets are regarded by many as unconventional.

However, given the fact that the Constitution leans heavily towards Christianity – particularly Roman Catholicism – there remains some doubt as to the reality of that equality and considerably more regarding parity between those of religious belief and those without.

- SECULARISM

The pervading Christian assumptions and consequent marginalising of secularism was illustrated in the recent query raised by the Advisory Group to the Forum on Patronage and Pluralism[86] questioning Rule 68 of the Rules for National Schools which states that 'a religious ethos should inform and vivify the whole work of the school', with its implied preferencing of Chritianity and discrimination against secularists. It was also apparent in the advice issued by the UN Human Rights Committee in 2014 that Ireland was breaching fundamental human rights of atheists and members of minority faiths – including freedom of conscience, equality before the law and freedom from discrimination – contrary to the International Covenant on Civil and Political Rights. The United Nations Committee on Economic, Social and Cultural Rights has similarly expressed concerns

---

85 [2011] IEHC 1, per Hogan J at para 27.
86 See, Report of the Advisory Group to the Forum on Patronage and Pluralism in the Primary Sector, April 2012, further, at: http://www.education.ie/.

regarding the failure of the Irish State to protect the human rights of atheists and secularists in the Irish Education system, discrimination against women under the right to health, and with regard to the blasphemy laws.

The right to manifest religion or belief

Article 44 of the Constitution declares 'the free practice and profession of religion . . . subject to public order and morality' to be 'guaranteed to every citizen'. While this 'free practice' clause has been subjected to some examination in the Irish courts,[87] there are no cases directly involving charities, although some decisions do serve to highlight the tension between charity law and human rights. In *Campaign to Separate Church and State v Min. for Education*[88] the court considered the presence of Catholic icons or artwork in classrooms. Barrington J then ruled that a publicly funded school is not obliged 'to change the general atmosphere of its school merely to accommodate a child of a different religious persuasion'. In the long run, however, it may be that the issue of what constitutes 'religion' and thereby entitles an adherent to manifest their beliefs – subject to the rights of others – will become particularly contentious in this jurisdiction.

Parental right regarding religious education of their children

This right, as supported by Article 2 of Protocol 1, is in theory respected in Irish charity law – which presumes that religious bodies are for the public benefit and entitled to charitable status – and in law more generally, but in fact has for many years been an area of contention. In Ireland, State education is faith based: some 98 per cent of primary schools and perhaps 50 per cent of secondary schools are managed by the Catholic Church;[89] the Catholic primary schools are generally owned by diocesan or parish trusts, by trustees on behalf of religious orders or lay trusts set up as limited companies and have charitable status; some 110 secondary schools, representing approximately 58,000 students (or one in six of all second level students) and 4,000 teachers and administrative staff, are members of the charity CEIST which is committed to embedding Catholic values in education. The assertion of Barrington J, in *Campaign to Separate Church and State v Min for Education*,[90] that 'the Constitution contemplated that if a school was in receipt of public funds any child, no matter what his religion, would be entitled to attend it'[91] has not always reflected reality. Indeed, exemption is expressly permitted by s.7(3)(c) of the Equal Status Acts 2000–2008 which enables schools

---

87 See, for example, *Quinn's Supermarket v Attorney General* [1972] IR 1 and *Campaign to Separate Church and State v Min. for Education* [1998] 3 IR 321.
88 [1998] 3 IR 321.
89 See, *Crowley v Ireland* [1980] IR 102, which clearly established that the State could support denominationally controlled education in discharging its obligation to provide for free primary education.
90 [1998] 3 IR 321.
91 Ibid., at p. 356.

to offer preferential treatment in admittance of pupils of certain religious backgrounds where 'the objective of the school is to provide education in an environment which promotes certain religious values', and by s.7(2) which enables a school to refuse admittance to a pupil who is not of its denomination where it can prove that 'the refusal is essential to maintain the ethos of the school'. This resulted, in early 2007, in a number of children of Nigerian origin failing to access any local schools in an area of north Co Dublin because they did not hold Catholic baptismal certificates.[92]

In the context of a national educational system of some 3,200 primary schools where only 2 per cent are multidenominational, the Educate Together initiative is worthy of note. This charity was founded in 1984 'to develop and support in Ireland the establishment of schools which are multi-denominational (i.e. with equal right of access for the children of Catholic, Protestant and other parents, and with the cultural and social background of each child held in equal respect)' and has grown from 40 schools in 2007 to 74 in 2014. This initiative would seem to be very much in keeping with Article 2 of Protocol 1.

Freedom of expression

This qualified right of freedom of speech is guaranteed by both Article 19 of the UDHR (ECHR, Article 10) and Article 40.6.1° of the Constitution. However, the latter is subject to certain caveats: 'the State shall endeavour to ensure that organs of public opinion' (such as the news media) 'shall not be used to undermine public order or morality or the authority of the State'; and 'the publication or utterance of blasphemous, seditious, or indecent matter' is specifically stated to be a criminal offence.[93]

In *Open Door and Dublin Well Woman v Ireland*, the ECtHR upheld the claim of the joint plaintiff charities that women had the right to receive information relating to birth control,[94] as protected by Article 10. While there are no other known charity law cases that address freedom of expression issues, this may in part be attributable to the prohibition on organisations with political purpose acquiring or retaining charitable status. Arguably, given the expectation that the socially disadvantaged should be able to rely on charities to act as advocates on their behalf, the prohibition constitutes a significant constraint on the exercise of this Convention right and must, for example, impede the capacity of the Irish Traveller Movement (ITMB) charity to campaign for changes in the law and policy relating to the Traveller community.

92 See: 'Is Your Child Catholic Enough to Get a Place at School?', *The Irish Times*, 1 May 2007; 'New Catholic School Policy could Produce Unintended "apartheid"', *The Irish Times*, 8 September 2007; 'Faith before Fairness', *The Irish Times*, 8 September 2007; and 'Ireland Forced to Open Immigrant School', *The Guardian*, 25 September 2007.
93 See, the Defamation Act 2009, introduced in response to the finding in *Corway v Independent Newspapers* (Ireland) Ltd [1999] 4 IR 484 that there was no coherent definition of this offence.
94 (1992) 15 EHRR 244.

Freedom of assembly and association

Protected by both Article 20 of the UDHR (ECHR, Article 11) and Article 40.6.1° of the Constitution, this freedom is fundamental to the right of charities to organise and act as such.

While, subject to 'public order and morality', the right of citizens to peaceful assembly 'without arms' and 'to form associations and unions' is guaranteed, the exercise of the latter right may be legally regulated 'in the public interest'.

As in England and Wales, the traditional reliance upon the charitable trust as the legal vehicle for giving effect to charity has been a constraint, as yet not similarly resolved, and considerable uncertainty has accompanied the political negotiations for introducing a European foundation that could offer a common legal structure for all charities and other nonprofit public benefit entities operating throughout Europe.

Equality and non-discrimination

The Workplace Relations Act 2015,[95] the Employment Equality Acts 1998–2011 and the Equal Status Acts 2000–2012 provide the relevant governing legal framework. Their provisions prohibit discrimination in employment, vocational training, advertising, collective agreements, the provision of goods and services, and other opportunities to which the public generally have access on nine distinct grounds: gender; civil status; family status; age; disability; race; sexual orientation; religious belief; and membership of the Traveller community. Other statutes may also be relevant: the Pensions Acts 1990–2008; the Unfair Dismissals Acts 1977–2007; the Social Welfare (Miscellaneous Provisions) Act 2004, which prohibits discrimination in the provision of occupational pensions; and the Prohibition on the Incitement to Hatred Act 1989, which criminalises hate speech.

A wider framework is provided by European Convention, EU Directives,[96] decisions of the ECtHR and of the ECJ as it interprets the Directives and rights under the EU Treaty. The approach now required by the Convention has become a good deal more rigorous since the more laissez-faire approach advocated by Henchy J in *Dillane v Ireland*.[97]

Religious discrimination

The basic principles governing discrimination are laid down in the Constitution, particularly Article 44.2.3, which prohibits the State from imposing any

---

95 Establishing the Workplace Relations Commission (WRC) which amalgamates and replaces the functions of the Equality Tribunal, the National Employment Rights Authority, the Labour Relations Commission, and the first instance functions of the Labour Court and the Employment Appeals Tribunal.

96 See, in particular, the Equal Pay Directive (75/117/EEC), the Equal Treatment Directive (76/207/EEC), and the General Framework Directive (2000/78/EC).

97 [1980] ILRM 167.

disabilities or making any discrimination on the ground of religious profession, belief or status. Any suggestion that the Constitution inferred preferential treatment for Christian religions was refuted by Walsh J in *Quinn's Supermarket v Attorney General*,[98] and subsequently by Barrington J in the Supreme Court case of *Corway v Independent Newspapers (Ireland) Ltd*.[99] However, there can be little doubt that the legislature's historical reluctance to address matters such as abortion, surrogacy, gay marriage and other LGBT issues has been largely due to the political realisation that the unmet needs of minority groups was a price worth paying if it avoided alienating a dominant Catholic electorate.

The religious exemption

There is clearly a tension between the assurance of Article 40.1 that 'all citizens shall, as human persons, be held equal before the law', and the exemption permitted by statutory and Convention provisions from the operation of that law available to those of religious belief.

Article 44.2.1 of the Constitution affords citizens the right to freely express their conscience, as well as the profession and practice of their religion, subject to public order and morality. However, any restriction on this right would have to be proportionate under the Constitution, meaning that the restriction would have to be rational, intrude as little as possible, and be proportionate to the aim that it seeks to achieve.[100] While, in *Quinn's Supermarket Ltd v Attorney General*[101] and in *re Article 26 and the Employment Equality Bill 1996*,[102] the Supreme Court confirmed that a religious action may be exempt from general laws if a failure to provide an exemption would restrict or prevent the free profession and practice of religion, it is clear that not every 'distinction necessary to achieve this overriding objective will be valid'.[103] In the latter case, the Supreme Court ruled that it was constitutionally permissible to discriminate on grounds of religious profession, belief or status if this is necessary to 'give life and reality' to the constitutional guarantee of freedom of religion.[104]

Under s.2 of the 2009 Act, as mentioned above, the definition of 'charitable organisation' grants a particular privilege to religious institutions, as does the exemption from registration, under s.48(6) of the 2009 Act for an 'education body'. In addition, the religious exemption principle underpins s.7(3)(c) of the

---

98 [1972] IR 1.
99 [1999] 4 IR 484, at p. 502.
100 *Heaney v Ireland* [1994] 3 IR 531.
101 [1972] IR 1.
102 [1997] 2 IR 321, at p. 358.
103 See, Casey J., *Constitutional Law in Ireland* (3rd ed.), Dublin, Round Hall Sweet & Maxwell, 2000 at p. 698.
104 The 1996 Bill was declared unconstitutional on other grounds but s.37(1) of the 1998 Act, its replacement, virtually replicates its predecessor. See, also, *Greally v Minister for Education (No 2)* [1999] 1 IR 1, [1999] 2 ILRM 296.

Equal Status Acts 2000–2012 which enables schools to offer preferential treatment in admittance of pupils of certain religious backgrounds where 'the objective of the school is to provide education in an environment which promotes certain religious values', and s.7(2) which enables a school to refuse admittance to a pupil who is not of its denomination where it can prove that 'the refusal is essential to maintain the ethos of the school'. Again, under s.37(1) of the Employment Equality Acts 1998–2012, it permits discrimination in employment for the purposes of maintaining, or the reasonable prevention of any undermining of, the religious ethos of an institution. Exemption is also evident in the freedom that permits many religious bodies to establish member only services: for example, Jah-Jireh homes are established and run wholly and solely to give accommodation and care to those members of the community of Jehovah's Witnesses.

It is clear from the relatively limited jurisprudence on the constitutional guarantee of freedom of religion that in practice the rights of individuals and of organisations will often have to give way to the protection of religious interests: the exemption privileges available to those of religious belief will trump the constitutionally guaranteed rights of others.

Discrimination (and exemptions) on other grounds

While the Constitution sets the overarching parameters for the law relating to discrimination in general, the provisions of the above-mentioned Equality Acts, CEDAW (ratified by Ireland in 1985) and various EU directives have a more direct bearing upon specific aspects of discrimination. The Equality Tribunal provides the primary adjudicative forum for determining allegations of discrimination,[105] though a new adjudicating body has now been established under the Workplace Relations Act 2015.

- GENDER DISCRIMINATION

Article 40.1 of the Constitution allows the State to have 'due regard to the differences of capacity, physical and moral, and of social function' between men and women. This has probably been a contributory factor in maintaining constraints upon women in Irish society that, as Buckley has pointed out, have only relatively recently been gradually eliminated:[106] not until 1973 was the ban on married women working in the civil service lifted; women were not allowed to sit on juries before that date; nor were single mothers entitled to social assistance; contraceptives became available to everyone only in 1984; divorce – limited – arrived in 1986; in 1991, it became illegal for a man to rape his wife; and two years

---

105 See, further, at: http://www.cipd.co.uk/global/europe/ireland/employment-law/recent-cases/equality-tribunal.aspx.
106 See, further, Buckley, S.-A., at: nuigalway.academia.edu/SarahAnneBuckley/.

later homosexuality was de-criminalised.[107] Even now, as illustrated in *Equality Authority v Portmarnock Golf Club*[108] when the court ruled that s.9 of the Equal Status Acts 2000–2012 permitted male-only clubs – as the principal purpose of the Portmarnock Golf Club was to cater only for the needs of men. Any charity established to promote gender equality or to advance the new charitable purpose – the integration of those who are disadvantaged, and the promotion of their full participation – will experience difficulties: the burden of proof on the plaintiff is considerable. However, the recent Gender Recognition Act 2015 provides for legal recognition to the acquired gender of transgender persons. This formal legal recognition is for all purposes, including dealings with the State, public bodies and civil and commercial society. It includes the right to marry or enter a civil partnership in the acquired gender and the right to a new birth certificate.

- RACIAL DISCRIMINATION

The 2012 report of the Equality Tribunal records that of all referrals to it, 'race continued to be the most frequently cited single ground'.[109] It is to be noted that membership of the Traveller community is a prohibited ground of discrimination under the equality code and the legislation provides a definition of 'Traveller community'.[110]

- SEXUAL DISCRIMINATION

Although, as yet, Ireland has made no legislative provision for same-sex marriage,[111] the Children and Family Relationships Bill 2015 has been signed into law, amending (among other acts) the Adoption Act 2010, enabling same-sex couples to jointly adopt children and step-children, which will undoubtedly lead to the same problems for Catholic adoption charities in this as in the neighbouring jurisdiction. The above-mentioned Gender Recognition Bill 2013 should also extend the ambit of legal prohibition from discrimination on sexual grounds. The Prohibition of Incitement to Hatred Act 1989 outlaws incitement to hatred based on sexual orientation.

---

107 Following *Norris v Ireland* (App No 10581/83) ECtHR 28 October 1988, when the court ruled that the criminalisation of male homosexuality in the Republic violated Article 8 of the Convention.
108 [2005] IEHC 235. Affirmed on appeal to the Supreme Court.
109 See, further, at: http://www.workplacerelations.ie/en/Publications_Forms/Equality_Tribunal_Annual_Report_2012.pdf.
110 Author thanks Gerard Whyte for drawing this to his attention (note to author, 22 July 2015).
111 Though a national referendum on 22 May 2015 cleared the way for such legislation, at present the Civil Partnership Act 2010 provides the only means available for same-sex couples to acquire formal legal recognition of their status.

• EMPLOYMENT DISCRIMINATION

There is no express constitutional protection for persons of no religious faith, as was illustrated in *Mulloy v Minister for Education*[112] which concerned a member of a religious order with charitable status who, on his return from a teaching service in Africa, failed to gain increments for his service in Africa on a par with similarly placed lay teachers. He succeeded in his claim that he was discriminated against on the grounds of his religious status under Article 44.2.3. The Supreme Court held that the term 'status' in Article 44.2.3 related to the position or rank of a person in terms of religion in respect to others, either of the same religion, or of another religion or of no religion. The decision shows that there is implied constitutional protection for persons of no religious faith in Article 44.2.3.

There are also LGBT-related discriminatory pension issues. The Pensions Act 1990, s.81E(5) as amended, prevents pensioners, who retired more than one year before the Civil Partnership Act 2010, from challenging the refusal of a survivor's pension in respect of their civil partner, whereas a corresponding claim in respect of a deceased spouse would not present such a problem.

• SERVICE PROVISION DISCRIMINATION

In recent years, religiously discriminatory practices in relation to the availability of abortion – which has long been prohibited by both the Offences Against the Person Act 1861, sections 58 and 59 and Article 40.3.3° of the Constitution – have been the subject of considerable national[113] and international controversy. In *A, B and C v Ireland*[114] the ECtHR held that the Article 8 rights of a Lithuanian national resident in Ireland, suffering from a rare form of cancer, had been violated due to her restricted access to abortion. As a direct consequence of this ruling, the government introduced the Protection of Life During Pregnancy Act 2013. This legislation will have implications for religious charities, as it provides for the termination of pregnancy in cases where there is a risk of loss of life from physical illness in an emergency or a risk of suicide. It does not provide directly for the termination of pregnancy as a result of rape or incest and it continues the long-standing discriminatory impact on those Irish women who face the forced change of either travelling abroad for an abortion or giving birth to an unwanted child. Inevitably, occasions will now arise when such charities will be faced with decisions to obey the dictates of either their religion or of human rights.

112 [1975] IR 88.
113 See, *Attorney General v X* [1992] IESC 1; [1992] 1 IR 1, which established the right of Irish women to an abortion if their life was at risk because of pregnancy, including the risk of suicide. The tragic death of Savita Halappanavar at the University Hospital in Galway in 2012 was attributed to a professional decision to deny her an abortion because Ireland was a Catholic country.
114 [2010] ECtHR (GC) (No 25579/05) (16 December 2010).

Surrogacy services are also problematic. There is, as yet, no specific legislation governing surrogacy:[115] while not illegal, surrogacy agreements are unenforceable;[116] consequently, it is estimated that there are now several hundred children living in Ireland born to surrogate mothers whose legal status is uncertain and their human rights seriously compromised,[117] a state of affairs which, the Supreme Court has pointed out, 'makes statutory law reform in this area more than urgent'.[118]

While discriminatory conduct in Ireland most often has an association with religious belief, frequently conflated with issues relating to sex or sexual orientation, the recent case involving the charity Pavee Point Traveller's Centre offers evidence that the jurisdiction also has a continuing problem with discrimination against the Traveller community. This case concluded with the Equality Authority finding that a Traveller family had suffered unlawful direct discrimination when they were refused access to a funeral home to repose the body of their son.[119]

- 'POSITIVE ACTION'

The decision in *Quinn's Supermarket* was unequivocally based upon a perceived need to extend 'positive discrimination' to the interests of a religious minority. Not only was the plaintiff's argument rejected – that special exemption for Jewish kosher butchers from the Sunday trading laws was discriminatory against non-Jewish shop keepers – but the exception was upheld on the basis that it was necessary in order to adequately protect the freedom of religion of the Jewish community. Again, in *Re Article 26 and the Employment Equality Bill 1996*,[120] s.12 of the Bill provided that the prohibition on religious discrimination would not apply to the selection of nurses or primary teachers for employment in any 'religious, educational or medical institution which is under the direction or control of a body established for religious purposes'. Such institutions were permitted to give 'favourable treatment' on grounds of religion to employees, and to prospective employees in terms of recruitment – if necessary 'to uphold the

115 See, further, at: http://www.citizensinformation.ie/en/birth_family_relationships/adoption_and_fostering/surrogacy.html.
116 See, the Report of the Commission on Assisted Human Reproduction, Dublin, 2005 which recommended that a child born through surrogacy should be presumed to be that of the commissioning couple. Also, see, *M.R. & Anor v An tArd Chlaraitheoir* [2013] IEHC 91.
117 See, further, at: http://www.aclsolicitors.ie/news-events/current-news/legal-status-of-surrogacy-in-ireland/.
118 *M.R. and D.R. (suing by their father and next friend O.R.) & ors v An t-Ard-Chláraitheoir & ors* [2014] IESC 60 (7 November 2014), per Hardiman J.
119 See, the Equality Tribunal (20 October 2014) at: http://www.equality.ie/en/IHREC%20welcomes%20decision%20by%20Equality%20Tribunal%20that%20refusal%20to%20allow%20a%20child,%20a%20member%20of%20the%20Traveller%20Community,%20to%20repose%20at%20a%20funeral%20home%20is%20direct%20discrimination.html.
120 [1997] 2 IR 321.

religious ethos of the institution'.[121] This was termed 'positive discrimination' by counsel for the Attorney General.

• CHARITIES AS PUBLIC BODIES

Section 3(1) of the 2003 Act places a statutory duty on 'organs of the State' (usually but not always public bodies) to 'perform its functions in a manner compatible with the State's obligations under the Convention provisions' unless there is a law stating that this is not required. There is thus a presumption that public bodies respect the requirements of the ECHR.

Arguably this gives rise to a significant problem in the field of education. The government retains responsibility for school funding and for curriculum development (excepting religious instruction) and staffing. Despite the views of Barrington J in *Campaign to Separate Church and State Ltd v Minister for Education*,[122] while government funding does not constitute 'endowment', it may suggest a level of involvement that, taken in conjunction with other factors, could indicate a controlling relationship. Given the extent of that control, in a relationship where the ownership of most schools rests with the Catholic Church, as does the management and delivery of educational services, it is at least arguable that the role of the Church in the national education system for children in Ireland can be construed as that of a public body. This is important because if that were the case, then, while functioning as such, that organisation cannot avail of the statutory exemption provided for religious bodies (that also have charitable status), and full Convention compliance would be required.

Conclusion

The preferential bias of the Constitution towards religion – Christianity in general and Catholicism in particular – as traditionally defined, has permeated Irish culture. Although this now seems increasingly like a legacy from a rapidly receding era, it continues to colour the nature and application of much Irish law. This is most evident where religious values conflate with sex and gender issues. For charity law, one consequence has been the recognition extended to a uniquely varied range of gifts, organisations and activities seen as advancing religion, coupled with a pronounced overspill into advancing education, and in the resistance to similarly conferring charitable status on other non-traditional belief systems. Nothing could more clearly highlight the continuing over-shadowing affect of the Constitution than – despite the many scandals noted by the UN relating to child abuse by paedophile priests, the Magdalene laundries, the mother and child homes in Tuam etc – the singling out of religious purposes as the only area of

---

121 Ibid., at p. 351.
122 [1998] 3 IR 321, [1998] 2 ILRM 81.

charity to be privileged, under the 2009 Act, with the legal presumption of being for the public benefit in contemporary Ireland.

The role of the public benefit test is compounded by the singular Irish twist that it is required to be interpreted subjectively, in accordance with the presumed intent of the donor. This characteristic alone would place Irish charity law at variance with the UDHR and ECHR which – in marked contrast to any subjective approach – put in place a platform of unequivocal standards for objectively determining when the conduct of persons, organisations or nations is human rights compliant. Irish charity law has been further distanced from both international instruments by the curious late removal from inclusion in the 2009 Act of a charitable purpose promoting human rights.

All in all, there are good reasons for concern regarding the future relationship between charity law and human rights in this jurisdiction. Perhaps in particular there is the probability that the protection afforded human rights is structurally flawed: the provisions of Article 8 and the Constitution are not in synch. The latter, being inherently discriminatory in its prejudicial treatment of families led by single parents or by same-gender couples relative to marital family units and by implicitly favouring Christianity, with an overlay of Roman Catholicism, is open to challenge on the ground of possibly adversely discriminating against all others including secularists.

6 The United States of America

Introduction

The US has 'the world's most generous tax concessions'[1] for philanthropy, and 'no other nation grants subsidies at such a high level or across so many types of activities'.[2] It also has a claim to be the first modern democracy founded explicitly on an agreed set of human rights – the first ten amendments to the Constitution (the Bill of Rights) came into effect on 15 December 1791, limiting the powers of the executive and protecting the rights of citizens. Nonetheless, its record of achievement in both charity and human rights is currently under attack: critics of its performance in relation to charity point, for example, to the wealth disparity in the population which has both millions living in poverty and contains the world's greatest number of billionaires;[3] critics of human rights point, for instance, to Guantánamo Bay, the use of drones, racial and religious discord and police shootings. This chapter looks to the case law to establish what now constitutes 'charity' and 'human rights' in the US and to examine how and when they intersect.

The federal nature of this jurisdiction is a complicating factor that must be borne in mind. The Tenth Amendment to the US Constitution – by which 'the powers not delegated to the United States by the Constitution, nor prohibited by it to the states, are reserved to the states respectively, or to the people' – creates difficulties in terms of overlapping federal and state powers. While each of the states has a statute governing nonprofit and charitable organisations, the federal government exerts substantial influence through its control of federal income tax and the related exemption for such organisations which, together with certain legislation and judicial decisions of the US Supreme Court, brings a degree of commonality to law and practice across all states.

Beginning with a brief overview of charity law, charitable purposes and the interface with human rights, the chapter then considers the relationship between

---

1 See, Clotfelter, C., 'Tax-Induced Distortions in the Voluntary Sector', *Case Western Law Review*, Vol 39 (1988/1989), pp. 663–694.
2 See, Weisbrod, B., 'The Pitfalls of Profits', *Stanford Social Innovation Review* (Winter 2004), at p. 45.
3 See, Forbes 400, at: http://www.forbes.com/forbes-400/.

government and the nonprofit sector, taking into account the prolonged and indeterminate charity law reform process. It outlines the contemporary legislative and regulatory framework for charity law and human rights together with a description of the remit and effect of related regulatory bodies. It summarises the human rights concerns expressed in recent UN reports. This leads into the main body of the chapter which applies the template to examine and assess the case law that illuminates issues and their jurisdiction specific characteristics along the charity law/human rights interface.

Background: a history inimical to human rights

To qualify as a charity for federal tax purposes, an organisation 'must be organized and operated exclusively for exempt purposes set forth in §501(c)(3), and none of its earnings may inure to any private shareholder or individual'.[4] Proof is required that an entity is established for, and its activities do in fact serve, purposes beneficial to the public interest.[5] A charitable organisation is entitled to receive tax-deductible contributions and is exempted from most forms of federal income tax, though any unrelated business income (UBIT) is taxable. Charitable intent has never been a necessary legal constituent of charitable status in the US; the utility of a gift may compensate for an absence of altruism.[6] The Internal Revenue Service (IRS) interprets 'exclusively' to mean 'primarily' or 'substantially';[7] and charity in the US has accommodated a considerable and distinctive 'private' dimension (the many private foundations being atypical of common law countries) alongside the public benefit benchmark, though the usual common law principles otherwise apply (see, further, Chapter 2).

Charity law and human rights: the early challenges

In this jurisdiction the distinction between public charities and private foundations (see, further, below) is of fundamental importance and one which the IRS has been at pains to police in order to copper-fasten the requirement that the purposes and activities of the former are absolutely committed to public benefit and to focus on possible continuing donor control in the latter.

Legal structures: charitable trusts

If an organisation is to qualify for charitable status under s.501(c)(3) of the Internal Revenue Code, it must be organised as a corporation, trust or unincorporated

---

4 See, IRS 'Exemption Requirements – §501(c)(3) Organizations' at: http://www.irs.gov/Charities-&-Non-Profits/Charitable-Organizations/Exemption-Requirements-Section-501(c)(3)-Organizations.
5 See, IRS document P557.
6 See, e.g., *Fire Insurance Patrol v Boyd*, 120 Pa. 624, 643 (1888).
7 Treas. Reg. ss.1.501(c)(3)–1(c)(1).

association;[8] the most popular is the nonprofit corporation. As has been noted, 'charities are usually created in one of two legal forms, corporations or trusts, with the corporation being the most common form utilized in the United States since the mid-twentieth century'.[9] The private trust or foundation, deeply rooted in the common law, has evolved to become a distinctive phenomenon and a significant feature of the US charity landscape.[10]

Constitution

Introduced in 1791, and then consisting of seven articles, the Constitution has since been subject to 27 amendments, of which the first ten comprise a Bill of Rights that address the balancing of legislative, executive and judicial powers and guarantee the fundamental rights of US citizens. The remaining 17 amendments largely address specific civil rights.

Exempt charities

Many religious congregations and thousands of churches are not required by law to register with the IRS and choose not to do so. Based on a interpretation of freedom of religion in the First Amendment, churches generally are presumed to be charitable and are tax-exempt.[11]

Political purposes

While public charities may engage in limited lobbying activity, private foundations are prohibited from engaging in any.[12] The limitation on lobbying is stated in s.501(c)(3): 'it may not be an action organisation i.e. it may not attempt to influence legislation as a substantial part of its activities and it may not participate in any campaign activity for or against political candidates'.[13] But the approach of US courts to political purpose trusts have been quite different from that adopted in other common law jurisdictions. As judicially noted, s.28 of the *Restatement (Third) of Trusts* comments that 'the mere fact, however, that the purpose of a

---

8 See the Revised Uniform Unincorporated Nonprofit Association Act (2008).
9 See, Fremont-Smith, M.R., *Governing Nonprofit Organisations: Federal and State Law and Regulation*, Harvard University Press, US, 2004, at p. 116.
10 The private foundation, in its present form, was largely defined by the Tax Reform Act 1969.
11 See, IRS Publication 1828, 'Tax Guide for Churches and Religious Organizations', at: http://www.irs.gov/pub/irs-pdf/p1828.pdf.
12 See, IRC Section 4945.
13 See, *Regan v Taxation with Representation of Wash* (1983) 461 US 540. See, further, at: http://www.irs.gov/Charities-&-Non-Profits/Charitable-Organizations/Exemption-Requirements-Section-501(c)(3)-Organizations.

trust is to advocate and bring about a *particular* change of law does not prevent the purpose from being charitable'.[14] As Barber explains:[15]

> The key question is whether a purpose that can *only* be achieved by a change in the law can possibly be 'charitable'. British law has long asserted that it cannot. In the US, such 'political' trusts have been permitted, though not without some controversy and lack of alignment in judicial decisions.

Should an entity intend non-violent conduct but illegal conduct, civil disobedience,[16] or engage in abusive or threatening behaviour, such activities would be incompatible with charitable status.[17]

Charitable purposes: a tangential relationship with human rights

Charity, as a legal concept, has not had quite the same meaning in the US as in other common law jurisdictions.[18] For some time now, the regulator has moved beyond the four heads of charity as established in *Pemsel*. Instead, charitable exempt organisations are of two types: public charities[19] and private foundations,[20] distinguished (loosely) by the 'public support test' that requires organisations to demonstrate a comparatively broad base of support to qualify for the status of 'public charity', both being eligible to receive tax-deductible contributions under federal law.[21]

The IRS explains that under s.501(c)(3) the term 'charitable' is used in its generally accepted legal sense and includes the following purposes.[22]

The relief of the poor, the distressed, or the underprivileged

In giving effect to this charitable purpose, neither the presence of an earned income nor the absence of poverty has proven to be an obstacle to charitable status. As has been noted,[23] 'charging fees would not necessarily remove plaintiff from the

---

14 The American Law Institute, *Restatement of the Law (3rd) of Trusts*, Thomson Reuters, 2010.
15 Note to author (11 July 2015).
16 Revenue Ruling 75–384, 1975–2 CB 204.
17 See, for example, *Bray v Alexandria Women's Health Clinic*, 506 US 263 (1993) and protests outside abortion clinics.
18 *Jackson v Phillips*, 96 Mass. 539, 556 (1867), quoted in Fremont-Smith, op. cit., at p. 119.
19 A public charity is defined in s.170(b)(1)(A)(i)–(vi).
20 See IRC ss.509, 501(c)(3). A private foundation is neither a public charity nor a supporting organisation.
21 See, IRC ss.170(c)(2), 501(c)(3), 2055(a)(2), 2106(a)(2)(A)(ii), 2522(a)(2) (West Supp 2008).
22 See, further, at: http://www.irs.gov/Charities-%26-Non-Profits/Charitable—Purposes.
23 *Methodist Old Peoples Home v Korzen* 233 NE 2d 537 – Ill Supreme Court 1968.

category of a charitable institution'[24] and 'charging fees and dispensing benefits to persons who are not necessarily poverty stricken would not destroy its charitable character'.[25] So, for example, the following were all found to be charitable: a home for aged and disabled men which paid for its running costs by requiring residents to manufacture and sell firewood;[26] a juvenile correction home where employed residents contributed to running costs;[27] a school, open to the public, charging students to cover running costs;[28] profit from sale of convalescent farm produce used to maintain a hospital;[29] and revenue from service users which paid for the upkeep of a school.[30] The fact that a charity discriminates in favour of a specific class or group is acceptable,[31] even although limited to 'worthy, deserving, poor, white, American, Protestant, Democratic widows or orphans residing in the town of Bridgeport'.[32] The idea that such discrimination is within limits was illustrated by *Bob Jones University v United States*[33] (see, further, below).

Where it is apparent that the role of charity is little more than to provide a shelter for tax-avoidance purposes, then charitable status will be denied.[34] For example, in *Selfspot Inc. v The Butler County Family YMCA*,[35] objections to the charity's 'plans to build a new 35,000 square foot, full-service fitness centre . . . which will feature a state-of-the-art health club and will operate as a tax-exempt charity' were upheld. This approach illustrates the bearing of a 'commerciality test' which functions as a cut-off threshold for charity.

The advancement of religion

As the Aspen Institute has noted, 'religiously affiliated colleges and universities, social service agencies, hospitals, and other institutions have been central actors in government-financed human service activities almost from the founding of the republic'.[36] Assumed to be for the public good, religious organisations are

---

24 Citing, *American College of Surgeons v Korzen*, 36 Ill 2d 340, 348; *People v Y.M.C.A.*, 365 Ill 118.

25 Citing, *People v Y.M.C.A.*, 365 Ill 118; *Sisters of Third Order of St. Francis v Board of Review*, 231 Ill 317. Also, see, *Estate of Carolyn E. Gray v Commissioner*, 2 TC 97 (1943).

26 *Patterson Rescue Mission v High*, 64 NJL 116, 118–119, 44 A 974, 975, 1899.

27 *House of Refuge v Smith*, 140 Pa 387, 1891.

28 *Trustees of Academy of Protestant Episcopal Church v Taylor*, 150 Pa 565, 1892.

29 *Contributors to Pennsylvania Hospital v Delaware County*, 169 Pa 305, 1895.

30 *Trustees of Kentucky Female Orphan School v City of Louisville*, 36 SW 921 (Ky Ct of App), 1896.

31 *Young Men's Christian Associations Retirement Fund, Inc. v Commissioner*, 18 BTA 139 (1929); acq. IV-1 CB 160.

32 See, Picarda, H., *The Law and Practice Relating to Charities* (4th ed.), at p. 51 citing *Beardsley v Selectmen of Bridgeport* 53 Conn 489 (1985).

33 461 US 574 (1983).

34 See, *New Dynamics Foundation v United States*, 70 Fed Cl 782 (Fed Cl 2006).

35 818 A 2d 58a7 (Pa Commw 2003).

36 Aspen Institute, *Religious Organizations and Government*, 2001, at p. 5, further, at: http://www.aspeninstitute.org/sites/default/files/content/docs/RELIGION.PDF.

presumed charitable and have been exempt from taxation since 1894.[37] While there is no definitive legal requirement placed upon religious organisations to demonstrate how their activities satisfy the public benefit test, the judiciary and the IRS have long been certain that closed and purely contemplative religious orders are unable to do so.[38]

As in other common law jurisdictions, testamentary dispositions subject to a religious discrimination condition have been found to be valid. In *Shapira v Union National Bank*,[39] for example, a father left his money to Israel, his wife and their three sons. The bequests to his sons were contingent on each son being married to a Jewish girl or marrying a Jewish girl within seven years of his father's demise. The court found that the father's unmistakable testamentary plan was that his possessions be used to encourage the preservation of the Jewish faith and blood and held that it was duty-bound to honour his intentions. Similarly, in *Re the Estate of Max Feinberg*,[40] the Illinois Supreme Court upheld a condition in the will of a deceased Chicago dentist which prohibited marriage outside the Jewish faith, with the effect of disinheriting his four grandchildren. However, where the testamentary disposition was made subject to a restrictive covenant that discriminated on a racial rather than a religious basis, then the courts took a different view (see, further, below).

The advancement of education or science

While the principles for determining charitable status in relation to this purpose are very similar to those applied in England and Wales, the case law reveals a heavy weighting towards tertiary education, often featuring grants to establish university chairs.[41] In this jurisdiction a significant proportion of local community public services (e.g. schools, universities, child care facilities and hospitals) have charitable status. Moreover, as scientific knowledge increases, so too does the scope of charity.[42] Again, poverty is not a determining factor, as 'a trust for educational purposes is charitable although the persons to be educated are not limited to the poor'.[43]

As elsewhere, an educational purpose must not stray into the realm of propaganda, which is what happened in *Slee v Commissioner*[44] when Judge Learned Hand advised that the American Birth Control League was not entitled to charitable status because it disseminated 'propaganda' to legislators and the public

37 Revenue Act 1894, ch 349, ss.27, 28 Stat 556.
38 See, further, at: http://www.irs.gov/pub/irs-tege/rp_1991–20.pdf.
39 39 Ohio Misc 28, 315 NE 2d 825 (1974).
40 (2009) 235 Ill 2d 256.
41 *LB Research and Education Foundation v The UCLA Foundation*, California Court of Appeal, 130 Cal App 4th 171, 29 Cal Rptr 3d 710, Cal App Dist (14 June 2005).
42 *Todd v Citizens Gas Company of Indiana*, 46 F 2d 855, 865 (7th Cir 1931) cert. den. 283 US 852.
43 Revenue Ruling 69–257, 1969–1 CB 151.
44 42 F 2d 184 (2d Cir 1930).

158   *Contemporary law, policy and practice*

when lobbying for the repeal of birth control laws (though Planned Parenthood's more recent acquisition of charitable status may indicate a change in interpretation of 'propaganda'). However, it may stray into the unworldly, as in *Re Kidd's Estate* when an Arizona court upheld as charitable a fund for research into proof that the human soul leaves the body at death.[45]

Erection or maintenance of public buildings, monuments, or works

Utility trumps altruism in this open market economy, as was demonstrated at an early stage in two state level decisions: *Read v Tidewater Coal Exchange, Inc.*,[46] when establishing a trade association to move coal efficiently through tidewater ports was found to be charitable; and *Fire Insurance Patrol v Boyd*,[47] when the fact that the provision of a fire patrol by an insurance company was commercially motivated did not negate its benefit to the public nor its eligibility for charitable status.

This charitable purpose overlaps with others, as the phrase 'erection or maintenance' in practice operates in conjunction with 'lessening of the burdens of government'. So, for example, the IRS has ruled that establishing and maintaining a public park, and the maintenance and improvement of public recreational facilities, lessens the burdens of government.[48]

In *Evans v Abney*[49] the discriminatory condition attached to a testamentary conveyance of land to the city for the creation of a park, restricting its use for the exclusive enjoyment of white people, was found to have nullified the general charitable intent necessary to create a trust. The different judicial approach to that adopted in the above testamentary dispositions subject to a religious condition is in part attributable to the fact that in this context the nature of the gift brings in public law (a park being a public utility) and with it the *locus standi* of the State, which is constitutionally barred under the Fourteenth Amendment from acting in a discriminatory manner.[50]

Lessening the burdens of government

Health and social care services, accessible only on a fee-paying basis, are often granted charitable status on the grounds that they lessen the burdens of government,[51] but this has generated considerable controversy.[52] In practice this

---

45 479 p2d 697 (1971).
46 13 Del Ch 195, 116 A 898 (1922).
47 120 Pa 624, 643 (1888).
48 Revenue Ruling 66–359, 1966–2 CB 218.
49 *Evans v Abney*, 224 Ga 826, 165 SE 2d 160, (1968), aff'd 396 US 435, 90 S Ct 628 (1970). Also, see, *Evans v Newton*, 382 US 296, 302 (1966).
50 See, Power, 'The Racially Discriminatory Charitable Trust: A Suggested Treatment', *St Louis U.L.J.*, Vol 9, 1965, pp. 495–496.
51 *Wexford Medical Group v City of Cadillac* 713 NW 2d 734 [Mich 2006].
52 See, for example, Carreyrou, J. and Martinez, B., 'Nonprofit Hospitals, Once for the Poor, Strike it Rich; With Tax Breaks They Outperform For-Profit Rivals', *Wall St Journal*, 4 April 2008 at A.1.

purpose accommodates many charities formed to promote health[53] and general social welfare. There is a considerable overlap between it and those that follow.

Lessening neighbourhood tensions

There have been many rulings issued by the IRS under a conjunction of this and other headings extending charitable status for activities such as providing assistance to low-income families to obtain improved housing,[54] teaching a specific sport to children[55] and establishing a recycling centre.[56]

Eliminating prejudice and discrimination

Again, rulings issued by the IRS have identified the following as eligible for charitable status: promoting racial integration in neighbourhoods;[57] educating the public on the need for housing available on a non-discriminatory basis;[58] promoting a lessening of racial and religious prejudice in the fields of housing and public accommodation;[59] eliminating the discrimination that restricted employment opportunities for qualified minority workers;[60] educating the public on the merits of racially integrated neighbourhoods;[61] and conducting investigations and research on discrimination against minority groups in housing and public accommodation.[62]

Defending human and civil rights secured by law

This cluster of purposes, particularly the present one, provides evidence of the US giving early recognition to the charitable status of organisations concerned with human rights issues, including advancing equal job opportunities[63] and promoting equal job rights for women.[64] The provision of legal services by a civil rights organisation 'to defend human and civil rights secured by law' is a charitable purpose because it promotes social welfare (the phrase 'secured by law' might be interpreted to mean that advocating for a change in related laws is not 'charitable'[65]). The charitable status conferred upon organisations that

53 Revenue Ruling 69–545, 1969–2 CB 117.
54 Revenue Ruling 67–138, 1967–1 CB 129 (4a).
55 Revenue Ruling 65–2, 1965–1 CB 227 (4b).
56 Revenue Ruling 72–560, 1972–2 CB 248.
57 Revenue Ruling 68–655, 1968–2 CB 213 (1, 2, 4a, 4b).
58 Revenue Ruling 67–250, 1967–2 CB 182 (1, 2, 3, 4a, 4b).
59 Revenue Ruling 68–438, 1968–2 CB 209 (1, 2, 3).
60 Revenue Ruling 68–70, 1968–1 CB 248.
61 Revenue Ruling 68–655, 1968–1 CB 248.
62 Revenue Ruling 68–438, 1968–2 CB 209.
63 Revenue Ruling 68–70, 1968–1 CB 248 (2).
64 Revenue Ruling 72–228, 1972–1 CB 148.
65 Putnam Barber, note to author (11 July 2015).

offer support to immigrants reveals a significant congruity between charity and human rights.[66]

Combating community deterioration and juvenile delinquency

Rulings issued by the IRS under this heading confer charitable status on activities such as investigation and education of the public on social problems,[67] and preventing potential community deterioration.[68] It has ruled that an organisation may qualify for exemption even though the community consists of an area where the median income level and quality of housing are higher than in many other parts of the city.

Native Americans

The history of indigenous people in the US, Canada and Australia is not dissimilar: abuse and containment on reservations;[69] a policy of enforced assimilation[70] involving the use of boarding schools; and the outlawing of their language and culture. Again, in keeping with their counterparts in Australia and Canada, a history of persecution followed by exploitation and then neglect has left Native Americans generally impoverished, with a greatly weakened cultural identity, suffering from widespread unemployment, poor housing conditions and prone to many health problems including a high incidence of alcoholism, heart disease and diabetes. Although many tribes have established successful licensed casinos, their involvement in the gambling industry has been at a price and, in some states, has brought with it the associated problems of addiction and family and community conflict. The Native Americans have for many generations constituted one of the most socially disadvantaged minority groups in the US. The United Nations Human Rights Committee has expressed concern regarding the lack of free prior and informed consent of indigenous people when state decisions are taken in relation to issues such as sacred sites and mineral extraction on their lands.[71]

Public benefit: civil society, charity and the State

The US is distinctive among the jurisdictions currently being considered in that not only is it without any trace of a welfare state tradition, but such are the

---

66 Revenue Ruling 76–205, 1976–1981 CB 154.
67 Revenue Ruling 68–15, 1968–1 CB 244 (1, 2, 4a, 4b).
68 Revenue Ruling 76–147, 1976–1 CB 151 (4a).
69 On 31 January 1876, the US government ordered all Native Americans into reservations.
70 As recently as the 1970s, the Bureau of Indian Affairs was still actively pursuing a policy of 'assimilation', the goal of which was to eliminate the reservations and steer Indians into mainstream US culture.
71 See, further, at: http://www.wired.com/2014/03/united-nations-human-rights-committee-considers-report-united-states/.

constitutional restrictions on State interventionism that it has always approached the business of public benefit provision with considerable caution: where the market or associational activity demonstrated a capacity to address social welfare concerns, then, at federal and state level, government would restrict its role to funding, regulating and calibrating the related tax regime (including applying UBIT) to facilitate provision by charities, other nonprofits and for-profit entities. This has been evident in the IRS policing of the public benefit requirement for charitable tax exemption – the hallmark of any civil society entity.

The Tax Reform Act 1969, for example, required hospitals to meet a 'community benefit' standard[72] which triggered much case law as the IRS sought to enforce the community benefit standard by requiring hospitals to declare the extent to which their services address this objective.[73] Another vehicle for generating civil society activity has been the community foundation. These have long provided a legal structure for charitable activity in this jurisdiction and have functioned as a particularly potent tool, involving cross-sections of society dedicated to undertaking specific local community improvements. The public benefit contribution of that characteristically American charity vehicle, the private foundation, has also done much to galvanise a sense of civic responsibility: the Rockefeller and Carnegie foundations, for example, have contributed greatly to shaping domestic developments in health, science and the arts, while, a century later, the Clinton and Gates foundations have done something similar in generating funds for targeted overseas aid. Then there are the s.501(c)(4) organisations which, though ineligible to receive tax-deductible donations from individuals, operate exclusively for the promotion of 'social welfare', addressing civic matters, with net earnings devoted exclusively to charitable, educational, or recreational purposes.

At bottom, the government approach rests on the premise that the public benefit provision of charities and others sufficiently compensates the State for lost tax revenues and that by reining in its interventionist powers it protects the independence of associational activity. Whether this in fact results in a more cohesive civil society is debatable.

Partnership

The political frame of reference that set the parameters for a relationship between government and charity in other common law countries, orchestrated through a negotiated charity law reform process, is largely absent in the US. The independence of lawful associations, in particular the right to establish and to manage them free from government interference, has been an enduring hallmark of society in this jurisdiction. The framing of the American Constitution and its

---

72 See, further, Lunder, E.K. and Liu, E.C., CRS Report for Congress, '501 (c)(3) Hospitals and the Community Benefit Standard' (November 2009).
73 See, revised Form 990 and the Pension Protection Act 2006.

Bill of Rights sought to ensure, among other things, that federal powers would not interfere with the independence of law-abiding individuals, communities and associational activity. This has not proved conducive to building a government/ charity partnership. Instead of any such structured relationship, a fluctuating web of service delivery contracts links government and nonprofits,[74] while a level of management is imposed through the medium of taxation as administered by the IRS.

Charity law reform and human rights: towards alignment

Law reform had been mooted for many years.[75] Its eventual commencement in the US, undertaken at federal level in the middle of the first decade of this century, was not really a process of charity law reform. It was not particularly concerned with charity law as that regime is understood elsewhere in the common law world: in the US, 'charity' is treated in law and for tax purposes very largely as just another form of nonprofit. Nor was law itself, let alone human rights, the focus of attention; it was rules and regulations, and the roles of the bodies involved in determining tax liability, that preoccupied most of the process. In contrast with other jurisdictions presently being considered, this was not seen as an opportunity for government to also engage in a strategic redistribution of responsibility for public benefit service provision, an ommission due in part to its relatively weaker sense of responsibility for providing, as opposed to regulating, such services.

The charity law reform process

Launched in 2004, with the US Senate Finance Committee hearings on *Charity Oversight and Reform: Keeping Bad Things from Happening to Good Charities*,[76] this process was and continues to be in the main a review of tax administration, and as such is the most comprehensive review of the governance, regulations, and operations of the charitable community undertaken for at least three decades.[77]

The process

At the federal level, the IRS sought reform to increase broad compliance with tax-exemption requirements, with greater transparency, accountability, and better

---

74 See, further, the National Council of Nonprofits at: www.councilofnonprofits.org.
75 See, for example, Fishman, J.J., 'The Development of Nonprofit Corporation Law and an Agenda for Reform', *Emory Law Journal*, Vol 34, 1985.
76 This contained proposals to tighten the definition of public charity, or simply to force all public benefit organisations to abide by the same strict self-dealing rules that currently apply only to private foundations. See further, 108th Cong. (2004), available at http://finance. senate.gov/sitepages/hearing062204.html.
77 See, Barber, P., 'Tending the Commons: Charities Reform in Britain and the United States at the Start of the 21st Century', *Exempt Organization Tax Review*, Vol 55, No 2, 2007.

surveillance of nonprofit funds. At the state level, the authorities were concerned about nonprofit governance, fundraising, and clarification of the responsibilities of the Attorney General. Charities and other nonprofits were focused mostly on the need to reduce reporting requirements, adjust taxes and improve fundraising capacity. Their collective response 'was a critically important consequence of this effort in spite of the fact that it was not a governmental initiative'.[78] Running alongside the latter stages of the tax administration reform process, a study group launched by the American Law Institute (ALI) in 2000 has been taking slow steps – still ongoing in 2015–to formulate and agree a 'Restatement of the Law: Charitable Nonprofit Organisations'. As explained on the ALI website, 'This Restatement clarifies the law governing charities. It addresses legal questions relating to the formation, governance, and termination of charities, as well as the duties of governing boards and individual fiduciaries.'[79]

Jurisdiction-specific outcomes

Throughout 2005 and early 2006, the Senate Finance Committee and Joint Committee on Taxation considered a number of proposals to expand IRS oversight of exempt organisations, particularly charitable organisations. One outcome of this process was the preparation by the National Conference of Commissioners of Uniform State Laws of a Model Protection of Charitable Assets Act, adopted in July 2011; the legislative intent was to strengthen the capacity of the Attorney General to protect the assets of charities.

In contrast to other charity law reform processes, as yet there have been no jurisdiction-specific outcomes at federal level in the US: no recasting of the 'public benefit' principle; no revision of political purposes; no re-interpretation of, or additions to, what may constitute a charitable purpose; and no statutory encoding of key common law concepts. At state level, there has been little more than inconclusive arguments 'about what is, and what shouldn't be, tax exempt, and whether some nonprofits should make payments in lieu of taxes (PILOTs)'.[80]

• INCREASED REGULATORY MEASURES

The Unified Registration Statement (URS) represents an effort to consolidate the information and data requirements of all states that require registration of nonprofit organisations performing charitable solicitations within their jurisdictions. Organised by the National Association of State Charities Officials and the

---

78 Barber, P., note to author (17 July 2015) citing the Panel on the Nonprofit Sector at: www. independentsector.org/panel.
79 See, Brody, E. et al., 'The Charitable Property-Tax Exemption and PILOTs', *Urban Institute*, Washington, DC, August 2012. Also, see, the American Law Institute at: https:// www.ali.org/projects/show/charitable-nonprofit-organizations/.
80 Putnam Barber, advice to author (10 July 2015).

National Association of Attorneys General, it is one part of the Standardized Reporting Project, the aim of which is to standardise, simplify and economise compliance under the states' solicitation laws.

Charity law and human rights purposes

In the US, recognition has long been given to 'defending human and civil rights secured by law' as a charitable purpose.[81]

Charity law and human rights: a contemporary framework for continuing dissonance

A modern domestic legislative framework, dealing specifically with charity and human rights, characteristic of most other jurisdictions currently being considered, is absent in the US.

Constitution, public policy and human rights

In the US, all law – whether statutory, judicial or administrative – occurs within and can be tested against the overarching provisions of the Constitution. Public policy and human rights must be similarly aligned.

   The Constitution, which took effect on 4 March 1789, has been an evolving instrument that in 1791 incorporated a Bill of Rights, a collective reference to the first set of ten amendments. These included such guarantees as the freedoms of religion and speech, a free press and a right of assembly; the right to keep and bear arms; freedom from unreasonable search and seizure and security of personal possessions; and certain justice rights. Together they have formed a legal context for shaping US public policy, a major strand of which has always focused on religious and racist discrimination, gradually expanding to address the range of incidences of inequality now known to law.

   In 1971, in keeping with the ruling in *Brown v Board of Education*[82] and the provisions of the Civil Rights Act 1964, the IRS published Rev. Rul. 71–447, 1971–2 CB 230 declaring its intention to be bound by the principle stated in the Restatement of Trusts (2d) that 'a trust for a purpose the accomplishment of which is contrary to public policy, although not forbidden by law, is invalid'.[83] Thereafter, it has taken the position that private educational institutions which discriminate on the basis of race, colour, national or ethnic origin, or are in other ways contrary to public policy, cannot acquire or retain charitable status. This principle would

---

81 Exempt Purposes – Internal Revenue Code, s.501(c)(3).
82 347 US 483 (1954). This landmark case ruled that racial discrimination in public educational facilities was unconstitutional.
83 The Restatement of Trusts (2d), section 377, comment c.

appear to have guided IRS determination of such status in relation, for example, to organisations associated with pro-life and pro-choice issues and gay relationships.

Public policy, charity law, overseas aid and anti-terrorism

It was in *United States v Carolene Producte Co.*[84] where Stone J, for the US Supreme Court, in his famous footnote 4, declared that one of the grounds on which legislation could be subjected to 'more exacting judicial scrutiny' was if it was directed at particular religious, national or racial minorities or expressed prejudice against 'discrete and insular minorities'.[85] This approach has since been followed by the IRS in a number of rulings which have upheld the charitable status of organisations that are set up: to eliminate the discrimination that limited employment opportunities for qualified minority workers;[86] to educate the public on the merits of racially integrated neighbourhoods;[87] to investigate the causes of deterioration in a particular community and informed residents and city officials of possible corrective measures;[88] and to conduct investigations and research on discrimination against minority groups in housing and public accommodation.[89] It was evident in *Bob Jones University v United States*,[90] when educational organisations that practise racial discrimination in their admissions policies were held to be ineligible for charitable status, and in *Home for Incurables of Baltimore City v University of Maryland Medical System Corporation*,[91] which concerned a medical rehabilitation centre that received a gift under charitable bequest for 'white patients' only and resulted in the racial restriction being struck.

• OVERSEAS AID

The US Agency for International Development (USAID) is the State vehicle for channelling much overseas humanitarian aid to those in need;[92] other assistance is politically determined and takes the form of military equipment and loans. Humanitarian aid is often transferred abroad through government funding of mediating charities. The IRS has long recognised that providing assistance to the

---

84 304 US 144, (1938). There are three aspects to this test – there must be a compelling state interest, the law or policy must be narrowly tailored to meet it, and the law or policy must be the least restrictive means for achieving it.
85 Ibid., at p.152.
86 See, Revenue Ruling68–70, 1968–1 CB 248.
87 See, Revenue Ruling 68–655, 1968–1 CB 248.
88 See, Revenue Ruling 68–15, 1968–1 CB 244.
89 See, Revenue Ruling 68–438, 1968–2 CB 209.
90 461 US 574 (1983).
91 797 A 2d 746 (Md 2002). Also, see, *Big Mama Rag, Inc. v United States*, 631 F 2d 1030 (DC Cir 1980).
92 See, further, http://www.usaid.gov/documents/1870/usaid-policy-framework-2011–2015.

foreign poor – the rural inhabitants of developing countries[93] and to the under-privileged in Latin America[94] – are charitable. However, in providing assistance a domestic charity must have real discretion in how to use the funds; if it is found to be merely a conduit for donations to a foreign charity, then, unlike the corresponding situation in Australia,[95] donations will not be tax-deductible.[96]

• ANTI-TERRORISM

The three principal directive measures taken by the US government, following the 9/11 terrorist attacks on the World Trade Center and the Pentagon, were (i) Executive Order 13224, Blocking Property and Prohibiting Transactions with Persons Who Commit, Threaten To Commit, or Support Terrorism (23 September 2001); (ii) the USA Patriot Act, Uniting and Strengthening America by Providing Appropriate Tools Required to Intercept and Obstruct Terrorism (24 October 2001); and (iii) the Treasury Department's, Anti-Terrorist Financing Guidelines: Voluntary Best Practices for U.S.-Based Charities (November 2002).[97] As elsewhere, the steady build-up of anti-terrorism powers has impacted upon the domestic and international work of charities.

In addition, its readiness to use the destructive powers of modern weaponry in some of the poorest countries of the world – together with the resort to torture in Iraq, Afghanistan and at Guantánamo Bay – has compromised the leadership role of the US in 'the war against terror' and added to the costs and complexity of the work of many, and directly impeded the activities of some, domestic and international charities in those countries.

The legislative and regulatory framework

In the absence of charity-specific legislation, the traditional roles and responsibilities of the IRS, the courts and the office of state attorneys general, reinforced by the customary range of ancillary regulatory bodies have, by and large, been seen as sufficient to maintain good practice in what is essentially treated as an aspect of tax administration. The National Association of State Charity Officials (NASCO), an association of state offices, is charged with oversight of charitable organisations and charitable solicitation. A similar absence of human rights-specific legislation has meant that for most purposes

---

93 Revenue Ruling 68–117, 1968–1 CB 251.
94 Revenue Ruling 68–165, 1968–1 CB 253.
95 *Commissioner of Taxation v Hunger Project* [2014] FCAFC 69 (13 June 2014).
96 See, Norton, L., *How to Be a Global Nonprofit: Legal and Practical Guidance for International Activities*, John Wiley & Sons, Hoboken, NJ, 2013.
97 See, US Department of the Treasury Antiterrorist Financing Guidelines: *Voluntary Best Practices for U.S.-Based Charities*, at http://www.treas.gov/press/releases/docs/tocc.pdf.
    Also, see, Sidel, M., *More Secure, Less Free?: Antiterrorism Policy & Civil Liberties after September 11*, University of Michigan Press, Michigan, US, 2007.

the Equal Employment Opportunity Commission is the regulatory body that arbitrates on equality issues arising under Title VII of the Civil Rights Act 1964, while the courts adjudicate on human rights issues and their constitutional implications.

Charity law

The distinct legal status of charity is recognised in law and by regulators in accordance with the usual common law principles governing 'exclusivity',[98] public benefit,[99] private benefit,[100] political activity[101] and public policy[102] (see, further, Chapter 2).

- THE CHARITIES REGULATOR: THE IRS

There is no charity specific regulator. One of the principal features of this regulatory framework is the dominance of the Treasury Department and the IRS in determining what is charitable: the periodic issue of new rulings ('Rev. Rul.') provide updates on its interpretation of 'charitable purpose'. Although state courts continue to play a role in this regard, it is the Tax Exempt and Government Entities (TEGE) Division of the IRS that is most directly involved in determining and monitoring charitable status. It maintains a register of all tax-exempt or nonprofit organisations, of which public benefit organisations (meaning 'charities' or 'charitable organisations') receive the highest level of tax benefits (including tax-preferred donations),[103] and it provides a level of supervision and accountability.

- ATTORNEY GENERAL

The state Attorney General is empowered to supervise and regulate charities and must oversee their liquidation and dissolution, whether voluntary or involuntary. Charities are responsible for filing reports with the Attorney General (or state equivalent) on a regular basis, and these are open to the public. In many

---

98 A charity's activities must be restricted to furthering its purpose or purposes as identified at registration.
99 Both the 'public' and the 'benefit' requirements must be satisfied: s.1.501(c)(3)–1(d)(1)(ii). See the influential decision in *Jackson v Phillips* 14 Allen (Mass) 539, 556 (1867).
100 A charity must ensure that no private benefit inures to any individual. See, *United Cancer Council v Commissioner* 165 F 3d 1173 (7th Cir 1999) and *Ginsberg v Commissioner* 46 TC 47 (1966).
101 IRC s.4911 imposes an 'excise tax' on excess lobbying expenses. See, *Christian Echoes National Ministry, Inc v United States*, 470 F 2d 849 (10th Cir 1972).
102 A charity must not violate fundamental public policy: Revenue Ruling 75–384, 1975–2 CB 204. See, for example, *Bob Jones University v United States* 461 US 574 (1983).
103 See, IRS, *Search for Charities, Online Version of Publication 78*, at: http://www.irs.gov/charities/page/0,id=15053,00.html.

states, however, this official has exercised little oversight over charities, leaving regulation to the IRS. Some states have enacted the Uniform Supervision of Trustees for Charitable Purposes Act 1996 which assigns certain responsibilities to the Attorney General's office. In July 2011, the National Conference of Commissioners of Uniform State Laws adopted a Model Protection of Charitable Assets Act intended to strengthen the protective capacity of the Attorney General.

Human rights

The US Constitution and its Bill of Rights (the first ten amendments), together with the Thirteenth, Fourteenth and Fifteenth Amendments, may be considered to provide a body of provisions equivalent to the ECHR, with nationwide application. In addition, the US has adopted the UDHR and the regional American Convention on Human Rights. In recent decades, of the ten core international human rights instruments, some with optional protocols, the US has become a signatory nation to most. As of summer 2015, it had signed and ratified the International Covenant on Civil and Political Rights (with reservations), the International Convention on the Elimination of All Forms of Racial Discrimination, and the Convention against Torture and Other Cruel, Inhuman or Degrading Treatment or Punishment; it has signed but not ratified the UN Convention on the Rights of the Child, the International Covenant on Social, Economic and Cultural Rights, the Convention on the Elimination of All Forms of Discrimination Against Women and the Convention on the Rights of Persons with Disabilities. In 2010, it declared its support for the United Nations Declaration on the Rights of Indigenous Peoples.

• THE HUMAN RIGHTS COMMISSION (HRC)

There is no such single national human rights institution in the US, though the State Department (which has no domestic role) does have a Bureau of Democracy, Human Rights and Labor, and in many states there are local HRCs, such as the one in Salt Lake City, Utah. The American Civil Liberties Union (ACLU), founded in 1920 and now with state branches nationwide, is very active in pursuit of its mission 'to defend and preserve the individual rights and liberties guaranteed to every person in this country by the Constitution and laws of the United States'.

• THE EQUAL EMPLOYMENT OPPORTUNITY COMMISSION (EEOC)

This federal agency administers and enforces civil rights laws. It is the regulatory body for matters arising under Title VII of the Civil Rights Act 1964 and, as such, determines all complaints of discrimination based on an individual's race, colour, national origin, religion, sex, age, disability or genetic information. Many states have equivalent agencies.

In 2006, the United Nations Committee on the Elimination of Racial Discrimination (CERD) issued a statement under its Early Warning and Urgent Action Procedure urging the US to 'freeze', 'desist' and 'stop' actions being taken, or threatened to be taken, against the Western Shoshone Nation. This unprecedented step was taken in response to a federal government claim to ownership of 90 per cent of tribal lands which it had been using for purposes that included underground nuclear tests, nuclear waste disposal and mining.[104]

The CERD's fourth US universal periodic review on the nation's implementation of the provisions of the ICCPR expressed a number of concerns, including the continuing detentions at Guantánamo Bay; the use of extensive data surveillance and collection by national security agencies; the lack of a national requirement to separate juveniles from adults in detention facilities and inclusion of 16- and 17-year-olds in adult criminal courts in some states; the criminalisation of homeless persons; the non-consensual use of psychiatric medication; the use of solitary confinement, particularly as it was applied disproportionately to people from minority backgrounds; mandatory deportation to countries that faced grave humanitarian challenges; the mandatory use of life without parole sentences for juvenile offenders or in cases where no murder had been committed; and concerns were also expressed regarding the increasing restrictions on women's right to abortion in some states.[105] In 2015, at the second UPR, there were direct challenges regarding the abortion restrictions that the US imposes on its foreign aid.

The contemporary charity law/human rights interface: a compliance audit

The following study of case law on the charity law/human rights interface uses benchmarks provided by the UDHR to identify and assess related points of interest.

Access to justice, legal process and principles

Any appraisal of the US in relation to such matters will necessarily be overshadowed by the political sanctioning of such breaches of human rights as indefinite detention without trial in Guantánamo Bay, unlawful rendition and the use of drones.

Access to justice

In recognition of obstacles presented by the high costs of litigation, the Department of Justice launched the 'Access to Justice Initiative' in March 2010 to

---

104 See, further, at: http://www.racism.org/index.php?option=com_content&view=article&id=548:soverign02&catid=121:articles-related-to-indigenous-peoples&Itemid=140.
105 See, further, at: http://www.wired.com/2014/03/united-nations-human-rights-committee-considers-report-united-states/.

address access issues in the criminal and civil justice system. It applies across federal agencies, and with state, local, and tribal justice system stakeholders to increase access to counsel and legal assistance for those unable to afford lawyers. This recent national human rights project aligns with the long-established IRS rulings granting charitable status to organisations that provide free,[106] or low-fee,[107] legal services to such persons.

As in other jurisdictions, the scandal of child abuse by clergy in the US has been accompanied by significant delay in official recognition of the extent of that abuse and in facilitating access to justice for the many victims.[108] The lack of a charity-specific regulator, accompanied by the exempt status of religious organisations and the legal presumption that they operate for the public benefit, have been factors in preventing a more timely and effective response from the legal system.

Due process

The Fourteenth Amendment – declaring that the states may not 'deprive any person of life, liberty, or property, without due process of law' – is important, as the courts have held that its protections are fundamental and therefore extend to the states' due processes of law. Unquestionably, this right has been breached by the US in the above-mentioned use of executive powers, but possibly the rampant practice of plea bargaining is also subverting due process, as the forced choice it presents for an implicated but non-culpable defendant can result in a false guilty plea.

Proportionality

As of 2014, the US had not ratified the Second Optional Protocol to the ICCPR on the abolition of the death penalty, which continues to be legislatively permitted in 32 states. Arguably, the 'three strikes' rule and the 'stand-your-ground' self-defence law that prevails in some states may also be viewed as disproportionate.

Respect for 'private life'

The above-mentioned clause in the Fourteenth Amendment of the US Constitution provides broadly the same protection as Article 12 of the UDHR. Its effectiveness has given rise to some contention.

It is in the context of the decades-long and ongoing culture wars that this principle has probably attracted most judicial attention. The pro-life/pro-choice litigation has at least twice given the US Supreme Court the opportunity to observe

---

106 Revenue Ruling 69–161, 1969–1 CB 149.
107 Revenue Ruling 78–248, 1978–2 CB 176.
108 See, for example, the John Jay College of Justice, *The Nature and Scope of the Problem of Sexual Abuse of Minors by Catholic Priests and Deacons in the United States* (the 'John Jay report'), 2004.

that 'if the right of privacy means anything, it is the right of the individual, married or single, to be free from unwarranted governmental intrusion into matters so fundamentally affecting a person as the decision whether to bear or beget a child'.[109] So, when ruling in favour of the plaintiff charity in *Planned Parenthood v Casey*,[110] it struck down the spousal notice requirement, finding that for many women this would impose a substantial obstacle in their path to have an abortion, and upheld the constitutional right to avail of that procedure. The principle was also a central rationale in striking down the Texas sodomy laws.[111]

Interest in the principle has not been confined to its bearing on domestic matters. For example, the covert surveillance of electronic communications on a worldwide basis by US intelligence agencies has caused the United Nations Human Rights Committee to question whether the US considers that the rights to privacy and to freedom of expression apply to those living outside its jurisdiction.[112] Clearly, also, some of the well-documented practices of the armed forces – sleep-deprivation, water-boarding, etc – breach this and other fundamental rights.

Freedom of religion and belief

Under the First Amendment of the Constitution, Congress is forbidden to enact a law 'respecting an establishment of religion or prohibiting the free exercise thereof', the latter clause being broadly in keeping with Article 18 of the UDHR. Recently, the US introduced reinforcing federal legislation: the Religious Freedom Restoration Act 1993;[113] the International Religious Freedom Act 1998; and the Religious Land Use and Institutionalized Persons Act 2000.

Church and State

The US Constitution is credited with erecting a wall to separate matters of Church and State. In particular, the First Amendment declared the two key rules for constraining State interference in religious affairs: 'the Establishment Clause'[114] and 'the free exercise clause'.[115] The first operates to prevent any attempt by Congress to identify an official or national church or collect taxes or provide public money to support any specific religion. The second prohibits Congress from interfering with the manner in which any person chooses to worship.

---

109 *Eisenstadt v Baird*, 405 US 438 (1972), per Brennan J and reiterated in *Planned Parenthood v Casey* 505 US 833 (1992).
110 Ibid.
111 *Lawrence v Texas*, 539 US 558 (2003).
112 See, further, at: http://www.wired.com/2014/03/united-nations-human-rights-committee-considers-report-united-states/.
113 See, *City of Boerne v Flores*, 521 US 507, 509 (1997).
114 See, *Everson v Board of Education*, 330 US: it cannot 'set up a church', or 'adopt . . . teach or practice religion', at pp. 15–16.
115 See, for example, *Sch. Dist. of Abington Twp., Pa. v Schempp*, 374 US 203, 305 (1963).

The aversion to 'established' religion in this jurisdiction is reflected in a history crammed with legislative and judicial evidence of a determination to keep seperate matters of Church and State. This has been particularly evident in the context of government funding of schools and religious charities, causing the courts to strike down many such funding arrangements.[116] However, in recent years the courts have moved towards interpreting the Establishment Clause as permitting funding but only in a manner that maintains a position of 'neutrality'.[117] As O'Scannlain J stated, in *Spencer v World Vision, Inc.*,[118] the Establishment Clause commands 'neutrality among religious groups.' So, for example, government grants currently provide two-thirds of the funding for Catholic Charities USA, and the Jewish Board of Family and Children Services receives 75 per cent of its funding from the government, for the non-discriminatory provision of contracted services. Justice O'Connor, in *Mitchell v Helms*,[119] employed 'the Lemon test'[120] in the following process of analysis. Firstly, does the programme of aid have a secular purpose? Secondly, does the programme of aid have the primary effect of advancing religion: is the aid actually diverted to religious indoctrination; does the programme define the eligibility of participating organisations without regard to religion; and does the programme create excessive administrative entanglement? She advised that religious organisations should monitor and 'compartmentalize' government funding received in the form of aid for education programmes. Where the aid is used for secular educational functions, then there would be no problem. If, however, the aid flowed into the entirety of an educational activity and some 'religious indoctrination [is] taking place therein', then that indoctrination 'would be directly attributable to the government'.[121]

In 2006, the InnerChange Freedom Initiative (IFI), an intensely religious rehabilitation programme delivered under the auspices of the Prison Fellowship Ministries, which required an enrolled prisoner to constantly satisfy an evangelical Christian program, was found to be 'pervasively sectarian'.[122] The following

116 See, for example: *Meek v Pittenger*, 421 US 349 (1975), government loans to religious schools; *Wolman v Walter*, 433 US 229 (1977), government loans for services away from the religious school campus; *Illinois ex rel. McCollum v Board of Education of School District* 333 US 203 (1948), disallowed the use of public buildings for optional religious instruction; *Bowen v Kendrick*, 487 US 589 (1989), disallowed the use of public buildings for optional religious instruction; and *Rosenberger v Rector and Visitors of Univ. of Va.*, 515 US 819 (1995), required that equal funding be granted to evangelical Christian groups.
117 The IRS treatment of churches and religious organisations has been judicially scrutinised to ensure compatibility with the 'neutrality principle': see, *Walz v Tax Commissioner*, 397 US 664 (1970) and *Committee for Public Education v Nyquist*, 413 US 756 (1973).
118 619 F 3d 1109 (9th Cir 2010). Also, see, *Epperson v Arkansas*, 393 US 97, 103–04 (1968).
119 530 US 793, 120 S Ct 2530 (2000).
120 See, *Lemon v Kurtzman* 403 US 602 (1971) which established criteria for justifying State legislative intervention in religious matters.
121 See, also, *Sch. Dist. v Ball*, 473 US 373, 398–400 (1985).
122 *Americans United For Separation of Church and State v Prison Fellowship Ministries*, 432 F Supp 2d 862 (S.D. Iowa 2006).

year, the civil rights group Freedom from Religion Foundation filed a lawsuit challenging the legality of the White House Office of Faith-Based and Community Initiatives, alleging that any such preferencing of religious organisations breached the Establishment Clause and violated the constitutional imperative that Church and State remain separate. The resulting decision of the Supreme Court in *Hein v Freedom From Religion Foundation*[123] ruled that taxpayers do not have the necessary *locus standi* to challenge the constitutionality of expenditures by the executive branch of the government, a decision that in effect gave the green light to further government faith-based initiatives.

Definition of 'religion': theism

It has been said that 'the theistic theme has always been well to the fore in definitions of religion in American cases'.[124] However, the courts in the US moved away from this earlier than their UK counterparts, and the IRS took a clear view that charitable trusts could not be restricted to those that declared their belief in one 'Supreme Being'.[125]

Definition of 'religion': belief system

The exclusively theistic approach was rejected in 1961 by Black J in *Torcaso v Watkins*[126] when the US Supreme Court struck down a Maryland law requiring officials to declare a belief in God in order to hold office in that state, and referred to a list of what could be termed 'religions' – including 'Buddhism, Taoism, Ethical Culture, Secular Humanism and others'. This was extended in *United States v Seeger*[127] to include 'a sincere and meaningful belief which occupies in the life of its possessor a place parallel to that filled by the God of those admittedly qualifying for the exemption'. In *Malnak v Yogi*[128] Adams J then described the criteria developed by US courts as first, a set of ideas that deal with the ultimate concerns of man; second, ideas that in toto constitute an integrated belief system; and third, forms and ceremonies that are found in accepted religions.

Equality of religions

The State cannot give precedence to any particular religion; this is specifically prohibited by the Establishment Clause. In this most open market of jurisdictions, government tends to regulate with a view to maintaining a level playing field between religions, and between those with and those without religious belief.

---

123 551 US 587 (2007).
124 Picarda, H., *The Law and Practice Relating to Charities* (3rd ed.), Butterworths, London, 1999, at p. 73.
125 *Torcaso v Watkins* 367 US 488 (1961).
126 Ibid.
127 380 US 163, 186 (1965).
128 (1979), 592 F 2d 197.

• SECULARISM

In keeping with the above principle, the State is required to hold a position of neutrality: favouring neither religion nor atheism; ensuring that it does not lend its resources or authority to preference adherents of any particular religion or of no religion; and proceeding, instead, on the basis of furthering an accommodation of diversity. Nonetheless, the national Pledge of Allegiance requires its citizens to proclaim their loyalty to 'one nation under God'.

The right to manifest religion or belief

The religious clauses of the First Amendment confer both a freedom to believe and a freedom to act, but while the former is absolute the latter is not.[129] The distinction has been the subject of many court cases. For example, in *Heffron v International Society for Krishna Consciousness,*[130] manifesting beliefs took the form of distributing pamphlets at a fair in defiance of a state ordinance prohibiting such behaviour, as it would interfere with the state's legitimate interest in ensuring the orderly movement and control of crowds. The ordinance was upheld: even if the plaintiffs peripatetic solicitation was part of a church ritual, it did not entitle church members to solicitation rights in a public forum superior to those of members of other religious groups that raise money but do not purport to ritualise the process.

Then, in 1990 the US Supreme Court[131] ruled that the State of Oregon could refuse employment to Native Americans who used peyote for religious reasons. The perceived threat posed by this decision to established religious freedoms led to Congress passing the Religious Freedom Restoration Act 1993, requiring the government to have a 'compelling reason' of the 'highest order' before interfering with a manifestation of religious belief of people with heartfelt attachments to religious customs, costumes, symbols and rituals.[132] Its effects were, perhaps, demonstrated 20 years after *Heffron* in *Watchtower Bible and Tract Society of New York v Village of Stratton,*[133] which concerned town ordinances that made it a misdemeanour to engage in door-to-door advocacy without first registering with town officials and receiving a permit. Jehovah's Witnesses argued that these ordinances violated their First Amendment right to canvass door-to-door as part of their religious belief that they should share the Gospel with others. The Supreme

---

129 *Reynolds v U.S.,* 98 US 145 (1978).
130 452 US 640 (1981). Also, see, *Int'l Society for Krishna Consciousness Inc v Lee* 505 US 672 (1992).
131 *Myke Freeman v State of Florida,* Department of Highway Safety and Motor Vehicles Case No 2002CA2828 (9th Cir).
132 See, Currier, P., '*Freeman v State of Florida*: Compelling State Interests and the Free Exercise of Religion in Post September 11th Courts', *Catholic University Law Review,* 53, Spring 2004, pp. 913–914.
133 122 S Ct 2080 (2002).

Court agreed and stated that the ordinances were 'offensive, not only to the values protected by the First Amendment, but to the very notion of a free society'.[134]

Parental right regarding religious education of their children

The US Supreme Court has often upheld the principle that parents have the fundamental right to direct the education and upbringing of their children.[135] For example, in applying the above-mentioned 'compelling interest' of the 'highest order' test, the Supreme Court has held that this was not satisfied where criminal penalties were imposed upon Amish parents for refusing to send their children to high school, the Amish claims being said to rest on 'deep religious conviction, shared by an organised group, and intimately related to daily living'.[136] In *Troxel v Granville*[137] the US Supreme Court reviewed the case law before concluding that 'it cannot now be doubted that the Due Process Clause of the Fourteenth Amendment protects the fundamental right of parents to make decisions concerning the care, custody, and control of their children'. The importance attached to the need for the State to stay at 'arm's length' from the scholastic environment was illustrated by a series of *School Prayer* cases which established that any memorial service sponsored or organised by a school and involving a prayer would compromise the neutrality of the public education system.[138]

Freedom of expression

The protections afforded this right in both the UDHR and the ICCPR are also guaranteed by the First Amendment to the US Constitution, which provides that 'Congress shall make no law . . . abridging the freedom of speech'.

This freedom is not absolute. In *Perry Educ. Ass'n v Perry Educators' Ass'n*,[139] while the court accepted that government can generally place time, place and manner constraints on its exercise, it added that such restrictions must be content neutral, narrowly tailored to serve a significant government interest, and leave open other channels of communication. Unless exercised in a manner that actually or potentially incites hatred or violence, is defamatory or is otherwise in breach of the law, the freedom to express views – however insulting – is constitutionally protected.

---

134 Ibid., at p. 2087.
135 See, for example: *Pierce v Society of Sisters*, 268 US 510 (1925); *Farrington v Tokushige*, 273 US 284 (1927); *Lehr v Robertson*, 463 US 248, 257–258 (1983); and *Hodgson v Minnesota*, 497 US 417 (1990).
136 *Wisconsin v Yoder* 406 US 205 (1972).
137 530 US 57 (2000).
138 See: *Santa Fe Indep. Sch. Dist. v Doe*, 530 US 290 (2000); *Lee v Weisman*, 505 US 577 (1992); *Wallace v Jaffree*, 472 US 38 (1985); *Sch. Dist. v Schempp*, 374 US 203 (1963); and *Engel v Vitale*, 370 US 421 (1962).
139 460 US 37, 45 (1983).

Such is the weight attached to this freedom that its influence moderates the traditional prohibition on political activity by charities. In recent years this has been particularly evident in the tensions between pro-life and pro-choice groups. The courts and the IRS[140] have been careful to respect the right to peaceful protest, even if abusive and provocative, that remains within the law.[141]

Freedom of assembly and association

The right to freedom of peaceful assembly and association in Article 20 of the UDHR closely resembles the First Amendment to the Constitution which declares:

> Congress shall make no law . . . abridging . . . the right of the people peaceably to assemble, and to petition the government for a redress of grievances.

It is a right reinforced by the US Supreme Court ruling in *Roberts v United States Jaycees*[142] that 'implicit in the right to engage in activities protected by the First Amendment' is a 'corresponding right to associate with others in pursuit of a wide variety of . . . ends'. Although, in that particular case, the court held that the right of a nationwide association to restrict its membership to males was outweighed by a compelling State interest in eradicating sex discrimination. Further, in *NAACP v Alabama ex rel. Patterson*,[143] it held that 'effective advocacy of both public and private points of view, particularly controversial ones, is undeniably enhanced by group association'. However, in *Boy Scouts v Dale*,[144] the court ruled that the plaintiff charitable organisation had a constitutional right, based on freedom of association, to exclude gays: this is difficult to reconcile with prior rulings which have held that the government has a compelling interest in ending discrimination, rulings which rejected claims of freedom of association as a basis for violating state laws prohibiting private clubs and groups from discriminating; it also seems to ignore IRS rulings which recognise 'eliminating prejudice and discrimination' as a charitable purpose.

Moreover, the lack of a positive obligation on the State to facilitate rights of association has led to the current position where there is no legal guarantee of

---

140 Note, however, the 2013 IRS decision to deny charitable status to Cherish Life Ministries because it was determined to be more 'political' than 'educational'.
141 See, *Griffin v Breckenridge*, 403 US 88 and *Bray v Alexandria Women's Health Clinic*, 506 US 263 (1993).
142 (1984) 468 US 609.
143 357 US 449 (1958).
144 120 S Ct 2446 (2000). Note that the Boy Scouts of America policy of denying membership to girls has also been upheld by the courts as not violating anti-discrimination laws.

trade union rights for agricultural and domestic workers, which has been a matter of concern to the UNHRC.[145]

Equality and non-discrimination

The assertion in the Declaration of Independence that 'all men are created equal', and reiterated by President Lincoln in his 'Gettysburg Address', provided a foundation stone for the world's most powerful democracy well before the protections of Article 14 of the UDHR and Articles 2 and 26 of the ICCPR were formulated.

On the one hand, this country has a considerable positive track record of giving effect to its constitutionally entrenched human rights principles in confronting slavery, racial discrimination and segregation, assimilating waves of immigrants and utilising those principles to address inequality in areas such as gender, age and disability. On the other, it has failed to treat health care as a fundamental human right: although the 'Obamacare' legislative initiative has improved the situation, there is still a wide gap in equality of access to health care between those who can afford health insurance, or who have it provided as an employee benefit, and those who do not. As of 2015, the world's most developed nation, with proportionately more billionaires, has also many millions of its citizens living in poverty; permits them to bear arms; imposes capital punishment; does not provide a universal right to abortion; has perhaps the highest percentage of its citizens in prison than any nation on earth, of which a disproportionate number are from minority groups (as with children in the public care system); and only in 2015 did it determine that same-sex marriage was a national right.

Religious discrimination

Religious discrimination occurs when someone is denied 'the equal protection of the laws, equality of status under the law, equal treatment in the administration of justice, and equality of opportunity and access to employment, education, housing, public services and facilities, and public accommodation because of their exercise of their right to religious freedom'.[146] For the purposes of this offence, 'religious discrimination' is broadly defined: 'religion' is not dependent on a belief in a supreme being;[147] it includes any belief that is sincere and that occupies in the life of the believer a place parallel to that of God in traditional religions,[148] but does not extend to racial supremist beliefs.[149]

---

145 See, further, at: http://www.wired.com/2014/03/united-nations-human-rights-committee-considers-report-united-states/.
146 US Commission on Civil Rights, *Religious Discrimination: A Neglected Issue; A Consultation Sponsored by the United States Commission on Civil Rights*, Washington, DC, 9–10 April 1979.
147 *Welsh v United States*, 398 US 333 (1970).
148 *United States v Seeger*, 380 US 163 (1965).
149 *Swartzentruber v Gunite Corp.*, 99 F Supp 2d 976 (ND Ind 2000).

Protection is afforded by Article 7 of the UDHR and by Articles 2(1) and 26 of the ICCPR. The relevant federal law is to be found in the Free Exercise Clause of the First Amendment, is included within the civil rights guaranteed by the Equal Protection Clause of the Fourteenth Amendment and also is in Title VII of the Civil Rights Act 1964. The Civil Rights Division of the Department of Justice lists the following range of laws protecting religious liberty:[150]

> laws barring discrimination based on religion in employment, public education, housing, credit, and access to public facilities and public accommodations;
> the Religious Land Use and Institutionalized Persons Act which bars zoning authorities from discriminating against houses of worship and religious schools;
> laws protecting the religious rights of institutionalized persons; and criminal statutes such as the Church Arson Prevention Act making it a federal crime to attack persons or institutions based on their religion, or otherwise interfere with religious exercise.

Title VII not only prohibits employers from discriminating against employees or prospective employees because of their religion, but it also requires employers to 'reasonably accommodate' the religious practices of employees, provided that such reasonable accommodations do not cause the employer 'undue hardship'.

The religious exemption

In 1987, the US Supreme Court in *Corp. of Presiding Bishop of Church of Jesus Christ of Latter-day Saints v Amos*[151] upheld the constitutionality of a law permitting religious organisations to exercise a religious preference when making employment decisions. Such action was found not to violate the Establishment Clause, at least when the discrimination occurs in connection with a religious organisation's nonprofit activities. Such exemption applies only to those institutions whose 'purpose and character are primarily religious'. It often refers to the tax-exemption status of such organisations, perhaps particularly with reference to property tax.[152] In recent years the exemption has been interpreted more narrowly: religious entities will not as a matter of course be able to claim immunity from state laws intended to have universal application.[153]

The legal complexities involved were well illustrated in *Spencer v World Vision Inc.*[154] which concerned a Christian humanitarian charity, established to address the causes of poverty and injustice, heavily funded by government, with more

150 See, further, at: http://www.justice.gov/crt/spec_topics/religiousdiscrimination/.
151 483 US 327, 329, 339 (1987).
152 See, for example, *Provena Covenant Medical Centre v Department of Revenue*, Docket No 107328 (Ill 18 March 2010).
153 For example, in *Alamo Foundation v Secretary of Labor* 471 US 290 (1985). Also, see, *United States v Lee* 455 US 252 (1982).
154 No 08–35532, 2011 WL 208356 (9th Cir 25 January 2011).

than 40,000 staff in nearly 100 countries. The case originated in a 2006 decision by World Vision to terminate the employment of three staff because they had ceased attending daily devotions and weekly chapel services held during the workday and because they had denied the deity of Jesus Christ. In 2007, the staff concerned sued World Vision for unfair dismissal, the latter responded by claiming that it was a religious entity and therefore exempt from Title VII, and the protracted court case got underway. The US Court of Appeals for the Ninth Circuit[155] eventually ruled that even though World Vision was not a traditional house of worship, it was entitled to the institutional religious liberty accommodation: as a 'religious corporation', it was exempt from a federal law that bars faith-based discrimination, and a petition for rehearing *en banc* was refused.

This important decision, confirming that religious organisations can legally factor religion into hiring decisions, was reinforced shortly afterwards by a Supreme Court ruling vindicating the right to hire and fire ministry personnel in accordance with the organisation's religious beliefs even where such action may conflict with the human rights of the personnel concerned.[156] Two years later, in *Burwell v Hobby Lobby*,[157] the US Supreme Court extended the exemption to commercial entities when it upheld the right of the evangelical Christian owners of Hobby Lobby not to provide health insurance cover, which included contraception, to their female employees. There remains some uncertainty, however, as to whether or not the law allows an organisation to avail of the exemption privilege when it uses federal money to deliver public services.

Discrimination (and exemptions) on other grounds

The US has signed and ratified the ICCPR and the International Convention on the Elimination of All Forms of Racial Discrimination (ICERD) and has signed but not ratified the Convention on the Elimination of All Forms of Discrimination against Women (CEDAW), the Convention on the Rights of the Child (CRC), and the Disability Convention, each of which requires US law to be Convention compliant. For most practical purposes, the law governing equality and diversity on a nationwide basis is to be found in Title VII of the Civil Rights Act 1964 which, as noted by Burger CJ in *Griggs v Duke Power*[158] where promotion opportunities were found to be biased in favour of white employees, 'proscribes not only overt discrimination but also practices that are fair in form but discriminatory in operation'.[159]

There are also a number of federal statutes (and much state specific legislation), some quite dated, that address matters of equality and diversity, including the

---

155 US Court of Appeals for the Ninth Circuit, No 08–35532, DC No 2:07-cv-01551-RSM (23 August 2010).
156 See, *Hosanna-Tabor Evangelical Lutheran Church & School v EEOC*, 132 S Ct 694 (2012).
157 573 US 134 S Ct 2751 (2014).
158 401 US 424, 91 S Ct 849 (1971).
159 Ibid., at 431.

Age Discrimination in Employment Act 1967, the Equal Pay Act 1963, and the Americans with Disabilities Act 1990.

• GENDER DISCRIMINATION

In *Roberts v United States Jaycees*,[160] a nationwide mens' only association was found to be unlawfully discriminating against women. Similarly, in *Board of Directors etc. v Rotary Club of Duarte*,[161] the court rejected the contention that the policy of excluding women by Rotary, a global charity, was protected by the First Amendment.[162]

• RACIAL DISCRIMINATION

In *Bob Jones University v United States*[163] the Supreme Court found that a university with a racially discriminatory admissions policy, and other policies relating to religious beliefs against interracial dating and marriage, was not charitable and therefore did not qualify for the tax exemption and other benefits available to charities. Justice Burger reasoned that, given the income tax privileges of charitable status, charities 'must serve a public purpose and not be contrary to established public policy'.[164] He concluded that there was 'no doubt' that a public policy against racial discrimination existed,[165] as 'few social or political issues' have 'been more vigorously debated and more extensively ventilated than the issue of racial discrimination'.[166] In *Trustees of University of Delaware v Gebelin*[167] and *Wooten v Fiztgerald*,[168] charitable gifts to educational institutions were restricted by racial conditions, but the courts could save the gift by using *cy-près* to eliminate the offending restrictions.

Currently, in the US, there is a widespread perception that African Americans and those of Hispanic origins suffer discrimination, a perception reinforced by their disproportionate representation in the statistics relating to victims of police shooting, convicted prisoners and children in the public care system.

• SEXUAL DISCRIMINATION

In *Baehr v Lewin*,[169] the Supreme Court of Hawaii, interpreting an express prohibition of sex discrimination in the Hawaii Constitution, held that denying

---

160 (1984) 468 US 609.
161 (1987) 107 S Ct 1940. Also, see, *Isbister v Boys Club* (1985) 40 Cal 3d 72 and *New York State Club Association v City of New York* (1988) 108 S Ct 2225.
162 See, further, McKenna, L.M., 'Freedom of Association or Gender Discrimination? *New York State Club Association v City of New York*', *The American University Law Review*, Vol 38, pp. 1060–1092.
163 461 US 574 (1983).
164 Ibid.
165 Ibid., at p. 588.
166 Ibid., at p. 596.
167 420 A 2d 1191 (Del Ch 1980) (racial restriction removed but not gender restriction).
168 440 SW 2d 719 (Tex Civ App 1969).
169 74 Haw 530, 852 P 2d 44 (1993).

same-sex couples the right to marry was *prima facie* sex discrimination and must be justified. Within the next 20 years, nine states in the US had legalised same-sex marriage, but not until *Obergefell v Hodges*[170] did it become legal nationwide. The potential impact of this decision for educational institutions with a religious ethos may be similar to that of *Bob Jones* on those with a racial one: the charitable status of the many faith-based schools, colleges and universities that continue to require adherence to traditional relationships as a condition of access to their courses, thereby discriminating against applicants whose relationships or beliefs comply with *Obergefell*, could be similarly forfeited. In all states where same-sex marriage has been legislatively introduced, the provisions impose no requirement upon religious organisations and their ministers to provide marriage services (i.e. a celebrant, use of church premises etc). Most such states include exemption clauses for religious organisations and their ministers (though not Massachusetts) and ensure that eligibility for tax-exempt status will not be adversely affected.

Christian Legal Society v Martinez[171] commenced with a suit filed in 2004 after California's Hastings College refused to recognise the student chapter of the Christian Legal Society (CLS): the College had a policy which required all student organisations to operate on an open membership basis, allowing participation regardless of a student's status or beliefs; the CLS required all its officers and voting members to agree with its basic Christian beliefs, and certain LGBT students objected when they were denied the opportunity to become voting members. The US Supreme Court upheld the College policy and denied CLS the protection of the First Amendment. Justice Stevens noted that CLS refused membership to those who engage in 'unrepentant homosexual conduct', and the same argument could be made by groups that 'may exclude or mistreat Jews, blacks, and women'.

- EMPLOYMENT DISCRIMINATION

As mentioned above, a raft of federal anti-discrimination legislation exists but in practice it is the Title VII exemption as regulated by the US Equal Employment Opportunity Commission (EEOC) that generates most litigation. Title VII expressly forbids employers with 15 or more employees to discriminate on the grounds of race, colour, sex, religion or national origin.[172] This prohibition was extended by EEOC case law in 2015 to include sexual orientation discrimination. Employers may not make any employment decisions based on such grounds, including hiring, firing, promoting, demoting, and determining assignments and workloads.

As in the other jurisdictions studied, the weight of case law concerns workplace issues arising from a conflation of religious and cultural conduct, including

---

170 576 US ___ (2015).
171 (No 08–1371) 319 Fed Appx 645 (2010).
172 Congress in 1972 added an exemption, codified in s.702 of the Act, for 'religious corporation[s], association[s], educational institution[s], or societ[ies]', to the prohibition against religion-based discrimination.

working on the Sabbath,[173] the swearing of oaths[174] and wearing certain apparel.[175] Employers have a duty to accommodate the religious beliefs of their employees. An employee's belief or practice can be 'religious' under Title VII even if the employee is affiliated with a religious group that does not espouse or recognise that individual's belief or practice, or if few – or no – other people adhere to it. Title VII's protection also extends to those who are discriminated against or need accommodation because they profess no religious beliefs. An exception to this rule exists if an individual's religion is a bona fide occupational qualification, as when it is an essential part of their job description. The law applies to federal, state and local employers.[176] Arguably, legal protection in the workplace is pervasively deficient by omission: it fails to provide entitlements taken for granted in other jurisdictions such as reasonable maternity leave and maximum hours for a working day.

- SERVICE PROVISION DISCRIMINATION

While Titles III and IV of the Civil Rights Act 1964 provide the main statutory protection from discrimination in accessing public services, Title II prohibits discriminatory practice by any establishment that leases, rents or sells goods or provides services.[177]

In recent years, the Catholic Charities have featured prominently in the contention regarding discriminatory service provision on the basis of sexual orientation. In February 2006, when it failed to gain exemption from the state's non-discrimination statute, Catholic Charities terminated its adoption work rather than continue to place children with gay couples. In 2010, the government declined to renew a contract with the US Conference of Catholic Bishops to provide services for human trafficking victims because Catholic Charities refused to provide referrals for contraception and abortion to sexual assault victims. In 2012, the Illinois Department of Children and Family Services revoked its contract with Catholic Charities after its refusal to provide adoption and foster-care services to same-sex couples, causing the transfer of more than 1,000 children from the charity's custody to secular agencies.

- 'POSITIVE ACTION'

The school voucher scheme, whereby public money is made available to pay for tuition at private schools, including religious schools with charitable status, has been contentious. In practice, most voucher recipients used their vouchers to transfer to

173 *EEOC v Covergys Corp.* (ED Mo 2011).
174 *Torcaso v Watkins,* 367 US 488 (1961).
175 *United States v Board of Educ. Sch. Dist. Phila.,* *911,* F 2d 882 (3d Cir 1990).
176 See, further, at: http://www.princeton.edu/hr/policies/appendix/a1/_1_1/.
177 See, for example, *Heart of Atlanta Motel Inc v U.S.,* 379 US 241 (1964) and *Katzenbach v McClung,* 379 US 294 (1964).

religious schools, triggering a complaint that public dollars were being funnelled to religious institutions and leading to the scheme being challenged in *Zelman v Simmons-Harris*.[178] The Supreme Court then found that the programme did not violate the Establishment Clause of the First Amendment, mainly because it was enacted for a secular rather than a religious purpose. The point of allowing parents to use public money to send their children to private schools was so that parents in poor areas with failing public schools could get a better education for their children.

In a ruling giving effect to the 'positive action' (or 'affirmative action') policy, the IRS granted charitable status to a job training programme that limited admissions to native Americans.[179] This was justified because the limitation (required by federal law governing funding of training programmes for Indians) was not racial discrimination, was not contrary to public policy and was not inconsistent with charitable exemption under IRC s.501(c)(3).

- CHARITIES AS PUBLIC BODIES

The decisions in both *Bowen v Kendrick*[180] and *Mitchell v Helms*[181] reveal a strong judicial awareness of circumstances in which a consequence of government funding could entail an imputing of functional responsibility from nonprofit service deliverer to government funder in accordance with the agent/principal rule. As Justice O'Connor warned in the latter case, when charities step wholly into the shoes of government in their delivery of core public benefit services (such as education), they are acting as agents of government, which may give rise to serious accountability issues for both parties.[182]

Conclusion

Although the interstices in human rights coverage and their enforcement can be problematic, the spread of those recognised as valid charitable purposes, and the duration of that recognition, are distinctive characteristics of this jurisdiction. Also distinctive are the number and thoroughness of judicial deliberations given to human rights issues, although those relevant to charity would seem to arise mainly in a religious context, conflated with sex orientation, and then tend to focus more on disentangling Church/State interests than upon rights of the individual. All in all, however, while the range of matters independently addressed by charity and human rights is extensive, the case law would seem to indicate that they intersect only at the margins.

178 536 US 639 (2002).
179 Revenue Ruling 77–272, 1977–2 CB 191.
180 487 US 589, 623 (1988).
181 530 US793, 120 S Ct 2530 (2000).
182 *Mitchell v Helms* 530 US 793, 120 S Ct 2530 (2000).

7   Canada

Introduction

The Constitution Act of 1867 confirmed the confederation of Canada.[1] In so doing, it also laid the foundations for jurisdictional difficulties that would grow to complicate the administration of the law in many respects including how it relates to charities and human rights. While the ten provinces and three territories are each vested with the authority to make laws regarding charities and human rights – resulting in replicated legislative and administrative frameworks across Canada – the federal government is in fact the regulator because of its taxation powers. Added complexity derives from Canada's bijural and bilingual heritage, coupled with the presence of a sizeable indigenous population comprising the First Nations, the Inuit and the Métis. It is frankly acknowledged that in the very space presently available, it is not possible to differentiate the application of the law between the various Canadian jurisdictions. Piecing together an overview that draws from judicial decisions – mainly those of the Supreme Court of Canada – supplemented by the policies and guidance of Canada Revenue Authority, is the limit of what is feasible.

Like the others, this chapter begins with a brief history of charity law and its interface with human rights. It considers the charity law reform process, the meagre outcomes and their implications for human rights. The contemporary legislative and regulatory framework is then outlined with reference to core institutions, followed by a summary of the more worrying and most relevant human rights issues identified in recent UN reports. This prepares the ground for the main section which applies the template to examine and assess the case law that illuminates the issues currently causing concern at the Canadian charity law/human rights interface.

Background: a history inimical to human rights

Canada applies the traditional common law approach to 'charity' which is broadly in keeping with that which prevailed in England and Wales prior to the reforms

---

1 Established by the British North America Act 1867, as re-enacted in 1982, s.92(7).

introduced in the latter jurisdiction by the Charities Act 2006: the key common law concepts, *Pemsel* purposes, rules and case law precedents have an equal relevance to charity law in both jurisdictions (see, further, Chapter 2). This source has been approved many times by Canadian courts, including the Supreme Court of Canada[2] where Iacobucci J has referred to the common law concept of charity in the Income Tax Act applying 'uniform federal law across the country'.[3]

Charity law and human rights: the early challenges

Given that the law relating to charity has remained embedded within traditional common law parameters – untouched by federal legislation, anchored upon very dated English precedents and only seldom considered by the Supreme Court of Canada – it is unsurprising that, as time passes, a lack of fit between that law, contemporary patterns of social need and human rights has become steadily more apparent.

Legal structures: charitable trusts

One aspect of the English common law that did not carry over into Canada was the reliance on the trust form for organising charities. Although trusts can be used, most Canadians incorporate their charities, either as nonprofit corporations or societies.

Constitution

The Constitution Act 1867[4] preceded the present Constitution Act 1982 (see, further, below) and initially provided an overarching framework of principles for Canadian charity law.

Exempt charities

While the exempt status for certain charities in England and Wales has not been adopted by the CRA, it does employ a partial version in its dealings with religious charities.[5] Also, in *Re Christian Brothers of Ireland in Canada (Re)*,[6] the Ontario Court of Appeal agreed with the court of first instance that there is no general doctrine of charitable immunity applicable in Canada, and consequently all assets

---

2 See, *Guaranty Trust Co. of Canada v Minister of National Revenue* [1967] SCR 133 and *Vancouver Society of Immigrant and Visible Minority Women v Minister of National Revenue* [1999] 1 SCR 10.
3 Ibid., at para 28.
4 Initially known as the British North America Act 1867.
5 See, CRA, 'Religious Charities – Exemption', Policy Commentary, CPC – O16 (17 October 2003).
6 2000 CanLII 5712 (ON CA). Also, see, *Rowland v Vancouver College Ltd.* [2000] BCJ No 1666 (QL).

of a charity, whether owned beneficially or held pursuant to a special purpose charitable trust, were available to satisfy claims by victims of historical child abuse on the winding-up of the religious organisation. The Supreme Court of Canada denied leave to appeal.[7]

Political purposes

Charities are not permtted to be established for political purposes[8] but may engage in public awareness campaigns in relation to their charitable purpose and participate in direct political activity – defined by the CRA as any activity that seeks to change, oppose or retain laws or policies – as long as this is ancillary and incidental to their charitable purpose and accounts for no more than 10 per cent of their resources.[9]

Charitable purposes: a tangential relationship with human rights

Essentially, at common law, an organisation will be deemed charitable only if its purposes are exclusively and legally charitable and it is established for the benefit of the public or a sufficient segment of it.[10] In making that determination, both the judiciary and the CRA have leant heavily on the long-established British precedents previously mentioned (see, further, Chapter 2).

The relief of poverty

The definition of this charitable purpose was considered in *Minister of Municipal Affairs of New Brunswick v (Maria F.) Ganong Old Folks Home*[11] when the Chief Justice of the New Brunswick court held that aged persons need not be poor to come within the Preamble to the Statute of Elizabeth.[12] This is consistent with other decisions.[13] Indeed, as recently as 2014, the CRA was advising (Oxfam) that 'preventing poverty could mean providing for a class of beneficiaries that are not poor' and that while relieving poverty is charitable, preventing it is not. This interpretation was evident also in *Re Denison*[14] in relation to a trust established for the relief of impoverished members of the legal profession and in *Jones v Executive Officers of the T. Eaton Co.*[15] when the Supreme Court of Canada held

---

7   [2000] SCCA No 277 (QL).
8   *N.D.G. Neighbourhood Association v Revenue Canada* 88 DTC 6279.
9   See, CRA, Policy Statement CPS-022, 'Political Activities', at: http://www.cra-arc.gc.ca/chrts-gvng/chrts/plcy/cps/cps-022-eng.html.
10 See, further, at: http://www.cra-arc.gc.ca/chrts-gvng/chrts/plcy/cps/cps-024-eng.html.
11 (1981), 129 DLR (3d) 655, at 663–64 (NB CA).
12 Ibid.
13 *Re Forgan* (1961), 29 DLR (2d) 585 (Alta SC).
14 (1974) 42 DLR (3d) 654.
15 [1973] SCR 635.

as valid a trust set up to assist 'any needy or deserving Toronto member of the Eaton Quarter Century Club'. In contrast, there would seem to be an absence of comparable case law addressing the endemic poverty that has characterised the Aboriginal communities for many generations.

The advancement of education

The system of Indian residential schools, funded by the federal government and administered by Christian charities – mainly emanations of the Catholic and Anglican Churches – might be seen as a distinctly perverse interpretation of this purpose. In a policy of 'cultural genocide'[16] consolidated by the Indian Act 1876, some 150,000 Aboriginal children were removed from their homes, communities and culture to residential educational institutions: the first such residential school being established in 1620 and the last closing in 1986, triggering what is now recognised as 'the beginning of an intergenerational cycle of neglect and abuse'.[17]

The promotion of peace and understanding has been rejected as a charitable purpose in Canada. *Toronto Volgograd Committee v M.N.R.*[18] concerned an organisation established to promote peace and understanding between Toronto and Volgograd in the USSR through education, public awareness, exchanges and meetings, which was denied charitable status because its activities and objects were viewed by the court as 'no more than propaganda'.[19] In contrast, a gift to the Ryerson Press for 'the purpose of assisting in publishing the work of an unknown Canadian author' was deemed charitable.[20]

For contemporary Canadian society, the *Vancouver Society of Immigrant and Visible Minority Women v M.N.R.*[21] – which among other things concerned the issue of how broadly the courts should interpret 'education' – was an important milestone. The court then took the view that a traditional interpretation restricted to formal teaching in a classroom was too limited. However, the approach of the plaintiff charity in simply providing an opportunity for people to educate themselves by making available materials with which this might be accomplished, but need not be, was not enough; activities could not constitute the promotion of education unless reasonably structured.[22] Organisations that provide

---

16 A phrase recently used by the Chief Justice of the Supreme Court, see p. 1 of the Summary of the *Final Report of the Truth and Reconciliation Commission of Canada* (2015) at: http://www.trc.ca/websites/trcinstitution/File/2015/Findings/Exec_Summary_2015_05_31_web_o.pdf.
17 See, Saskatchewan Child Welfare Review Panel Report, 'For the Good of our Children and Youth: A New Vision, a New Direction', at p. 18. See, further, at: http://saskchildwelfarereview.ca/CWR-panel-report.pdf.
18 [1988] 1 CTC 365, 88 DTC 6192 (FCA).
19 See, also, *Positive Action Against Pornography v MNR* [1988] 2 FC 340 (CA).
20 *Re Shapiro* HC WN CIV-2010–485–1275.
21 [1999] 1 SCR 10.
22 *News to You Canada v Minister of National Revenue* 2011 FCA 192.

information[23] or promote a point of view, as their sole or main activity, cannot qualify as a charity under this *Pemsel* head. In terms of the charity law/human rights interface, this case paved the way for a more accommodating approach to the work of community development organisations with immigrant minority cultures. The Canadian courts, in *A.Y.S.A. Amateur Youth Soccer Association v Canada*,[24] further extended this *Pemsel* heading to include trusts set up to benefit amateur sports.

The advancement of religion

According to the CRA website:[25]

> To advance religion in the charitable sense means to promote the spiritual teachings of a religious body and to maintain doctrines and spiritual observances on which those teachings are based. There must be an element of theistic worship, which means the worship of a deity or deities in the spiritual sense.

While the presumption of public benefit has almost always ensured that Canadian religious institutions have charitable status, this has not stretched to accommodate polytheistic religions nor trusts for 'ethics' organisations like the Free Masons. In *Wood v Whitebread*,[26] for example, the court rejected the claim that a gift for the Theosophical Society was a trust for the advancement of religion, although it did recognise that 'the study of comparative religion, philosophy and society is prima facie charitable'.[27]

The range of gifts deemed charitable under this *Pemsel* head are much the same as in England and Wales.[28] It is perhaps worth noting that both jurisdictions also share the same approach towards 'closed' religious orders. In holding that they fail the public benefit test – as no tangible benefit can be said to accrue to the general public from the private devotional prayerful activity of such

---

23 *Travel Just v Canada (Revenue Agency)* 2006 FCA 343, [2007] 1 CTC 294.
24 *A.Y.S.A. Amateur Youth Soccer Ass'n v Canada*, 2007 SCC 42.
25 Still in force and available at: http://www.cra-arc.gc.ca/chrts-gvng/chrts/plcy/csp/csp-r06-eng.html.
    See, also, two more recent guidances Promotion of Health and Charitable Registration (CG-021) and How to Draft Purposes for Charitable Registration (CG-019), both issued in 2013. Author acknowledges advice from Carters on this matter (note to author, 28 August 2015).
26 (1969) 68 WWR 132, (Sask QB).
27 Ibid., at p. 284.
28 CRA guidance as to what constitutes the advancement of religion includes two recently released policies: *Applicants Assisting Ethnocultural Communities*, and *Guidelines for Registering a Charity: Meeting the Public Benefit Test*. Also, see *Promotion of Health and Charitable Registration* (CG-021) and *How to Draft Purposes for Charitable Registration* (CG-019).

communities – they are both equally vulnerable to the charge that by making a distinction between public and private worship, they are discriminating against such closed religious orders. As Grattan and Conway have convincingly demonstrated,[29] discrimination is also very evident in a considerable body of Canadian case law, featuring bequests made subject to religious conditions imposed by testators, which have been upheld by the judiciary.[30] Parachin has also catalogued many such discriminatory bequests.[31]

Beneficial to the community, not falling under any of the preceding heads

Canadian judicial creativity, as evidenced in the above *Vancouver Society* case, has also often been demonstrated in relation to decisions taken under the fourth *Pemsel* head.

For example, the court in *Re Vancouver Regional Free Net Association and Minister of National Revenue*[32] utilised the 'spirit and intendment' rule to confirm the charitable status of an organisation established to provide free community access to the internet; the rationale – that the service could, by analogy, be viewed as a contemporary public utility equivalent to the 'highways' declared charitable in the Preamble – would seem to parallel the human rights approach. In *Everywoman's Health Centre Society v Canada*,[33] a society established to provide 'necessary medical services for women for the benefit of the community as a whole' and carrying on 'educational activities incidental to the above' in the form of a free-standing abortion clinic was found to be eligible for registration as a charity.

However, the approach taken to the charitable status of organisations that support immigrants has been equivocal. While in *Re Fitzgibbon*[34] a bequest to the 'Women's Welcome Hostel', established for the assistance of immigrant girls, was held to be charitable, in *Vancouver Society* the Supreme Court of Canada ruled that this was not the case in relation to assisting immigrant women to integrate into society by helping them to obtain employment.

---

29 See, further, Grattan, S. and Conway, H., 'Testamentary Conditions in Restraint of Religion in the Twenty-first Century: An Anglo-Canadian Perspective', *McGill Law Journal*, Vol 50, 2005, p. 511.

30 See, for example: *Laurence v McQuarrie* (1894), 26 NSR 164 (forfeiture condition in the event of the beneficiary 'embracing the doctrines of the church of Rome'); *Re Patton* [1938] OWN 52 (CA), ('is and proves himself to be of the Lutheran religion'); and *Re Curran*, [1939] OWN 191 (HCJ). ('is at that time a member of a Roman Catholic Parish').

31 See, Parachin, A., 'The Definition of Charity and Public Law Equality Norms', Paper Presented at Conference Private and Public Law – Intersections in Law and Method, the T C Beirne Law School at the University of Queensland, Brisbane, July 2011.

32 (1996) 137 DLR (4th) 206 Federal Court of Appeal. Also, see, *Everywoman's Health Centre Society v Canada* [1991] 2 CTC 320, 92 DTC 6001 (FCA).

33 [1991] 2 CTC 320, 92 DTC 6001 (FCA).

34 (1916) 27 OWR 207 (HC).

The First Nations

Given the well-documented history of neglect affecting the Aboriginal communities, the absence of any related case law – excepting *Native Communications Society v M.N.R*[35] (development of radio and television productions relevant to native peoples, etc.) – is noticeable. This may be partly attributable to the historical effect of the charity law rule requiring the 'public' arm of the public benefit test to be interpreted to the exclusion of those conjoined in a nexus of kinship relationships: the 'class within a class' problem, typical of Aboriginal communities.[36] This approach has been ameliorated, to an uncertain degree, by the CRA policy announced in 2005, with regard to ethnocultural communities, where it concedes that it may be acceptable for charities to limit services to a particular ethnocultural or grouping of ethnocultural communities – under other purposes beneficial to the community – if the reasons for doing so are justified by the purposes.

Public benefit: civil society, charity and the State

Pluralism has prevailed as Canada's preferred mode of nation-building. However, this has proved particularly challenging due to problems that include managing a bijural, bilingual, federated State; acknowledging and addressing the needs of different cultural groups, including the Catholic and separatist Quebecois; the presence of sizeable and largely impoverished indigenous communities; and a population containing a high proportion of first generation immigrants. Given that context, it seems singularly unhelpful that the CRA continues to reject the promotion of multiculturalism as a charitable purpose: an approach reinforced by the decision in *Canada UNI Assn. v Canada (Minister of National Revenue – MNR)*.[37] Such factors, together with the added complications of geography and distance, have combined to reduce pluralism to the loose administration of regions and cultures. This has inevitably impeded the growth of a more cohesive civil society.

Canada suffered less than most of the developed nations that slipped into economic recession in 2007/08. Nevertheless, government continues to rely heavily upon charities and other nonprofits for the delivery of public benefit services. As a consequence it may indeed be the case that 'Canadian charities face pressure to align their programs with the public policy agenda of the incumbent government, and feel powerless to resist'.[38]

---

35 [1986] 3 FC 471. Also, see, *Gull Bay Development Corp. v The Queen* [1984] Ex CR 159, 62 DTC 1099.

36 See, CRA, 'Policy Statement, Benefits to Aboriginal Peoples of Canada', CPS-012, 1997, at http://www.cra-arc.gc.ca/tax/charities/policy/cps/cps-012-e.html.

37 [1992] FCJ No 1130 (CA), 151 NR 4.

38 See, Chan, K., 'The co-optation of charities by threatened welfare states', *Queen's Law Journal*, Vol 40, 2015, p. 34.

Partnership

In keeping with the experience elsewhere, as the government reduced its support for public service provision, so, in the last decades of the 20th century, Canada experienced a resurgence in community-based health and social care charities. Consequently, Canadian government embarked on charity law reform as a means of both tightening the regulatory framework for the sector and of redistributing the responsibility for future public benefit service provision. This proceeded with little evidence of mutual commitment to simultaneously building a government/sector partnership: the sector was unable to put forward representative bodies authorised to negotiate on issues identified as of strategic importance to it; government baulked at putting in place the institutions and processes necessary to bridge the gap between it and the sector; and the obstacles presented by a federated political context seemed to defeat coherent planning.

Charity law reform and human rights: towards alignment

In the aftermath of the failed Ontario Law Reform Commission,[39] when its proposals for a principled basis on which government and sector could jointly embark on modernising charity law were rejected, there was a period of regrouping which, in 1995, saw 12 national umbrella organisations covering most parts of the voluntary sector coming together as the Voluntary Sector Roundtable. The preparatory work of this body led to the creation of the Voluntary Sector Initiative (VSI). This promised the beginning of a new stage in government/sector relations.

The charity law reform process

As has been pointed out, 'the fact that a dated body of largely English common law decisions dictates the range of organisations that are granted both federal and provincial charitable tax benefits has never generated any significant debate'.[40]

The process

The 1998 interim report of the VSI, 'Helping Canadians Help Canadians: Improving Governance and Accountability in the Voluntary Sector', and the final report, 'Building on Strength: Improving Governance and Accountability in Canada's Voluntary Sector' (the Broadbent Report), made 41 substantive recommendations aimed at increasing good governance and accountability. Significantly, the Broadbent Report recommended that the CRA have 'enhanced' authority to

---

39 See, the Ontario Law Reform Commission Report 1996.
40 See, Chan, K., 'Charitable According to Whom? The Clash Between Quebec's Societal Values and the Law Governing the Registration of Charities', *Les Cahiers de droit*, Vol 49, No 2, 2008, pp. 277–295, at para 10.

regulate charities, and that an 'advisory' agency be developed that would encompass the advisory functions of an entity like the English Charity Commission. Following the release of that report, the federal government, in co-operation with the voluntary sector, set up seven 'joint tables' to discuss ways in which the government and the sector could work together more effectively.

In addition to various recommendations, the VSI produced an 'Accord Between the Government of Canada and the Voluntary Sector,' signed in 2001, the purpose of which was to strengthen the ability of both the voluntary sector and the Government of Canada to better serve Canadians.[41]

Jurisdiction specific outcomes

There are few indications that any of the above will lead to the government making significant changes to the law. As Strayer J remarked, in the *Human Life International* case,[42] charity 'remains an area crying out for clarification through Canadian legislation for the guidance of taxpayers, administrators and courts'. There is no sense in which there has been any of the following: recasting of the public benefit principle; changes to the political purposes rule; alteration to the categories of purposes recognised as charitable; nor any federal or provincial statutory definition of charity or any encoding of common law concepts. Despite some protest,[43] the attenuated Canadian charity law reform process has been allowed to quietly peter out.

- INCREASED REGULATORY MEASURES

The reforms ultimately introduced by government were based on recommendations made in the 2003 report 'Strengthening Canada's Charitable Sector: Regulatory Reform',[44] all but six of which were accepted and subsequently incorporated into the Income Tax Act,[45] none being of any real significance – though the introduction of hybrid social enterprise legal structures (restricted to British Columbia and Nova Scotia) has proved durable. Unlike other common law jurisdictions, however, no legislative steps have been taken to transfer either the lead regulatory responsibility to a charity specific national agency or the common law

---

41 See, 'Accord between the Government of Canada and the Voluntary Sector', at http://www.vsi-isbc.org/eng/relationship/the_accord_doc/index.cfm.

42 *Human Life International in Canada Inc. v Canada (Minister of National Revenue)* [1998] 3 FC 202 (FCA).

43 See, for example, Tsao, D., Stoffman, Z., Lloyd-Smith, G. and Mohomoud, K., 'Tax Audits of Environmental Groups: The Pressing Need for Law Reform', *Environmental Law Centre*, University of Victoria, 2015, at: http://desmog.ca/sites/beta.desmogblog.com/files/Modernizing-Canadian-Charitable-Law.pdf.

44 See, further, at: http://www.vsi-isbc.org/eng/regulations/reports.cfm.

45 For an updated version of the Income Tax Act (Canada) see: http://laws-lois.justice.gc.ca/eng/acts/I-3.3.

definitional matters to statute. Thus the long-standing deficiencies of this regulatory regime continue largely unabated.

Charity law and human rights purposes

There is no specific statutory recognition for the advancement of human rights as a charitable purpose in this jurisdiction, although *Re Lewis's Estate*[46] and *Lewis v Doerle*[47] provide authority for the proposition that a trust to promote the enjoyment of existing civil rights (as opposed to securing new ones) is charitable. However, the Charities Directorate acknowledges that activities which uphold human rights can further charitable purposes under all four heads of charity, and also that upholding human rights can be a charitable purpose in and of itself under the fourth head.[48] Its authority for finding this to be charitable derives from the decision in *McGovern*.[49]

Given the well-documented concerns of the UN (see, below), there is a noticeable absence of recognition given by regulator or judiciary to charitable purposes that specifically address those concerns.

Charity law and human rights: a contemporary framework for continuing dissonance

The modern legislative and regulatory framework for human rights in this jurisdiction compares sharply with its charity law counterpart.

Constitution, public policy and human rights

The Constitution Act 1982, with its Canadian Charter of Rights and Freedoms, was signed into law by Queen Elizabeth II on 17 April 1982. Its Preamble declares that 'Canada is founded upon principles that recognize the supremacy of God and the rule of law', and the Charter goes on to include the following declarations:[50]

> 2.　Everyone has the following fundamental freedoms:
>
> > (a) freedom of conscience and religion;
> > (b) freedom of thought, belief, opinion and expression, including freedom of the press and other media of communication.

46　25 A 878 (1893).
47　(1898) 25 OAR 206.
48　See, 'Upholding Human Rights and Charitable Registration Guidance', CG-001, 15 May 2010, at: http://www.cra-arc.gc.ca/chrts-gvng/chrts/plcy/cgd/hmn-rghts-eng.html.
49　*McGovern et al. v Attorney-General et al.* [1981] 3 All ER 493.
50　See, Schedule B to the Canada Act 1982 (UK), 1982, c.11. The Canadian Charter of Rights and Freedoms was introduced partly as a consequence of the decision in *Gay Alliance Toward Equality v Vancouver Sun*, 1979 CanLII 225 (SCC).

7. Everyone has the right to life, liberty and security of the person and the right not to be deprived thereof except in accordance with the principles of fundamental justice.

15. (1) Every individual is equal before and under the law and has the right to the equal protection and equal benefit of the law without discrimination and, in particular, without discrimination based on race, national or ethnic origin, colour, religion, sex, age or mental or physical disability.

In *Dore v Barreau du Quebec*[51] the Supreme Court of Canada confirmed that administrative decisions – which include those of the CRA – have to comply with the Charter.

Public policy, charity law, overseas aid and anti-terrorism

An interesting aspect of public policy in relation to charity in this jurisdiction is the singularly generous approach of the State towards donors: a system of tax credits and donor incentives, directly tied into a government programme of specified public benefit services, enables government to channel charitable donations towards its social priorities. Arguably, such government preferencing (of donors and services) gives rise to equity issues for those not favoured.

A charity's activities must be legal and cannot be contrary to public policy.[52] While the case law indicates that charities encountered public policy difficulties at an early stage,[53] probably no single case did more to draw attention to the issues than *Canada Trust Co v Ontario Human Rights Commission*.[54] This concerned a trust established in 1923 for the provision of scholarships, which limited recipients to 'a British Subject of the White Race and of the Christian Religion in its Protestant form' and included a statement that the 'progress of the World depends in the future, as in the past, on the maintenance of the Christian religion'.[55] The management and administration of the fund was also subject to racial and religious restrictions. Such a trust, premised on notions of racism and religious superiority, clearly contravened contemporary public policy imperatives.[56] The court therefore ordered a striking-out of all

---

51 2012 SCC 12 (CanLII), at para 56.
52 See, *Everywoman's Health Centre Society (1988) v Canada (Minister of National Revenue)*, [1991] FCJ 1162 (FCA) and *Scarborough Community Legal Services v The Queen*, [1985] 2 FC 555.
53 See, for example, *Re Drummond Wren* [1945] 4 DLR 674 (restrictive covenant prohibiting the sale of land to 'Jews or persons of objectionable nationality' against public policy) and *Lord's Day Alliance of Canada v Attorney General of British Columbia* [1959] SCR 497 (prohibition on Sunday gambling a valid exercise of the criminal law).
54 (1990), 69 DLR (4th) 321 (ON CA).
55 Ibid., at p. 328.
56 Ibid., at p. 334.

references to and restrictions regarding race, colour, creed or religion, ethnic origin and sex.

The Canadian Charter of Rights and Freedoms, with its s.2 guarantees of freedom of conscience and religion and s.15 guarantee of equality, seemed to inaugerate a new era. As Galligan J commented, '[i]t is now settled that it is against public policy to discriminate on grounds of race or religion'.[57] However, while it is broadly true that purposes that are contrary to public policy are now prohibited,[58] the courts and regulators have equivocated, to some degree, with the principle that a trust in breach of public policy cannot acquire or hope to retain charitable status. For example, in *University of Victoria v British Columbia (A.G.)*,[59] the court upheld a scholarship for practising Roman Catholics, reasoning that a 'scholarship or bursary that simply restricts the class of recipients to members of a particular religious faith does not offend public policy'.[60] Currently there is growing frustration with the archaic legal constraints on the contribution charities may make to matters of public policy in Canada.[61]

• OVERSEAS AID

Over the past decade Canada has consistently been the seventh-largest annual provider of government humanitarian assistance to countries in need; currently this amounts to some $700 million or 0.3 per cent of gross national income.[62]

The CRA has long accepted that organisations engaged in such work are eligible for charitable status. However, its ruling in 2014 requiring Oxfam Canada – which spends about $32 million annually on humanitarian aid in Africa, Asia, and Central and South America – to remove 'preventing poverty' from its declaration of charitable purposes in order to be registered as a charity, is clearly worrying both in its own right and as regards implications for all other similar charities. The Canadian Council for International Co-operation, representing some 70 groups which work to alleviate poverty and defend human rights in other countries, is challenging the CRA on this matter.

---

57 See, *Fox v Fox Estate* (1996), 28 O.R. (3d) 496, 88 O.A.C. 201 (C.A.), per Galligan J at p. 502.
58 *Canadian Magen David Adom for Israel v Canada (MNR)*, (2002) 218 DLR (4th) 718 (FCA) at para 57.
59 [2000] BCJ No 520.
60 Ibid. at para 25, per Maczko J.
61 See, for example, the open letter 'Enhancing the Role of Charities in Public Policy Debates in Canada, Request for a Platform Commitment' (10 February 2015) at: http://voices-voix.ca/en/news/open-letter-enhancing-role-charities-public-policy-debates-canada-request-platform-commitment.
62 See, further, at: http://www.globalhumanitarianassistance.org/countryprofile/canada.

- ANTI-TERRORISM

A human rights concern for Canada, as for all jurisdictions currently being considered, has been the impact of anti-terrorism legislation on the activities of charities – among others.[63] In particular, the Anti-Terrorism Act 2001[64] specifically enacted the Charities Registration (Security Information) Act to suppress and prevent support for terrorism and to protect the integrity of the registration system for charities under the Income Tax Act.

In *International Relief Fund for the Afflicted and Needy (Canada) v Canadian Imperial Bank of Commerce*[65] the plaintiff organisation was deregistered as a charity by the CRA for allegedly supporting or funding Hamas, which Canada designates as a terrorist organisation. Otherwise, in the very few relevant anti-terrorism cases, Charter rights have been consistently held to trump anti-terrorism legislation.[66] The Ontario Superior Court, for example, voided a section of the legislation defining terrorism as a crime committed with religious, ideological or political motives, stating that the definition is 'an essential element that is not only novel in Canadian law, but the impact of which constitutes an infringement of certain fundamental freedoms,' including 'those of religion, thought, belief, opinion, expression and association'.[67]

The legislative and regulatory framework

The jurisdictional split between government at federal and provincial levels affects the legislation and regulatory machinery for this area of law as it does for all others.

Charity law

Instead of a nationwide statutory regime, various provinces have their own definitions of what constitutes a charitable purpose. In practice, however, charities are administered on a nationwide basis by the CRA, utilising the common law conceptual framework within a remit which confines it to applying the Income Tax Act. The Canada Not-for-profit Corporations Act 2009 may also be relevant.[68]

---

63 See, for example, Bill C-36, *An Act to amend the Criminal Code, the Official Secrets Act, the Canada Evidence Act, the Proceeds of Crime (Money Laundering) Act and other Acts, and to Enact Measures Respecting the Registration of Charities, In Order to Combat Terrorism*.
64 See, also, the Anti-Terrorism Act 2015–07–16. For more information on the implications for charities see: http://www.carters.ca/pub/bulletin/charity/2015/atchylb39.pdf.
65 2013 ONSC 4612.
66 See, *Charkaoui v Canada (Citizenship and Immigration)* [2007] 1 SCR 350, 2007 SCC 9; available at http://scc.lexum.umontreal.ca/en/2007/2007scc9/2007scc9.html.
67 *R v Khawaja*, 2005 CanLII 63685 (ON SC) at para 7; available at http://www.theglobeandmail.com/special/audio/Rutherford.pdf.
68 SC 2009, c 23.

- THE CHARITIES REGULATOR: THE CRA

There is no charity-specific regulator. The Charities Directorate of the CRA assumes regulatory responsibility for charities and for determining charitable status, in accordance with s.248(1) of the Income Tax Act,[69] and explains that 'as the Act does not define what is charitable, we look to the common law for both a definition of charity in its legal sense as well as the principles to guide us in applying that definition'.[70] The CRA, assisted by very occasional judicial intervention, provides the only consistent framework for monitoring and guiding the development of Canadian charities.

- ATTORNEY GENERAL

The *parens patriae* authority of the Attorney General to intervene in matters relevant to charities seems has become nominal at federal and province level and is now largely of procedural interest only.[71]

Human rights

This term, as the CRA has explained, refers to those individual rights and freedoms, within their prescribed limitations, set out in:[72]

Canadian law, including:

the Canadian Charter of Rights and Freedoms,
the Canadian Bill of Rights,
the Canadian Human Rights Act,
provincial and territorial human rights legislation; and

International treaties to which Canada is a party that come within the following categories:

United Nations human rights covenants, conventions, and protocols,
International Labour Organisation conventions, and
Geneva conventions and protocols.

Canada signed and ratified the UDHR in 1948[73] together with its two Optional Protocols,[74] and in 1977 the federal parliament passed the Canadian Human

---

69 *Income Tax Act*, RSC 1985 (5th Supp), c.1, s.248 (1).
70 See, Revenue Canada, Information Circular CPS – 022 – *Political Activities*, 2003 at para 4.
71 See, Chan, K., 'The Role of the Attorney General in Charity Proceedings in Canada and in England and Wales', *Canadian Bar Review* Vol 89, 2010, p. 373, at pp. 398–399.
72 See, 'Upholding Human Rights and Charitable Registration Guidance', CG-001, 15 May 2010, at: http://www.cra-arc.gc.ca/chrts-gvng/chrts/plcy/cgd/hmn-rghts-eng.html.
73 The provinces and territories quickly followed with supporting legislation: Saskatchewan (1947), Ontario (1962), Nova Scotia (1963), Alberta (1966), New Brunswick (1967), Prince Edward Island (1968), Newfoundland (1969), British Columbia (1969), Manitoba (1970) and Quebec (1975).
74 The International Covenant on Economic, Social and Cultural Rights and the International Covenant on Civil and Political Rights.

Rights Act.[75] The principles of the UN International Convention on the Elimination of All forms of Racial Discrimination[76] were absorbed into the Canadian Bill of Rights 1960 and subsequently into the Canadian Human Rights Act 1985, which on a federal basis (broadly replicated at province and territory levels) prohibits discrimination on the grounds of national or ethnic origin, colour, race, religion, age, sex, sexual orientation, marital status, family status, disability and conviction for which a pardon has been granted or a record suspended. Canada has also ratified the UN Convention on the Rights of the Child 1990, The Hague Convention on Protection of Children and Co-operation in Respect of Intercountry Adoption 1993, and the Convention on the Rights of Persons with Disabilities 2010, but, along with the US, Australia and New Zealand, has declined to endorse the United Nations Declaration on the Rights of Indigenous Peoples 2005 and has not signed the American Convention on Human Rights. In addition, the Canadian government has introduced a set of regulations – the Federal Contractors Program 1986[77] – and the Employment Equity Act 1996[78] which promotes equity in the workplace of the four designated groups: women, Aboriginal peoples, persons with disabilities, and members of visible minorities.

In this federated jurisdiction, while the primary body of authority for human rights is to be found in the Constitution, these rights derive added protection from province level legislation. The Supreme Court has advised that courts should develop the common law, which remains the basis for determining charitable status in Canada, 'in a manner consistent with the fundamental values enshrined in the Constitution'.[79]

• THE CANADIAN HUMAN RIGHTS COMMISSION (CHRC)

The CHRC, an independent body established at federal level, was created to administer the Canadian Human Rights Act 1977 and subsequently undertook responsibility for ensuring compliance with the Employment Equity Act 1996. It has initiated some important projects.[80] The Canadian Association of Statutory Human Rights Agencies (CASHRA) is the national association of Canada's statutory agencies. It administers federal, provincial and territorial human rights legislation and aims to co-ordinate its member agencies to provide a national voice on human rights issues of common concern.

75 RSC 1985, c. H-6.
76 Opened for signature by the United Nations General Assembly on 21 December 1965 and entered into force on 4 January 1969.
77 Only applies to provincially regulated suppliers (with more than 100 employees bidding on federal contracts of $1,000,000) to the federal government.
78 Only applies to federally regulated organisations.
79 See, *Retail, Wholesale and Department Store Union, Local 580 v Dolphin Delivery Ltd*, [1986] 2 SCR 573, 1986 CanLII 5 (SCC), per McIntyre J at para 39.
80 See, for example, the *Report on Equality Rights of Women* (2014) and further at: http://www.chrc-ccdp.ca/eng/content/publications.

• THE CANADIAN HUMAN RIGHTS TRIBUNAL

This Tribunal was established under the Canadian Human Rights Act 1977. It is independent of the Canadian Human Rights Commission which refers cases to it for adjudication under the Act.

• THE UN REPORTS

Canada's human rights record was subject to UN review in July 2015 for the first time since 2005.[81] The Committee then expressed its concern regarding persisting gender inequalities particularly in relation to the pay gap, which disproportionately affects minority and indigenous women, and to the continued high prevalence of domestic violence which mostly affects such women. It again drew attention to the issue of murdered and missing indigenous women and girls and called for a national inquiry, as recommended by the Committee on the Elimination of Discrimination Against Women. It urged that anti-terrorism legislation should contain adequate legal safeguards to ensure that rights protected under the Covenant are not undermined. It expressed regret that any migrant or asylum seeker designated as an 'irregular arrival' would be subject to mandatory indefinite detention. Interestingly, the Committee also identified as a matter of concern the treatment of non-governmental organisations registered as charities whose activities are considered as political activities when they relate to the promotion of human rights.

Other matters of concern included the following: prison conditions and the disproportionately high rate of incarceration of indigenous people, including women; increased repression of mass protests and the disproportionate number of arrests of participants; the abuse of indigenous land rights and titles; and a general concern about the situation of indigenous peoples and their access to health and social care services. This echoed the earlier reports[82] which had concluded that the condition of Aboriginal people in the country was the most pressing human rights issue facing Canada. A decade later, a follow-up report[83] noted that – in relation to the earlier recorded gap between indigenous and non-indigenous Canadians in health care, housing, education and social services – 'there has been

---

81 See, UN International Covenant on Civil and Political Rights, *Concluding Observations on the Sixth Periodic Report of Canada* at: http://tbinternet.ohchr.org/_layouts/treatybodyexternal/ SessionDetails1.aspx?SessionID=899&Lang=en#sthash.XzzyC1Bz.dpuf. For an analysis, see further at: http://www.carters.ca/pub/update/charity/15/aug15.pdf.
82 See: Fourth Periodic Report (4 October 2004) at: http://docstore.ohchr.org/SelfServices/ FilesHandler.ashx?enc=6QkG1d%2fPPRiCAqhKb7yhskswUHe1nBHTSwwEsgdxQH I6vc94nw71CNYrJ2nvKUH4Wd2NVQnnz2XHUXSaW2TImdtTfP7zV51sd1XBmr %2b%2bF4o9JIM4WU8jU0Yr%2bQQU%2ffPx and Fifth periodic report (27 October 2004) at: http://docstore.ohchr.org/SelfServices/FilesHandler.ashx?enc=6QkG1d%2 fPPRiCAqhKb7yhskswUHe1nBHTSwwEsgdxQHI6vc94nw71CNYrJ2nvKUH4Wd2N VQnnz2XHUXSaW2TImdtTfP7zV51sd1XBmr%2b%2bF4o9JIM4WU8jU0Yr%2bQQ U%2ffPx.
83 At: http://unsr.jamesanaya.org/country-reports/the-situation-of-indigenous-peoples-in-canada.

no change in that gap' and 'it is difficult to reconcile Canada's well-developed legal framework and general prosperity with the human rights problems faced by indigenous peoples in Canada that have reached crisis proportions in many respects'.[84]

The contemporary charity law/human rights interface: a compliance audit

The following study of the charity law/human rights interface uses the UDHR as the most suitable international instrument for examining contemporary law and practice in Canada. Like the other chapters in this section, it concentrates on those cases that involve or have direct relevance for charities.

Access to justice, legal process and principles

The UDHR, Article 10, declares that 'everyone is entitled in full equality to a fair and public hearing by an independent and impartial tribunal, in the determination of his rights and obligations and of any criminal charge against him'. This largely corresponds to provisions in the Canadian Charter of Rights and Freedoms and the Canadian Human Rights Act 1985.

Access to justice

Of the recent government initiatives to address issues associated with access to justice,[85] the implementation of Bill C-21 in 2008 to facilitate the protection of Aboriginal people under the Canadian Human Rights Act was probably the most significant.[86] This is offset by conspicuous failings.

Canada's inability to endorse the United Nations Declaration on the Rights of Indigenous Peoples 2007, for example, clearly disadvantages the Canadian indigenous communities, relative to similar communities in signatory States, and may deprive them of access to significant safeguards. Indeed, many Aboriginal people are simply unaware of the protections guaranteed by the Canadian Human Rights Act, the procedures for filing a complaint, or the remedies that might be available. In this context it is also important to note that promoting, preserving or fostering a particular culture is not considered to be a charitable

---

84 See, also, Canada's Second Report under the UPR 2013 at: http://www.international. gc.ca/genev/mission/UN_Per_Rev_Sec_Rep_Canada_2013-Deux_Rap_Ex_Pol_NU_ Canada_2013.aspx?lang=eng.
85 See, for example, the National Action Committee on Access to Justice in Civil and Family Matters, launched by Canada's Chief Justice in 2008 and, in 2012, the Government of British Columbia launched the BC Justice Reform Initiative.
86 See, further, the Canadian Human Rights Commission Special Report to Parliament on the impacts of Bill C-21 (September 2014) at: http://www.chrc-ccdp.ca/eng/content/ special-report-parliament-impacts-bill-c-21.

purpose in Canada.[87] Confidence in the justice system has not been helped by the long-running scandal of missing and murdered Aboriginal women (including many from Vancouver's Downtown Eastside) who disappeared between 1997 and 2002, which was officially ignored for a decade.[88]

Canada's justice system faces an indictment of a higher order. This lies in the sustained intransigence demonstrated by government in the face of mounting evidence of serious harm perpetrated on children in the context of both the residential schools policy for Aboriginal children and in the historical child abuse practised by members of religious orders. The scale and duration of that systemic abuse – mostly conducted by or under the management of charitable religious orders – has only been addressed in recent years. Given that the residential schools were implementing an enforced assimilation policy from at least the Indian Act 1876[89] and continued to do so for the next century, while records of child sexual abuse by Catholic Church clergy date back to Newfoundland in the 1980s and earlier, the processes of justice have been slow. In terms of the charity law/human rights interface, these are matters that, at the very least, highlight the social cost of not having in place an assertive charity specific regulatory body charged with ensuring that the activities of every entity awarded charitable status do in fact benefit the public.

A failure to positively assert human rights principles was also apparent in *Action by Christians for the Abolition of Torture (ACAT) v The Queen & al.*[90] On the one hand, reassuring evidence of congruity between charity law and human rights was demonstrated when the Federal Court of Appeal then clearly stated: 'it is evident, on its face, that the abolition of torture is an objective that is itself eminently laudable and that an organisation devoted to it is, *prima facie*, a charity'. On the other hand, it is discouraging to note that the organisation was denied charitable status because it was held to have political purposes: by both trying to change the law, particularly in relation to the death penalty, and by engaging in political activity that exceeded the limits allowed by the Income Tax Act.

Due process

In *R v Guindon*[91] the Federal Court of Appeal of Canada was concerned with an appeal from a judgment of the Tax Court of Canada relating to a fraudulent charity donation scheme. The Federal Court held that the Tax Court did not

87 Canada Revenue Agency, *Policy Statement – Applicants Assisting Ethnocultural Communities, No CPS-023* (effective date 30 June 2005), at para 24.
88 Since 2010, the independent Missing Women Commission of Inquiry in British Columbia has been examining this matter and the associated police investigation but, as of May 2015, with little result.
89 Not until 2008 did Parliament amend the Canadian Human Rights Act to give full human rights protection to those subject to the Indian Act.
90 2002 FCA 499.
91 2013 FCA 153 CANLII. An appeal was subsequently dismissed by the Supreme Court of Canada.

have the jurisdiction to take the action it did and had strayed into a constitutional matter without adhering to proper processes. Due process was also a key issue in *International Relief Fund for the Afflicted and Needy (Canada) v Canadian Imperial Bank of Commerce*[92] in which the plaintiff, having been compulsorily deregistered as a charity, was challenging the decision of the Bank to terminate its banking services to the Fund. Having painstakingly reviewed the processes followed by the Bank – and found these to be fair, appropriate and fully explained to the plaintiff – the court dismissed the requested injunction against the Bank.

Proportionality

The importance of this principle was stressed 20 years ago by Lamer CJ, in *Dagenais v Canadian Broadcasting Corporation*:[93]

> When the protected rights of two individuals come into conflict . . . Charter principles require a balance to be achieved that fully respects the importance of both sets of rights.

Shortly afterwards, in *B. (R.) v Children's Aid Society of Met. Toronto*,[94] the court applied the principle to override Jehovah's Witness parents who had refused blood transfusions for which their one-year-old daughter was in urgent need. More recently, the principle was again in play when the Supreme Court of Canada determined a freedom of religion issue in *Alberta v Hutterian Brethren of Wilson Colony*.[95] The case concerned the Alberta government's decision to withdraw an exemption previously available to Hutterites (whose religious beliefs prohibited them from willingly allowing their pictures to be taken) from the requirement that their drivers' licences include photographs. In rejecting the applicants claim, McLachlin CJ acknowledged the perspective of the religious claimants rights but went on to state, 'this perspective must be considered in the context of a multi-cultural, multi-religious society where the duty of state authorities to legislate for the general good inevitably produces conflict with individual beliefs'. This right is one that has since been variously iterated in the human rights legislation of the provinces and it is there that much related case law has recently been generated.[96]

Respect for 'private life'

Article 12 of the UDHR states:

> No one shall be subjected to arbitrary interference with his privacy, family, home or correspondence, nor to attacks upon his honour and reputation.

---

92 2013 ONSC 4612.
93 [1994] 3 SCR 835 at para 31. See, also, *R v Oakes* [1986] 1 SCR 103, per Dickson CJ.
94 [1997] 1 SCR 315.
95 2009 SCC 37, [2009] 2 SCR 567.
96 See, for example, *Syndicat Northcrest v Amselem*, [2004] 2 SCR 551.

Everyone has the right to the protection of the law against such interference or attacks.

There are a range of privacy cases but so far none are known to directly involve charity law or charities in general, although possibly the *Hutterite* case, above, may be seen as being about an unwarranted intrusion into personal privacy. However, many cases impact indirectly and, without doubt, in the future more will do so directly.

Freedom of religion and belief

Article 18 of the UDHR states:[97]

> Everyone has the right to freedom of thought, conscience and religion; this right includes freedom to change his religion or belief, and freedom, either alone or in community with others and in public or private, to manifest his religion or belief in teaching, practice, worship and observance.

This resonates with the broadly similar 'fundamental freedoms' section of the Charter of Rights and Freedoms under the above-mentioned s.2(a). The freedom of religion and belief has thus been locked into the Constitution via the Charter, and s.2(a) of the latter specifically prevents the legislature from discriminating against religious minorities. Section 1 of the Charter qualifies the right proclaimed in s.2 with the provisio that it be exercised subject to such 'reasonable limits prescribed by law as can be demonstrably justified in a free and democratic society'. The right has been examined by the Supreme Court of Canada in *Reference Re Same Sex Marriage*.[98] In rejecting the notion that allowing same-sex couples to marry infringed the religious freedom of those opposed to same-sex marriage, the Court advised that:

> the mere recognition of the equality rights of one group cannot, in itself, constitute a violation of the rights of another. The promotion of the equality rights of one group cannot in itself constitute a violation of the rights of another.[99]

Church and State

In *R. v Big M Drug Mart Ltd* the court declared that:[100]

> whatever else freedom of conscience and religion may mean, it must at the very least mean this: government may not coerce individuals to affirm a

---

97 Also, see, Article 18 of the ICCPR.
98 [2004] 3 SCR 698. See, also, *R. v Big M Drug Mart Ltd* [1985] 1 SCR 295 at paras 94–96 and *Gay Alliance Toward Equality v Vancouver Sun*, 1979 CanLII 225 (SCC), [1979] 2 SCR 435.
99 Ibid., at para 47. See, also, *Loyola High School v Quebec (Attorney General)*, 2015 SCC 12.
100 Op. cit., at p. 362.

specific religious belief or to manifest a specific religious belief or to manifest a specific religious practice for a sectarian purpose.

In Canada, as elsewhere, this sentiment has surfaced in a contentious debate as to where the line should be drawn between government funding of schools and respecting the independence and equality of charitable institutions. The fact that the establishment of denominational schools is permitted in the Constitution Act 1867[101] – and that 'the Canadian Charter, unlike the US Constitution, does not explicitly limit the support the state can give to a religion'[102] – has not prevented dissension.

The decision in *Adler v Ontario*[103] is worthy of note because of the Supreme Court's finding that the provision of State funding for Catholic charitable schools did not violate the human rights principle of freedom of religion nor the equality rights of other religions. However, in *Waldman v Canada*[104] the UNHRC came to the opposite view when it found that the provision in the Ontario Education Act for such funding was a violation of the equality provisions (Article 26) of the ICCPR. Accordingly, the Committee held that public funding should either be withdrawn or also be made available to other minority religious communities. This was reinforced on 5 November 1999, when the UNHRC condemned Canada and Ontario for the violation, and again on 2 November 2005, when it published its Concluding Observations regarding Canada's fifth periodic report and observed that Canada had failed to 'adopt steps in order to eliminate discrimination on the basis of religion in the funding of schools in Ontario'.

The Canadian courts have firmly declared that an indirect subsidy achieved through the conferring of charitable status with associated tax privileges does not constitute an affirmation by the State that one religious view is superior to another.[105] In that context, *Trinity Western University v Nova Scotia Barristers' Society*[106] is interesting because the plaintiff, a private university founded in 1962 by the Evangelical Free Church of America, had (and has) a policy enshrined in its mandatory Community Covenant prohibiting its students from engaging in sexual intimacy outside a traditionally defined marital relationship, a policy to which the respondents, advocating on behalf of the LGBT community, objected.

---

101 The Constitution Act, 1867 (UK), 30 & 31 Victoria, c. 3.
102 See, *S.L., et al. v Commission scolaire des Chênes, et al.* [2012] 1 SCR 235, per Deschamps J at para 27.
103 [1996] SCR 609.
104 Comm No 694/1996.
105 See, *Re Mackay and Manitoba* (1986), 24 DLR 4th 587 (Man CA) and *Edward Books and Article Ltd. et al. v the Queen*, [1986] 2 SCR 713 at 34.
106 2015 NSSC 25. Also, see, *Trinity Western University v The Law Society of Upper Canada*, 2015 ONSC 4250, which dealt with similar facts and came to an opposite conclusion. The TWU chain of case law is still ongoing with inevitable appeals (from both sides) and upcoming legislation in British Columbia. Author acknowledges advice from Carters on this matter (note to author, 28 August 2015).

Cambell J upheld the plaintiff's right to manifest its beliefs in this fashion and admonished the respondents as follows:

> The *Charter* is not a blueprint for moral conformity. Its purpose is to protect the citizen from the power of the state, not to enforce compliance by citizens or private institutions with the moral judgments of the state . . . The refusal to accept the legitimacy of institutions because of a concern about the perception of the state endorsing their religiously informed moral positions would have a chilling effect on the liberty of conscience and freedom of religion.

The courts in Canada, as in the other jurisdictions currently studied, are reluctant to be drawn into Church affairs. This was recently demonstrated in *Diaferia v Elliott*[107] when the court drew the line at reviewing decisions taken by the members; it had 'no intention of getting involved in how the ultimate meeting of the Church members proceeds . . . this court must circumscribe the extent to which it becomes involved in the internal affairs of a religious organisation'.[108] The ruling is in keeping with the approach generally adopted in other common law jurisdictions, though among the lessons to be drawn from the litany of historical child abuse cases involving the clergy is that a more interventionist stance is often warranted.

Definition of 'religion': theism

Religion, as the Supreme Court of Canada explained in *Fletcher v A.G. Alberta*, 'involves matters of faith and worship, and freedom of religion involves freedom in connection with the profession and dissemination of religious faith and the exercise of worship'.[109] However, freedom of 'belief' sits alongside that of religion. As Wilson J declared in the Supreme Court some 30 years ago, 'in a free and democratic society "freedom of conscience and religion" should be broadly construed to extend to conscientiously-held beliefs, whether grounded in religion or in a secular morality'.[110] Nonetheless, the distinction holds when it comes to eligibility for charitable status under the third *Pemsel* head together with the presumption of public benefit.

Definition of 'religion': belief system

The Supreme Court of Canada, in *Syndicat Northcrest v Anselem*,[111] stated that freedom of religion was to be interpreted in a 'broad and expansive' manner and should not be prematurely narrowly construed. Another decision in the same year reinforced this approach. In *Reference Re Same-Sex Marriage*[112] the court

---

107 2013 ONSC 1363.
108 Ibid., per Edwards J at p. 22J.
109 [1969] SCR 383, 1969 CanLII 64 (SCC) at 393.
110 See, *Morgentaler v R* [1988] 1 SCR 30, per Wilson J at para 251.
111 2004 SCC 47, [2004] 2 SCR 551.
112 [2004] 3 SCR 698, 2004 SCC 79.

held that, in the event of a conflict between the freedom of religion and another Charter freedom, the courts should give s.2(a) an expansive interpretation. These and other similar judicial pronouncements have brought the jurisdictions of Canada and England and Wales into closer alignment in terms of construing 'belief systems' for charity law purposes.

In *Blackmore v The Queen*[113] the presenting issue was eligibility for privileged tax treatment under s.143 of the Canadian Income Tax Act, which deals with communal organisations. To be eligible a community had to satisfy all four tests set out in the definition of 'congregation' in the Act. The appellant was the leader of a group called Bountiful which had an established community in British Columbia, was an offshoot of the fundamentalist Latter-day Saints, and practised polygamous marriage. The court held that the community did not meet any of the criteria because it was not a 'religious organisation' as defined in the Act, and its members were too integrated into the community, despite their practise of polygamy.

Equality of religions

Judicial rulings on the equality of religions have a long and consistent history in Canada. In 1955, the Supreme Court of Canada ruled in *Chaput v Romain*,[114] a case concerning Jehovah's Witnesses, that all religions have equal rights. In *R. v Big M. Drug Mart*,[115] Dickson CJ then said that religious freedom in Canada includes 'the right to entertain such religious beliefs as a person chooses, the right to declare religious beliefs openly and without fear of hindrance or reprisal, and the right to manifest religious belief by worship and practice or by teaching and dissemination'.

- SECULARISM (*LAÏCITÉ*)

The Preamble to the Charter of Rights and Freedoms declares 'Canada is founded upon principles that recognize the supremacy of God and the rule of law' and arguably thereby discriminates against all those who are atheists, or hold non-theistic or polytheistic beliefs. Reassurance that they, along with adherents from mainstream and minority religions, would be given equal recognition and protection in law was offered by Cambell J in *Trinity Western University v Nova Scotia Barristers' Society*.[116] Among many other cogent observations, he notes:

> Canada is a 'secular society'.[117] The state remains neutral on matters of religion. It does not favour one religion over another. And it does not favour

---

113 2013 TCC 264 (CanLII).
114 [1955] SCR 834.
115 [1985] 1 SCR 295.
116 2015 NSSC 25. See, also, *R. v Big M. Drug Mart* [1985] 1 SCR 295, per Dickson CJ at p. 354.
117 Ibid., at para 19, citing Taylor, C., *Dilemmas and Connections; Selected Essays*, The Belknap Press of Harvard University Press, Cambridge, MA, 2011, at p. 306.

either religion or the absence of it. While the society may be largely secular, in the sense that religion has lost its hold on social mores and individual conduct for many people, the state is not secular in the sense that it promotes the process of secularisation. It remains neutral.

This approach was re-affirmed by the Supreme Court, in *Loyola High School v Quebec (Attorney General)*,[118] which commented that secularism includes 'respect for religious differences' and that 'through this form of neutrality, the state affirms and recognizes the religious freedom of individuals and their communities'.[119]

The right to manifest religion or belief

In *Trinity Western University v British Columbia College of Teachers*[120] the Supreme Court asserted that 'the freedom to hold beliefs is broader than the freedom to act on them'.[121] When a conflict does erupt – as when demonstrating religious belief infringes the human rights of others – the approach adopted by the judges of the Canadian Supreme Court would essentially seem to be one of accommodation. As the Chief Justice has explained, the courts must then 'carve out a space within the rule of law in which religious commitment and claims to authority – sometimes wholly at odds with legal values and authority – can manifest and flourish'.[122] The Supreme Court in a leading constitutional decision has explained that the obligation to choose the option calculated to cause minimal impairment to the rights of the parties before it does not require the government to employ the least intrusive measures available.[123] 'Rather, it only requires it to demonstrate that the measures employed are the least intrusive, in light of both the legislative objective and the infringed right.'

Parental right regarding religious education of their children

There is no doubt that parents have a constitutionally protected right to raise their children in accordance with their religious beliefs. This was acknowledged in *B(R) v Children's Aid Society of Metropolitan Toronto*[124] where the court referred to a 'protected sphere of parental decision-making which is rooted in the

118 2015 SCC 12.
119 Ibid., at paras 43–44. See, further, at: http://www.carters.ca/pub/seminar/charity/2015/Renderings2015.pdf.
120 [2001] 1 SCR 772. See, also, *Trinity Western University v Nova Scotia Barristers' Society*, op. cit.
121 [2001] 1 SCR 772 at paras 36 and 37.
122 McLachlin, B., 'Freedom of Religion and the Rule of Law: A Canadian Perspective' in Farrow, D. (ed.), *Recognizing Religion in a Secular Society: Essays in Pluralism, Religion, and Public Policy*, McGill-Queen's University Press, Montreal & Kingston, 2004, pp. 12–34, at p. 19.
123 *RJR-McDonald v Canada* [1995] 3 SCR 1999.
124 1 SCR 315.

presumption that parents should make important decisions affecting their children both because parents are more likely to appreciate the best interests of their children and because the State is ill-equipped to make such decisions itself'.[125]

In *S.L., et al. v Commission scolaire des Chênes, et al.*,[126] the Supreme Court of Canada heard an appeal from a decision of the Quebec Court of Appeal concerning whether parents in a public school can exempt their children from participation in Quebec's 'Ethics and Religious Culture' course designed to promote, in a religiously neutral way, the 'understanding of several religious traditions whose influence has been felt and is still felt in our society today'. The question for the Supreme Court was whether the mandatory nature of the course interfered with the freedom of religion of the Catholic parents who requested exemption for their children because its content was considered incompatible with their family beliefs. Deschamps J, while endorsing the desirability of religious neutrality as a policy of the State, dismissed the appeal:[127]

> The suggestion that exposing children to a variety of religious facts in itself infringes their religious freedom or that of their parents amounts to a rejection of the multicultural reality of Canadian society and ignores the Quebec government's obligations with regard to public education.

Freedom of expression

Article 19 of the UDHR states:

> Everyone has the right to freedom of opinion and expression; this right includes freedom to hold opinions without interference and to seek, receive and impart information and ideas through any media and regardless of frontiers.

This is broadly the same as s.2(b) of the 'fundamental freedoms' section of the Charter of Rights and Freedoms. As the Supreme Court of Canada acknowledged in *Native Women's Assn of Canada v Canada*,[128] 'this case does not involve the typical situation of government action restricting or interfering with freedom of expression in the negative sense' and 'the respondents are requesting the Court to consider whether there may be a positive duty on governments to facilitate expression in certain circumstances'. In considering the Association's claim that the government had an obligation to financially support it in constitutional negotiations, as it had supported others, the court took into account that a consequence of the government's actions might be to limit Aboriginal women's free

---

125 Ibid., at p. 319.
126 [2012] 1 SCR 235.
127 Ibid., at para 40.
128 [1994] 3 SCR 627.

speech, but nevertheless government retained the freedom to choose and fund its advisors on matters of policy. While the Supreme Court agreed discussions with the government was 'unquestionably' a form of expression, the government did not seem to be guilty of suppressing any expression, and thus the claim was dismissed.

The decision of the Supreme Court of Canada in *Saskatchewan (Human Rights Commission) v Whatcott*,[129] that some flyers promoted hatred against gays and lesbians, strengthened the hand of the LGBT charities representing their interests, while upholding the limits on free speech intended more generally to shield vulnerable groups from discrimination and violence. The court emphasised the need to pursue true hate speech, not just offensive language.

Alliance for Life v MNR[130] is important because it illustrates the difficult tension between charity law and human rights when it comes to advocacy. Alliance had been a registered charity but CRA was proposing to revoke that status because of its grass roots political activity. It was agreed with CRA that Alliance would set up a nonprofit 'sister' organisation to pursue its political activities. This was done, but Alliance nonetheless was eventually deregistered because it continued to use funds raised by the charity for its political activities. More recently, the tension has been ratcheted up by an ongoing political activities audit launched by CRA into the work of charities such as PEN Canada, the Canadian Centre for Policy Alternatives, Canada Without Poverty, Environmental Defence, and Amnesty International Canada, all of which candidly admit that advocacy lies at the heart of their charitable identity. If their right to freedom of expression were to be further muffled by the 'chilling effect' of CRA surveillance, as it almost certainly will be – if only in terms of the reputational damage associated with being the subject of a public enquiry – it is hard to see the net gain to either the public benefit or human rights in Canada.[131]

Freedom of assembly and association

Article 20 of the UDHR states:

Everyone has the right to freedom of peaceful assembly and association.

This is replicated in the 'fundamental freedoms' section of the Charter of Rights and Freedoms which, under s.2(c), guarantees everyone the freedom of peaceful assembly and, under (d), the freedom of association.

There are no known charity law related cases on the freedom of peaceful assembly, although any imposed restraints are likely to also impact upon

129 [2013] 1 SCR 467.
130 *Alliance for Life v MNR* [1999] 3 FC 504, available at http://decisions.fca-caf.gc.ca/en/1999/a-94-96/a-94-96.html.
131 See, further, http://www.carters.ca/pub/bulletin/charity/2015/chylb361.pdf.

the ability of charities to protest on behalf of the groups whose needs they represent.[132]

The freedom of individuals to form associations is as crucial for charitable activity in Canada as it in all other common law jurisdictions. The corollary is also true: individuals are equally free not to associate.[133] The fact that this jurisdiction has never been as reliant upon the trust form for organising charitable activity as in Ireland and England and Wales has resulted in a correspondingly reduced need for more appropriate corporate structures.

Equality and non-discrimination

Article 2 of the UDHR states:

> Everyone is entitled to all the rights and freedoms set forth in this Declaration, without distinction of any kind, such as race, colour, sex, language, religion, political or other opinion, national or social origin, property, birth or other status.

This is virtually repeated in the Charter of Rights and Freedoms, s.15(1), where it is followed by a 'positive discrimination' caveat:

> (2) Subsection (1) does not preclude any law, program or activity that has as its object the amelioration of conditions of disadvantaged individuals or groups including those that are disadvantaged because of race, national or ethnic origin, colour, religion, sex, age or mental or physical disability.

The Canadian Human Rights Act,[134] the Federal Contractors Program 1986 and the Employment Equity Act 1996 are also relevant, while each of the provinces has its own parallel body of equality and human rights legislation.

Religious discrimination

This was most clearly evident in the above-mentioned *Canada Trust* case[135] when the court found it was 'to expatiate the obvious' that a trust premised on notions of racism and religious superiority was discriminatory and therefore void.

---

132 See, report by Maina Kai, the UN Human Rights Council's Special Rapporteur, on her criticism of Canada for breaches of the freedom of peaceful assembly (21 June 2012). Also, see, *Health Services and Support – Facilities Subsector Bargaining Assn. v British Columbia* [2007] 2 SCR 391.

133 See, *R. v Advance Cutting & Coring Ltd.* [2001] 3 SCR 209, 2001 SCC 70.

134 RSC 1985, c. H-6.

135 See, *Re Canada Trust Co v Ontario (Human Rights Commission)*; *Re Leonard Foundation; Canada Trust Co v Ontario Human Rights Commission* (1990) 69 DLR (4th) 321.

Trinity Western University v British Columbia College of Teachers[136] illustrates the difficulties that arise on the many occasions when religious belief conflates with sex and gender issues. In 1995, Trinity Western University (TWU), a private institution associated with the Evangelical Free Church of Canada, was refused accreditation for its Teacher Training Program by the British Columbia College of Teachers (BCCT) because of a TWU requirement that its students sign a Community Standards Contract signalling their condemnation of homosexual behaviour. TWU complained that this was an infringement of their right to freedom of religion and association. The Supreme Court of Canada explained that the existence of the Community Standards contract, signed by the students, was insufficient to support the conclusion of BCCT that TWU graduates would behave in a discriminatory manner towards future homosexual students and there was no evidence that this in fact had ever occurred. Delivering the majority verdict in favour of TWU, Iacobucci and Bastarache JJ noted that 'for better or worse, tolerance of divergent beliefs is a hallmark of a democratic society'.[137]

The religious exemption

As Cambell J pointed out in *Trinity Western University v Nova Scotia Barristers' Society*,[138] the plaintiff university, 'like churches and other private institutions, . . . does not have to comply with the equality provisions of the Charter'.

When the Civil Marriage Act[139] was introduced, which extended the meaning of marriage to include same-sex relationships under Canadian federal law and inserted s.149.1(6.21) into the Income Tax Act,[140] it provided that charities organised for the advancement of religion would not have their charitable registration revoked solely because they or any of their members exercised freedom of conscience and religion in relation to the meaning of marriage. The Supreme Court of Canada had also ruled to similar effect in *Reference Re Same Sex Marriage*.[141] All of which was in keeping with an established acceptance, clearly evident in testamentary dispositions, that religious beliefs conferred a degree of immunity from the customary non-differentiating application of the law.

Heintz v Christian Horizons[142] was a province-level case that illustrated the implications for practice arising from the religious exemption. Christian Horizons,

---

136 (2001), 39 CHRR D/357. 2001 SCC 31.
137 Ibid., at p. 44.
138 2015 NSSC 25 at para 10. Note that the Charter only applies to federal and provincial governments and matters within the authority of those governments; see s.32 of the Charter. Author acknowledges advice from Carters on this matter (note to author, 28 August 2015).
139 SC 2005, c. 33.
140 RSC 1985, (5th Supp.), c. 1, as amended.
141 [2004] 3 SCR 698.
142 2008 HRTO 22, 2010 ONSC 2105 (Div Ct). See, also, *Ontario Human Rights Commission v Christian Horizons*, 2010 ONSC.

a government-funded charity which provided housing, care and support to some developmentally disabled individuals, required each employee to sign a Statement of Faith and a Lifestyle and Morality Policy. Connie Heintz, a staff member whose same-sex relationship breached that policy and who was forced to resign, alleged that her employment had been terminated because of her sexual orientation. The initial Tribunal finding, endorsed by the Divisional Court, was that because Christian Horizons provided a service to a broader community than Evangelical Christians, and because the general care of the disabled residents did not require religious observance, adherence to the group's religious doctrine and prohibitions against sexual orientation were not a necessary part of the job and the particular constraint imposed on Ms Heintz was unwarranted. In upholding the appeal, however, the Ontario Divisional Court stated that for employers there is an entitlement to exemption from the law barring discriminatory hiring 'if they are primarily engaged in serving the interests of their religious community, where the restriction is reasonable and bona fide because of the nature of the employment'.[143]

Loyola High School v Quebec (Attorney General)[144] now stands as a landmark case for the competing tensions facing religious charities currently operating on the charity law/human rights interface in Canada. The issue was not dissimilar to that which lay at the heart of the above-mentioned *SL v Commission scolaire des Chênes*[145] and resonates also with *Trinity Western University v Nova Scotia Barristers' Society*.[146] It concerned the Quebec government's mandatory core curriculum for high schools, the Program on Ethics and Religious Freedom (ERC). In 2008, the principal of a private Catholic high school in Quebec objected not so much to the ERC – which required schools to teach a range of religious and non-religious ethical systems – but to the accompanying obligation to do so impartially. Approval had been sought and refused to teach the objectives of the ERC from a Catholic rather than a neutral perspective. Ultimately, the Supreme Court of Canada unanimously found the refusal to release Loyola in any way from the requirement of strict neutrality in the teaching of the ERC disproportionately interfered with the religious freedom of the Loyola community. It reasoned that 'requiring Loyola's teachers to take a neutral posture even about Catholicism means that State is telling them how to teach the very religion that animates Loyola's identity', which amounts to 'requiring a Catholic institution to speak about Catholicism in terms defined by the State rather than by its own understanding of Catholicism'.[147] While the court had divided views regarding the secondary issue – that Loyola should adopt an objective stance when teaching about the *ethics* of other religions – the majority held that it was constitutionally sound to require the Catholic school to teach the ethics of other religions in as

---

143 *Ontario Human Rights Commission v Christian Horizons*, 2010 ONSC 2105 (ONSC) at para 52.
144 2015 SCC 12.
145 [2012] 1 SCR 235.
146 2015 NSSC 25.
147 Ibid., at para 63.

neutral a manner as possible. The minority view, which rejected the idea that Loyola must present all religious perspectives as 'equally legitimate and equally credible' and suggested that instead it should be allowed to treat other systems of religious ethics from a Catholic perspective, would seem more consistent with the court's earlier unanimous finding. This decision, with clear implications for other religion-specific schools, underpins the accuracy of Campbell J's observation in *Trinity Western*:[148]

> Equality rights have not jumped the queue to now trump religious freedom. That delineation of rights is still a relevant concept. Religious freedom has not been relegated to a judicial nod to the toleration of cultural eccentricities that don't offend the dominant social consensus.

Discrimination (and exemptions) on other grounds

Article 7 of the UDHR states:

> All are equal before the law and are entitled without any discrimination to equal protection of the law. All are entitled to equal protection against any discrimination in violation of this Declaration and against any incitement to such discrimination.

This right largely finds domestic authority in the provisions of the Canadian Charter of Rights and Freedoms, the Employment Equity Act 1996 and other similar provincial human rights and employment legislation with application to the groups as listed above.

- GENDER DISCRIMINATION

Gender equality is protected under s.15 of the Charter, by the Canada Labour Code 1985 and by CEDAW, which Canada was one of the first countries to sign and ratify. The government is proud of its commitment to gender equality:[149]

> Canada is a world leader in the promotion and protection of women's rights and gender equality. These issues are central to Canada's foreign and domestic policies. Canada is committed to the view that gender equality is not only a human rights issue, but is also an essential component of sustainable development, social justice, peace, and security.

The Supreme Court of Canada has ruled that an onus rests on employers to show that any gender discrimination is justified as a bona fide occupational

---

148 2015 NSSC 25 at para 196.
149 See, further, at: http://www.international.gc.ca/rights-droits/women-femmes/equality-egalite.aspx?lang=eng.

requirement;[150] a refusal of membership in a men's organisation is, rather surprisingly, not a discriminatory denial of services;[151] and an employee disability plan, which denied certain benefits to pregnant employees, discriminated against them.[152]

• RACIAL DISCRIMINATION

Canada became a signatory State to the International Convention on the Elimination of All Forms of Racial Discrimination in 1966. As currently stated in CRA guidance:[153]

> Organisations whose purpose is to educate about, or to promote racial equality can qualify for registration as a charity. Promoting racial equality includes efforts to eliminate racial or ethnic discrimination. It also includes promoting positive race relations by, for example, working to improve relations between any racial and/or ethnic groups in Canada.

So far, no issues on charity law and racial discrimination have come before the Canadian courts.

• SEXUAL DISCRIMINATION

Issues which most frequently tend to cause this right to be breached relate to same-sex marriages, abortion services, and a range of gay,[154] lesbian and transgender[155] lifestyle choices or the consequences thereof,[156] but seldom directly engage non-religious charities or charity law.

• EMPLOYMENT DISCRIMINATION

By far the majority of complaints received by the CHRC and its provincial counterparts concern employment matters.

In 2014, two landmark decisions by the Federal Court of Appeal confirmed that parental childcare obligations fall within the scope and meaning of the

---

150 *British Columbia (Public Service Employee Relations Comm.) v B.C.G.E.U.* (1999), 35 CHRR D/257 (SCC).
151 *Gould v Yukon Order of Pioneers* (1996), 25 CHRR D/87 (SCC).
152 *Brooks v Canada Safeway Ltd.* (1989), 10 CHRR D/6183 (SCC).
153 See, further, at: http://www.cra-arc.gc.ca/chrts-gvng/chrts/plcy/cps/cps-021-eng.html.
154 See, *Egan v Canada* (1995) 2 SCR 513, where a statutory definition of 'spouse' which excluded homosexual partners was deemed to discriminate against a homosexual couple.
155 See, for example, *Vancouver Rape Relief Society v Nixon*, 2005 BCCA 601.
156 See, *P. (S.E.) v P. (D.D.)*, 2005 BCSC 1290, where the British Columbia Supreme Court ruled that the definition of adultery should include affairs between two people of the same gender.

ground 'family status' in the Canadian Human Rights Act. Both *Canada (Attorney General) v Johnstone*[157] and *Canadian National Railway Company v Seeley*[158] concerned female employees whose requests for their work schedules to be adjusted to allow them to care for a family member were refused by their employer. Upholding the employees' discrimination complaints, these rulings reaffirm that employers have an obligation to accommodate their staff when the latter can demonstrate a need to care for a family member, and by broadening the application of human rights law they have the potential to affect millions of Canadian family carers and many associated charities.

- SERVICE PROVISION DISCRIMINATION

The difficulties, uncertainties and extent of litigation generated in regard to discriminatory service provision can be seen in the many lengthy court battles resulting in anti-abortion groups[159] and an anti-pornography group[160] losing their charitable status, largely due to the perceived bias of their materials and activities,[161] while abortion clinics[162] and abortion rights groups have maintained such status. For example, in 1991, the Minister for National Revenue refused to register an abortion clinic, the Everywoman's Health Centre Society, as a valid charity, largely on the grounds that there was no consensus as to whether an abortion clinic met the public benefit test. The Federal Court of Appeal disagreed, holding that the Society was incorporated to provide 'necessary medical services for women for the benefit of the community as a whole', and to 'carry on educational activities incidental to the above'.

More recently, in 2007, the First Nations Child and Family Caring and the Assembly of First Nations filed a human rights complaint against the government of Canada alleging that the federal government discriminates against First Nations children on the basis of their race.[163] It maintained that the federal government underfunds child welfare services on reserves, depriving vulnerable and disadvantaged First Nations children of core benefits that are readily accessible in off-reserve communities: in short, that the federal government's programmes for child welfare services on reserves are inequitable. Evidence in support of such allegations was adduced from the following: Statistics Canada data, which

---

157 2014 FCA 110.
158 2014 FCA 111.
159 E.g., *Human Life International in Canada Inc. v Canada (Minister of National Revenue)* FCJ No 365, 18 March 1998 and *Alliance for Life v Canada (MNR)* 1999 FCJ No 658, 5 May 1999.
160 See, *Positive Action Against Pornography v MNR* [1988] 3 FC 202, 1 CTC 232.
161 See, *Interfaith Development Education Association, Burlington v MNR*, 97 DTC 5424.
162 *Everywoman's Health Centre Society (1988) v Canada (MNR)* [1992] [1992] 2 FC 52, 136 NR 380 (FCA). See, also, *Moore v British Columbia (Ministry of Social Services* (1992), 17 CHRR D/426 (BCCHR).
163 See, The Canadian Human Rights Tribunal on First Nations Child Welfare (Docket: T1340/7708).

shows that almost half (48.1 per cent) of all children in foster care are Aboriginal although they represent only 7 per cent of all children in Canada; the 2008 Auditor General report, which found the on-reserve funding formula did not take into account the disproportionate rate at which First Nations children on reserves are taken into care; and the 2011 Auditor General report, which concluded that the delivery of services to First Nations was limited due to structural impediments in the funding system.

• 'POSITIVE ACTION'

The equality provision in the Canadian Charter of Rights and Freedoms, s.15(1), is subject to the s.15(2) exception that it 'does not preclude any law, program or activity that has as its object the amelioration of conditions of disadvantaged individuals or groups including those that are disadvantaged because of race, national or ethnic origin, colour, religion, sex, age or mental or physical disability'.

In the above-mentioned *Canada Trust* case[164] Justice Tarnopolsky stated that scholarships could be restricted to 'women, aboriginal peoples, the physically or mentally handicapped, or other historically disadvantaged groups', a view subsequently endorsed by the CRA.[165] This view was also endorsed in *Canadian Centre for Torture Victims (Toronto) Inc v Ontario*,[166] which concerned a centre for the assistance of torture victims, the majority of whom were dependent on social assistance, lived in poverty and were mostly refugees. In confirming its charitable status, Lax J considered that the intended purpose was to assist those whose 'poverty is linked to circumstances unique to them as refugees who have been victims of torture, or whose family members have been tortured'.[167]

This approach, representing an acknowledgement by court and regulator that groups defined along such lines may have distinct needs that are most effectively and efficiently addressed by expert organisations permitted to engage exclusively with the target community, has since been adopted in a number of cases.

• CHARITIES AS PUBLIC BODIES

Arguably, the closer the government/charity relationship approximates that of principal/agent,[168] the stronger the presumption that the charity is functioning in law, for all intents and purposes, as a public body.

In *Heintz v Christian Horizons*,[169] for example, Christian Horizons was wholly public-funded and operated almost exclusively as a service provider for government.

---

164 Op. cit. Also, see, *Canadian National Railway Co. v Canada (Human Rights Comm.)* and *Action travail des femmes* (1987), 8 CHRR D/4210 (SCC).
165 Canada Revenue Agency CPS-023 and CPS-024.
166 (1998) 36 OR (3d) 743.
167 Ibid., at para 10.
168 See, *Gay Alliance Toward Equality v Vancouver Sun* 1979 CanLII 225 (SCC), [1979] 2 SCR 435.
169 2008 HRTO 22, 2010 ONSC 2105 (Div Ct).

It nevertheless successfully relied upon the statutory exemption clause to shield its employment practices from the normal requirements of equality and human rights law, despite Ms Heinz being employed in a peripheral role. Some may question the diversion of taxpayers' revenue to subsidise the running costs of a partisan organisation the beliefs of which many taxpayers may prefer not to support.

Conclusion

The present regulatory framework for charity law in Canada and its interface with human rights law demonstrates why other jurisdictions perservered with charity law reform and why those processes concluded with much the same outcomes. There is an obvious need to synthesise these two areas of law. This probably cannot be achieved until a modern governing framework – with designated institutions, appropriate legal functions and co-ordinating processes – is in place. Unless the mechanics are re-engineered to build a more coherent national legal system, it is hard to see how human rights can be wholly integrated with charity law. This is not to imply that the CRA and the CHRC are currently doing a terrible job, just that the present systems are not as helpful as they might be. How else do we explain a spectrum of human rights failings that at one end muffles the advocacy and dissent of eminent charities trying to speak on behalf of the socially disadvantaged and at the other a decades-long inability to address issues of indigenous abuse and neglect that are of international concern?

8   Australia

Introduction

Political volatility in this federated jurisdiction provides a more uncertain context for legislative development than it does in most other common law countries. This fact is well illustrated by the protracted and turbulent gestation of charity law reform but evident also in an equivocating approach towards embedding human rights and to addressing some long-standing related issues.

Beginning with a brief background history of charity law in Australia, this chapter considers the early indicators of a problematic relationship with human rights. It examines the charity law reform process, its implications for human rights and the vulnerability of its substantive legislative outcomes. It outlines the current legislative and regulatory framework with particular reference to the Constitution, the new statutes, the lead regulator and the changed role of the Australian Taxation Office (ATO). As with other chapters in this section, there then follows the core business which applies the template to examine and assess the case law that illustrates the characteristics of the contemporary charity law/human rights interface in Australia.

Background: a history inimical to human rights

The courts in Australia,[1] broadly following the *Pemsel* classification, had come to recognise the following as charitable purposes: the relief of poverty, the relief of the needs of the aged, the relief of sickness or distress, the advancement of religion and the advancement of education. The law continued the public benefit presumption in relation to the first three *Pemsel* heads, and as regards the common law definitional concepts as they were applied in England and Wales before charity law reform (see, further, Chapters 2 and 4).[2]

---

1   See, further, O'Connell, A., 'A Short History of the Taxation of Charities in Australia' in Tiley, J. (ed.), *Studies of the History of Tax Law*, Vol 5, Bloomsbury Publishing, London, 2011.

2   *Navy Health Ltd v DFC of T* 2007 ATC 4568.

Charity law and human rights: the early challenges

The lack of opportunity for judicial consideration of charitable matters, coupled with the natural reluctance of the Australian Tax Office to extend the definition of charitable purpose and thereby undermine the nation's tax revenue base, resulted in the legal interpretation of 'charity' slipping further out of synch with contemporary patterns of social need. As Australia subscribed to a sequence of international treaties, conventions and protocols detailing protection for human rights, this slippage became ever more pronounced.

Legal structures: charitable trusts

Australia, unlike England and Wales, moved away from dependency on trusts as the designated legal structure and instead cultivated the corporate model as the preferred vehicle for charitable activity. There is, however, a growing call for the introduction of new legal structures such as the UK CICs to provide legal structures to facilitate social enterprise.

Constitution

The Australian Constitution came into effect on 1 January 1901. It limits the legislative capacity of the Commonwealth Parliament: neither charity nor human rights are among the 'heads of power' available to Parliament for legislative purposes.[3] While this does not prevent Parliament legislating on some aspects of such matters, it can only do so incidentally.

Exempt charities

The privileges traditionally accorded to religion and religious organisations in Australia have been continued by the Charities Act 2013, excusing them from requirements that now accompany the mandatory registration of all charities. Churches and 'basic religious charities' are exempted from complying with governance standards and from submitting annual financial reports, and the Commissioner has no power to suspend or remove their directors or trustees.

Political purposes

The traditional rule prohibiting charities from advocating change in law or policy[4] as their primary purpose was illustrated in case law such as in *Re Cripps*,[5] when

---

3 Author acknowledges advice from Myles McGregor-Lowndes on this point (note to author, 9 August 2015).
4 See, Taxation Ruling TR 2005/21, at para 111, which declares that 'a purpose of seeking changes to government policy or particular decisions of governmental authorities is also not charitable'.
5 [1941] Tas SR 19.

establishing a trust for the purpose of promoting temperance through the introduction of legislation was denied charitable status for being essentially political. However, in *Re Blyth*,[6] the Queensland Supreme Court ruled that a bequest for 'the elimination of war' was charitable; but not until 2010 did the High Court decision in *Aid/Watch Inc v Federal Commissioner of Taxation*[7] finally make this aspect of charity law compliant with human rights (see, further, below).

Charitable purposes: a tangential relationship with human rights

While generally following English precedents, Australian courts have also at times exercised a creative independence enabling them to find a wide range of purposes – such as the preservation of native fauna and flora,[8] the elimination of war,[9] the Church of Scientology,[10] adopting electronic commerce,[11] and the promotion of a culture of innovation and entrepreneurship[12] – to be charitable.

The relief of the poor, aged and impotent

The interpretation of 'poverty', the class of poor persons, the spectrum of impoverished circumstances and the variety of means by which poverty may be relieved have been very largely dictated by case precedents established in England and Wales. Much the same is true of the interpretation given to 'aged' and 'impotent'.

An interesting initiative, with clear implications for human rights and in marked contrast to current policy, was the decision in *Re Wallace*[13] that a trust to support immigrants arriving in Australia was charitable because, in the words of Hood J, 'a bequest in aid of immigration might probably be for the direct benefit of this community'.[14] This decision was followed in *Re Stone*.[15]

At an early stage, charity law in Australia split to create a unique two-tiered interpretation of charity. *The Perpetual Trustee Co. Ltd. v Federal Commissioner of Taxation*[16] introduced the concept of a public benefit institution (PBI), later entrenched by statute, which it defined as an 'institution organised for the relief of

---

6 [1997] 2 Qd R 567.
7 (2010) 241 CLR 539.
8 *Attorney General (NSW) v Satwell* [1978] 2 NSWLR 200.
9 *Southwood v AG* [1998] 40 LS Gaz R 37.
10 *The Church of the New Faith v The Commissioner of Pay-roll Tax* (Victoria) (1983) 154 CLR 120.
11 *Tasmanian Electronic Commerce Centre Pty Ltd v FC of T* (2005) 142 FCR 371; 2005 ATC 4219; (2005) 59 ATR 10.
12 *FC of T v The Triton Foundation* 2005 ATC 4891 (2005) 60 ATR 451.
13 [1908] VLR 636 (SC).
14 Ibid., at p. 640.
15 (1970) 91 WN (NSW) 704 (SC).
16 [1931] 45 CLR 224, per Starke J at p. 232. See, also, *Public Trustee (NSW) v Federal Commissioner of Taxation* (1934) 51 CLR 75 and *Maughan v Federal Commissioner of Taxation* (1942) 66 CLR 388.

poverty, sickness, destitution or helplessness'. While all PBIs are charities, only a third of the latter qualify as a PBI: all charities are eligible for tax exemption, but a PBI is also eligible for a tax donation deduction. PBI status requires evidence that an entity's charitable purposes include a commitment to directly relieve such 'poverty, sickness, destitution or helplessness', the prioritising of which has endorsed a very traditional and conservative supplicant/benefactor dynamic as an appropriate interpretation of contemporary philanthropy in Australia. This focus on 'relieving' categories of the 'poor' or otherwise disadvantaged is restated in the Charities Act 2013, s.7, and while it clearly functions to prioritise the chanelling of funds from donor and government towards those in greatest need, it is open to criticism: it would seem to foreclose a strategic approach aimed at structural and embedded causes of social deprivation; it provides a means of narrowing the charity definition of 'poverty' to symptom relief rather than prevention; it suggests that a reliance on charity rather than on legal rights might be appropriate and sufficient; it targets donor discretion and funds towards addressing the government social policy agenda rather than promoting 'choirs, advocacy or advancing religion etc';[17] and for recipients it may be more condescending and patronising than empowering.

This approach has, however, been adjusted by the recent decision in *Commissioner of Taxation v Hunger Project*[18] which found that the 'direct' requirement insisted upon by the ATO for many decades is unnecessary. Hunger Project was part of a global network of organisations collaborating to work towards a sustainable end to world hunger. Within that network, the chief function of Hunger Project in Australia was to conduct fundraising and to pass the proceeds to other network members in developing countries to use for hunger relief programmes that directly provided relief.[19] While its charitable status was not challenged by the ATO, the latter contended that because Hunger Project Australia's predominant activity was fundraising, it did not directly provide relief from hunger and therefore could not be a PBI, but ultimately the court ruled otherwise. While the implications of this important decision have yet to be fully explored,[20] the basic distinguishing characteristics of a PBI would seem to be retained.[21]

---

17 *Mines Rescue Board of New South Wales v Commissioner of Taxation* (Cth) (2000) 44 ATR 107 at p. 30. Also, see, *Perpetual Trustee Co Ltd v FC of T* op. cit., per Evatt J who described the recipients of charity as:

> Those who receive aid or comfort in this way are the poor, the sick, the aged, and the young. Their disability or distress arouses pity, and the institutions are designed to give them protection.

18 [2014] FCAFC 69 (13 June 2014).
19 Following the rationale in *Commissioner of Taxation v Word Investments* (2008) 236 CLR 204.
20 But see, Murray, I. and Martin, F., 'The Blossoming of Public Benevolent Institutions: From Direct Providers to Global Networks', University of Western Australia, Faculty of Law Research Paper No 2015–1.
21 See, ACNC, Commissioner's Interpretation Statement: The Hunger Project case, at: https://www.acnc.gov.au/ACNC/Pblctns/Interp/ACNC/Publications/Interp_HungerProject.aspx.

The advancement of education

The courts have tended to construe the word 'education' widely, and when interpreting what constitutes the advancement of education they have closely followed English precedents. As in that jurisdiction, education can accommodate what might be viewed as more elitist accomplishments such as the following: the bequest for 'the Litchfield Award for Literature';[22] 'to encourage the performance of orchestral compositions and concert works';[23] for the best composition of a song cycle from a 'Viennese or Austrian' composer;[24] for the publication of works by the testatrix on the poet Henry Kendall;[25] and to fund annual portrait painting competitions.[26] Similarly, gifts to establish museums and art galleries,[27] public libraries and observatories[28] have been upheld as charitable.

The lacuna permitting 'charitable' to be interpreted as allowing preference to be given to members – of a class of beneficiaries – who are related to the donor is evident in Australian charity law.[29] It also accommodates discriminatory gifts to, for example, those of a particular religion, to a specific Law Society library,[30] for women lawyers in Victoria[31] and for workers in a particular industry.[32] Where recreation or amateur sport can be linked to an educational purpose, as in 'fostering the sport of Rugby Union in Sydney University'[33] or, most tenuously, providing a rose garden named after the testatrix in the grounds of a specific university,[34] then it is eligible for charitable status.

The advancement of religion

The Charities Act 2013 simply encoded in statute the long-established definition of this charitable purpose. While to be charitable, the organisation or gift must 'advance' religion, in practice once the entity concerned was recognised as religious by the ATO, then it was presumed to be charitable; this continues to be the case. In making both determinations – that the entity is religious and is advancing religion – the ATO, and now the Australian Charities and Not-for-Profit

---

22 *Re Litchfield* (1961) 2 FLR 454. Subject to the caveat that 'under no circumstances may any award be given for writings which glorify the sordid, ugly, vulgar under-world types'.
23 *Canterbury Orchestra Trust v Smitham* [1978] 1 NZLR 787.
24 *Re Lowin (deceased)* [1967] 2 NSWLR 140.
25 *Re Hamilton-Grey* (1938) 38 SR (NSW) 262.
26 *Perpetual Trustee Co Ltd v Groth* (1985) 2 NSWLR 278.
27 *Public Trustee v Nolan* (1943) 43 SR (NSW) 169 and *Re Gwylim (deceased)* [1952] VLR 282.
28 *Attorney-General v Marchant* (1866) LR 3 E 424 and *Incorporated Council of Law Reporting (Qld) v Federal Commissioner of Taxation* (1971) 125 CLR 659.
29 *White v Principal and Councillors of St Andrew's College* (1886) 17 LR (NSW) (Eq) 40.
30 *Re Mason (deceased)* [1971] NZLR 714.
31 *Victorian Women Lawyers' Association Inc v Commissioner of Taxation* [2008] FCA.
32 *Attorney-General (NSW) v Perpetual Trustee Co Ltd* (1940) 63 CLR 209.
33 *Kearins v Kearins* [1957] SR (NSW) 286.
34 *McGrath v Cohen* [1978] 1 NSWLR 621.

Commission (ACNC) – have relied heavily on case precedents established in England and Wales.

This has been particularly noticeable with regard to the principle of a testator's right to make a bequest subject to an overtly discriminatory religious condition.[35] So the bequest to sons, conditional upon their wives converting to Protestantism, in *Trustees of Church Property of the Diocese of Newcastle v Ebbeck*[36] was valid in itself, and the court declared the general validity of testato – marriage, such as preventing marriage to a person of a particular religious denomination, race, ethnicity or class, have also been upheld.[37]

There are, however, some notable jurisdictional differences. For example, the approach to 'closed' religious orders is different. Initially the courts seemed persuaded by the ruling in *Gilmore v Coats*,[38] but by 1967, in *Assoc. of Franciscan Order of Friars Minor v City of Kew*[39] and thereafter, *Coats* was rejected, and ever since charitable status has been awarded to such religious entities[40] as now endorsed by the Charities Act 2013. Again, and in keeping with the principle that public benefit can be derived from the practice of intercessory prayer, masses for the dead – even if said in private and for the donor – were found to be charitable in Australia though not in England and Wales.[41]

Beneficial to the community, not falling under any of the preceding heads

In this jurisdiction, gifts 'for the benefit of the community' have long been recognised as a general heading for other purposes, deemed charitable on the grounds of being within the 'spirit and intendment' of the Preamble but not fitting under any other *Pemsel* head.

As in similar jurisdictions, the Australian regulatory approach towards entities claiming charitable status within this category has tended to be generous, many being hospitals and various health and social care services such as 'a maternity home to be available to young women who have erred for the first time'.[42] Mostly, charitable status for such public utility infrastructure is justified on the basis that the discretionary provision of that which government would otherwise have to fund 'lessens the burden on government' and reduces taxes.[43] On the

35 See, for example, *Omari v Omari* [2012] ACTSC 33. See, further, Butt, 'Testamentary Conditions in Restraint of Religion', (1977) 8 *Sydney LR* 400.
36 (1960) 104 CLR 394; [1961] ALR 339.
37 *Seidler v Schallhofer* [1982] 2 NSWLR 80.
38 [1949] AC 426 (HL).
39 (1967) VR 732.
40 *Council of the Municipality of Canterbury v Moslem Alawy Society Limited* (1987) 162 CLR 145 and *Crowther v Brophy* [1992] 2 VR 97, 100.
41 *Nelan v Downes* (1917) 23 CLR 546, 571.
42 *Re Wyld* [1912] SALR 190.
43 *Monds v Stackhouse* (1948) 77 CLR 232.

other hand, the granting of charitable status to environment conservation entities is very much in keeping with a modern human rights rationale; though this has proved politically contentious (see further below).[44]

The fact that services are provided on a for-profit basis,[45] are accessible only by fee payment,[46] or otherwise produce a benefit to members,[47] has never been a bar to charitable status, even if politically contentious – e.g. for the promotion of a Jewish settlement in Israel.[48] This was acknowledged in *Commissioner of Taxation (Cth) v Word Investments Ltd*[49] where the majority emphasised that the existence of a goal of profit, as a relevant purpose, does not exclude a characterisation of an institution as charitable. The inclusive approach also produced some contentious interpretations of 'charity' including gifts: in favour of those who may be quite prosperous because 'an organisation may be beneficial to the community without delivering a *community service*';[50] establishing a telecommunications infrastructure;[51] promoting football for the benefit of the communities within the state;[52] the promotion of a culture of entrepreneurship for the benefit of Australian society;[53] 'to promote the interests of the Keren Kayemeth Limited';[54] and the promotion of a global grain exporting business with an approximate $15 billion annual turnover.[55]

There are areas in which the potential effectiveness of charities under this head have been constrained. Until rectified by the Charities Act 2013, a group belonging to a minority culture forming an organisation to preserve and promote its cultural heritage was likely to be regarded as essentially social and of insufficient benefit to the community;[56] self-help groups were found not to have the necessary

44 *Australian Conservation Foundation Inc v Commissioner of State Revenue* [2002] VCAT 1491.
45 *Commissioner of Taxation (Cth) v Word Investments Ltd* [2008] HCA 55; (2008) 236 CLR 204.
46 *Taylor v Taylor* (1910) 10 CLR 218; *Re Chamber of Commerce and Industry of Western Australia (Inc) and Commissioner of State Revenue* [2012] WASAT 146.
47 *Federal Commissioner of Taxation v Co-Operative Bulk Handling Ltd* [2010] FCAFC 155; (2010) 189 FCR 322.
48 *Re Stone (deceased)* (1970) 91 WN (NSW) 704.
49 Op. cit., at p. 24.
50 *Victorian Women Lawyers' Association v Commissioner of Taxation* [2008] FCA 983; (2008) 170 FCR 318.
51 *Tasmanian Electronic Commerce Centre Pty Ltd v Commissioner of Taxation* [2005] FCA 439; (2005) 142 FCR 371.
52 *Northern NSW Football Ltd v Chief Commissioner of State Revenue* [2009] NSWADT 113.
53 *Federal Commissioner of Taxation v Triton Foundation* [2005] FCA 1319; (2005) 147 FCR 362
54 *Re Stone* (1970) 91 NSWWN 704.
55 *Grain Growers Ltd v Chief Commissioner of State Revenue (NSW)* Supreme Court of New South Wales, 14 July 2015.
56 See, for example, *Attorney-General (NSW) v Cahill* [1969] 1 NSWR 85 and *Latvian Co-operative Society v Commissioner of Land Taxes (Vic)* (1989) 20 ATR 3641.

'public' element, or their activity or facility was construed as being essentially for member benefit,[57] or was too vague or imprecise.[58] A discretionary gift can be charitable even if open to abuse, as in one to the Worshipful Master for the time being of a masonic lodge for the purposes of paying for the advancement, preferment and benefit of a boy selected by him leaving the Masonic Baulkham Hills School for Boys for the purpose of setting up in life, by either furthering the said boy's education or putting him into some trade or profession, preference being given to a boy who was a son of a member or past member of the said lodge.[59]

The indigeous people

The legal fiction of *terra nullius* permitted the wholesale transfer of English law to Australia without the necessity for any concession to indigenous law, custom or practice.[60] Charity and the associated law – as legislatively derived from the 1601 Act, developed by judicial precedent and applied by the regulatory body – formed part of that transfer. Then, as now, it had little relevance for the most deprived people in Australia.

The fact of their deprived circumstances has attracted judicial attention. As Gyles J commented in *Trustees of the Indigenous Barrister's Trust: The Mum Shirl Fund v FC of T*:[61]

> In my opinion, the undisputed evidence leads to a finding that, at the time the Trust was settled, and for the foreseeable future, many, indeed most, indigenous persons in Australia could properly be described as 'disadvantaged'.

This charity law case marks an important milestone in the development of the law relating to indigenous people. It endorsed existing judicial notice of the fact that they are per se within the definition of 'necessitous circumstances'[62] but went a significant step further to construe activity, intended to provide more strategic leverage, as being worthy of charitable status. This rationale represented a synergy between charity law and human rights that is clearly

---

57 See, *In re Income Tax Acts (No 1)* [1930] VLR 211.
58 The ATO relies on the decision in *Inland Revenue Commissioners v Baddeley* [1955] 1 All ER 525.
59 *Perpetual Trustee Co Ltd v Ferguson* (1951) 51 SRNSW 256 (cited by Poirier, D., *Charity Law in New Zealand*, at p. 267, see, further: https://www.charities.govt.nz/assets/Uploads/Resources/Charity-Law-in-New-Zealand.pdf).
60 Not until the decision in *Mabo v Queensland (No 2)* [1992] HCA 23; (1992) 175 CLR was the doctrine finally overruled.
61 (2002) ATC 5055. Citing in support: *Re Mathew* [1951] VLR 226 at 232; *Re Bryning* [1976] VR 100 at 101–102; *Aboriginal Hostels Ltd v Darwin City Council* (1985) 75 FLR 197 at 211–212; and others. See, also, *Northern Land Council v Commissioner of State Taxes* [2002] NTCA 11, where the Council, which acted as a representative body for Indigenous People, was held to be a PBI.
62 *Re Bryning (deceased)* [1976] VR 100.

transferable not just to other indigenous communities in other countries but, arguably, to all minority groups that share the same status of 'necessitous circumstances'. Nonetheless, the charity law framework – with its established restrictions that prevent groups and communities bound by a 'blood-link' from satisfying the public benefit test – continuously failed to adequately address the needs of indigenous people.

Public benefit: civil society, charity and the State

The early, substantial and sustained leadership in basic public benefit service provision offered by religious charities – mainly emanations of the Catholic and Anglican churches – enabled the sector to achieve a partnership with government on such matters that is possibly unique in the common law world. Government has consequently largely confined its role to funding the delivery of public benefit services by charities and allowed civil society entities to evolve in their wake.

This policy has been facilitated by the deliberate blurring of government/ charity responsibilities, as can be seen in the many cases that have come before the Australian courts in relation to bodies such as ambulance, fire brigade and mine rescue authorities.[63] By introducing the concept of PBI, and manipulating related tax concessions and donation incentives, the government injected real support to charities and targeted the most socially disadvantaged. In replicating the English Recreational Charities Act 1958, the government in some states extended tax exemption to a wide range of 'civil society' type organisations, thereby generating healthy civic interaction and new sources of support in local communities. However, until a strategy is found and followed that allows the indigenous people and all other Australians to share resources and living standards more equitably, a coherent civil society will remain unattainable.

Partnership

The transition from a Liberal to a Labor government in 2007 saw a transition also in government/sector relations. Among the steps taken by the incoming government to demonstrate its commitment to building a new working relationship with the sector was that of issuing the Productivity Commission in 2009, with terms of reference requiring it to examine how government could engage the sector efficiently and effectively in providing public benefit services, and to assess the related regulatory framework. This was followed by the Henry tax review, by a private bill, and by the Economics Legislation Committee report into the Tax Laws Amendment (Public Benefit Test) Bill 2010.

---

63 *Metropolitan Fire Brigade Board v The Commissioner of Taxation* (1990) 27 FCR 279; *Mines Rescue Board (NSW) v The Commissioner of Taxation* (2000) 101 FCR 91; *Ambulance Service of New South Wales v Deputy the Commissioner of Taxation* (2003) 130 FCR 477.

Charity law reform and human rights: towards alignment

The pace, outcomes and durability of charity law reform in Australia have been, and continue to be, dictated by domestic party politics. The need to include a human rights dimension, however, has never been seriously challenged.

The charity law reform process

This process has lurched through many phases over a great many years.[64] An early foray concluded with the Australian Industry Commission Report, *Charitable Organisations in Australia*, 1995, which was shelved by the government without legislative outcome nor any recommendations being implemented. The last and seemingly wholly successful endeavour wound to a close in 2013 with the legislative introduction of a comprehensive programme of substantive change – but it remains to be seen whether this will survive in the currently volatile Australian political climate.

The process

The Inquiry into the Definition of Charities and Related Organisations was launched in September 2000 amid much political rhetoric regarding the need to strengthen regulatory processes, update common law concepts and improve sector capacity. The submission of a report in 2001[65] led to the drafting of a Charities Bill, withdrawn in May 2004 and triggering the collapse of this reform process, leaving behind only the bare remnants to be salvaged by the 2004 Act.[66] Revived in 2009, the reform process saw government and sector thoroughly engaged in a new and meaningful phase of sustained negotiations that concluded on 27 June 2013 with a set of formative statutes.

Jurisdiction-specific outcomes

The Charities Act 2013 (Cth), now defines and extends the *Pemsel* charitable purposes and encodes in statute the existing common law concepts and rules; this includes some adjustment to the public benefit presumption. It also includes the statement in the Explanatory Memorandum that the 'common law . . . will . . . remain relevant for the purposes of interpreting those principles, concepts and terms that have been derived from the common law and utilised in the statutory definition'.[67]

---

64 There have been at least five major reviews in the past 20 years.
65 See, Sheppard, I., Fitzgerald, R. and Gonski, D., *Inquiry into the Definition of Charities and Related Organizations*, CanPrint Communications Pty Ltd, Canberra, 2001.
66 The Extension of Charitable Purpose Act 2004 did no more than extend the *Pemsel* list to include child care, self-help groups, and contemplative religious orders.
67 Explanatory Memorandum, Charities Act 2013 (Cth) 10 at 1.19.

• INCREASED REGULATORY MEASURES

The new regime is headed by the ACNC, displacing the ATO as lead regulator, and is now statutorily charged with registering and regulating not-for-profit
entities (initially charities eligible for federal tax concessions) and maintaining a
related register. The registration of charities is dependent upon the new statutory
definition of 'charity' to be found in the Charities Act 2013 and the Charities
(Consequential Amendments and Transitional Provisions) Act 2013.

• RECASTING PUBLIC BENEFIT

The Charities Act 2013, s.6(1), effects little change; it mainly encodes the existing common law. A purpose is held to be for the public benefit if (a) the achievement of the purpose would be of public benefit and (b) the purpose is directed
to a benefit that is available to the members of (i) the general public or (ii) a
sufficient section of the general public. Section 7 declares that the following are
presumed to be for the public benefit, unless there is evidence to the contrary:
preventing and relieving sickness, disease or human suffering; advancing education; relieving the poverty, distress or disadvantage of individuals or families; caring for and supporting the aged or people with disabilities; and the purpose of
advancing religion. In relation to open and non-discriminatory self-help groups,
and closed or contemplative religious orders that regularly undertake prayerful
intervention at the request of members of the public, the Charities Act 2013,
s.10, explicitly states that the public benefit test is to have no application. In relation to indigenous people only, s.9 makes an important change by directing that
where a purpose – which applies to native title or to traditional rights of ownership, occupation, use or enjoyment of land – would be for the public benefit if
it were not for the relationships between the indigenous individuals to whose
benefit the purpose is being applied, then this will not prevent that purpose from
being charitable.

Section 6(2)(b) includes a new caveat which warns that in determining public
benefit, consideration must be given to any possible detrimental consequence
that may arise.

• POLITICAL PURPOSES

The Charities Act 2013, s.11, endorsed a recent important change in established
law. It includes a note declaring that 'a purpose of promoting or opposing a
change to any matter established by law, policy or practice in the Commonwealth, a State, a Territory or another country may be a charitable purpose'.[68]
The 'change' is confined to any matter that falls within the definition of charitable

68 The inclusion of this provision was necessitated by the decision in *AID/WATCH Incorporated v Commissioner of Taxation* [2009] FCAFC 128.

purpose in s.12(1), whether in Australia or overseas. It has already generated contention in respect of the many registered charities – such as Friends of the Earth – that include campaigning for environmental causes among their purposes, leading to political confrontations with the fossil fuel extraction industry.[69]

- *PEMSEL* PLUS CHARITABLE PURPOSES

The categories of charitable purposes are now as stated in the Charities Act 2013, s.12(1): advancing health; advancing education; advancing social or public welfare; advancing religion; advancing culture; promoting reconciliation, mutual respect and tolerance between groups of individuals that are in Australia; promoting or protecting human rights; advancing the security or safety of Australia or the Australian public; preventing or relieving the suffering of animals; advancing the natural environment; any other purpose beneficial to the general public that may reasonably be regarded as analogous to, or within the spirit of, the above purposes; and promoting or opposing a change to law, policy or practice as defined above.

- STATUTORY ENCODING OF KEY COMMON LAW CONCEPTS

The conceptual elements long held to constitute the definition of charity are now encoded in the new legislation.

Charity law and human rights purposes

Specific statutory recognition for the promotion of human rights as a charitable purpose is provided in the free-standing purpose of 'promoting or protecting human rights' by the Charities Act 2013, s.12(1)(g). Section 3 states that 'human rights has the meaning given by the Human Rights (Parliamentary Scrutiny) Act 2011' (see, below).

Considering the torturous process that culminated in the above statutory list of charitable purposes, it is noticeable that it excludes any that specifically address matters of concern to the UN (see, further, below).

Charity law and human rights: a contemporary framework for continuing dissonance

There is considerable slippage in the fit between charity law and human rights in this jurisdiction.

---

69 On 26 March 2015, the House of Representatives Standing Committee on the Environment adopted an inquiry, referred by the Minister for the Environment, asking the Committee to inquire into and report on the Register of Environmental Organisations.

Constitution, public policy and human rights

The Constitution does not contain a 'bill of rights'; in fact, Australia has the singular distinction of being the only modern democratic country without such protection,[70] but it does provide, directly or implicitly, for certain rights and freedoms. For present purposes, the most relevant of these are s.116, freedom of religion, and s.117, freedom from non-discrimination.

Public policy, charity law, overseas aid and anti-terrorism

The Charities Act 2013, s.11, specifically identifies the following as a 'disqualifying purpose' and incompatible with charitable status: '(a) the purpose of engaging in, or promoting, activities that are unlawful or contrary to public policy; or (b) the purpose of promoting or opposing a political party or a candidate for political office'. It adds that 'activities are not contrary to public policy merely because they are contrary to government policy'.

Immigration has long played a prominent role in Australian public policy. It has included the transporting of many thousands, perhaps hundreds of thousands of children, by charties such as Barnardos, from the UK and Ireland to welcoming new homes in Australia[71] and elsewhere throughout the latter half of the 19th and the first half of the 20th centuries. An inverted form of this policy would seem to have been introduced by the Migration Amendment Act 1992 which provides for the mandatory detention of all persons entering the country without a valid visa. This has resulted in many thousands of people, including children, being held indefinitely[72] in facilities on the Australian mainland or on designated islands (the 'Pacific Solution' policy which began in 2012), with consequent numerous and repeated breaches of the Convention on the Rights of the Child.[73] The contemporary response of charity to this issue would seem to be politically constrained by the clause in the Charities Act 2013 restricting the remit of a purpose to 'in Australia' or the 'Australian public', which may exclude 'asylum seekers' from being the subject of a charitable purpose.[74]

The general common law rule, that to have or retain charitable status an entity must not breach public policy, was stretched to a considerable degree by Santow J in *Public Trustee v Attorney General of New South Wales*[75] where he expressed

---

70 See, further, Saunders, C., 'The Australian Constitution and our Rights', *Future Justice*, 2010, at pp. 117–135.

71 See, Bean and Melville, *Lost Children of the Empire*, Unwin Hyman, London, 1989.

72 As of May 2014, a total of 8,521 people, including 1,731 children, were in detention centres.

73 See, the HREOC *National Inquiry into Children in Immigration Detention*, April 2004, at: http://www.humanrights.gov.au/publications/commission-website-national-inquiry-children-immigration-detention-115; also, see, *Al-Kateb v Godwin* (2004) 219 CLR 562.

74 See, Field, O., *By Invitation Only: Australian Asylum Policy*, Human Rights Watch, 2002.

75 (1997) 42 NSWLR 600.

the view that 'persuasion directed to political change is part and parcel of a democratic society in which ideas and agendas compete for attention and allegiance'.[76] Noting that some states in Australia had not legislated to remove racial discrimination, he ruled that a trust which had such removal as an object could nevertheless be charitable. Santow J distinguished between trusts that were 'contrary to the established policy of the law' and trusts whose object is to 'introduce new law consistent with the way the law is tending'. This ruling pushes back the boundary at which trusts risk being denied such status due to a breach of public policy.

- OVERSEAS AID

Australia's record of making significant annual contributions to overseas aid has a current focus on the Indo-Pacific region. The government is committed to the implementation of the Millennium Development Goals, and its major political parties agreed to a target allocation of 0.5 per cent of gross national income to official development assistance by 2015. The stated purpose of its aid programme is 'to promote Australia's national interests by contributing to sustainable economic growth and poverty reduction'. The congruity with human rights is evidenced not just in the poverty reduction aim but also in the declared intention to invest in matters such as 'gender equality and empowering women and girls'.[77] At the launch of the Australian Charities 2013 Report (the 'Curtin Report'), the ACNC Commissioner noted that it revealed 17 per cent of registered charities are involved overseas – through directly operating in another country, or by helping people outside Australia – and that they operate in more than 100 countries.[78]

- ANTI-TERRORISM

The Australian Anti-Terrorism Act 2005 (revised), intended to hamper the activities of any potential terrorists, includes measures – such as anti-money laundering and financing provisions, banning of organisations and criminalisation of membership of certain associations aiming to control suspect nonprofit organisations – that necessarily also impact upon charities. The 2015 meeting of the Financial Action Task Force (FATF) considered the different roles of government and nonprofit organisations in protecting the sector from terrorist financing abuse and ways to mitigate the terrorist financing risks faced by NPOs delivering services in the field.[79] The freedoms of association and expression, crucial to the work of charities, are consequently open to potential abuse by government and

76 Ibid., at p. 621.
77 See, further, at: http://dfat.gov.au/aid/Pages/australias-aid-program.aspx.
78 See, further, at: http://www.probonoaustralia.com.au/news/2014/10/regulator-watch-funds-overseas-aid-charities#.
79 See, FATF and APG 'Anti-money laundering and counter-terrorist financing measures – Australia', 2015. See, further, at: http://www.fatf-gafi.org/documents/news/npo-consultation-march-.

regulators in Australia. The ACNC Commissioner, on the occasion of the launch of the above-mentioned Curtin Report, drew attention to the 'need to reduce the risk of misuse of funds sent overseas, including through charities'.

The legislative and regulatory framework

Establishing a framework of federal legislation that accommodates both human rights and charity law, with the latter extended to include all nonprofit entities, constitutes a singular and significant achievement for this jurisdiction.

Charity law

The federal legal framework for determining charitable status and for regulating charities now consists of the following: the Charities Act 2013 and the Charities (Consequential Amendments and Transitional Provisions) Act 2013; the common law definitions, concepts, rules and case precedents largely continue in effect; the Income Tax Assessment Act 1997[80] (as amended) continues to apply to charities and all other nonprofits; as do sundry specialised legislation, such as the Corporations Act 2001 or a state equivalent. However, the Charities Act 2013 applies only to the Commonwealth not to the states.[81]

The Charities Act 2013, s.5, declares that 'an entity is a charity if it satisfies the following criteria: it is not-for-profit; it has all charitable purposes (other than ancillary or incidental purposes that further or aid the charitable purpose) that are for the public benefit; it does not have disqualifying purposes; and it is not an individual, a political party or a government entity'.

- THE CHARITIES REGULATOR: ACNC

This new national regulator, which commenced on 2 December 2012,[82] now bears responsibility for regulating all charities wishing to avail of federal tax exemptions, and in due course intends to extend its remit to the entire Australian nonprofit sector.

- ATTORNEY GENERAL

In each state and territory this official exercises the traditional *parens patriae* role in relation to charitable trusts but the role is devoid of any regulatory functions. This is partly due to the fact that the bulk of charitable activity is undertaken not through trusts but by corporate entities, and therefore falls outside the *parens patriae* jurisdiction.

80 In conjunction with the Tax Laws Amendment (2005 Measures No 3) Act 2005.
81 Author acknowledges advice from Myles McGregor-Lowndes on this point (note to author, 9 August 2015).
82 See, further at the ACNC website: http://www.acnc.gov.au/.

• THE ATO

The determination of charitable status and eligibility for tax exemption rested with the ATO until December 2012. Having transferred that role to the ACNC, the Australian Taxation Office retains responsibility for determining eligibility for income tax exemption and associated concessions (Tax Concession Charity status) and Deductible Gift Recipient status (DGR).

Human rights

The Human Rights (Parliamentary Scrutiny) Act 2011, s.3(1), states that 'human rights' means the rights and freedoms recognised or declared by the following: the International Convention on the Elimination of All Forms of Racial Discrimination 1965;[83] the International Covenant on Economic, Social and Cultural Rights 1966;[84] the International Covenant on Civil and Political Rights 1966;[85] the Convention on the Elimination of All Forms of Discrimination Against Women 1979;[86] the Convention Against Torture and Other Cruel, Inhuman or Degrading Treatment or Punishment 1984;[87] the Convention on the Rights of the Child 1989;[88] and the Convention on the Rights of Persons with Disabilities 2006.[89] Australia is a party to all the above.

This jurisdiction has neither a formal bill of rights nor as extensive a human rights legislative base as can be found in most European countries. It has yet to ratify the Optional Protocol Against Torture, but in 2009 it became a signatory nation to the UN Declaration of the Rights of Indigenous People 2007. The Constitution is unable to ensure rights to equality and non-discrimination:[90] since it was enacted in 1975, for example, the Racial Discrimination Act has been modified three times. There is only limited legislative protection of human rights at a federal level and this is largely confined to broad protections against discrimination. The individual states and territories each have their own corresponding equality and anti-descrimination legislation.

However, Australia does have a human rights commission at federal and at state levels. Further, the Human Rights Framework in 2010 led to the Human Rights (Parliamentary Scrutiny) Act 2011 (Cth) which took effect on 4 January 2012 and requires all new legislation introduced to the federal parliament to be assessed for compatibility with human rights. It also established a new

---

83 [1975] ATS 40.
84 [1976] ATS 5.
85 [1980] ATS 23.
86 [1983] ATS 9.
87 [1989] ATS 21.
88 [1991] ATS 4.
89 [2008] ATS 12.
90 See, further, See, Williams, G., *Human Rights under the Australian Constitution*, Melbourne, Oxford University Press, 1999.

parliamentary joint committee on human rights and a National Action Plan for implementing related commitments was launched in 2012.

At Commonwealth level, the Fair Work Act 2009 (Cth) extends the specific legal protection previously given to religious non-discrimination in the workplace.

- THE AUSTRALIAN HUMAN RIGHTS COMMISSION (AHRC)

Established under the Human Rights and Equal Opportunity Commission Act 1986 (Cth), and previously known as the Human Rights and Equal Opportunity Commission, this is a national independent statutory body with responsibility for investigating matters protected by Australia's anti-discrimination legislation.[91] These include 'discrimination on the grounds of age, race, colour, or ethnic origin, racial vilification, sex, sexual harassment, sexual orientation, gender identity, intersex status, marital or relationship status, actual or potential pregnancy, breastfeeding or disability'.

The Australian Council of Human Rights Authorities[92] is the body that provides a unified voice for all Commonwealth, State and Territory anti-discrimination and human rights agencies. The AHRC issues annual reports, on behalf of the Australian Council of Human Rights Authorities, giving an account of progress made towards meeting concerns recorded at the last UPR.

In addition, a National Children's Commissioner (2013) and a Race Discrimination Commissioner (2014) have been appointed.

- THE UN REPORTS

In 2009, the UNHR Committee reported its concern that 'the rights to equality and non-discrimination are not comprehensively protected in Australia in federal law'.[93] The unacceptable level of disadvantage experienced by Aboriginal and Torres Strait Islander peoples has been a consistent theme: although constituting only 2.3 per cent of the adult population, they represent over a quarter of the adult prison population and are currently imprisoned at a rate which is over 11 times higher than for non-indigenous people (as at 30 June 2013); their life expectancy is 18–19 years less and the death rate from diabetes is about eight times the national rate.[94] At the last UPR, many countries called upon Australia to ensure the full and effective implementation of the UN Declaration on the

91 See, *Brandy v HREOC* (1995) 183 CLR 245 which held that HREOC was constitutionally barred from exercising any judicial power.
92 See, the Australian Council of Human Rights Authorities, *Australia's Universal Periodic Review, 2013 Progress Report*, December 2013 at: http://www.uprinfo.org/sites/default/files/document/australia/session_10__january_2011/ahrc_upr_progress_report_2013.pdf.
93 See, UNHR Committee, Concluding Observations: Australia (2009) at para 12.5.
94 See, 'Close the Gap' campaign for Indigenous health equality and the National Aboriginal and Torres Strait Islander Health Plan 2013–2023 (2014).

Rights of Indigenous Peoples, and there was strong lobbying for a commitment to amend the Australian Constitution so as to provide specific recognition for Aboriginal and Torres Strait Islander people.[95] Concern was also expressed about such matters as the following: the treatment of asylum seekers; the high level of violence against women;[96] the rights of people with disability;[97] the need for greater promotion and protection of the rights of people who are lesbian, gay, bisexual, trans, gender diverse and intersex (LGBTI); and the use of enforced sterilisation procedures.[98]

In May 2011, the UN High Commissioner[99] urged 'a fundamental rethink of the measures being taken under the Northern Territory Emergency Response' and called upon Australia to intensify efforts to reduce the life expectancy gap between indigenous and non-indigenous Australians and increase the commitment to reducing socio-economic inequalities. In June 2012, Australia appeared before the UN Committee on the Rights of the Child but, as yet, has not responded to the Committee's Concluding Observations. In August 2013, the UN's Human Rights Committee found 150 breaches of the International Covenant of Civil and Political Rights in the government's treatment of 46 asylum seekers, which 'cumulatively inflict[ed] serious psychological harm'.[100]

The contemporary charity law/human rights interface: a compliance audit

The UDHR provides the basic international benchmarks for the following scrutiny of the current charity law/human rights interface in Australia.

Access to justice, legal process and principles

For charities engaging with the disadvantaged, meaning mainly those with PBI status, the existence of a readily accessible framework of human rights – within which charities can pursue their public benefit mission – is clearly crucial.

---

95 See, the Aboriginal and Torres Strait Islander Peoples Recognition Act 2013 which is a step towards their constitutional recognition.
96 See, the first *Progress Report to the Council of Australian Governments 2010–2012* on the National Plan to Reduce Violence against Women and their Children (2013).
97 See, the subsequent National Disability Strategy 2010–2020 as formally endorsed by the Council of Australian Governments (2011).
98 See, further, Australian Human Rights Commission, *The Involuntary or Coerced Sterilisation of People with Disabilities in Australia* (2012), at: http://www.humanrights.gov.au/submissions/involuntary-or-coerced- sterilisation-people-disabilities-australia.
99 See, statement by the United Nations High Commissioner for Human Rights, Navi Pillay, Canberra, 25 May 2011.
100 See, further, at: http://www.ohchr.org/EN/NewsEvents/Pages/DisplayNews.aspx?NewsID=13648&LangID=E.

Access to justice

In terms of the interface between charity and human rights, the 'stolen generations' scandal is a significant milestone. This was a process which, beginning with the Aboriginals Ordinance 1918 (NT) and officially ending at least in New South Wales in 1967, mandated the removal of some 30,000 Aboriginal children from their parents for adoption with white families. While this was a government policy, enforced directly by official agencies which denied Aboriginal access to the courts, its implementation depended greatly on the role of church missions and other religious charitable bodies to arrange the adoption placements.[101]

More recently, the systemic abuse of children by clergy has been a matter of grave concern. Religion and charitable status would seem to have screened the extent of such abuse from public awareness, and may account also for the delay in launching official enquiries and for the prolonged failure of the legal system to bring justice for victims and perpetrators.[102] The Royal Commission into Institutional Responses to Child Sexual Abuse, for example, noted in July 2015 that Jehovah's Witnesses (with approx 70,000 Australian members) had failed to report any of its 1,006 alleged offenders over six decades of recorded child abuse.[103]

Finally, the Commission's 2014 report, *Equal Before the Law*, has expressed concern about access to justice in the criminal justice system for people with disabilities.[104]

Due process

The policy of enforced sterilisation procedures clearly constitutes an abuse of due process and the criminalisation of same-sex relationships in some parts of Australia may also do so.

---

101 See, the Human Rights and Equal Opportunity Commission, *Bringing Them Home: A Guide to the Findings and Recommendations of the National Inquiry into the Separation of Aboriginal and Torres Strait Islander Children from their Families*, Australian Government Publishing Service, 1997. On 13 February 2008, Prime Minister Kevin Rudd delivered an official apology on behalf of the Parliament of Australia to those affected by the Stolen Generations policy.

102 For example, only in 2012 did the Cummins Inquiry identify concerns regarding the handling of criminal child abuse in religious organisations in Victoria, which then prompted the government to set up a joint investigatory Family and Community Development Committee.

103 See, further, at: http://www.childabuseroyalcommission.gov.au/media-centre/media-releases/2015–07/public-hearing-into-the-jehovah's-witnesses.

104 See, further, at: https://www.humanrights.gov.au/sites/default/files/document/publication/2014_Equal_Before_the_Law.pdf.

Proportionality

As of 31 October 2014, 3,084 asylum seekers were being detained in Australia, with a further 2,151 held in offshore processing centres.[105] The 'warehousing' of refugees, currently including some 800 children, for periods that can extend to years, on the Pacific states of Nauru and Papua New Guinea as part of the 'Pacific Solution' is open to many criticisms, including that of being a disproportionate response, and was the subject of a 2015 report by the Human Rights Commissioner.[106]

Also disproportionate was the treatment of the plaintiff in *Coleman v Power*[107] who had been convicted for giving a public address on a 'political matter' in a pedestrian mall without a permit. The Human Rights Committee found that, given the lack of any evidence that the plaintiff's conduct had been unduly disruptive, his arrest, conviction and sentence were disproportionate and constituted a violation of Article 19 of the ICCPR.[108]

Respect for 'private life'

The right not to be subjected to arbitrary interference with privacy, family, home or correspondence, nor to attacks upon honour and reputation, is protected by Article 12 of the UDHR.

The ruling in *Alice Springs Town Council v Mpwetryerre Aboriginal Corp, et al*[109] would seem wholly compliant with this right. The court then held that in providing town camps for the large population of transient Aboriginal persons and families, the associations were fulfilling a charitable purpose. Further, they also fulfilled a charitable purpose in relation to the permanent dwellers in the camps, because such persons were neither nomadic nor urban but were culturally disadvantaged, and the associations represented their method of determining their own cultural development. In stark contrast, a UN Special Rapporteur reported in 2010 that the Emergency Response policy was discriminatory and breached the human rights of Aboriginal people in the Northern Territory.[110]

---

105 Department of Immigration and Border Protection, *Immigration Detention and Community Statistics Summary 31 October 2014* (2014), at: http://www.immi.gov.au/About/Documents/detention/immigration-detention-statistics-oct2014.pdf.
106 See, the Human Rights Commission, *The Forgotten Children: National Inquiry into Immigration Detention 2014*, at: https://www.humanrights.gov.au/our-work/asylum-seekers-and-refugees/publications/forgotten-children-national-inquiry-children.
107 (2004) 209 ALR 182.
108 UN Doc CCPR/C/87/D/1157/2003, (2006) 14 IHRR 49, IHRL 1582 (UNHRC 2006), 17 July 2006, Human Rights Committee (UNHRC).
109 (1997) 115 NTR 25. See, also, *Aboriginal Hostels Ltd v Darwin City Council* (1985) 55 LGRA 414 and *Tangentyere Council Inc v Commissioner of Taxes* (1990) 99 FLR 363.
110 Anaya, J., *Observations on the Northern Territory Emergency Response in Australia* (February 2010).

The methods then employed by the federal government to address alleged rampant child abuse in some Aboriginal communities required exemption from the Racial Discrimination Act 1975 and breached the principles of the UN Declaration on Indigenous Peoples. This heavy-handed intervention, involving the use of the police and army, resonated for many with the 'stolen generations' debacle and represented a State intrusion on culture, a limitation on 'individual autonomy',[111] and was at odds with the charitable purpose of 'advancing culture' newly introduced by the Charities Act 2013, s.12(1).

Freedom of religion and belief

Mason ACJ and Brennan J asserted in *Church of the New Faith* that 'freedom of religion, the paradigm freedom of conscience, is of the essence of a free society' and stressed that the protection of s.116 extends to those without religious belief and can accommodate all nascent minority religions that may yet emerge.[112] It is also guaranteed by Article 18 of the UDHR.

Among the retrospective objections to the Aboriginals Ordinance 1918 (authorising the forcible 'removal of Aboriginal and half-caste children from their communities') was the argument that in so doing it breached their right to the free exercise of religion under s.116 of the Constitution, but patently not an argument advanced to any avail on their behalf at the relevant time.[113]

Church and State

The protections relating to religion are as stated in s.116:

> The Commonwealth shall not make any law for establishing any religion, or for imposing any religious observance, or for prohibiting the free exercise of any religion, and no religious test shall be required as a qualification for any office or public trust under the Commonwealth.

The High Court of Australia has advised that the only laws invalidated under the Establishment Clause are those which entrench 'a religion as a feature of and identified with the body politic', 'constitute a particular religion or religious body as a State religion or State church' or require 'statutory recognition of a religion as a national institution'. Moreover, its constitutional protection applies only to the Commonwealth not to the states. It has not impeded the parliamentary standing orders from requiring a full recitation of the Lord's Prayer by the Speaker of the House of Representatives and the President of the Senate at the commencement of each day's business.

---

111 See, further, at: http://www.abc.net.au/worldtoday/content/2010/s2828921.htm.
112 *Church of New Faith v Commissioner of Pay-Roll Tax* (1983) 154 CLR 120.
113 See, *Kruger v Commonwealth*, op. cit., per Gaudron J. Note the provision made in the 2013 Act for an Aboriginal Association.

Definition of 'religion': theism

The Charities Act 2013 offers no definition of religion, no reference to the need or otherwise for a god or gods, and makes no reference to non-religious forms of belief. The High Court of Australia in *The Church of the New Faith v Commissioner of Pay-roll Tax*[114] considered whether a particular set of beliefs and practices would constitute a religion, with Mason ACJ and Brennan J suggesting that:[115]

> for the purposes of law, the criteria of religion are twofold: first, belief in a supernatural Being, Thing or Principle; and second, the acceptance of canons of conduct in order to give effect to that belief, though canons of conduct which offend against the ordinary laws are outside the area of any immunity, privilege or right conferred on the grounds of religion.

They took the view that the weight to be placed upon tenets and doctrines was a matter of no great importance.[116]

This approach was evident more recently in *OV and OW*,[117] a charity law case that is significant from many perspectives including for its exploration of what constitutes a religion. The Wesley Mission had sought to rely upon the 'fundamental Biblical teaching that "monogamous heterosexual partnership within marriage" is both the "norm and ideal"', but the Tribunal (NSWADT) found, given the diversity of views across Christendom on this issue, that 'it does not follow, and nor is it asserted, that that belief can properly be described as a doctrine of the Christian religion'. The Court of Appeal held that the search for such a doctrine and the need to establish its conformity or otherwise with the act or practice of the Mission, was 'misguided'[118] and referred the issue back to the Tribunal. In reconsidering the matter, the NSWADT took the view that 'doctrine' was broad enough to encompass not just formal doctrinal pronouncements such as the Nicene Creed, but effectively whatever was commonly taught or advocated by a body, including moral as well as religious principles, in a contemporary timeframe rather than as traditionally prescribed. Much the same approach was adopted by Hampel J in another charity law case – *Cobaw Community Health Services Limited v Christian Youth Camps Limited & Anor*.[119] Having heard expert evidence from theologians on the meaning of 'doctrines of religion', and the interpretation that should be given to 'conforms with the doctrines of the religion', she found that the plenary inspiration (the words of the Bible must be

---

114 [1983] HCA 40; (1983) 154 CLR 120 (27 October 1983) at p. 137.
115 Ibid., at p. 74.
116 Ibid., at p. 126.
117 *OV v QZ (No 2)* [2008] NSWADT 115; *Member of the Board of the Wesley Mission Council v OV and OW (No 2)* [2009] NSWADTAP 57; *OV & OW v Members of the Board of the Wesley Mission Council* [2010] NSWCA 155.
118 Ibid., at para 40.
119 [2010] VCAT 1613 (8 October 2010).

believed and acted upon) is a doctrine of the Christian religion. However, as the evidence showed no reference to marriage, sexual relationships or homosexuality, in the creeds or declarations of faith adhered to by members of the Christian Brethren, she held that their beliefs about these matters could not be construed as 'doctrines of the religion'. The judicial finding included the observation that not everything in the Scriptures amounts to 'doctrine'; the prevailing cultural beliefs at the time must also be taken into account.[120]

It remains the case that where the purpose of an organisation is to work against already established religions, or against the idea of religion, this cannot itself be a religious purpose and hence the organisation cannot be a charity.[121]

Definition of 'religion': belief system

In *Church of the New Faith* the court considered whether the doctrines and beliefs of Scientology could be construed as meeting the definition of religion, thereby enabling the organisation to claim charitable status. Although unable to agree on what might constitute such a definition, there was consensus that it should extend to philosophies which 'seek to explain, in terms of a broader reality, the existence of the universe, the meaning of human life and human destiny'.[122]

For human rights purposes, it is worthy of note that charity law reform failed to produce provisions designed to recognise and accommodate the dreamtime rites that constitute the religious beliefs of indigenous people – despite judicial notice having earlier been taken of that fact: 'the Aboriginal people of the Northern Territory, or at least some of them, had beliefs or practices which are properly classified as a religion'.[123]

Equality of religions

That the courts are not in a position to assess the validity of any religion, or to differentiate between them, was established by the High Court of Australia in *Church of the New Faith*.[124] Shortly after, in *Canterbury Municipal Council v Moslem Alawy Society Ltd*,[125] McHugh JA added: 'the preservation of religious equality has always been a matter of fundamental concern to the people of Australia and finds its place in the Constitution, s.116'.

The issue of government funding for faith-based charities has generated controversy in the context of education. In *Attorney-General (Vic) (Ex rel Black) v Commonwealth*,[126] the plaintiffs (Defence of Government Schools' organisation)

---

120 Also, see, *Ananda Marga Pracaraka Samgha Ltd v Tomar (No 6)* [2013] FCA 284.
121 *Re Jones* [1907] SALR 1990 (Incorporated Body of Freethinkers of Australia).
122 *Church of New Faith v Commissioner of Pay-Roll Tax* (1983) 1 VR 97, at para 13.
123 *Kruger v Commonwealth* (1997) 190 CLR 1, per Gaudron J.
124 (1983) 154 CLR 120.
125 (1985) 1 NSWLR 525.
126 (1981) 146 CLR 559. Also known as the State Aid or Defence of Government Schools (DOGS) case.

sought a court order declaring that State funding of Church schools breached the Constitution. The court rejected the plaintiff's petition and ruled that s.116 of the Constitution does not prevent the 'giving of aid to or encouragement of religion' and therefore could not prevent the government from providing financial assistance to schools operated by religious organisations on the same basis as that assistance was provided to other private schools. Indeed, the ruling permits the preferential treatment of one religion over another, providing this falls short of the establishment of religion.

There has been a long-running controversy regarding the appointment of chaplains to the armed forces which require that the prospective appointee be 'a member of a church or faith group approved by the Religious Advisory Committee to the services'. This, clearly being a 'religious test', has triggered debate as to whether it can be s.116 compliant. So, for example, as in *Kruger v Commonwealth*,[127] the question arose as to whether non-Christians or atheists, caught between the Regulations and s.116, are thus unfairly treated.

• SECULARISM

Similar controversy attended *Williams v the Commonwealth of Australia*[128] which concerned the National School Chaplaincy Program, introduced in 2007, and uses federal money to fund school chaplaincy services to nearly 3,000 schools across Australia. Debate focused on the provision of a service that is religious (almost exclusively Christian) and which is paid for by taxpayers, some of whom are atheists, agnostics or belong to non-Christian religions, and many of whom argue that schools should be strictly secular. Mr Williams's claim that he had a right to secure a secular education for his children was rejected by the High Court.

The right to manifest religion or belief

This right is protected by Article 18 of the UDHR[129] and by Article 18(1) of the ICCPR, as ratified by Australia in 1980. Also relevant is the Declaration on the Elimination of All Forms of Intolerance and of Discrimination Based on Religion or Belief,[130] which elaborates upon the right in Article 18 of the ICCPR to 'manifest' one's religion. It is also protected by the Australian Constitution. Latham CJ, in *Adelaide Company of Jehovah's Witnesses Inc v Commonwealth*,[131] was clear

127 (1997) 190 CLR 1, 161.
128 [2012] HCA 23. See, further at: http://www.hcourt.gov.au/cases/case-s307/2010.
129 See, the Human Rights and Equal Opportunity Commission, *Article 18*, report of an inquiry into freedom of religion and belief in Australia, 1998, at: https://www.humanrights.gov.au/sites/default/files/content/pdf/human_rights/religion/article_18_religious_freedom.pdf.
130 GA Res 36/55, UN GAOR, 36th sess, UN Doc A/36/684 (25 November 1981).
131 (1943) 67 CLR 116, 124.

that the protection afforded by s.116 extended beyond beliefs to include manifestations of such beliefs, as were Mason ACJ and Brennan J in *Church of the New
Faith v Commissioner of Pay-roll Tax (Vict).*[132]

The Australian courts have, on a number of occasions, found a disconnect
between the beliefs of a religious organisation and the means by which it chooses
to manifest those beliefs. So, the following are among the activities found insufficient to warrant charitable status: a 'Catholic daily newspaper';[133] the 'formation and advancement of a Catholic Boys' Club';[134] and camping activities.[135]
Conflicts between the right to religious freedom and the right to freedom of
speech are not uncommon.[136] In *Catch the Fire Ministries Inc v Islamic Council
of Victoria Inc*[137] the Victorian Court of Appeal considered whether the conduct of the charity Catch the Fire Ministries contravened s.8 of the Racial and
Religious Tolerance Act 2001 (Vic). The conduct concerned statements made
at a seminar in 2002, in a newsletter in 2001 and in an article on their website
in 2001 that included the following: the Koran promotes violence and killing;
the Koran teaches that women are of little value; Allah is not merciful; that Muslims practising Jihad are following the Koran; and a number of other similar
statements. The ruling that there had been no incitement to hatred of Muslims
because of their Islamic faith is in keeping with the generous latitude traditionally
allowed to proselytising religious entities in charity law.[138]

Parental right regarding religious education of their children

Article 26(3) of the UDHR provides that 'parents have a prior right to choose
the kind of education that shall be given to their children'.

The lack of any firm constitutional separation of Church and State (due, perhaps, to the fact that Australia is not a republic) allows private religious schools
to flourish and to receive government support at federal and state level, such
funding being deemed constitutionally compliant in the 1981 *Defence of Government Schools* case because it is intended for educational rather than religious
purposes.[139] This does not fit very well with the rejection of the plaintiff's claim

132 (1983) 154 CLR 120, 135.
133 *Roman Catholic Archbishop of Melbourne v Lawlor* (1934) 51 CLR 1.
134 *Attorney-General v Cahill* [1969] 1 NSWR 85.
135 *Cobaw Community Health Services Limited v Christian Youth Camps Limited & Ano*
     [2010] VCAT 1613.
136 See, for example: *Fletcher v Salvation Army Australia (Anti Discrimination)* [2005]
     VCAT 1523 (1 August 2005); *Bropho v Human Rights and Equal Opportunity Commission*
     [2004] FCAFC 16; *Judeh v Jewish National Fund of Australia Inc* [2003] VCAT 1254;
     and *John Fairfax Publications Pty Ltd v Kazak* [2002] NSWADTAP 35.
137 [2006] VSCA 284 3751.
138 See, further, Parkinson, P., 'Enforcing Tolerance: Vilification Laws and Religious Freedom
     in Australia', 2005, at: http://sydneyanglicans.net/blogs/indepth/enforcing_tolerance_
     patrick_parkinson.
139 *Attorney-General (vic) (Ex rel Black) v Commonwealth* (1981) 146 CLR 559.

in *Williams v the Commonwealth of Australia*[140] that he had a right to secure a secular education for his children.

Freedom of expression

Article 19 of the UDHR and Articles 19 and 20 of the ICCPR assert the right to freedom of opinion and expression. While not expressly protected by the Australian Constitution, the High Court of Australia has found freedom of expression to be an implied constitutional right, so far as public and political discussion are concerned (arguably, not quite the same thing as freedom of speech),[141] and it is specifically protected in state legislation. In *Australian Capital Television Pty Ltd v The Commonwealth*[142] the High Court decided that a right to freedom of political communication was essential to the system of representative government provided for in the Constitution and noted that the proposed new part IIID of the Broadcasting Act would severely hinder groups such as charities which may wish to make political statements. Although not an absolute right, it cannot be legislatively restricted without good cause.

That the Constitution carries an implied right of political communication was reinforced in *Coleman v Power*[143] (see, also, above) where the conduct of the plaintiff was both plainly 'political' and a legitimate exercise of freedom of expression which could not to be curtailed by State powers except in extenuating circumstances. This, and other associated rulings, prepared the ground for the *AidWatch* controversy which was ultimately responsible for the change introduced by the Charities Act 2013, s.11, to the traditional charity law prohibition on charities engaging in political activities. The controversy began with the ATO decision to revoke the 12-year-old charitable status of AidWatch, an organisation which it conceded had wholly charitable objectives except for three deemed political: urging the Government to put pressure on the Burmese regime; delivering an ironic 60th anniversary birthday cake to the World Bank; and raising concerns about developmental impacts of the US–Australia Free Trade Agreement. It ended with the High Court decision reinstating charitable status – accompanied by the judicial admonishment that 'in Australia there is no general doctrine which excludes from charitable purposes *political objects*'[144] – thereby setting charity law in this jurisdiction on a different course to that established in England and Wales.

That course was not without its problems. In 2015, a parliamentary inquiry into environmental organisations registered as charities triggered protest from

---

140 [2012] HCA 23. See, further at: http://www.hcourt.gov.au/cases/case-s307/2010.
141 *Unions NSW v New South Wales* [2013] HCA 58. Also, see, *Nationwide News Pty Ltd v Wills* (1992) 177 CLR 1.
142 (1992) 177 CLR 106.
143 (2004) 209 ALR 182. See, also, *Mulholland v Australian Electoral Commission* (2004) 209 ALR 582 and *Lange v Australian Broadcasting Corporation* (1997) 189 CLR 520.
144 *AID/WATCH Incorporated v Commissioner of Taxation* [2009] FCAFC 128, per Kiefel J.

244 *Contemporary law, policy and practice*

advocacy bodies, such as Friends of the Earth, alleging that the government's intention seemed to be to deregister more than 100 environment groups because of their outspoken opposition to fossil fuel development in Australia.[145]

Freedom of assembly and association

Article 20(1) of the UDHR proclaims the right of everyone to freedom of peaceful assembly and association, as do Articles 21 and 22 of the ICCPR, subject to certain broadly stated restrictions. The Fair Work Act 2009 protects freedom of association in the workplace. This right is as crucial to the forming of charitable organisations and their activities in Australia as it is elsewhere. Interestingly, not only is there no general right to freedom of association and assembly in Australian law, but many laws, such as anti-terrorism legislation (see, above), impose specific restrictions.

The fact that the Charities Act, s.12(1)(f) and (g), expressly accommodates the purpose of promoting reconciliation, mutual respect and tolerance between groups of individuals in Australia and the purpose of promoting or protecting human rights, respectively, offers a much increased assurance of future compatibility between charity law and human rights on contemporary associational issues. This new approach was demonstrated in *Kostka v the Ukranian Council of New South Wales Incorp*[146] when Young AJ was prepared to find that:

> In 21st century New South Wales a trust in favour of a group of women of a particular ethnicity, who seek more than mere recreation and social intercourse but also to assist people of the same ethnic group and spread that culture to further the community purposes of a group of Australians of a certain ethnic origin, is a charitable gift.

The principle is one that clearly extends to Aboriginal communities.

Equality and non-discrimination

Article 14 of the UDHR provides for the right not to suffer discrimination and is supported by Articles 2 and 26 of the ICCPR which assert rights of equality and non-discrimination. The AHRC has statutory responsibility for investigating any alleged breach of such rights, including discrimination on the grounds of age, race, colour, or ethnic origin, racial vilification, sex, sexual harassment, sexual orientation, gender identity, intersex status, marital or relationship status, actual or potential pregnancy, breastfeeding or disability.

---

145 Author acknowledges advice from Myles McGregor-Lowndes on this matter (note to author, 22 July 2015). See, further, at: http://www.abc.net.au/news/2015–04–10/environment-groups-could-lose-tax-concession-status/6384554.
146 [2013] NSWSC 222, at paras 44–45.

In 2011, the Human Rights Law Centre noted that Australia has a number of laws that address discrimination and viewed this piecemeal protection of the right to non-discrimination as deficient because the laws are reactive and complaints-based, fail to actively promote equality or address systemic discrimination, do not address all grounds of discrimination or intersectional discrimination (e.g. sexual orientation, gender identity, religion or social status) and are ineffective in areas that have been granted permanent exemptions. Comprehensive federal legislation that consolidates Commonwealth equality and anti-discrimination laws would seem to be a pressing necessity.[147]

Religious discrimination

Article 7 of the UDHR grants an entitlement to protection against any discrimination and against any incitement to such discrimination, while Articles 2(1) and 26 of the ICCPR protect the right not to be discriminated against on the basis of religion. In general, such discrimination is usually prohibited with respect to employment, the provision of goods and services, accommodation, education, membership of clubs and participation in sporting activity, and provision of government services.

In its report on Article 18, the Human Rights and Equal Opportunity Commission recommended that the Commonwealth Parliament enact religious freedom legislation which would (i) recognise and give effect to freedom of religion and belief in Australia, and (ii) make unlawful direct and indirect discrimination on the ground of religion and belief in areas of public life. It also recommended that 'religion and belief' should be broadly defined, to encompass theistic, non-theistic and other beliefs, including the traditional belief systems of indigenous people.[148] The Human Rights and Anti-Discrimination Bill 2012, currently suspended, promised to address these matters and provide a consolidated body of federal anti-discrimination provisions.

Both the above-mentioned *OV and OW*[149] and *Cobaw Community Health Services Limited v Christian Youth Camps Limited & Anor*[150] were cases that centred on alleged religious discrimination by charities. The first concerned the right of the Wesley Mission to withhold services, by not accepting an application to place a child in the foster care of a same-sex couple, on the grounds that its religious beliefs would be breached if it treated them the same as it did those whose

---

147 See, further, at: http://www.humanrightsactionplan.org.au/nhrap/focus-area/equality-and-non-discrimination-laws.
148 See, further, at: https://www.humanrights.gov.au/sites/default/files/content/pdf/human_rights/religion/article_18_religious_freedom.pdf.
149 *OV v QZ (No 2)* [2008] NSWADT 115; *Member of the Board of the Wesley Mission Council v OV and OW (No 2)* [2009] NSWADTAP 57; *OV & OW v Members of the Board of the Wesley Mission Council* [2010] NSWCA 155.
150 [2010] VCAT 1613. See, further, at: www.austlii.edu.au/au/cases/vic/VCAT/2010/1613.html.

status complied with the core Wesleyan doctrine of 'monogamous heterosexual partnership within marriage'. Ultimately, the court rejected the allegation of discrimination on finding that the Wesley Mission was able to avail of the statutory exemption as, at the relevant time, its doctrines were binding upon the Mission and could be construed as religious (see, further, above). In the second, the issue was whether Christian Youth, a religious charity, could withhold services to people because of their sexual orientation, but claim statutory exemption from what would otherwise be discriminatory practice. Hampel J concluded that it was not necessary for the respondents to refuse the booking in order to comply with their genuine religious beliefs and in taking that step they had discriminated in breach of the Act.

The religious exemption

The Sex Discrimination Amendment (Sexual Orientation, Gender Identity and Intersex Status) Act 2015 has now amended the Sex Discrimination Act 1984 by inserting new protections from discrimination on the basis of sexual orientation, gender identity and intersex status.

In the lengthy proceedings that constituted the above *OV and OW* case and *Cobaw Community Health Services Limited v Christian Youth Camps Limited & Anor*,[151] the entitlement to exemption from the prohibition on discrimination provided for 'religious bodies' was clearly central. Perhaps the finding of most significance in both cases is that when a legal issue arises, which makes it necessary to ascertain the doctrines of a religion, it will be the formulation of those doctrines at the time the issue arose which is crucial.

The exemption privileges traditionally exercised by religious charities must now be revised in the light of the Sex Discrimination Amendment (Sexual Orientation, Gender Identity and Intersex Status) Act. However, the exemption privileges will continue to allow religious bodies – or their emanations such as Sanitarium (which produces the cereal Weet-Bix and is owned and operated by the Seventh-Day Adventist church) – to discriminate in staff selection criteria.

Discrimination (and exemptions) on other grounds

At Commonwealth level, anti-discrimination provisions are to be found in the Age Discrimination Act 2004, the Disability Discrimination Act 1992, the Racial Discrimination Act 1975, the Sex Discrimination Act 1984 (as amended) and the Australian Human Rights Commission Act 1986. Some legislation, such as the Fair Work Act 2009 (Cth), offers limited protection against discrimination on the basis of religious belief. In November 2012, the government released a draft of its Human Rights and Anti-Discrimination Bill 2012, which was intended to consolidate Commonwealth anti-discrimination law and replace the above-listed

151 [2010] VCAT 1613 (8 October 2010).

five existing Acts. Instead, the Bill has been suspended and the government has settled for amending the more deficient features of the Sex Discrimination Act. As of summer 2015, Australian legislation still fails to comprehensively address human rights and equality issues.

• GENDER DISCRIMINATION

Achieving gender equality in the workplace has been a particular policy concern in this jurisdiction, but one that has seen recent legislative progress. The Workplace Gender Equality Act 2012 (Cth) (previously the Equal Opportunity for Women in the Workplace Act 1999 (Cth)) provides in particular for the reporting of matters in accordance with specified gender equality indicators. The related regulatory agency has been renamed the Workplace Gender Equality Agency. However, as noted by the Sex Discrimination Commissioner, there remain issues of gender inequality in the following: average weekly earnings; leadership positions in both public and private sector workplaces; retirement incomes and savings; and as regards victims of domestic violence.[152]

• RACIAL DISCRIMINATION

The primary international source of authority prohibiting racial discrimination is provided by the UDHR, Article 2, and reinforced by the International Convention on the Elimination of All Forms of Racial Discrimination. Domestic provisions are to be found in the quite dated federal law provided by the Racial Hatred Act 1995, the Human Rights and Equal Opportunity Commission Act 1986 and the Racial Discrimination Act 1975; an overall lack of co-ordination is compounded by the existence of a varied array of state statutes.

In the main, relevant Australian case law has been concerned with both direct and indirect discrimination[153] against Aboriginal people, of which the *Mabo* decisions[154] were major landmarks as they finally extinguished the doctrine of *terra nullius* and instead established the basis for official recognition of native title to land,[155] which provided the basis for more equitable land-leasing contracts. The decision in *Public Trustee v Attorney-General of New South Wales*[156] was something of a setback when the trust to remove racial discrimination and advance the interests of Aborigines and Torres Strait was found to be non-charitable. In this

---

152 See, further, at: https://www.humanrights.gov.au/news/speeches/face-gender-based-discrimination-australian-workplaces.
153 *Laalaa v Director General, Department of Education and Training (EOD)* [2009] NSWADTAP 56.
154 *Mabo v Queensland (No 1)* (1988) 166 CLR 186 and *Mabo v Queensland (No 2)* (1992) 175 CLR 1.
155 *Western Australia v Commonwealth* (1995) 183 CLR 373.
156 (1997) 42 NSWLR 600.

context, it might also be noted that a requirement banning the display of tattoos could amount to a breach of the Racial Discrimination Act 1975, in the case of a tattoo that was representative of ethnic or cultural affiliation.

The rather anomalous case of *Kay v South Eastern Sydney Area Health Service*[157] is worthy of note. It concerned a testatrix's gift on trust to the Children's Hospital at Randwick of $10,000 for treatment of white (underlined twice) babies. Young J found the condition to be valid, an integral part of the gift, and that in its entirety the gift did not breach public policy on the grounds of racism, as both the Racial Discrimination Act 1975 (Cth), s.8 and the Anti-Discrimination Act 1977, s.55, expressly provide that any charitable disposition is not subject to the Act, a blanket exemption which questions the synthesis achieved in public policy and human rights. The vilification of Jews has also been held to constitute racial discrimination.[158]

- SEXUAL DISCRIMINATION

Australia has recently made considerable legislative progress in this area. In 2013, the Australian Government passed the Sex Discrimination Amendment (Sexual Orientation, Gender Identity and Intersex Status) Act 2013 (Cth) which amends the Sex Discrimination Act 1984 by inserting new protections from discrimination, and extending the ground of marital status to marital or relationship status, to provide protection from discrimination for same-sex de facto couples. It will ensure that the future provision of care services for the elderly by religious charities (which constitute approximately one-third of total aged care provision in Australia) will no longer be subject to opt-out caveats that previously permitted a refusal of services to those whose sexual orientation or gender identity offended the beliefs of service providers.

Despite the well-documented Australian history of non-traditional family units, including polygamy,[159] it was not until *Toonen v Australia*[160] that same-sex relationships became de-criminalised and civil unions then became possible in Queensland, Tasmania, Victoria, New South Wales and ACT. The consequences were illustrated in cases such as *Young v Australia*,[161] in which the plaintiff and same-sex partner of a deceased war veteran was denied a pension to which a veteran's dependant was entitled, on the grounds that 'partner' was not legislatively intended to include a same-sex relationship. The Committee found that Mr Young had been discriminated against under Article 26 of the ICCPR. The Freedom to Marry Bill 2014, introduced into the Australian Senate on 26 November

---

157 [2003] NSWSC 292.
158 *Jones v Tonen* [2002] FCA 1150.
159 See, further, Evans, C. and Gaze, B., 'Between Religious Freedom and Equality: Complexity and Context', *Harvard International Law Journal*, Vol 49, 2008.
160 Communication No 488/1992, U.N. Doc CCPR/C/50/D/488/1992.
161 Communication No 941/2000: Australia 09/18/2003. CCPR/C/78/D/941/2000.

2014, amended the Marriage Act 1961 (Cth) to enable all Australians regardless of sex, sexual orientation, or gender identity to marry. In keeping with practice elsewhere, it exempts religious organisations from a statutory obligation to either conduct same-sex wedding ceremonies or allow their churches to be used for that purpose.

- EMPLOYMENT DISCRIMINATION

Discrimination in employment is prohibited by the International Labour Organisation's Discrimination (Employment and Occupation) Convention, ratified by Australia in 1973, which requires the removal of employment-related discrimination on the grounds of race, colour, sex, religion, political opinion, national extraction or social origin. In 1989, Australia added the grounds of age, medical record, criminal record, impairment, marital status, mental, intellectual or psychiatric disability, nationality, physical disability, sexual preference, and trade union activity. The Discrimination Act 1991, s.10, further prohibited discrimination by an employer in relation to the terms and conditions on which employment is offered, is undertaken or is terminated, or that subjects the employee to any other detriment.

Bell v De Castella and Rob de Castella's Smartstart for Kids Ltd,[162] an example of the latter, concerned a national health promotion charity whose employee alleged unlawful discrimination under the Discrimination Act 1991 (ACT) by his employer on the s.7 grounds of race, political conviction and profession. Ultimately, as the plaintiff could not establish a causal link between his allegations of unfavourable treatment and discrimination on the basis of the attributes designated in the Act, his evidence was rejected as 'subjective, self-serving or hearsay' and his claim dismissed.

The Fair Work Amendment Act 2013 (Cth) expands the right to request a flexible working arrangement (beyond parents of children under school age and children with a disability).[163]

- SERVICE PROVISION DISCRIMINATION

While each state and territory has roughly similar legislation, the range of federal statutes addressing such discrimination is limited.[164] The Disability Discrimination Act 1992, s.24, prohibits discrimination by a provider of goods or services on the ground of a user's disability: by refusing to provide such goods, services or facilities; or in the terms or conditions of their provision; or in the manner in which they are provided. Controversy has tended to focus on matters such as government funding of faith-based health facilities that refuse to provide vasectomy services on religious grounds.

---

162 [2013] ACAT 27. See, further, at: https://wiki.qut.edu.au/display/CPNS/Discrimination+cases.
163 See, for example, *Poppy v Service to Youth Council Incorporated* [2014] FCA 656.
164 However, see the development of the National Disability Strategy (2010–2020).

- 'POSITIVE ACTION'

An example of such a strategy for preferencing the disadvantaged can be seen in the Charities Act 2013, s.9, which specifically exempts indigenous people from the traditional constraint that excludes kinship relationships from constituting the 'public' dimension of the 'public benefit' test. Charity law also provided a somewhat perverse interpretation of positive action when, the above-mentioned *Kay v South Eastern Sydney Area Health Service*,[165] a fund for the treatment of white babies was upheld as charitable. In reaching its decision, the court relied not just on the fact that charities are expressly exempt from anti-discrimination legislation but also added the banal rationale that 'the receipt of a fund to benefit white babies would just mean that more of the general funds of the hospital would be available to treat non-white babies so that, in due course, despite the testatrix's intention things will even up'.

- CHARITIES AS PUBLIC BODIES

In Australia the government has never sought to supplant the well-established public benefit service provision of charities: the policy has consistently been one of working in partnership with them, maintaining their role with financial support.[166] This policy was demonstrated in the *Central Bayside* case when, on appeal,[167] the court declared:

> The appellant's purpose is charitable. It remains charitable even though the government is the source of the funds it uses to carry out that purpose.

Moreover, it has been specifically continued into the new regulatory regime by the inclusion of a provision stating 'funding charity-like government entities does not prevent a contributing fund from being charitable for the purposes of Commonwealth law'.[168]

From a human rights perspective, this blurring of the distinction between charitable and government purpose is a matter of concern: it may well strengthen the position of those charities – particularly religious entities – that seek the protection of exemption privileges for an ever-extending ambit of employment and service provision arrangements; but it may also impute to government responsibility for the inequitable practice of charities acting on its behalf.[169]

---

165 [2003] NSWSC 292.
166 Note that in *Ambulance Service of New South Wales v Deputy Commissioner of Taxation* [2002] FCA 1023 Allsop J found that the Ambulance Service of New South Wales was too governmental to be a public benevolent institution.
167 *Central Bayside Division of General Practice Ltd v Commissioner of State Revenue* (2005) 60 ATR 151.
168 See, Charities Act 2013.
169 See, the comments of Matthews, J in the *Murgha* case in May 1979. Also, see, *Baird v State of Queensland* [2005] FCA 495 at: https://wiki.qut.edu.au/display/CPNS/Discrimination+cases.

Conclusion

Some long-standing sources of tension on the Australian charity law/human rights interface have recently been de-activated: the kinship network problem that has obstructed charitable intervention in indigenous communities would seem to be statutorily neutralised by the Charities Act, s.19, while s.11 has removed the prohibition on political activities by charities that are 'contrary to government policy'. This has been reinforced by the statutory recognition now given to the importance of human rights by the inclusion of 'promoting or protecting human rights' as a charitable purpose in the Charities Act 2013, s.12(1)(g), and by such legislative initiatives as the Workplace Gender Equality Act 2012 (Cth), the Sex Discrimination Amendment (Sexual Orientation, Gender Identity and Intersex Status) Act 2013 (Cth) and the Freedom to Marry Bill 2014. To some this might seem offset by the absence of a bill of rights, or equivalent constitutional protection, and by the statutory concessions to religion – the institutional structures of which are so prominent in the nonprofit sector of this jurisdiction – particularly, retention of the public benefit presumption favouring all such entities, a presumption extended to 'closed' or contemplative communities, and the exemption from discrimination laws granted to their educational and health and social care emanations.

As of July 2015, the threatened repeal of the Charities Act 2013, coupled with the indefinite suspension of the Human Rights and Anti-Discrimination Bill 2012, leaves the Australian charity law/human rights interface looking particularly fragile and unsettled.

9   New Zealand

Introduction

New Zealand is rightly proud of its human rights record. This began 130 years ago when it became the first nation to give women the right to vote in national elections and has evolved to include ratification of seven of the nine core key human rights treaties. It has also more recently completed a charity law reform process which concluded with the Charities Act 2005 to put in place the country's first charity-specific regulatory framework. It should, therefore, provide a promising exemplar of how modern developed nations marry the provisions of charity law and human rights.

This chapter follows the same format as its five predecessors. Beginning with a background history that explains the development of charity law and its social context in this jurisdiction, it draws attention to case law that illustrates principles in play that are at variance with a human rights ethos. It then examines the charity law reform process, identifies the outcomes and considers the extent to which they have nudged charity law into a closer alignment with human rights. The current legislative and regulatory frameworks for both bodies of law are outlined and their lack of synthesis noted. This leads into the main part of the chapter which conducts an audit of the various points at which charity law and human rights intersect, or otherwise, and assesses the implications arising from that exercise.

Background: a history inimical to human rights

By the time this jurisdiction acquired a measure of independence in 1840, the development of its legal framework for charities[1] was rooted in common law principles. The Religious, Charitable, and Educational Trusts Act 1856 was the first statute regulating charitable trusts. The common law test then established for determining whether a purpose was charitable had retained its currency by the

---

1 See, Dal Pont, G., *Charity Law in Australia and New Zealand*, Oxford University Press, Melbourne, 2000, at p. 78 et seq.

time the Court of Appeal in *Latimer v Commissioner of Inland Revenue*[2] defined it as follows:

(i) Is the purpose for the public benefit; and, if so,
(ii) Is it charitable in the sense of coming within the spirit and intendment of the preamble to the Statute of Charitable Uses Act 1601 (43 Eliz c4) ('the Preamble').

This heritage, as extended by following case law precedents established in England and by broadening its contemporary relevance under the 'spirit or intendment' rule[3] within the *Pemsel*[4] classification of charitable purposes, formed the foundation for the development of charity law in this jurisdiction. The Religious, Charitable and Educational Trusts Act 1908, as subsequently amended in 1928, consolidated the law relating to charitable trusts and, as Dal Pont notes, under s.3 it defined 'charitable purpose' as every other purpose which in accordance with the law of England is a charitable purpose.[5]

Charity law and human rights: the early challenges

Given that the law relating to charity remained embedded within traditional common law concepts, confined by arcane rules and a definition of charitable purpose that broadened only with glacial slowness to accommodate newly emerging forms of social need, it is unsurprising that its development in this jurisdiction, as in others, largely failed to take into account the relatively modern phenomenon of human rights.

Legal structures: charitable trusts

The transfer of charity law from England to New Zealand included the same preference being given to the charitable trust as the preferred legal structure for charity. However, in due course the incorporated society grew to become the legal vehicle of choice.

Constitution

There is no New Zealand constitution as such (see, further, below). However, the Treaty of Waitangi,[6] a founding document, provides a broad statement of

---

2 [2002] 3 NZLR 195 (CA) 10 at para 32.
3 *Commissioner of Inland Revenue v Medical Council of New Zealand* [1997] 2 NZLR 297.
4 *Income Tax Special Commissioners v Pemsel* [1891] AC 531.
5 See, Dal Pont, G., *Charity Law in Australia and New Zealand*, op. cit., at p. 81.
6 Signed on 6 February 1840 by representatives of the British Crown, and Māori chiefs from North Island at Waitangi on the Bay of Islands in New Zealand and eventually consolidated by the Treaty of Waitangi Act 1975.

254 Contemporary law, policy and practice

principles for the building of a nation state and government. It offers a 'constitutional' basis for recognising legal rights and for testing government policy in respect of all citizens, but 'has to be seen as an embryo rather than a fully developed and integrated set of ideas'.[7]

Exempt charities

There is no New Zealand equivalent to the traditional English category of 'exempt charities' which removed many large institutions, in particular religious entities, from the Charity Commission's regulatory requirements. In this jurisdiction every charitable entity, including Churches, wishing to claim tax-exemption privileges must register and be regulated.

Political purposes

Until very recently, the law relating to charity and political purposes in New Zealand had remained true to the *Bowman* ruling.[8] For example, in *Molloy v Commissioner of Inland Revenue*,[9] the Society for the Protection of the Unborn Child was denied charitable status because its main object was to preserve the current law on the subject, which fatally compromised its charitable purpose. Similarly, in *Knowles v Commissioner of Stamp Duties*[10] an organisation ostensibly established to promote temperance in alcoholic consumption was determined to be non-charitable on the grounds that its main purpose was in fact to effect changes in the law. However, in *Latimer v Commissioner of Inland Revenue*,[11] the purpose of providing the Waitangi Tribunal with research findings to assist it in adjudicating on disputes between Māori and the Crown was deemed charitable as 'it is directed towards racial harmony in New Zealand for the general benefit of the community. That is not an object which can legitimately be regarded as political in nature and thus disqualified.'[12] Although this decision was distinguished from its predecessors, thereby avoiding conflict with *Bowman*, two very recent cases met that challenge head-on. The decisions in *Greenpeace*[13] and *Family First*[14] have now ended the established embargo on charities having political purposes in this jurisdiction (see, further, below).

Charitable purposes: a tangential relationship with human rights

The Charitable Trusts Act 1957 consolidates previous legislation. In s.2 it broadly defines and confines the meaning of 'charitable purpose' to the *Pemsel* classification;

---

7 *New Zealand Maori Council v Attorney-General*, op. cit., per Cooke P.
8 *Bowman v Secular Society Ltd* [1917] AC 406.
9 [1981] 1 NZLR 688.
10 [1945] NZLR 522.
11 [2002] 3 NZLR 195.
12 Ibid., per Blanchard J at p. 209.
13 *Re Greenpeace of New Zealand Inc* [2015] 1 NZLR 169 (SC).
14 *Family First New Zealand* [2015] NZHC 1493.

therefore, the range of activities, organisations, gifts and bequests found to be charitable is not disimilar to that in the generated under the 1601 Act (see, further, Chapter 2), though a specific list of instances of charitable activity funded by voluntary donations is incorporated in s.38. Unsurprisingly, it is a range that from an early stage reflected with the progenitor charity law jurisdiction a shared disjunction in alignment between charitable purpose, contemporary patterns of need and a human rights ethos.

The relief of poverty

In New Zealand this first *Pemsel* head consists of much the same spectrum of charities, resting on similar interpretations of 'poverty', the means for its 'relief,' and subject to the same political purpose constraint as in England and Wales and other common law jurisdictions (see, further, Chapter 2). Similar tendencies are also evident in discriminatory bequests to restricted classes (e.g. a trust for the indigent blind of the Jewish persuasion in London[15] and to members of a specific regiment[16]).

The means for relief have long included gifts for the benefit of the inhabitants of a parish or town,[17] though lately this has become somewhat controversial. In *Re Centrepoint Community Growth Trust,*[18] it was held that 'in contemporary New Zealand poverty can quite readily be equated with lack of affordable accommodation',[19] but in *Canterbury Development Corporation v Charities Commission*[20] the Corporation's goal of promoting the general economic wellbeing of the Canterbury area, through assisting businesses and promoting economic development, was judged to provide insufficient public benefit, a decision that conflicts with the not dissimilar Canadian case *Travel Just v Canada.*[21] This more stringent approach towards community infrastructure development as a means of poverty relief was reinforced by MacKenzie J when in *Queenstown Lakes Community Housing Trust*[22] he commented that while housing was a basic need and a right, home ownership was not: as the Trust had not only failed to restrict its activities to the poor but in fact excluded those with less than 140 per cent of the median family income, it was denied charitable status.

15 *Re Trusts of the Will of Jacob Joseph decd* (1907) 26 NZLR 504, 9 GLR 329.
16 *Re Booth* [1954] NZLR 114.
17 *Lysons v Commissioner of Stamp Duties* [1945] NZLR 738; *D V Bryant Trust Board v Hamilton City Council* [1997] 3 NZLR 342.
18 [2000] 2 NZLR 325.
19 Ibid., per Cartwright J at p. 343.
20 [2010] 2 NZLR 707.
21 2006 FCA 343. See, further, at: http://www.globalphilanthropy.ca/images/uploads/2006-10-24_Travel_Just_v._Canada_(Canada_Revenue_Agency).pdf.
22 [2011] 3 NZLR 502 (HC).

The advancement of education

This charitable purpose is presumed to be for the public benefit[23] and again is constituted by much the same range of organisations, activities and gifts in New Zealand as elsewhere in the common law world, including provision for the following: structured education[24] by establishing the customary range of educational entities; ancillary sport and recreation facilities; and learned societies, libraries, publications, orchestras, museums, art galleries etc (see, further, Chapter 2). Service access subject to fee payment is permissible at a level that does not exclude the less well-off,[25] and the customary line is drawn between information giving that is educational and charitable[26] and that which is merely propaganda.[27]

This jurisdiction has also made its own challenging contribution to the interpretation of 'charity' under this head, including the following: Auckland Women Lawyers; for a law library and 'all kinds of books' for the Auckland Law Society';[28] orchestral compositions and concert works;[29] and a bequest to provide 'a coach for improving back play and place kicking in the game of rugby football among the scholars'.[30]

In the leading case of *Commissioner of Inland Revenue v Medical Council of New Zealand* the court confirmed the charitable status of the Medical Council, which registers and supervises medical professionals, on the grounds that while its primary purpose was to provide for the interests of the public through ensuring high standards in the practise of medicine and surgery, any benefits to registered practitioners were considered incidental. Much the same rationale was applied in determining the publication and sale of law reports for the benefit of those engaged in the administration or practice of law in New Zealand to be charitable.[31]

The advancement of religion

As Mallon J noted in *Liberty Trust*,[32] in relation to gifts or organisations for the advancement of religion, 'the starting assumption is that it has a public benefit'.

In New Zealand, much the same range of gifts, activities and organisations have been deemed charitable or otherwise under this *Pemsel* head as in England and Wales, including the following: advancement of religion in general;[33] for repairs

---

23 *Re Education New Zealand Trust* (2010) 24 NZTC 24,354.
24 Ibid.
25 *D V Bryant Trust Board v Hamilton City Council* [1997] 3 NZLR 342.
26 *Auckland Medical Aid Trust v Commissioner of Inland Revenue* [1979] 1 NZLR 382.
27 *Re Draco Foundation (NZ) Charitable Trust* (2011) 25 NZTC 20032 (HC).
28 *Re Mason (deceased)* [1971] NZLR 714.
29 *Canterbury Orchestra Trust v Smitham* [1978] 1 NZLR 787.
30 *Nelson College v Attorney-General*, HC Nelson 40/1986 (unreported) per Heron J.
31 *Commissioner of Inland Revenue v New Zealand Council of Law Reporting* [1981] NZLR 682.
32 *Liberty Trust v Charities Commission* [2011] 3 NZLR 68 (HC), per Mallon J at para 125.
33 *Centrepoint Community Growth Trust v CIR* [1985] 1 NZLR 673 (HC).

to church tower or spire;[34] for an organ for a Methodist church;[35] for the support of active and retired ministers of religion and their dependants;[36] for the erection or maintenance of tombs;[37] and that Freemasonry does not advance religion[38] but gifts for masses to be said for the soul of the dead does.[39] In *Presbyterian Church of New Zealand Beneficiary Fund v Commissioner of Inland Revenue*[40] the High Court held that a superannuation scheme for the benefit of retired ministers of the church and their widows was charitable under the advancement of religion. Mallon J seemed to adopt the same approach in *Liberty Trust v Charities Commission*[41] when she considered that confining the advancement of religion 'to praying, preaching and building churches or looking after priest, minister, nuns and the like' was outdated.[42] She took the view that the Trust was not engaged in a purely secular activity by promoting budgeting and financial advice: its loan scheme was a practical outworking of the Christian faith and, therefore, it was 'advancing religion'; and 'it is not for the Court to say that teaching biblical financial principles is not a public benefit'.[43]

Bequests subject to a condition that the prospective beneficiary 'be of the Lutheran religion'[44] or be 'in the Protestant faith'[45] were initially acceptable charitable bequests in this jurisdiction as they were elsewhere in the common law world. However, by mid-20th century, Smith J in *Re Lockie*,[46] when considering a gift accompanied by a condition that discriminated on grounds of religion, took quite the opposite approach and refused to recognise such a gift as charitable on the grounds that the testator's blatant religious discrimination had irredeemably corrupted any charitable intent. This approach was then followed in relation to attached conditions intended to prevent 'contracting marriage outside the Jewish faith'.[47] The absence of rulings upholding the right of testators to make testamentary dispositions subject to discriminatory religious conditions is a noticeable feature of New Zealand case law which differentiates it from that of countries such as England, Canada and Ireland.

---

34 *Brown v Public Trustee* [1927] GLR 456 and *Rowe v Public Trustee* [1928] NZLR 51.
35 *Methodist Theological College Council v Guardian Trust and Executors Co. of New Zealand Ltd* [1927] GLR 294.
36 *Hester v Commissioner of Inland Revenue* [2005] 2 NZLR 172.
37 *Re Budge (deceased)* [1942] NZLR 350 and *Filshie (deceased), Raymond v Butcher* [1939] NZLR 91, [1939] GLR 41.
38 *Re The Grand Lodge of Antient Free and Accepted Masons in New Zealand* [2011] 1 NZLR 277 (HC).
39 *Carrigan v Redwood* (1910) 30 NZLR 244.
40 [1994] 3 NZLR 363.
41 Op. cit.
42 Ibid., at p. 89.
43 Ibid., at p. 102.
44 *Re Carleton* [1909] 28 NZLR 1066.
45 *In Re Gunn* [1912] 32 NZLR 153.
46 [1945] NZLR 230, at p. 240.
47 *Re Biggs, Public Trustee v Schneider* [1945] NZLR 303, 307 and *Re Myers, Perpetual Trust Estate and Agency Co of New Zealand v Myers* [1947] NZLR 828, 834.

Beneficial to the community, not falling under any of the preceding heads

The spread and volume of charities registered under this *Pemsel* head is unwieldy, but perhaps the majority can be grouped as follows: health and social care including the provision of hospitals, clinics etc;[48] public utilities; local community development; protection of the environment; animal care; and agricultural or industrial development. What they have in common, to paraphrase Hammond J in *D V Bryant Trust Board v Hamilton City Council*,[49] is that they do not fit under any other *Pemsel* head but are beneficial to society and meet the necessary public benefit test.[50]

The latter case is significant, for present purposes, as Hammond J then refers to a component that resonates with the human rights approach: the aged (over 70), by virtue of that fact, regardless of whether they are also in poverty or have other needs, are *ipso facto* eligible for charity; the question to be asked is whether or not the proposed charitable purpose appropriately addresses that status (of being aged). This approach is clearly transferable to other needs that confer a similar status (e.g. child, disabled etc) and has been so applied, as Poirier[51] has pointed out, for example in relation to the following: establishing a home for aged women,[52] an institution for boys who are destitute orphans,[53] a Methodist Church children's home[54] and a convalescent home for children;[55] for an old men's home;[56] relief of the indigent blind;[57] a sheltered workshop for the handicapped;[58] and a gift to the Presbyterian Orphanage for Girls at Christchurch for providing financial assistance for all or any girls from time to time leaving the Presbyterian Orphanage to seek their fortunes.[59] Facilities and services clearly established to address circumstances of vulnerability – rather than designated groups of the vulnerable – are equally assured of charitable status (e.g. lifeguards, lifeboats, fire brigades etc), as are environment protection organisations, reforestation schemes and open access public amenities such as parks, swimming pools, botanical gardens etc.[60] Equally clearly, this approach rules out a purpose that

---

48 *Auckland Medical Aid Trust v Commissioner of Inland Revenue* [1979] 1 NZLR 673.
49 [1997] 3 NZLR 342.
50 Ibid., at p. 350.
51 See, Poirier, D., *Charity Law in New Zealand*, Chapter 13, at: https://www.charities.govt.nz/assets/Uploads/Resources/Charity-Law-in-New-Zealand.pdf.
52 *Re Bingham* [1951] NZLR 491.
53 *Dilworth v Commissioner of Stamps* (1898) NZPCC 578; [1898] AC 99.
54 *Re Hook*, High Court, Wellington, A 8/83, 25 October 1984, per Ongley J.
55 *Re List* [1949] NZLR 79; [1948] GLR 541.
56 *Re Palmer* [1939] NZLR 189; [1939] GLR 138.
57 *Re Elliot* (1910) 102 LT 528.
58 *Re Clark*, High Court, Auckland M 1271/186, 10 November 1989, per Sinclair J.
59 *Re Mitchel* [1963] NZLR 934.
60 *Waitemata County v Commissioner of Inland Revenue* [1971] NZLR 151; *Morgan v Wellington City Corporation* [1975] 1 NZLR 416; *Grant v Commissioner of Stamp Duties* [1943] NZLR 113.

(i) does not address that status as such but is merely ancillary, incidental or otherwise fails to directly relate to and further it or (ii) restricts access by fees that exclude the poor.

Again, there are cases that illustrate a quirkish interpretation of 'charity', such as a bequest for the rehabilitation of those discharged from the navy or airforce with preference for men who were farmers or proposed to become farmers,[61] an annual hot air balloon festival – the 'Balloons Over Waikato' charitable trust[62] – and an amateur radio clubroom facility.[63]

New Zealand, in keeping with early decisions in Australia, adopted a similar human rights compliant approach to immigrants when, in *Re Cohen*,[64] a bequest to a society to assist Jewish refugees was held to be charitable under this *Pemsel* head.

Māori

The indigenous Māori people are the largest non-European ethnic group, accounting for 14.6 per cent of the population of New Zealand. For Māori, in common with indigenous people generally, religion and culture are closely interwoven: their religious or spiritual beliefs form shared reference points for daily life. However, poorer health outcomes and fewer positive life opportunities for Māori and Pasifika people are a continuing problem with significant human rights implications.[65] In December 2012, Māori constituted 51.4 per cent of all prison inmates but less than 15 per cent of the New Zealand population. Māori are very over-represented as both victims and perpetrators of violence in families, with considerably lower life expectancies and higher unemployment rates than non-Māori.

The public benefit test in charity law has for generations constrained ameliorative intervention to effect change in such circumstances. As with indigenous populations elsewhere, the fact that prospective beneficiaries are joined in a nexus of extended kinship relationships – arranged around the essentially 'closed' social units of *iwi* and *hapu* – breaches the 'public' arm of the test, resulting in some otherwise charitable organisations, bequests or other such entities being denied that status by court or regulator and probably very many such schemes being abandoned at an early stage. The fact that not until very recently was any legislative initiative taken to correct this well-known lacuna in the law[66] that clearly had an adverse discriminatory effect on Māori relative to non-Māori – as it did

---

61 *Re Elgar* [1957] NZLR 1221 (CA).
62 See, further, at: http://www.balloonsoverwaikato.co.nz/about-bow.
63 *Clarke v Hill and Granger*, High Court, Auckland, 2 February 2001 per Priestley J, CP 68-SD99.
64 [1954] NZLR 1097 (SC).
65 See, Bell, S., 'The Right to Health' in Bedggood, M. and Gledhill, K. (eds.), *Law into Action: Economic, Social and Cultural Rights in Aotearoa New Zealand*, Thomson Reuters, Wellington, 2011, at p. 96.
66 Acknowledged by government in *The Taxation of Māori Organisations*, April 2002.

in respect of indigenous people and settled communities in all common law countries – says something about altruism as a driving force in charity law and underlines the tangential relationship between it and human rights.

In recent years some government initiatives have been taken to address Māori inequity, prompted by judicial notice given to the doctrine of Aboriginal title which was used to protect customary Māori fishing rights[67] and provided the basis for Māori claims to the foreshore and seabed.[68] For example, in 2009 the government reviewed the Foreshore and Seabed Act 2004, in response to international and domestic concerns about its discriminatory effect on Māori, replaced it with the Marine and Coastal Area (*Takutai Moana*) Act 2011.

However, in the 2013 CERD report, the Committee expressed concern that the 2011 Act contained provisions that may restrict the full enjoyment by Māori communities of their rights under the Treaty of Waitangi, such as the provision requiring proof of exclusive use and occupation of marine and coastal areas without interruption since 1840, and urged further review.[69] It also expressed continuing concern regarding the inadequacy of the consultations conducted with Māori communities before awarding drilling contracts, under circumstances that may threaten enjoyment of their rights to land and other resources traditionally owned or used, and before pursuing negotiation of Free Trade Agreements that could similarly affect their rights. Although, it must be noted that the Special Rapporteur on the Rights of Indigenous Peoples has drawn attention to the New Zealand system for settling historical land claims – the Treaty settlement process – describing this as one of the most important examples in the world of addressing historical and ongoing grievances.[70] Nonetheless, there is some way to go before human rights can hope to strategically redress the current imbalance between the health and socio-economic circumstances of Māori and non-Māori communities.

Public benefit: civil society, charity and the State

In New Zealand the government has had a long-standing formal policy, embedded as a fundamental premise in the Treaty of Waitangi, of working in partnership with Māori.[71] This experience coloured the slowly evolving government/sector relationship. In the late 1990s, government broadened its approach when, following political developments in the UK, it also pursued the 'third way' democratic

---

67 *Te Weehi v Regional Fisheries Officer* [1986] 1 NZLR 680 (HC).
68 *Attorney-General v Ngati Apa* [2003] 3 NZLR 643 (CA).
69 See, further, at: http://www2.ohchr.org/english/bodies/cerd/docs/co/CERD-C-NZL-CO-18–20_en.pdf.
70 See, statement by Professor James Anaya, at the Tenth Session of the UN Permanent Forum on Indigenous Issues, New York, (19.05.2011), further, at: http://www.un.org/esa/socdev/unpfii/documents/session_10_statement_sr_anaya_%202011.pdf.
71 Author acknowledges advice from Sue Barker on this matter (note to author, 8 September 2015).

pluralist policy by leading Māori, other ethnic organisations and the nonprofit sector more generally, towards assuming a growing share of responsibility for planning and delivering public benefit service provision. By 2000, the government was beginning to place greater emphasis on ways in which 'community-government partnerships . . . help create social capital and social cohesion'.[72]

Partnership

The appointment of a Minister with specific responsibility for the nonprofit sector in 1999, the Statement of Government Intentions for an Improved Community-Government Relationship (SOGI) in 2001, and the creation of the Office for the Community and Voluntary Sector in 2003, all illustrated a movement towards closer government/sector relationships epitomised by the launch of *He Waka Kotuia – Joining Together on a Shared Journey*[73] and other actions documented in *A Community-Government Relationship: The Road to a Cross-Sectoral Forum*.[74] A range of other initiatives followed, such as increased tax relief for contributions to nonprofit organisations.[75] The context was set for the charity law reform process.

Charity law reform and human rights: towards alignment

Until the partial introduction of the Charities Act in July 2005, there was no system of registration, no regulatory framework and no central regulatory body for charities in New Zealand. There was also little approximating an assimilation of the human rights ethos into charity law.

The charity law reform process

Following on from its largely tax-centred attempts at reform in 1979, 1989 and 1998, the government launched the charity law reform process in June 2001 with the issue of its discussion document *Tax and Charities*,[76] and in October the Minister for Finance announced a decision in principle to introduce registration,

---

72 Ministry of Social Policy (2000) *Models of Community-Government Partnerships and their Effectiveness in Achieving Welfare Goals: A Review of the Literature*, Ministry of Social Policy, Wellington.

73 See, Community-Government Relationship Steering Group, *He Waka Kotuia – Joining Together on a Shared Journey*, Community Policy team, Ministry of Social Policy, Wellington, 2002.

74 See, Office for the Community and Voluntary Sector, *A Community-Government Relationship: The Road to a Cross-Sectoral Forum*, Office for the Community and Voluntary Sector, Wellington, 2007.

75 See, further, Gousmett, M., 'The History of Charitable Purpose Tax Concessions in New Zealand', the *New Zealand Journal of Taxation Law and Policy*, 2013, pp. 139–174.

76 See, Community-Government Relationship Steering Group, *He Waka Kotuia – Joining Together on a Shared Journey*, Community Policy Team, Ministry of Social Policy, Wellington, 2002.

reporting and monitoring requirements for charities. In 2003, a taskforce was established – later named the Community Sector Taskforce – as a way of progressing recommendations made by *He Waka Kotuia*.

The process

The Office for the Community and Voluntary Sector was created within the Ministry of Social Development in 2003 'to address overarching issues affecting the community and voluntary sector and to raise the profile of the sector within government'.[77] It acted as the central hub for co-ordinating the government's engagement with the sector and worked closely with the Community Sector Taskforce. The Office had responsibility for, among other matters, the overall management of public discussions and negotiations with the sector that constituted the brief life of the charity law reform process.

Jurisdiction specific outcomes

The charity law reform process concluded with the launch of the Charities Act 2005. This achieved little more than the following: the statutory encoding of already established common law rules and principles, thereby, in keeping with the UK and Irish jurisdictions, giving the legislature the future capacity to amend and extend the *Pemsel* list and adjust the public benefit rules; the introduction of a now defunct Charities Commission and a register for charities (although not mandatory, eligibility for tax exemption is conditional upon registration); and some tactical amendments to the Income Tax Act 2007. There was no attempt to broaden the traditional *Pemsel* list of charitable purposes.[78] Nor were steps taken to revise the political purpose rule or to alter the presumption of public benefit in regard to the first three heads; it remains the case that 'the question whether a gift is or may be operative for the public benefit is a question to be answered by the Court by forming an opinion on the evidence before it',[79] whereas it must be expressly proven in respect of the fourth.[80]

- INCREASED REGULATORY MEASURES

Decoupling the responsibilities for determining charitable status and eligibility for tax exemption has been the principal reform outcome, with the Inland

---

77 As stated on the website of OCVS, see further at http://www.ocvs.govt.nz/about-us/index.html#Ourrole1.
78 Amateur sporting clubs were added in 2006, and subsequently the definition of 'charitable purpose' in the Charities Act was amended to include an entity that promotes amateur sport, if the purpose is 'expressed to be, and is in fact, the means by which a charitable purpose (such as the promotion of health or education) will be achieved'.
79 *Molloy v Commissioner of Inland Revenue* [1981] 1 NZLR 688 at p. 695.
80 *Canterbury Development Corporation v Charities Commission* [2010] 2 NZLR 707.

Revenue Department transferring the power to grant charitable status to the Charities Commission which was to implement and maintain a system for registering, reporting and monitoring charities and for investigating complaints. The new statutory regime requires charities to submit annual returns (s.41), and the charities regulator to inquire into charities (ss.50–55) and to consider a charity's activities (s.18) so they can be monitored to ensure they continue to act in accordance with their charitable purposes.[81]

Charity law and human rights purposes

The outcome of the charity law review process did not include any reference to human rights as a charitable purpose. Nonetheless, in general the promotion of human rights can be charitable, especially where an entity has educational purposes, promotes research and disseminates the findings; Amnesty International for example, is a registered charity in this jurisdiction.

Charity law and human rights: a modern framework for continuing dissonance

The associational structures of Māori society formed a relatively intact, homogenous culture. While this has undoubtedly loosened up during the course of the latter part of the 20th century, the preceding centuries of experience in dealing with the cultural gap between the social institutions of the immigrant population and the *tangata whenua*[82] have given the government many opportunities to develop the strategies necessary to construct and sustain a pluralist society. The resulting success in building a civil society infrastructure is not, arguably, reflected in the current framework that emerged from a forced desultory marriage between charity law and human rights.

Constitution, public policy and human rights

New Zealand does not have a constitution as such,[83] though collectively the following constitute a body of law with an overarching constitutional effect:[84] the Treaty of Waitangi; the Constitution Act 1986; the Imperial Laws Application Act 1988; the New Zealand Bill of Rights Act 1990; and the Human Rights Act 1993. The Constitution Act 1986, New Zealand's primary constitutional legal instrument, consolidated the institutional and statutory powers necessary to

---

81 See, Barker, S., at para 10, at: http://www.lawnewzealand.co.nz/resources/Appealing%20 decisions%20of%20the%20charities%20regulator.pdf.

82 This Māori term loosely translates as 'people of the land'.

83 See, further, at: http://www.justice.govt.nz/policy/constitutional-law-and-human-rights/ consideration-of-constitutional-issues-1/members-of-the-constitutional-advisory-panel.

84 See, further, Ekins, R. and Tomkins, D., *Constitutional Theory for the Constitutional Review*, Maxim Institute, Auckland, 2013.

clarify its relationship with the UK government and monarchy, provide for more coherent domestic governance and affirm its (relatively) independent status.

Public policy, charity law, overseas aid and anti-terrorism

Charitable status is required to be public policy compliant. The public benefit presumption will not save the otherwise charitable status of an organisation, its activities or gift dedicated to it, where this is found to be illegal,[85] immoral or in breach of the prevailing public policy.

The latter is probably dominated, in human rights terms, by issues relating to the disparity between the health and lifestyle oppportunities of Māori and non-Māori communities, responding to illegal immigrants and asylum seekers, managing the narrowing of the gender gap in its various manifestations and addressing difficulties arising in the field of equality. While these are all areas in which logic and morality might dictate that charity law would have a central role, it is evident from the case law (and its absence in relation to certain matters) discussed in the following section that the impact of charitable organisations is not always direct and effective. This is attributable, at least in part, to charity law and human rights being at times out of synch.

- OVERSEAS AID

The OECD Development Assistance Committee Peer Review 2015 of New Zealand's aid shows that since 2011, New Zealand has consistently increased its focus on sustainable economic development in the Pacific region, working in environments that are vulnerable, high risk, disaster-prone and fragile.[86] However, while its approach to reducing and responding to disaster risks in the Pacific is commended to other donors, the report also notes that New Zealand's overseas development aid budget is only equivalent to 0.27 per cent of gross national income and has not exceeded 0.3 per cent in recent years (in relation to the average 0.39 per cent of other Development Assistance Committee (DAC) member countries and an agreed DAC commitment of 0.7 percent), and that it needs to demonstrate that its programmes make a positive difference to the lives of poor and vulnerable people. Approximately 11 per cent of charities registered in New Zealand are involved in overseas aid – working independently or on behalf/ in conjunction with government, including UNICEF, Red Cross, the Salvation Army and Save the Children. Religious charities constitute some 60 per cent of those working overseas and contribute the largest proportion of total funds.[87]

---

85 See, for example, abortion and *Auckland Medical Aid Trust v Commissioner of Inland Revenue* [1979] 1 NZLR 382, per Chilwell J at p. 395.
86 See, the Income Tax Act 2007, Sched. 32.
87 See, further, CharityWatchNZ at: http://charitywatchnz.blogspot.co.uk/2012/08/nz-charities-with-overseas-purposes.html.

• ANTI-TERRORISM

The Terrorism Suppression Act 2002 contains a range of procedures relating to the protection of human rights and observance of international obligations. These have been bolstered by the Countering Terrorist Fighters Legislation Act 2014 which allows the Security Intelligence Service to carry out surveillance and interception operations in respect of local Islamic State supporters. There are misgivings about potential breaches of civil liberties, as the police now have extensive powers to justify intrusion into private homes and business premises. Local charities with overseas programmes, perhaps particularly those representative of Islamic interests, have concerns regarding the possible continuous surveillance of staff, communications and records.

The legislative and regulatory framework

The Charities Act 2005 may appear somewhat anodyne, but it has put in place, for the first time, the basic components of a charity-specific regulatory system that began with the registration process on 1 February 2007. In conjunction with the human rights legislative provisions, largely resulting from endorsement of international conventions and treaties etc, New Zealand has established modern legal frameworks for both charity and human rights, though they fail to intersect effectively.

Charity law

On 24 February 2012, the Charities Amendment Act 2012 disestablished the Charities Commission and transferred its functions to the Department of Internal Affairs (the Department) and the Charities Registration Board. The 2012 Act, together with the Charities Act 2005 and the Income Tax Act 2007, now provide the legislative framework for charities (in conjunction with the Incorporated Societies Act 1908, the Trustee Act 1956, the Charitable Trusts Act 1957 and the Companies Act 1993).[88]

The 2005 Act neither repealed nor significantly amended any previous legislation.[89] The Charitable Trusts Act 1957, which had consolidated earlier legislative provisions, continues to provide the rudiments of a supervisory system. Section 2 of the 1957 Act explains that 'charitable purpose' means every purpose which in accordance with the law of New Zealand is charitable, including, within the terms of Parts I and II, every purpose that is religious or educational, whether or not it is charitable according to the law of New Zealand. Section 61A specifically retains the principle that a trust or institution must be for the public benefit to be charitable.

---

88 There are also private statutes such as the Royal New Zealand Foundation of the Blind.
89 However, it inserts slight amendments to the Estate and Gift Duties Act 1968, the Incorporated Societies Act 1908, the Tax Administration Act 1994, the Income Tax Act 2004, the Crown Entities Act 2004 (2004 No 15) and the Ombudsmen Act 1975 (1975 No 9).

• THE CHARITIES REGULATOR: THE CHARITIES REGISTRATION BOARD

The disestablishment of the Charities Commission was followed by the creation of a statutory three-person Charities Registration Board which is now responsible for the registration and deregistration of charities, while the Department of Internal Affairs (DIA) is responsible for monitoring, investigating, and prosecuting. Amendments to the Income Tax Act 2007 and the Estate and Gift Duties Act 1968 have ensured that since July 2008 only those registered as 'charitable entities' are exempted from income tax, and gift duty is now entirely abolished.[90]

• ATTORNEY GENERAL

In *Kaikoura County v Boyd*[91] it was stated that 'we feel we should add that it seems generally desirable that the Attorney-General should be a party at least to any action concerning a charitable trust of substantial value for the benefit of the general public or a section of them'. It is, therefore, as Sue Barker has pointed out, 'a mystery why the Attorney-General has not been joined as a party in any of the Charities Act cases to-date',[92] adding, 'the involvement of the Attorney-General is essential in the public interest. In every Charities Act case, the question of whether the Attorney-General should be served should at least be asked.'[93]

Human rights

Although a party to most international treaties and conventions,[94] not until 2010 did New Zealand decide to support the UN Declaration of Rights of Indigenous Peoples.[95] It now has in place a typical platform of domestic equality legislation including the Human Rights Act 1993, the New Zealand Bill of Rights Act 1990, the Privacy Act 1993, the Equal Pay Act 1972 and the Employment

---

90 See, further, Gousmett, M., 'Examinations and Inquiries into Charities', *New Zealand Law Journal*, 2013, pp. 97–106.

91 [1949] NZLR 233 (SC and CA) at p. 262. See also *Wallis v Solicitor-General* (1902–1903) NZPCC 23 (PC).

92 See, Barker, S., para 103 at: http://www.lawnewzealand.co.nz/resources/Appealing%20 decisions%20of%20the%20charities%20regulator.pdf.

93 Ibid., at para 107.

94 New Zealand has ratified the: International Convention on the Elimination of All Forms of Racial Discrimination; International Covenant on Civil and Political Rights; International Convention on the Elimination of All Forms of Discrimination Against Women; International Convention on the Rights of the Child; International Convention Against Torture and Other Inhuman or Degrading Treatment; International Covenant on Economic Social and Cultural Rights; and Convention on the Rights of Persons with Disabilities. See, further, at: http://www.hrc.co.nz/report/chapters/chapter09/religion02.html.

95 On 13 September 2007, the General Assembly adopted a landmark declaration outlining the rights of the world's estimated 370 million indigenous people and outlawing discrimination against them: 143 Member States voted in favour; 11 abstained and 4 – Australia, Canada, New Zealand and the US – voted against the text.

Relations Act 2000 (which repealed the Employment Contracts Act 1991), and has introduced other legislative and policy frameworks to promote equality.[96] The 1990 Act provides for 'Democratic and Civil Rights' including the freedoms of thought, conscience, and religion (s.13); expression (s.14); religion and belief (s.15); peaceful assembly (s.16); association (s.17); movement (s.18); non-discrimination (s.19); minority rights (s.20); and a number of rights relating to justice and the legal system. It also requires the Attorney General to alert Parliament if any draft legislation appears inconsistent with human rights obligations (s.7).

A recent academic report claims that the country's reputation as a global leader in human rights is at risk, as it is slipping behind in areas such as child poverty, gender equality, the systemic disadvantages of Māori, and the rights of disabled people to challenge the State. It suggests 13 recommendations to help New Zealand retain human rights leadership, including a comprehensive rewrite of human rights legislation, a new parliamentary select committee to deal with human rights, and the urgent repeal of non-human rights compliant legislation to reinstate the rights of all New Zealanders to complain about discrimination.[97]

- THE HUMAN RIGHTS COMMISSION, *TE KAHUI TANGATA*

The Human Rights Act 1993 established the Human Rights Commission which was subsequently restructured by the Human Rights Amendment Act 2001. The changes then introduced included setting up the Office of Human Rights and merging the Office of Race Relations Conciliator into the Commission. The Commission's main functions are (i) to provide advocacy and support for human rights, cultural diversity and for equal employment opportunities, (ii) to advise on the law and practice relating to the statutory grounds for unlawful discrimination and (iii) to resolve or adjudicate upon any issues arising in the latter context.

New Zealand also has a Children's Commissioner.[98]

- THE EMPLOYMENT RELATIONS AUTHORITY

The task of interpreting and applying the Employment Relations Act 2000 falls to the Employment Relations Authority, the Employment Court and the New Zealand Court of Appeal.

---

96 Citizenship Act 1977; Immigration Act 1987; State Sector Act 1988; Ethnic Perspectives in Policy 2003.
97 McGregor, J., Bell, S. and Wilson, M., *Fault lines: Human rights in New Zealand*, at: http://www.aut.ac.nz/__data/assets/pdf_file/0010/536572/NO-watermark-Fault-lines-Human-rights-in-New-Zealand.pdf.
98 Author acknowledges advice of Michael Gousmett on this matter (note to author, 5 August 2015).

• THE UN REPORTS

In 2014, at the second New Zealand UPR, recorded concerns included the following: the delay in signing or ratifying certain Conventions; the lack of any overarching protection for human rights; disparities experienced by Māori as demonstrated by key social and economic indicators and the extent of family violence and violence against women and children; gender inequality; and child poverty. The above-mentioned 2015 academic report concluded that New Zealand's human rights legislation – the New Zealand Bill of Rights Act and the Human Rights Act – 'were problematic and didn't prevent the passing of other laws, which breach rights'.

The contemporary charity law/human rights interface: a compliance audit

As with the preceding jurisdiction specific chapters, this one also takes the UDHR to be the most basic and appropriate international instrument and applies it to identify and examine issues arising along the charity law/human rights interface.

Access to justice, legal process and principles

In this as in many modern developed nations, access to justice and to the legal process is constrained by increasing costs and delay.[99] Given that charities tend to be litigation-averse, and those they represent are almost by definition unlikely to be able to bear the costs of court proceedings, the current difficulties are certain to disadvantage and discourage such prospective litigants relative to all others.

Access to justice

In *EB v New Zealand*[100] the Human Rights Committee, in its second finding against New Zealand, found that extended delay of proceedings denied EB access to her children and there had been a violation of Article 14 of the ICCPR. This problem is clearly not confined to family law issues. The restricted time limit available to lodge an appeal under s.59 of the Charities Act 2005 is likely to adversely affect charities and those they represent.[101]

---

99 See, for example, Righarts, S. and Henaghan, M., 'Public Perceptions of the New Zealand Court System: An Empirical Approach to Law Reform', *Otago Law Review*, Vol 12, No 2, pp. 329–344.
100 CCPR/C/89/D/1368/2005 (views adopted 16 March 2007).
101 Author acknowledges advice from Sue Barker on this matter (note to author, 8 September 2015).

Due process

New Zealand, in common with some other countries currently being considered, has been accused by international bodies of denying asylum seekers due process. In its 2013 CERD report, the Committee recalled its General Recommendation No 30 (2004) on discrimination against non-citizens, noted that the Immigration Amendment Bill 2012 provided for the mandatory detention of asylum seekers, and urged New Zealand to ensure that the Bill accords to international standards in the treatment of persons in need of international protection and does not unfairly and arbitrarily discriminate against asylum seekers.

Proportionality

The 2013 CERD report expressed concern regarding the over-representation of Māori in the criminal justice system, despite the introduction of the 'Better Public Services' programmes, the 'Drivers of Crime' initiative and reforms to the jury selection system.[102] Noting its previous recommendations on this matter, the Committee urged that efforts be intensified to address the over-representation of members of the Māori and Pasifika communities at every stage of the criminal justice system.

Respect for 'private life'

No provision is made for privacy rights in the New Zealand Bill of Rights 1990, but the Privacy Act 1993, in keeping with a restricted interpretation of Articles 12 of the UDHR and 17 of the ICCPR, promotes and protects the right of an individual to privacy of information. It establishes principles to govern the collection, use, disclosure and storage of personal information by agencies, and the accessing of personal information by individuals. It also sets out the functions and powers of the Privacy Commissioner.

In New Zealand the law would not appear to offer the same recognition of and protection for the right to private life as, for example, would be available under the ECHR; there is no case law corresponding to that litigated before the ECtHR and no evidence that the courts in this jurisdiction have examined the nuances of this right – and its implications for individuals, family life and for charity law – as necessitated elsewhere by a range of associated issues.

Freedom of religion and belief

As a signatory nation to the UDHR, New Zealand is bound by Article 18(1) which is essentially replicated in the New Zealand Bill of Rights Act 1990. This

---

102 See, further, at: http://www2.ohchr.org/english/bodies/cerd/docs/co/CERD-C-NZL-CO-18–20_en.pdf.

declares the right to freedom of thought, conscience, religion and belief (including the right to hold and embrace views without interference), protects the right to express religion and belief in worship, observance, teaching and practice and affirms the right of minorities to be free from discrimination. In addition, Articles 2 and 3 of the Treaty of Waitangi provide protection for Māori to observe and practice their religions and beliefs: the first does so by reference, in the Māori version, to *taonga*, that is, 'everything that is held precious'; the second by providing for Māori to have 'the same rights as those of the people of England'.

Church and State

The Constitution Act 1986 fails to provide for the separation of Church and State but also refrains from 'establishing' a specific religion. However, the courts have taken judicial notice of such a separation, as illustrated, for example, by Mabon J in *Marshall v National Spiritual Assembly of the Bahá'is of New Zealand Inc*[103] when he referred to the court's duty to adopt an approach 'reflecting the separation of church and state' before reaching its decision.

Definition of 'religion': theism

The leading Australian case, *Church of the New Faith v Commissioner of Pay-roll Tax*,[104] has been followed by the New Zealand judiciary. Of particular note are the requirements as then stated by Mason ACJ and Brennan J for 'first, belief in a supernatural Being, Thing or Principle and second, the acceptance of canons of conduct in order to give effect to that belief' – which were to be interpreted broadly and flexibly.[105] As Dal Pont has noted, the other members of the Bench – Wilson and Deane JJ – added three further indicia of a religion: 'that its ideas relate to man's nature and place in the universe and his or her relation to things supernatural; that its adherents constitute an identifiable group or groups; and that its adherents themselves see the collection of ideas and/or practices as constituting a religion'.[106] Dal Pont makes the point that, given the Pacific Rim cultural context of Australia and New Zealand, the judiciary in this and other cases can be seen interpreting religion so as to give recognition to the fact 'that some, mostly Eastern religions are not theistic which (sic) thereby releases the law from Judeo-Christian notions'. This prompted the New Zealand and Australian judiciary to digress from the traditional formulaic definition of religion at an earlier stage than their contemporary English counterparts[107] (see, also, Chapter 4).

103   [2003] 2 NZLR 205 at paras 31–34.
104   (1983) 154 CLR 120.
105   Ibid., at p. 136.
106   See, Dal Pont, G., *Charity Law in Australia and New Zealand*, op. cit., at p. 148.
107   Ibid., at p. 149.

Tomkins J applied the Mason and Brennan JJ principles in *Centrepoint Community Growth Trust v Commissioner of Inland Revenue*,[108] which concerned an incorporated community of like-minded persons who shared the common purpose of advancing the spiritual education and humanitarian teachings of Herbert Thomas Potter and 'of all the messengers of god'. The court found that, while some members of the community believed in a supernatural being, others held 'a belief in the supernatural in the sense of reality beyond that which can be perceived by the senses'. Included in such beliefs were concepts that related not only to man's relationship to man but also to his relationship to the supernatural in the sense of a Being or a reality beyond sensory perception. The court held that in terms of their formal association and beliefs and practices, the members satisfied the definition of religion.[109]

Definition of 'religion': belief system

A broad view of what constitutes religion in New Zealand is reflected in the record (limited though it may be) of instances in which recognition of charitable status has been extended to organisations at a time when this was likely to have been denied in the UK and elsewhere.

For example, in December 2002 the New Zealand Inland Revenue notified the Church of Scientology that 'the advancement of Scientology meets the requirements of the definition of Charitable Purpose in . . . the Income Tax Act of 1994', and 'the Church of Scientology of New Zealand is a "society or institution established exclusively for charitable purposes"'. The New Zealand Humanist Society was also awarded charitable status. However, the *Exodus Ministries Trust Board* and other cases involving religious charities coming before the Commission (or Board, as it now is) have led the latter to comment that religious status alone may not constitute tangible public benefit under the terms of the Charities Act sufficient to warrant registration as a charity. This warning is one that acknowledges the continuing presumption of public benefit in relation to religious charities but is also a reminder that, presumption or not, all charities must nonetheless benefit the public.

Equality of religions

As Cooper J declared in *Carrigan v Redwood*,[110] 'the Roman Catholic Church is, therefore, in New Zealand in the same legal position as the Anglican Church or any other religious denomination'. This sentiment was echoed by Gresson J in *Watch Tower Bible and Tract Society v Mount Roskill Borough*:[111] 'every person is

---

108 [1985] 1 NZLR 673.
109 Ibid. Citing as a guiding precedent, the earlier ruling in *Church of the New Faith* in the High Court of Australia.
110 (1910) 30 NZLR 244 at p. 252.
111 [1959] NZLR 1236 at p. 1241.

free to choose the context of his own religion and it is not for a Court, in a field in which it can profess no competence, to disqualify upon some a priori basis certain beliefs as incapable of being religious in character'. This was not always the case: the Tohunga Suppression Act 1907 specifically discriminated against Māori spiritual beliefs.[112]

- SECULARISM

As the Human Rights Commission points out, 'New Zealand is a secular State with no State religion, in which religious and democratic structures are separated',[113] albeit within a distinct Christian colonial heritage.

The right to manifest religion or belief

The New Zealand Bill of Rights Act 1990, s.15, provides for the right of any person to manifest their religion or beliefs through worship, observance, practice, or teaching, either individually or in community, in public or in private. This right is one that under s.5 'may be subject only to such reasonable limits prescribed by law as can be demonstrably justified in a free and democratic society'.

One such manifestation of religious belief, which has caused difficulty for the Jewish community in this and other jurisdictions, is the requirement that the slaughter of animals for human consumption be conducted without stunning. The New Zealand animal welfare code states that all animals set for commercial consumption must be stunned prior to slaughter so that they are treated 'humanely and in accordance with good practice and scientific knowledge'. While this requirement accords with the expectations of the rest of society, it offends the Jewish community because their kosher laws necessitate slaughter by shechita or without stunning. In November 2010, the New Zealand Jewish community reached agreement with the Minister of Agriculture enabling the shechita of poultry to continue in New Zealand, and orders putting that agreement into effect were issued by the High Court in Wellington.

The s.15 right, specifically extended under s.20 to provide protection for the cultural practices of minorities, has given rise to issues in New Zealand and elsewhere regarding the wearing of the burqa by parties when giving evidence in court proceedings.[114] Such a conflation of cultural practice and religious belief is a challenge for law per se but also impacts directly upon charity law, particularly in those jurisdictions where the promotion of human rights (and/or 'cultural identity', 'diversity') is recognised as a distinct charitable purpose.

---

112 7 Edw. VII No 13. The Act was not repealed until 1962.
113 See, further, at: http://www.hrc.co.nz/report/chapters/chapter09/religion02.html.
114 See, for example, *Police v Abdul Razamjoo* [2005] DCR 408.

Parental right regarding religious education of their children

Young J, in *Re Draco Foundation (NZ) Charitable Trust*,[115] noted that 'the essence of the advancement of education is that learning must be passed on to others'. The wide range of schools in this jurisdiction – single-sex schools, private schools, integrated religious schools, Kura Kaupapa Māori schools (immersion schools) and the correspondence school (for those unable to attend a local school due to geography, illness, disability or exclusion) – gives ample scope for parents to choose one that ensures appropriate religious values are passed on to their children.

The Education Amendment Act 1964, s.78, makes provision for religious instruction and observances in New Zealand's basically secular primary schools. If parents require religious instruction for their child, this is generally made available in State schools by voluntary instructors outside normal teaching hours. If they wish to avoid religious instruction, parents are permitted to exclude their child from a particular class on religious or cultural grounds. Technically, however, s.78 authorises State schools to provide religious instruction and this provision overrides the right to religious freedom under the New Zealand Bill of Rights Act 1990, s.4. The parental right seldom gives rise to issues and would not seem to have generated any case law.

Freedom of expression

This right, guaranteed by Article 19 of the UDHR and Article 19 of the ICCPR, also finds protection in the New Zealand Bill of Rights Act 1990, s.14, which states that:

> Everyone has the right to freedom of expression, including the right to seek, receive, and impart information and opinions of any kind in any form.

It has been declared that this section is 'as wide as human thought and imagination'[116] but also that 'it would not be in society's interests to allow freedom of expression to become a licence irresponsibly to ignore or discount other rights and freedoms'.[117] The Court of Appeal has held that any restriction on free speech must be proportionate to the objective sought to be achieved; the restriction must be rationally connected to the objective; and the restriction must impair the right to freedom to the least possible amount.[118] The right is supported by the Human Rights Act 1993, ss.61 and 131, which prohibit hate speech.

The right to freedom of expression has recently been thoroughly explored in two charity law cases. In 2012, Greenpeace of New Zealand Inc won its case to

---

115 HC WN CIV-2010–485–1275.
116 *Moonen v Film and Literature Board of Review* [2000] 2 NZLR 9 at para 15.
117 *Hosking v Runting* [2005] 1 NZLR 1.
118 *Moonen v Film and Literature Board of Review*, op. cit.

have its charitable status reconsidered after the Court of Appeal set aside an earlier ruling by the Charities Commission rejecting such recognition. The Charities Commission had ruled that Greenpeace's objectives, which included

> the promotion of conservation, peace [and] nuclear disarmament; and the promotion of legislation, policies, rules, regulations and plans which further the objects of the Society . . . and support their enforcement or implementation through political or judicial processes as necessary

constituted a political purpose which was not 'charitable' under the Charities Act 2005. That decision was upheld by the High Court in 2011,[119] which followed the ruling in *Molloy*,[120] but was then overturned by the Court of Appeal.[121] The latter stated that it would not depart from *Molloy*, which it said had effectively been endorsed by the Charities Act 2005 and had established that a society established for contentious political purposes is not established principally for charitable purposes. It held that while the prohibition on political purposes no longer applied in Australia, following the *Aid/Watch* decision,[122] it remained part of the current law of New Zealand. In August 2014, the Supreme Court[123] upheld an appeal against that ruling. Conceding that political purposes and charitable purposes were not mutually exclusive if the political purpose is itself charitable, the court went on to explain:[124]

> More importantly, it is difficult to see that all advocacy for legislative change should be excluded from being recognised as charitable. Promotion of law reform of the type often undertaken by law commissions which aims to keep laws fit for modern purposes may well be properly seen as charitable if undertaken by private organisations even though such reform inevitably entails promotion of legislation. Such advocacy may well constitute in itself a public good which is analogous to other good works within the sense the law considers charitable.

The second case concerned Family First, a charity known for its open espousal of partisan political allegiances and for lobbying in support of causes such as the parental right to administer corporal punishment and against gay marriage. As it explained on its website:[125]

> a 'natural family', not the individual, is the fundamental social unit . . . [a] 'natural family' is: . . . the union of a man and a woman through marriage

119 *Re Greenpeace New Zealand Inc* [2011] 2 NZLR 815.
120 *Molloy v Commissioner of Inland Revenue* [1981] 1 NZLR 688 (CA).
121 *Re Greenpeace New Zealand Inc* [2012] NZCA 535.
122 *Aid/Watch v Commissioner of Taxation* [2010] HCA 42.
123 *Re Greenpeace of New Zealand Inc* [2014] NZSC 105.
124 Ibid., at para 62.
125 See, further, at: https://www.familyfirst.org.nz/about- us/frequently-asked-questions/.

for the purposes of sharing love and joy, raising children, providing their moral education, building a vital home economy, offering security in times of trouble, and binding the generations.

Early in 2013, before the decision in *Greenpeace*, the Charities Registration Board deregistered Family First on the grounds that its main purpose was to promote particular points of view about family life, which, the Board concluded, was a non-charitable political purpose without public benefit. A notice of appeal was filed in the High Court in May 2013 and an interim order made under s.60 of the 2005 Act allowing Family First to remain registered until after the Supreme Court delivered its judgment in Greenpeace, which was delivered on 6 August 2014. In the light of that decision, the High Court allowing the appeal advised, 'in view of the Supreme Court's explanation that political purposes are not irreconcilable with charitable purposes, it is appropriate for the Charities Board to reconsider the position of Family First'.[126] The implications of this case have been summarised as follows:[127]

> The decision is that the purposes of Family First are charitable (in the same manner as those in the Greenpeace case), and so it should be registered as a charitable entity in New Zealand. This continues New Zealand's move to settle the question of whether purposes which are political, including those that advocate certain views, can be charitable. In *Greenpeace*, the Supreme Court of New Zealand, by a majority of three to two, held that there should no longer be a political purpose exclusion applied to New Zealand charities. This finding accords with the legal position in Australia.

Freedom of assembly and association

Article 20 of the UDHR guarantees the right to peaceful assembly and to freedom of association. Protection is also to be found in Articles 21 and 22 of the ICCPR, Article 8(1)(a) of the International Covenant on Economic, Social and Cultural Rights (ICESR) and in the New Zealand Bill of Rights Act 1990, ss.16 and 17.

The 1990 Act requires that any interference with the right to peaceful assembly be reasonable, to the least extent necessary to preserve some other proper interest, and be justified in law. For any organisation engaged in advocacy as a means of representing the interests of minority groups, such as those mentioned above, this is a crucial right and one which should not be constrained by arcane rules specifically intended to subject charities to restrictions that the law would not

126 *Family First New Zealand* [2015] NZHC 1493, at pp. 84–85.
127 See, McGregor-Lowndes, M. (ed.), *The Australian Nonprofit Sector Legal and Accounting Almanac 2015*, at: http://eprints.qut.edu.au/61386/.

tolerate being imposed upon ordinary citizens. This was emphasised in *Bradford v Police*:[128]

> in any free society, the factor of protest is part of daily activity. It is a right for everyone, whether their cause is attractive or unattractive and whether the form of protest is attractive or unattractive.

As in some other common law countries, such as Ireland, the limited range of legal structures available and suitable for contemporary charitable activity can impose restrictions on the right of association for charities in New Zealand.

Equality and non-discrimination

The 1990 Act, as noted above, prohibits discrimination on various grounds: s.19 guarantees freedom from discrimination on the grounds set out in the Human Rights Act 1993 (sex, marital status, religious belief, ethical belief, colour, race, ethnic or national origins, disability, age, political opinion, employment status, family status and sexual orientation), and s.20 provides protection for the culture, religion, and language of individuals who belong to ethnic, religious and linguistic minorities.

Discrimination, as Tipping J said in *Quilter v Attorney-General*,[129] can be discerned in 'the difference of treatment in comparable circumstances. For discrimination to occur one person or groups of persons must be treated differently from another person or group of persons', each case turning on its own set of facts.[130] The customary distinction between direct or indirect discrimination applies in this jurisdiction, as does the caveat favouring 'affirmative action' to counteract structural inequality.

The New Zealand courts, while maintaining a conservative approach that seldom strays far from mainstream common law jurisprudence, have cautiously sought to make links between national statutory human rights provisions and the developing international law on discrimination and equality. In *Quilter v Attorney-General*,[131] for example, the Court of Appeal noted that equality is one of the core principles underlying New Zealand's law on discrimination, even though that law contains no express reference to equality.

Religious discrimination

Under the Human Rights Act 1993, s.21(1) (as amended), discrimination is expressly prohibited in relation to religious belief and ethical belief (which also

---

128 [1995] 2 HRNZ 405, per Robertson J.
129 [1998] 1 NZLR 523.
130 *Orlov v Ministry of Justice and Attorney-General* [2009] (NZHRRT 28, 14 October 2009).
131 [1998] 1 NZLR 523.

means the lack of religious belief, whether in respect of a particular religion or religions or all religions), in employment, in partnerships, in access to places, vehicles and facilities, in the provision of goods and services and in the provision of land, housing and accommodation.[132]

The religious exemption

The Human Rights Act 1993, s.28, provides specific 'exceptions for purposes of religion'. The potential ambit of that discretion is uncertain due to both the broad legal interpretation now given to religion and to Mallon J's generous interpretation in *Liberty Trust* of activities that may be construed as 'outworkings' of religious faith.

Section 28(3) requires employers to accommodate the religious or ethical belief practices of an employee as long as any adjustment required 'does not unreasonably disrupt the employer's activities'. This has to be balanced against health and safety considerations in the work environment. An example of a breach of this provision occurred in 2003 when the Office of Human Rights Proceedings determined a case concerning a Seventh-Day Adventist who had been required, by his employer, to work on his Saturday Sabbath contrary to his religious beliefs. Exemption is also available under the Marriage Act 1955, s.29(2), which excuses Churches from the obligation to solemnise marriages contrary to their religious beliefs; a similar exemption exists in relation to religion and conscience in the Contraception, Sterilization and Abortion Act 1977, s.46.

While exemption from the prohibition against discrimination in relation to employment is specified in s.28, provision for educational establishments to be maintained wholly or principally for students of one religious belief is to be found in s.58(1).

The 1993 Act allows churches to discriminate on grounds of sex (including sexual orientation) with respect to the engagement of clergy. This exemption gave rise to an issue heard by the Human Rights Tribunal in *Gay and Lesbian Clergy Anti-Discrimination Society Inc v Bishop of Auckland*[133] which concerned a gay man who alleged he had been barred from training to become an Anglican priest because he was in an 'active' homosexual relationship. To become a priest in the Anglican Church, an applicant must be either single and celibate or in a heterosexual marriage, which the court found to be a valid requirement notwithstanding the introduction of the Marriage (Definition of Marriage) Amendment Act 2013. It further found that s.39(1) provided an exemption for the Church (and all organised religions) in their ordaining of ministers but did not allow sexual orientation (unlike sex and religious belief) to be a ground of discrimination for a qualifying body (i.e. the Anglican Church). Placing decisive weight on the

---

132 See, Mooney Cotter, A.-M., *Heaven Forbid: An International Legal Analysis of Religious Discrimination*, Ashgate, Surrey, 2009.
133 [2013] NZHRRT 36. See, further, at: http://www.justice.govt.nz/tribunals/human-rights-review-tribunal.

doctrines of the Anglican Church, the importance of clearly separating the remit of Church and State, and ensuring that the court did not trespass into either, the plaintiff's claim of indirect discrimination was dismissed.

Discrimination (and exemptions) on other grounds

The Human Rights Amendment Act 2001 introduced additional safeguards against discrimination on grounds such as age, disability or sexual orientation in the policies and the practices of government agencies.

• GENDER DISCRIMINATION

New Zealand ratified CEDAW in 1985 and its optional protocol in 2000. Nonetheless, the Human Rights Act 1993 does not explicitly prohibit discrimination on the basis of gender and, as Professor Judy McGregor recently pointed out:[134]

> we keep telling the United Nations we were the first to grant women the vote, but we still don't have equal pay for women or pay equity for carers. Nor do we have adequate paid parental leave, and we continue to suffer completely unacceptable levels of violence against women.

This is in keeping with comments made by the Human Rights Commission that although the country is making some progress as regards the role of women in the workforce,[135] women remain under-represented in areas of public life such as law, governance and corporate sector leadership, and the gender pay gap in 2014 was 9.9 per cent. In 2014, New Zealand was ranked 13th out of a total of 142 countries in the Global Gender Gap Report which ranks countries in terms of gender equality under four heads: economic participation, health, education and political empowerment.[136] The likelihood of current socio-economic gender disparity being redressed in the short term suffered a setback when the National Council of Women of New Zealand Incorporated was controversially deregistered as a charity in 2010, reregistered in 2012, and that registration eventually backdated (to 2010) by the High Court in 2014.[137] That such a society, with a record of striving to improve the status and conditions of women since its founding in 1896, should have to undergo a public ordeal on the basis of what proved to be the unwarranted charge that it was not established and maintained exclusively for charitable purposes – as it had a purpose of political advocacy which

---

134 See, further, at: http://www.news.aut.ac.nz/news/2015/april/new-zealands-human-rights-reputation-at-risk.
135 Human Rights Commission 'New Zealand Consensus of Women's Participation 2012' at p. 2.
136 See, the World Economic Forum's annual report on the global gender gap at: http://www.weforum.org.
137 *The National Council of Women of New Zealand Inc v Charities Registration Board* [2014] NZHC 3200.

could not be considered to be ancillary to its other charitable purposes – adds weight to the HRC concerns.

- RACIAL DISCRIMINATION

The Race Relations Act 1971, which made incitement to racial disharmony a criminal offence, presaged the setting up of the Office of the Race Relations Commissioner in 1972, which was merged with the Human Rights Commission in 2002.

In 2013, the UN Committee on the Elimination of Racial Discrimination made 15 recommendations for improving race relations in New Zealand and expressed its particular concern regarding reports of persistent discrimination against migrants, particularly of Asian origin, in the labour market, and that the Human Rights Amendment Bill would abolish the designation of Race Relations Commissioner and make the role subject to the direction of the Chief Human Rights Commissioner.[138] It noted with regret that, despite previous recommendations, the Treaty of Waitangi was still not a formal part of domestic law, even though held to be the founding document of the nation, and urged the adoption of a National Action Plan on Human Rights which would includes plans on how to combat racial discrimination. The Committee recommended that efforts be intensified to improve the outcomes of Māori and Pasifika in the fields of employment and health, and in the administration of criminal justice by, inter alia, addressing the existing structural discrimination in New Zealand.

In *Haupini v SRCC Holdings Ltd*[139] a company which required a Māori employee to cover her tattoo was found not to be racially discriminatory, as fellow Māori employees were not asked to cover their tattoos and in her case the request was linked to a particular workplace function. Interestingly, the Tribunal noted that the outcome might have been different if the claim had been based on culture.

- SEXUAL DISCRIMINATION

Both the Human Rights Act 1993 and the New Zealand Bill of Rights Act 1990 prohibit discrimination on the basis of sex.

Following a succession of cases in which the judiciary wrestled with new definitions of family and with the problems entailed in transposing familiar concepts into a reconfigured and more challenging social and legal landscape,[140] the Court of Appeal in *Quilter*[141] considered same-sex marriage and held that the Marriage Act 1955 was

---

138 See, further, at: http://www2.ohchr.org/english/bodies/cerd/docs/co/CERD-C-NZL-CO-18–20_en.pdf.

139 [2011] NZHRRT 20.

140 See, for example: *VP v PM* (1998) 16 FRNZ 61 (lesbian mother retains custody of two children); *Re An Application by T* [1998] NZFLR 769 (second parent adoption by lesbian mother of partner's child by donor insemination refused); *A v R* [1999] NZFLR 249 (non-biological mother in *Re An Application by T*, ibid., held liable for child support payments as a step-parent); and *Re application of AMM and KJO to adopt a child* [2010] NZFLR 629 ('spouse' includes de facto heterosexual couples).

141 *Quilter v Attorney-General* [1998] 1 NZLR 523 1.

incompatible with the anti-discrimination standards set out in s.19 of the 1990 Act and s.21 of the 1993 Act. Consequently, on 17 April 2013, the New Zealand Parliament passed the Marriage (Definition of Marriage) Amendment Act 2013 enabling gay, bisexual, lesbian, transsexual and intersex marriages to be legal.[142]

* EMPLOYMENT DISCRIMINATION

The Human Rights Act 1993, s.21, prohibits discrimination in employment on the grounds of age (from 16 years), colour, disability, employment status, ethnic belief, ethnic or national origin, family status, marital status, political opinion, race, religious belief, sex (including childbirth and pregnancy) and sexual orientation. The Employment Relations Act 2000, in conjunction with the Employment Contracts Act 1991, provides employees with the right to take allegations of discrimination to the Employment Court.

The Court of Appeal decision in *Ministry of Health v Atkinson*[143] had considerable potential significance for the many domestic care charities and a wide range of families caring for dependants. The court then held that a government policy, making family members providing support services for their disabled children ineligible for payment, was discriminatory on the basis of family status. That decision, promptly overturned by the Public Health and Disability Amendment Act 2013, was duly followed in *Child Poverty Action Group Incorporated v Attorney-General*,[144] by a decision to similar effect. The alleged discriminatory provisions in the Income Tax Act 2007, prohibiting families receiving income benefits or accident compensation from being eligible for tax credits, were then found to be justified under the New Zealand Bill of Rights Act 1990, s.5. Such decisions lend weight to the charge made by some academics that New Zealand takes a 'needs-based' rather than a 'rights-based' approach to the administration of social security.[145]

* SERVICE PROVISION DISCRIMINATION

The Human Rights Act, s.44, prohibits discrimination in the provision of goods and services; however, this prohibition does not apply to access to membership of a club or to the provision of services or facilities to members of a club.

The Marriage (Definition of Marriage) Amendment Act 2013 is problematic in terms of guaranteeing gay couples access to a marriage service. While it is clear that a religious organisation is now enabled to conduct such a marriage ceremony, it remains somewhat uncertain as to what happens if celebrant clergy refuse to officiate and/or the couple are denied the use of their chosen Church.

---

142 Note also, the Human Rights Commission, *To Be Who I Am: Report of the Inquiry into Discrimination Experienced by Transgender People*, January 2008.
143 [2012] 3 NZLR 456.
144 [2013] NZCA 402.
145 See, Geiringer, C. and Palmer, M., 'Human Rights and Social Policy in New Zealand' *The Social Policy Journal of New Zealand*, Vol 30, 2007, pp. 91–108.

In New Zealand, as in many other common law countries, this is fraught with religious discrimination issues.

The 2013 Act also gives rise to adoption issues, as same-sex married couples will now be eligible to apply jointly to adopt a child. This will present traditional faith-based adoption charities with the same forced choice as faced by their counterparts in the US and UK. Catholic Social Services in Christchurch and the Latter-day Saints Social Services, for example, are restricted by their religious beliefs in the range of services they can offer. Specifically, although both engage in ancillary adoption work, their discriminatory beliefs exclude the possibility of contracting with same-sex prospective adopters and they are therefore excluded from registration and regulation by government as adoption agencies.

Adoption was also central to the proceedings in *Keelan v Peach*[146] which concerned the disposition of an estate involving a *whangai* child.[147] As this form of adoption is specifically declared by the Adoption Act 1955 to have no legal effect, the court was unable to find that the plaintiff could be a person entitled to claim under the Family Protection Act 1955, s.3, as a 'child of the deceased'. Arguably, this failure to place a child adopted in accordance with well-established cultural practice on the same legal footing as one adopted in accordance with the provisions of a very dated statutory framework is at least a disparity that requires legislative correction to redress the consequent disadvantages that inevitably accrue to a *whangai* child and to avoid further compromising the adoption charities involved.

- 'POSITIVE ACTION'

The New Zealand Bill of Rights Act 1990, s.19(2), provides for exceptions to the prohibition on discrimination in respect of 'measures taken in good faith for the purpose of assisting or advancing persons or groups of persons disadvantaged because of discrimination'. This and similar provisions in the Human Rights Act 1998 require, as a pre-condition, that any such measures are actually needed: the intended recipients must be disadvantaged relative to others, and they must need, or be reasonably supposed to need, assistance in order to achieve equality.

In *Amaltal Fishing Co Ltd. v Nelson Polytechnic (No 2)*[148] the plaintiff alleged that the defendant's policy of reserving a quota of places in their fishing cadet course for Māori and Pasifika applicants constituted discrimination against its employees whose applications had been unsuccessful. In reaching its decision, the court focused on the prerequisite that the target group did not occupy an equal place with others in a particular community and that the intended measure was necessary for them to achieve that equality. It concluded that, in the absence of

146 [2003] NZFLR 727 (CA).
147 For centuries Māori have had a practice known as *whangai* or *atawhai* or customary adoption whereby a collective decision is taken, usually as a result of ongoing consultation between all members of the extended families or communities involved, that a particular child would be given to relatives for them to raise.
148 *Amaltal Fishing Co Ltd. v Nelson Polytechnic (No 2)* (1996) 2 HRNZ 225.

sufficient evidence from the defendant to that effect, the positive action grounds were not substantiated. This principle, of compensatory intervention justified by the relative disadvantages of the recipients' circumstances, also underpinned the decision in *Avis Rent A Car Ltd v Proceedings Commissioner.*[149] In a religious charity context, the Partnership Schools/*Kura Hourua* project provides an example of positive action. In June 2013, following the passing of the Education Amendment Act 2012, the legal framework was created for a third type of state-funded school, Partnership Schools/*Kura Hourua* which are to be accountable to government for raising achievement through a contract to deliver specific outcomes. In return they will have more flexibility to make decisions about how they operate and use funding. In addition, the religious charity Sanitarium together with Fonterra will expand their free breakfast programme to such schools.

• CHARITIES AS PUBLIC BODIES

Government activities are required to be compliant with anti-discrimination standards, including discrimination on grounds of sexual orientation, as set out in s.19 of the New Zealand Bill of Rights Act 1990 and s.21 of the Human Rights Act 1993.[150] The extent to which religious organisations, when delivering public services on behalf of government are thereby acting as public bodies and are similarly bound by the same provisions, is an open question.

Conclusion

Charity is the antithesis of rights, and the distance between them has yet to be satisfactorily bridged in this jurisdiction.

The Charities Act 2005, unlike equivalent legislation in England and Wales, failed to make any reference to human rights as a charitable purpose. Indeed, that statute can perhaps be seen as New Zealand continuing to follow the lead set by England and Wales – though at some remove – as it essentially did little more than adopt the model established by the Charities Act 1960. The Human Rights Act 1993, the New Zealand Bill of Rights Act 1990, together with other domestic legislation and ratification of international treaties and conventions, does not add up to a coherent assertion of human rights law. However, judicial deliberation in the recent and important cases of *Greenpeace* and *Family First* has brought into clearer focus issues which have for many decades helped distance charity law from human rights.

---

149 *Avis Rent A Car Ltd v Proceedings Commissioner* (1998) 5 HRNZ 501. The Tribunal then held that the practice of rental car companies of passing on to the client the higher insurance cost they incurred by hiring vehicles to drivers under the age of 25 was justified, provided that the difference could be established by reference to statistical or actuarial data.
150 See, the Human Rights Amendment Act 2001.

Part III

Contrasting tensions and political implications

10 Characteristic tensions and alternative perspectives

Introduction

Part II demonstrated that even in some of the more developed common law nations, the persistence of poverty, inequality, discrimination and other forms of inequity testify to the fact that neither individually nor in conjunction have charity or legal rights proved sufficient to ensure a fair and adequate distribution of opportunities for their citizens. In all probability such social engineering is beyond the reach of law: it lies more with politics, with the government of the day and with social policy choices to be taken in the light of other exigencies. While both bodies of law are thus politically confined – and the onus to address injustice will always remain the core business of human rights – charity nonetheless has a proud history of advocacy on behalf of the disadvantaged, and charity law has had a long if problematic association with political purposes. Moreover, charity and rights share with politics the same broad public benefit *raison d'être* with a focus on rectifying the effects, at least, of social disadvantage. It might, therefore, be reasonable to expect that they would intersect frequently on matters of importance to those adversely affected by birth, circumstance or prejudice, a supposition not borne out by the case law.

This final chapter reflects on the gulf between the concerns recorded by the UN Human Rights Council in its national universal periodic reviews and the type of human rights issues addressed by charity law as revealed in the case law. This leads into an appraisal of the tensions involved and of related alternative perspectives. So, beginning with an overview of the major issues noted by the Human Rights Council, the chapter gives particular attention to their nature, duration and severity before identifying and contrasting some jurisdictional themes. This picture is then set against an analysis of charity law functions, each accompanied by illustrative case law, in order to gauge the nature and extent of slippage between such functions and human rights outcomes. Having established the fact and characteristics of the disjunction, the chapter then turns to examine the principle of public benefit which clearly should provide common ground for both bodies of law. The chapter concludes by considering the significance of cultural context as a possible cause of the current lack of synthesis between charity law and human rights and briefly explores some alternative judicial perspectives that may be representative of cultural differences.

Human rights: the UN reports and charity law

The UPRs conducted by the UN Human Rights Council provide a candid appraisal of a nation's shortfall in meeting its human rights obligations. This and other mechanisms for ongoing audit clearly reveal the extent to which each nation is attempting to remedy that shortfall.

Human rights deficit

There are some themes in the agenda of deficits noted in the Council appraisals of the six common law jurisdictions studied. One such is the plight of the indigenous communities, relative to the socio-economic advantages of their respective 'host' societies in Australia, New Zealand, Canada, the US and to some extent also in Ireland with regard to the Travellers. This particular cross-jurisdictional human rights deficit is notable because of the very marked degree of social inequality it represents, its systemic and embedded nature, and also because it has repeatedly attracted Council censure to little or no avail. Other prominent themes include the following: child poverty (UK, Canada and New Zealand); treatment of migrants and asylum seekers (UK, Ireland and Australia); abuse or inequality in the treatment of women (Ireland, Australia and New Zealand); disability rights (Ireland, Canada and Australia); and historic child abuse by clergy (all jurisdictions).

Issues of interest, due more to their singular association with a particular jurisdiction than to any cross-jurisdiction relevance, include the following: UK (no FGM prosecutions, the impact of inadequate water and poor sanitation, abuse of anti-terrorism powers and incidence of human trafficking); US (abuse of anti-terrorism powers, data surveillance, detention and imprisonment, death penalty, racism and access to abortion); Ireland (access to abortion, treatment of women (particularly single mothers), lack of non-denominational schools); Australia (treatment of asylum seekers, the high level of violence against women, the rights of LGBT persons and the use of enforced sterilisation procedures); and New Zealand (violence against women and children, and gender inequality).

Charity law relevance

Insofar as there is a hierarchy of laws, charity must be rated quite low: some of the jurisdictions studied do not have any charity-specific legislation; for most, the transition from common law to statute law has occurred only recently and then was largely confined to simply encoding the common law. Its weighting relative to human rights law is very weak: there is no body of international charity law; there is no provision for it in any nation's constitution; nor does it usually merit its own designated regulatory body. Arguably it only just qualifies as public law.

To suppose, therefore, that charity law is currently in a position to succeed – or make any real impact – where human rights law has failed, in relation to the above matters, would be naïve. Although it has often made an ameliorating contribution, its substantive role has lain more in the breadth and sustainability of its enrichment of society, its encouragement of altruism and in fostering social capital. In relation to deep-seated social disadvantage, however, as the preceding chapters have noted, the law as opposed to the concept of 'charity' is both subject to serious constraints and is inherently flawed in certain respects.

Constraints

The law relating to charity has long been constrained in ways which restrict its capacity to make much impact on the sort of human rights issues mentioned above that have been of concern to the Council. Most obviously, there are the political purposes and the public policy constraints, but others such as those due to concerns arising from its common law origins also inhibit effectiveness.

- THE POLITICAL PURPOSES CONSTRAINT

The strong historical record of charities leading social campaigns to end slavery, introduce votes for women etc has been eclipsed for decades by their relative silence on contemporary issues such as child abuse by clergy. It would be hard to overstate the enduring suppressing effect on the natural advocacy role of charities that followed the judicial rulings in *Bowman*[1] and *McGovern*[2] (see, further, Chapter 2), rulings that now seem wholly at variance with the right to freedom of expression. Given that the judiciary in New Zealand have recently decided to adopt the approach of their colleagues in Australia and break from the political purposes constraint, the voice of protest from charities on important social issues should in future be heard – at least in those countries.

- THE PUBLIC POLICY CONSTRAINT

Where an entity is in breach of the law, then plainly it cannot be charitable. The same rule applies in relation to charities and public policy, but its application can be more complicated and inconsistent. When, as in Canada, a gift to fund a scholarship is restricted to white Protestants,[3] or, as in the US, one to 'further the development of the Irish Republic',[4] then the fact that they are in breach of public policy and therefore cannot be charitable is readily understood. But public policy to a greater extent that law is more likely to differ between jurisdictions. In Australia, for example, the judiciary, in contrast to their Canadian counterparts, seemingly had no difficulty in recently finding a gift for the treatment of white (underlined twice) babies compatible with public policy.[5] However, in an encouraging development with implications for other jurisdictions,

1 *Bowman v Secular Society Ltd* [1917] AC 406.
2 *McGovern v Attorney General* [1981] 3 All ER 493.
3 *Canada Trust Co v Ontario Human Rights Commission* (1990) 69 DLR (4th) 321.
4 *Re Killen* 124 Mic 720, 209 NY Supp 206 (1925).
5 *Kay v South Eastern Sydney Area Health Service* [2003] NSWSC 292.

the Australian judiciary in distinguishing between trusts that are 'contrary to the established policy of the law' and trusts whose object is to 'introduce new law consistent with the way the law is tending' have given permission for charities to push the public policy boundaries.[6] Again, in the antipodes, judicial initiative may permit the voice of charities to be heard in future on the sort of issues that have been of concern to the Council.

- COMMON LAW RULES

As previously mentioned, there are common law principles and rules that bind and restrain the role of charity, not always in ways that are logical or defensible.

Foremost of these are the charitable purposes: an entity simply cannot qualify as charitable unless its purposes conform to one of the four *Pemsel* heads as extended by analogy or by statute. Inevitably this means there is a time lag between the emergence of a new social problem and a ruling by court or regulator that it can or cannot be interpreted as coming within the legal definition of 'charitable purpose'; a time lag which may render obsolete the intended object of the charity (e.g. leprosy[7]). The public benefit test (with its varying presumption in relation to different charitable purposes) and the exclusivity rule then come into play, and, should the entity acquire charitable status, there follows the issue of which of the few legal structures available is suitable to give effect to the charity. Among the many other legal constraints that also contribute to limit the application of charity are the founder's kin rule and the anomaly which permits discriminatory bequests in restraint of religion (see, further, Chapter 2).

Inherent flaws

The above constraints have combined with certain inherent flaws in charity law to obstruct the latter's capacity to adopt an effective interventionist role with potential to impact the Council's concerns.

- POVERTY

Charity, in law as in concept, does have a redistributive function: donor gifts and the tax system combine to produce that result, for example in the funding and consequent impact of the Gates and Clinton foundations on disease in Africa, and, when combined with government funds, can make the overseas aid delivered by charities a potent anti-poverty weapon. However, in law this function is otherwise strictly constrained: it is not axiomatic that charity lessens poverty. The fact that it has been restricted to addressing effects rather than causes (though no longer in the UK) must have inhibited its capacity to effect change in many

---

6 *Public Trustee v Attorney General of New South Wales* (1997) 42 NSWLR 600, per Santow J at p. 621.
7 *A-G v Hicks* (1810) 3 Bro CC 166n.

of the circumstances noted above by the Council, including that of indigenous communities with which charities have been engaged for centuries; indeed, some charities, emanations of religious orders, have worsened such circumstances by inflicting generations of child abuse. Even when dealing with the effects of poverty, as in the case of responding to the plight of asylum seekers, charities would seem to be having little impact. Although the issue is clearly more one for politics and justice than for charity, the latter have over the past few years shown an inability to effectively intervene in the flow of migrants, manage the distribution of resources and people, mediate on behalf of the most vulnerable and advocate on behalf of those facing detention or deportation.

In fact, although all charitable purposes have always been required to be for the public benefit (some presumptively), that test has never been interpreted as importing a requirement for poverty relief; while the poor must not be excluded as possible beneficiaries, it has never been necessary to demonstrate that a charity will lessen their poverty. The fact that child poverty and child welfare charities co-exist indefinitely in the UK, for example, may question the effectiveness of charities but not their legal definition as such. Moreover, not only are charities legally excused from any obligation to lessen poverty, they are also permitted to make profits and – in an increasingly competitive contract culture – many do so.[8] Some, as mentioned earlier – by imposing fee-paying limits to access elite schools, hospitals, opera houses etc – may well exacerbate the effects of poverty.

• INEQUALITY

Many charities are to the fore in addressing inequality, but some accommodate it while for others inequality is mandatory. Indeed, there is a sense in which the charitable sector itself perpetuates a culture of inequality, one of its characteristics being the number of charities that cluster around the same purpose, as happens in relation to many of those concerned with health (e.g. cancer research) or child welfare. There is a definite 'pecking order' within each group, which encourages competition for public donations, government grants, media attention and for staff, while discouraging the sharing of resources and information. Further, as noted, there is among some charity executives in some jurisdictions an 'entitlement culture' that gives permission for levels of remuneration that rival those available at the highest levels of government. Such divisiveness, siphoning of resources and wasteful duplication has long been recognised and sets an unfortunate example, particularly in relation to those that share an equality and human rights platform.

The fact that religious organisations and their emanations have exemption from statutory equality provisions is problematic. Arguably, while this may be understandable in the context of traditional prescribed roles, integral to religious

8 See, for example, the large number of fee-paying hospitals with charitable status such as St George's Hospital in Christchurch, New Zealand, and the for-profit concerns of religious bodies such as Sanitarium (an emanation of the Seventh Day Adventist Church) which has a multimillion business producing weet-bix in that country.

ceremonies, it is less so in relation to activities performed as outworkings of religion: not just as regards proselytism but also in schools, hospitals and other services – often in mainstream commerce – managed under religious auspices. The exercise of such overt inequality – mainly in relation to gender and sexual orientation – perpetuates such practices in some of the more important institutions of contemporary society, provides an inconsistent message that may undermine the legal obligation of their religious adherents and, in all probability, dilutes civic resolve to eradicate inequality in the treatment of women and LGBT persons.

The propensity for some charities to accommodate inequality can be obscured by an ethos of promoting diversity and multiculturalism. Respect for culture specific practices can, in some instances, be pernicious and may well be at least a contributory factor in accounting for the lack of FGM prosecutions in the UK, a blindness to honour beatings and the tolerance extended to arranged marriages, 'child brides' etc. There may also be some latent cultural factor in play that accounts for the fairly widespread phenomenon of gender inequality: not just the pay gap, and the implication of lower status, but in the level of actual violence endured by women. There is little evidence that charities have been able to make much difference in attitudes and behaviour that continue to permit this insidious undercurrent in the daily life of developed nations.

• DISCRIMINATION

Given the lead role successfully played by charities, mainly in the US but also in the other jurisdictions studied, in campaigning for the introduction of laws providing for universal suffrage, ending racial segregation and prohibiting discrimination, it is an uncomfortable fact that discrimination – especially in relation to race and religion – retains its hold in attitudes and practices, perhaps particularly in the US. This has not been helped by perpetuating the traditional latitude given to testators' bequests subject to a discriminatory condition.

Paradoxically, it is the social role played by religious charities that often exacerbates rather than alleviates discriminatory practice, and nowhere more so than in the US. As charity law licenses an ever-growing spread of assorted belief systems within the definition of 'religion' – each presumed to be for the public benefit (except in the UK), entitled to charitable status and exemption from equality laws – an escalation in associated discrimination with fragmentary consequences for civil society seems unavoidable. Conflation of religious values with contemporary medical and science issues is responsible for the difficulties noted by the Council relating to accessing abortion services and further extends social divisions. Added to this is the threat from Islamic terrorism and large-scale migration. As these combine to challenge the culture, values and resources of western nations, such nations are experiencing a worrying revival of anti-semitism and racial discrimination.

More generally, while charities have undoubtedly done much to facilitate the workplace integration of those placed at a competitive disadvantage by age, disability, gender, sexual orientation, race etc, where this has been by means of a 'quota system', such over-compensation may also risk introducing an accompanying stigma as an indirect form of discrimination.

Charity law: core business and human rights

The core business of charity law has always been confined to its charitable purposes, as defined in *Pemsel* and thereafter extended by analogy, and in some jurisdictions with statutory additions as an outcome of charity law reform. These are crucial aspects of its 'trust' legacy, and together with other common law rules they remain integral to the definition of 'charity' but restrict its scope. They are given effect by means of a specific set of legal functions, the limited terms of reference of which help explain the current relationship between charity law and human rights.

Dissonance: nature of the disconnect

As is evident from the six jurisdiction-specific chapters, charity law and human rights rarely intersect and when they do it tends to be only at the margins: the most striking aspect of the case law is the peripheral relevance of charity law to major human rights issues. The reasons for this would seem to be rooted in the long history of the trust, which gave rise to the straightjacket of charitable purposes, as administered in recent years by national Revenue agencies.

Charity: the trust approach

The Statute of Charitable Uses 1601, as the title suggests, was concerned with 'uses' – the precursor of 'trusts'. In England and Wales the trust became the legal structure for giving effect to charity, so, in due course, it was transferred to all common law jurisdictions, though some to a much lesser extent than others. Trusts, in general, were characterised by their specificity (except for charitable trusts, they were all private in nature and established for the benefit of identified individuals or a small and discrete class of persons) and subject to the courts of Chancery which developed a body of jurisprudence based upon principles of equity.[9] These stand as powerful reminders of the principled basis on which Chancery resolved disputes and clearly resonate with some of the more fundamental human rights.[10] The charitable trust, in particular, was focused on purpose, and

---

9 See, for example, Wylie, J.C.W., *A Casebook on Equity & Trusts in Ireland* (2nd ed.), Dublin, 1998, chap 1 'Fundamental Principles'.

10 These were as follows:

Equity follows the law.
Equity will not suffer a wrong to be without a remedy.
Equity acts *in personam*.
He who seeks equity must do equity.

most distinctively it was established for the public benefit. The Charity Commission[11] operated a regulatory regime that primarily policed the interpretation of trust objects to ensure conformity with charitable purpose. The weight of case law and key precedents clearly reveal the extent to which the body of charity law jurisprudence, shared among all the common law nations, grew and solidified around principles relating to charitable purpose. For centuries, the courts and regulators, when exercising their equity jurisdiction in respect of charities, focused on how trustees gave effect to their duties in respect of a donor's charitable purpose.

Charity: the Revenue approach

In the US, Canada, New Zealand and Australia there was never the same commitment as in England and Wales to trusts as the preferred legal structure, nor to the body of principles associated with trusts and trustees. Incorporation was always viewed as a more secure basis for charitable activity, and an early reliance upon the charitable corporation became a distinctive feature in the development of their charity law. In those jurisdictions, the Revenue was the lead regulatory agency, with a focus on income and no particular brief for charitable purposes other than as a threshold for tax exemption.

The defensive attitude of Revenue towards charity was clearly evident in its endeavours to 'fence in' such exemptions to prevent tax evasion (or avoidance) and it only reluctantly conceded incremental extensions to charitable status. It never had any incentive to seriously examine charitable purpose as a principled rationale that could be developed to provide a potential source for producing a public benefit outweighing the tax loss. It treated the charitable purposes classification simply as a litmus test for tax exemption together with a routine application of the ancillary common law rules regarding public benefit and exclusivity. Not until the turn of the century, as demographic trends combined with economic recession and the cost of combating terrorism and managing large scale migration forced a re-appraisal of future public benefit provision, did governments see

---

He who comes into equity must come with clean hands.
Delay defeats equity.
Equality is equity.
Equity looks to the intent rather than the form.
Equity looks on that as done which ought to have been done.
Equity imputes an intention to fulfil an obligation.
Where the equities are equal, the first in time prevails.
Where the equities are equal, the law prevails.

See, further, Ronan Keane, J, 'The Maxims of Equity' in *Equity and the Law of Trusts in Ireland*, Dublin, 1988, at p. 27.

11 Following the success of the Brougham Inquiry 1819–1837, the government in England passed the Charitable Trusts Act 1853, amended in 1855 and 1860, to establish a permanent Charity Commission to supervise charitable activity.

the need to examine charitable purpose as offering a way of spreading the costs of that provision and consider the merits of removing determination of that status from the Revenue.

The legal functions of charity law and implications for human rights

As argued in *Charity Law & Social Policy*,[12] the principal legal functions of charity law are protection, policing, mediation and adjustment, and support. They are a mix of those inherited from the Courts of Chancery and the law of trusts, developed through centuries of exercising the wardship jurisdiction for the support and protection of charities (and such other vulnerable subjects of the King as children and lunatics), and those required to provide a level of scrutiny sufficient to deter or detect abuse within the tax regime. Clearly evident from the outset, they have held fast in the common law jurisdictions over the past 400 years, though in the post–law reform era the emphasis now given to each varies somewhat from country to country. They are not untypical of the functional balance to be found in other bodies of law in a democratic legal system.

Protection

This, the original legal function, had its beginnings in the law of trusts and in the concern of the Court of Chancery to ensure that the value and purpose of a donor's gift was respected after his death, both for the encouragement of future donors and because of the sacred nature of a trust with its initial strong religious connotations. The special protection accorded to charities in law was recognised at a very early stage by entrusting responsibility for safeguarding charitable trusts to the Attorney General and the High Court. In England and Wales, the Charity Commission and trustees also had and continue to have a role in protecting charitable interests. By establishing through important precedents the particular legal characteristics of charity, mostly followed throughout the common law world, the judiciary together with the Charity Commission made a significant contribution towards protecting the integrity and autonomy of charities.

As charitable status became more attractive, carrying as it did a prestigious hallmark of social respectability and entitlement to generous tax exemptions, so this legal function has grown more sophisticated in terms of guarding the distinction between charity and other nonprofit entities. However, its effectiveness diminished in all common law nations as court involvement in charitable matters steadily faded, the number and range of nonprofit entities other than charities proliferated and more charities became incorporated and thus moved outside the reach of the Attorney General.

---

12 O'Halloran, K., McGregor-Lowndes, M. and Simon, K., *Charity Law and Social Policy*, Springer, The Netherlands, 2008, at pp. 99–104.

• CHARITY LAW REFORM AND CONSEQUENCES FOR HUMAN RIGHTS

Reform outcomes in the jurisdictions concerned cannot be said to have leant any extra weight to this legal function. A primary challenge for all national charity law reform processes was whether or not to adopt the admittedly expensive Charity Commision regulatory model which required a decoupling of the responsibilities for regulating charitable status and for policing tax-exemption privileges, with a statutory assigning of the former to a Commission. Few opted to do so.

Government reluctance may have been less to do with the additional expense involved and more about wishing to avoid introducing a possibly complicating layer of protective oversight. As governments move towards cultivating charities as public service providers, it may be that they would prefer to leave charities available and dependent upon direct contractual relations with them rather than interpose a mediating agency; this, along with the constraints on political activity and imposed by registration, may help explain the recent surge towards social entrepreneurship and new hybrid legal structures for philanthropy. It may also account for government failure to reboot the role of Attorney General, though no other country went quite as far as Ireland and excised that role.

The implications for human rights of this diminution in the protective function's effectiveness can be sensed in a general charity tendency towards subdued compliance and a muting of dissent within that cohort of service delivery charities. As such charities are drawn closer to government they may have good reason to fear that outspoken advocacy, on behalf of the disadvantaged group whose needs they represent, may jeopardise their eligibility for future government contracts. In addition, the prevailing climate of anti-terrorism has greatly increased charity exposure to surveillance and accountability mechanisms which again reduce the likelihood of their challenging government policy. The net result has been to erode charity independence and suppress their freedom of expression.

Policing

The legal function of policing, which from at least the introduction of taxation[13] has existed alongside protection, plays a prominent role in preventing abuse in relation to charities. The loss of tax revenue occasioned by an award of charitable status ensured that governments placed policing at the heart of their regulatory frameworks. The existence of a charities register, criteria for registration, and a designated government agency charged with responsibility for monitoring/ supervising the activities of charities, are essential preconditions for a policing function. In all countries, except for England and Wales, that responsibility was vested almost exclusively in the Revenue agency which has given effect to it mainly by rigorous application of the 'public benefit' test and 'exclusively charitable' rules.

---

13 Introduced in England and Wales by the Income Tax Act 1799.

In England and Wales, the Charity Commission has been the gatekeeper to charitable status more or less since established to do so under the 1601 Act.[14] In determining whether organisations and their activities comply with the definition of charity, it has relied less upon a defensive application of rules and more on a broad interpretation of contemporary public benefit.

• CHARITY LAW REFORM AND CONSEQUENCES FOR HUMAN RIGHTS

Reform outcomes in several jurisdictions (three UK nations, Ireland, New Zealand and Australia) gave effect to this function, in compliance with UDHR requirements (mainly Articles 7, 8, 11, 12, 19 and 20), by the following: establishing a statutory regulatory body, independent and with a specific brief for charities, to determine charitable status and provide for de-registration, with an appeal process; a formal and mandatory charities register to differentiate charities from other entities, and provide publicly accessible data in accordance with standards of transparency and accountability; and provisions for ensuring compliance with contemporary law and public policy (e.g. equality and non-discrimination).

However, while the initial incentives for charity law reform may have been progressive, with intentions that included broadening the capacity to respond to contemporary patterns of social need, all governments responded to the sudden outbreak of international terrorist attacks by rapidly recalibrating to ensure a priority focus on the need for a more stringent scrutiny of charities and the non-profit sector generally: policing moved swiftly to centre-stage. Government concern that charities and others could unwittingly become conduits for the transfer of funds to terrorist organisations led to all jurisdictions introducing tighter regulatory controls (tracking funds, communications surveillance etc) ensuring mandatory registration and accountability procedures with reduced exemptions. The imposed restrictions have undoubtedly hindered the work of charities in general but in particular have obstructed the overseas aid work of those with a humanitarian relief role in countries where terrorist insurgencies are rife. The inhibiting effect on freedom of expression is illustrated by the current ongoing intrusive scrutiny conducted by the CRA into Canadian charities such as PEN and Amnesty International, and the parliamentary inquiry into the charitable status of up to 100 advocacy organisations in Australia. This climate of suspicion was possibly also responsible for the disappearance of the promotion of human rights as a charitable purpose from the expected outcomes of the Irish charity law reform process. Moreover, a latent government preference for maintaining control may account for both the general move towards statutory encoding (thereby giving legislators, rather than reserving to the judiciary, the power to redefine charitable purposes) and the absence of an extended *Pemsel* plus list of such purposes in some post-reform charity legislation. It must also be acknowledged that

---

14 The Statute of Charitable Uses 1601 established a body of Commissioners with powers to supervise and inspect charitable trusts.

the removal in some countries of the centuries-old prohibition on charities pursuing political purposes has been a positive development for both charities and human rights.

Mediation and adjustment

This legal function, a legacy of the approach developed in the Courts of Chancery with an ameliorating effect on the more traditional adjudicative focus of the common law, has become an extremely important operational aspect of charity law. The varying extent to which jurisdictions provide for it, as apparent from institutional arrangements and case law, reflects the corresponding political will to facilitate the capacity of charity to address contemporary social issues and ease the burdens of government.

In a common law regulatory environment, it was only when the public benefit test and the spirit and intendment rule were employed to introduce a flexible interpretation of charitable purpose that pressing social policy issues such as the causes of poverty and cultural affirmation for minority groups could be addressed by charity law. Otherwise, charity law tended to ossify around traditional judicially established precedents. The availability and willingness of relevant agencies (e.g. the Charity Commission in England and Wales) to broaden the interpretation of charitable purposes to meet emerging patterns of social need has been critical to realising this legal function's potential, not just in the UK but also in the nations studied which adopted almost all precedents established in that jurisdiction. In the absence of such a specially designated agency to offset the traditional tax-driven concerns of charity law, little weight could be given to the mediation/adjustment function.

- CHARITY LAW REFORM AND CONSEQUENCES FOR HUMAN RIGHTS

Reform outcomes in some jurisdictions (three UK nations, Ireland and Australia) gave effect to this function, in compliance with UDHR requirements (mainly Articles 7, 12, 18, 19, 20, 22, 25, 26 and 27), by the following: establishing a regulatory body with powers/duties to develop the definition and capacity of charity; introducing statutory provisions to correct traditional constraints (e.g. broadening definition of 'religion' to accommodate non-theistic beliefs); and introducing *Pemsel* plus charitable purposes to confer eligibility on new classes of the 'socially disadvantaged'.

Decoupling the determination of charitable status from policing tax liability was, as mentioned above, probably the main charity law reform challenge for those governments whose Revenue authority continued to bear both sets of responsibilities. It was a challenge underpinned by a recognition that maintaining the traditional status quo entailed placing the Revenue in a position of increasing conflict of interest. As protector of the nation's tax revenue base, that agency guarded against more organisations becoming tax exempt and a drain on the pool of taxable entities, perhaps particularly in relation to human rights advocacy organisations, the activities of which might well be embarassing for government and could generate further claims for charitable status.

While three UK jurisdictions followed, not unnaturally, the lead of the fourth and established a Charity Commission, other countries were less enthusiastic: in Ireland it was the chosen model but launching was deferred for five years; in New Zealand, it was chosen, implemented and scrapped within a very short period; Australia launched a more ambitious model for all nonprofit entities, but is now preparing to abandon it; while neither Canada nor the US gave the prospect serious consideration. The result could lead to a two-speed charity law regime: those with the Commission model being able and willing to flexibly develop charitable purposes that address emerging areas of social need, while the rest maintain a more defensive approach that places a priority on defending the nation's tax revenue base by allowing the Revenue to stringently ration the awarding of charitable status. Faced with the absence of a Commission, and the increased marginalisation of the Attorney General, this legal function will be given effect by agencies for which it is at best a secondary concern and, if the current experience in Canada is anything to go by, will in all probability be superseded by the policing function, to the detriment of human rights organisations.

Support

Finally, in modern democracies the coercive or rule-enforcing effect of law tends to be balanced by supportive or enabling provisions. This being 'soft' law, however, such enabling statutory provisions are often expressed in general and discretionary terms. An explicit statutory duty requiring a named and appropriately resourced, independent agency, such as the Charity Commission, to provide specific services (e.g. assisting with administration, providing operational advice and guidance, promoting good governance and other measures to encourage the efficiency of charities) gives the best assurance of effective support being available for charities.

- CHARITY LAW REFORM AND CONSEQUENCES FOR HUMAN RIGHTS

There is little evidence that any reform outcomes were specifically designed to strengthen this legal function, though a positive by-product has been a general increase in the issue of practice guidance advice by regulators.

However, support requires a regulatory system that provides for transparency, accountability and inspires public confidence. In those jurisdictions which completed their reform process, the outcomes included modernised legislation and a charities register. In addition, some introduced a range of appropriate legal structures to facilitate corporate philanthropy and modern bespoke incorporated hybrid entities (Community Interest Companies, Charitable Incorporated Organisations etc) which provide flexibility and increase charity effectiveness. Such developments improve the environment for charities in general, including those with human rights purposes.

Public benefit: the principle as the way forward

Central to both charity law and human rights, and sharing common ground with the contemporary social democratic politics of all Part II jurisdictions, is the concept of public benefit which, as Fullagar J expansively declared in *Re Belcher*,[15] can be found in 'purposes whose fulfilment may reasonably be thought to minister to the safety or happiness or well-being or good conscience of the community'. In practice this should translate into addressing areas of social need such as poverty and humanitarian relief; homelessness, persecution and asylum; unemployment and exploitive terms of employment; access to health, care and education services and to basic public utilities such as drinking water; civil liberties; and environmental protection. They, or permutations thereof, constitute the bulk of the above matters of concern to the Council and, together with a myriad of associated issues, could equally justify intervention from any one or all three frames of reference.

Charity law and human rights: public benefit and the political dimension

At a minimum, human rights are about putting in place and giving effect to a platform of basic rights, while charity law is about chanelling donor gifts and associated tax privileges to further specific charitable purposes. While both might be expected to converge for the benefit of the disadvantaged, such as in the above-mentioned areas of social need, in practice they rarely intersect. The reasons for this have been noted, as has the fact that the pattern of non-convergence is largely replicated across all jurisdictions studied.

As the two bodies of law are characteristic features of the jurisdictions studied, which share a common political ethos, a strategic realignment of charity law and human rights would seem both sensible and possible. Arguably, a more coherent and balanced framework that allows the law to govern and give effect to these two important strands of social democracy – equally relevant to contemporary stresses in both domestic and international contexts – in a mutually supportive manner, is becoming a pressing necessity. Their combined terms of reference, driven by the political will representative of the jurisdictions concerned, offers the best chance of addressing issues such as those repeatedly raised by the Council.

The choice of regulator, and the associated institutional infrastructure for applying the functions of law, are crucial determinants of the latter's net public benefit. However, as evidenced in Part II, they are subject to considerable national variation. This can obstruct the functioning of both bodies of law and reduce any likelihood of achieving complementarity on a domestic basis while generating inconsistency and ineffectiveness in an international context. In contrast, where

---

15 (1950) VLR 11 at p. 13.

there are formal worked-through partnership arrangements between government and other sectors, this would seem to offer a political context more conducive to developing charity law, embracing the challenge of embedding human rights and thereby consolidating civil society.

Government/sector partnerships

Partnership arrangements between government and other sectors, such as established in the UK and Ireland and to a lesser extent in Australia and New Zealand, provide interesting examples of the mix of opportunities and risks afforded by this particular political context. Only the first three countries, where formal government/sector partnerships were in place, produced legislative extensions to the traditional *Pemsel* classification of charitable purposes – which represent a public benefit agenda of matters assigned or franchised out to charity – together with a Charity Commission regulator. They also have domestic human rights legislation and Commissions and are signatory nations to most international human rights treaties, conventions and protocols. However, the current defensive political climate would seem to be discouraging even their governments from developing further public benefit partnership initiatives and from attempting any co-ordination of charity law and human rights.

- ENGLAND AND WALES

This jurisdiction is distinctive because government has worked with representative sector bodies for many decades to cultivate a participative model of governance that promotes a shared approach to formulating social policy. The resulting multilayered government/sector partnership is notable because it is accompanied by a complex institutional infrastructure which has been sustained for some decades. The Office for Civil Society in the Cabinet Office has oversight of the 'compacts' and codes of practice at national, regional and local authority levels (the 'local strategic partnerships') that set out principles and review processes for resourcing and implementing public benefit strategies, particularly those associated with government/charity service provision. It also has responsibility for the Charity Commission, which has a central mediating role in relation to public benefit law, policy and practice. Of particular relevance, as noted in Chapter 4, is the fact that reformed charity law now accommodates not just a revised public benefit test and poverty prevention as a charitable purpose but also 'the purposes of the advancement of human rights, conflict resolution or reconciliation or the promotion of religious or racial harmony or equality and diversity'. This jurisdiction, therefore, is quite advanced in terms of forging a framework that encourages cross-sectoral planning and implementation of public benefit service provision. In so doing, it is creating a political context favourable to a synthesis of charity law and human rights, albeit one that remains compromised by the political purposes constraint and by a more generalised cultural resistance to the pursuit of rights.

• IRELAND

Not far removed from its neighbour in many respects, including in terms of building and sustaining a similar partnership, Ireland has recently developed a more centralised form of governance – perhaps in response to a severe economic crisis. Government retreat from a previous more open and participative cross-sectoral approach to social policy was demonstrated by the unilateral decision to mothball the charities legislation that it had spent years negotiating with the sector to finalise. That it should also delete an agreed provision to establish the advancement of human rights as a charitable purpose and expunge the protective role of the Attorney General from charity law indicates just how fragile its partnership arrangements have now become. While the need to continue reducing costs will push government further towards sharing responsibility for public benefit service provision with the sector, and it can now do so from a position of having finally implemented the Charities Act 2009, it would seem unlikely that in the short term this will include a greater accommodation for human rights.

• AUSTRALIA AND NEW ZEALAND

Both antipodean jurisdictions concluded their charity law reform processes with legislation that seemed to demonstrate government conviction that the UK regulatory model and associated arrangements offered the best way of maximising public benefit outcomes. Both have since resiled from that position: New Zealand having abandoned its short-lived Commission, and Australia formally announcing its intention to do likewise.[16] In neither country has the government/sector partnership endured for so long, been so thoroughly tested and grown to become so institutionalised as in the UK, and in both the retraction of legislative reforms may be attributed at least in part to underdeveloped trust and mutuality in that partnership.

In Australia, the uneasy government/sector relationship set within a characteristically volatile domestic political context has led to a curiously equivocal approach to human rights. On the one hand, this country has the dubious distinction of being the only modern democracy without a bill of rights incorporated into its constitution. On the other, it has statutorily extended the *Pemsel* charitable purposes to specifically include 'promoting or protecting human rights' and, unlike the UK, it has removed the prohibition on charities having political purposes. In New Zealand, the charity law reform process failed to introduce statutory recognition for human rights as a charitable purpose and to repeal the political purposes embargo; although, in the latter case the judiciary have now compensated for the legislature's omission. In neither jurisdiction does the

16 In both countries, while the reforming legislation remains in place, the intended Charity Commission role of the regulator has already been, or in the case of Australia is threatened to be, considerably reduced.

government/sector relationship currently have the synergy and momentum necessary to initiate a collaborative strategy for future public benefit provision, nor would there seem to be a political will to further embed human rights let alone consider ways of harmonising the functions of rights and charity law.

• US AND CANADA

Neither of these federated jurisdictions has a nationwide government/sector partnership with the sophistication and lifespan of that in England and Wales: in the US there is no evidence of government intent or sector capacity to construct such a model; in Canada tentative efforts to begin such work have made little progress. The fact that the nonprofit sector in both countries is not as coherent and politically mature as in the UK is reflected in the more enabling than negotiating role played by their respective umbrella organisations which lack the leadership required to identify key sector interests, rally organisations around a clearly identified national agenda and sustain the momentum necessary to negotiate a working relationship with government. The corollary is that the sector has been of insufficient political weight to attract serious attention from government. Consequently, in both, charity law reform has been largely relegated to increasing the efficiency, effectiveness and security of the taxation system.

Human rights jurisprudence, on the other hand, is well developed in both countries but unaccompanied by any closer relationship with charity law. While the US provides federal recognition for the defence of human rights as a charitable purpose, there is no equivalent specific recognition in Canadian law. In both, the traditional common law constraint on charities having political purposes remains largely in place: the former permits limited advocacy for public charities to bring about a particular change in law or policy but denies private foundations any equivalent right; the latter prohibits it unless it is ancillary and incidental and accounts for no more than 10 per cent of income. The strong anti-welfare political stance in the US together with the characteristically pragmatic politics of Canada militate against the likelihood of either initiating a more holistic exploration of charity law as a field for sourcing further public benefit output or of engineering a closer alignment between it and human rights.

Charity law and human rights: the public benefit principle as a basis for synthesis

Charity – with the public benefit as its USP – is morally obligated to address social disadvantage and therefore should be more relevant than it currently is to the above-mentioned Council concerns. While ultimately the responsibility to ensure lasting change in the causal factors producing disadvantage lies with human rights and/or politics, the onus to be a first responder and to at least ameliorate its effects must rest with charity.

Titmuss: charity, rights and discrimination

In his final chapter 'The Right to Give', Titmuss suggested that donor anonymity, lack of personal reward and inability to select recipients amounted to more than merely the characteristics that distinguished the UK National Blood Transfusion Service from its US counterpart. He argued that it was precisely such freedom of choice – enabling an individual to give for the benefit of others, coupled with constraints preventing them from doing so on a basis that may discriminate on grounds of country, religion, gender, locality etc – which was to be valued in a democracy. As he then explained:[17]

> It was the explicit or implicit institutionalization of separateness, whether categorized in terms of income, class, race, colour or religion, rather than the recognition of the similarities between people and their needs which causes much of the world's suffering. By not doing something – by not giving donors a 'right' to prescribe the group characteristics of recipients – the Service thus presumes an unspoken shared belief in the universality of need.

At first sight this argument seems equally irreproachable from the perspectives of both charity law and human rights. The 'universality of need' from the former perspective may, for example, indicate intervention for the advancement of religion, or from the latter it may suggest a right to religious freedom. But in either case, it is the particular circumstances that defines the need and in so doing sets the eligibility criteria for relief; any number and variety of persons may at any time fit within such circumstances, and, should this be verified, they thereby gain legal recognition as legitimate claimants for intervention. The question that then arises is – should the response be from charity or human rights?

Charitable purposes do, of course, 'prescribe the group characteristics of recipients': donors are specifically required to select from the *Pemsel* classification; only those who can fit their needs within a designated charitable purpose may qualify for assistance; and the regulator ensures that intervention is appropriately targeted. Human rights are similarly classified and the claimant must select from the spectrum available: the judiciary or HRC ensure that intervention is appropriate. Specificity and matching are undeniably present in both. While the 'universality of need' and a corresponding eligibility to claim intervention is accepted, it is politics that determines whether any such intervention should follow and, if so, whether it should take the form of executive government action and/or be sanctioned by charity law and/or human rights. Contrary to the Titmuss perspective, it then falls to government, regulator or judiciary – applying specificity and matching criteria – to decide whether a claimant becomes a recipient.

This still leaves unanswered the more basic questions: whether the response should be from charity or human rights; what role should politics play; and are

17 Titmuss, R.A., *The Gift Relationship: From Human Blood to Social Policy*, Allen and Unwin, London, 1970, at p. 238.

these modes of intervention mutually exclusive? As of summer 2015, these were questions urgently demanding answers in the face of the rolling disaster that constituted the migrant crisis confronting Europe.

Cultural context

The Titmuss concept of the 'universality of need' is redolent of the welfare state and of the cultural context typified by Britain in the decades that preceded the Thatcher era. Such language now seems quite anachronistic in Britain, was always inappropriate in the US, and is currently of little relevance in the other social democracies, as they lean increasingly towards neo-liberalism. However, humanitarian emergencies such as the 2015 migrant crisis in Europe demonstrate that in some circumstances no other concept is as viable or appropriate. Whether classified as 'asylum seekers' or 'economic refugees', their needs and impact upon host communities are the same and, in the absence of any other factors, impoverished migrants must be equally entitled to benefit from political, charitable and human rights intervention.

The concept, like the public benefit principle, is central to charity law and human rights. It can be understood, as Titmuss intended, free of cultural conotations but domestic politics determine the response it generates from contemporary nation states. Arguably, within the common law world, this in turn is contingent upon the extent of a nation's welfare state experience which did much to shape and ultimately to differentiate the understanding of citizenship in the jurisdictions studied, with corresponding implications for their current approach to both charity law and human rights.

The welfare state model

The jurisdictional differences noted in Part II would seem to correlate with a proximity to the welfare state ideology. Although this model was adopted, to a varying degree, in Ireland, New Zealand, Australia and Canada, it never wholly transcended its UK origins (nor, perhaps, its health care and welfare benefits focus).

The fact that, among the common law countries, the welfare state experiment was implemented most fully in the UK set that jurisdiction somewhat apart from the others in terms of subsequent national expectations as to an extensive spectrum of public benefit services that should be provided by government. In so doing, it also, perhaps, introduced an egalitarian acceptance that the accompanying sense of civic 'entitlement' was collective: it was not just that services would be available to the disadvantaged on a non-stigmatising basis but that the same service would be available to all, regardless of income or class; you would 'wait your turn' and there would be no 'queue-jumping'. Again, perhaps, this was coupled with an acceptance that service specification and quality was a government matter: a dutiful reliance on 'government knows best' when it came to identifying social need, service design and matching service to need. This model was not so very different from that in place in other welfare or centrist states of western and northern Europe.

Arguably, a consequence of prolonged exposure to this dynamic inculcated a civic attitude prejudicial to self-assertion: the intuitive response to need, whether personal or social, being that government will fix it, accompanied by a sense that it would be improper to push for something not available to others with similar needs but also by an anxiety that resources were limited and there was only so much to go around. The corollary being that a mutual acceptance of the need for an element of give-and-take emerged in the working relationship between government and citizen; preparing the ground for a future government/sector partnership. This has, perhaps, militated against the full and prompt embedding of human rights in the UK. In jurisdictions such as Ireland, Australia and New Zealand the commitment to the welfare state model was considerably less, and the civic perception of matters that could or should be left to government or to charity or pursued through an assertion of human rights has varied accordingly. In all these countries the government/charity nexus has a history of proving more workable than government/rights or charity/rights.

The 'open market' model

The above welfare state model grew from the particular political context of post-war England. Seen as being tainted with national socialism, it was not an initiative that other governments readily or wholly embraced. In fact, this model was rejected by the welfare-adverse US which has always inclined towards accommodating disparity, letting the market decide what services at what price should be available, and a 'user pays' approach. Responsibility for health and social care was a matter for the citizen as 'consumer', not for government: the latter ensured the existence and regulated the standards of a modern welfare infrastructure comprising the usual range of hospitals, medical staff etc, but service access remained the responsibility of the individual to be either bought directly or in conjunction with such third parties as employers and insurance companies. The initiative for getting the right service when needed rested with the consumer, for whom choice and queue-jumping, at a price, were also available. The corrolary was that for the millions of US citizens without the means to privately access health care, charity was a familiar option but one that incurred greater stigma in this competitive environment than in other common law nations. This public/private division extended to include educational facilities at all levels, and utilities such as highways, prisons and emergency services. Indeed, the 'open market' ethos meant that typical public benefit welfare state services could often be available to US consumers from government, charity, a commercial outlet or from all three sources.

The welfare-adverse approach of the US has long been accompanied by an acute rights awareness. This most litigious of nations was essentially founded on a Bill of Rights (ratified in 1792) which enumerated core human rights – such as the freedoms of religion, speech, press, assembly and the right to keep and bear arms – that have ever since provided its citizens with countless opportunities for self-assertion. No other developed nation has as strong a reputation for upholding personal rights and forcing adjudication on clashes of rights. Those common law countries that are closer to the US than the UK on the welfare state spectrum – such as Canada and Australia – tend to share, though to a lesser degree, in the associated rights awareness. It is an environment in which the government/rights nexus has an established primacy over government/charity or charity/rights.

Charity and human rights: developments conducive to civil society

For Judt, the contemporary approach of US government towards public benefit provision was cultural and rooted in 'the American combination of economic insecurity, social inequality, and reduced or minimal government intervention in the field of welfare legislation'.[18] He concluded that, therefore, 'the US model is not exportable'.[19] However, the evidence in recent years has been to the contrary. As charity law makes adjustments to accommodate human rights, and in all jurisdictions government becomes more accustomed to franchising out public benefit service provision to charity, while the UN ratchets up its monitoring of human rights compliance and issues evermore treaties, conventions and protocols, there are signs of gradual jurisdictional convergence – at least among the developed common law nations – and the convergence is towards the US approach. The case law trends are revealing.

Religion

Rapidly becoming the single most potent source of contemporary social controversy – between adherents of different religions and beliefs, and between them and secularists – in both domestic and international contexts, religion is reclaiming its age-old role as simultaneously both the best and the worst force for generating social capital. This time, however, it would seem that the courts are developing an interesting approach which – at least on a domestic basis – may help diffuse confrontation and inject some perspective into what must otherwise build up to the traditional inflammatory stand-off between the parties concerned.

In Australia, the *ratio decidendi* of cases such as *OV and OW*[20] and *Cobaw Community Health*[21] indicate that the judiciary are not prepared to rubber-stamp traditional religious beliefs as providing sufficient good cause for exemption from the requirements of equality legislation; it is necessary to also factor in contemporary values. The *Trinity Western* series of cases reveal the Canadian judiciary

---

18 Judt, T., *Reappraisals*, Vintage Books, London, 2008, at p. 420.
19 Ibid.
20 *OV & OW v Members of the Board of the Wesley Mission Council* [2010] NSWCA 155.
21 *Cobaw Community Health Services Limited v Christian Youth Camps Limited & Anor* [2010] VCAT 1613.

working along the same lines,[22] and similar is happening in England and Wales.[23] The striving to ensure an equitable and balanced approach towards the traditional religions and the growing mix of belief systems is particularly evident in British case law. It was emphasised in *McFarlane*[24] and given effect in the recognition extended to spiritualists, Druids and Wiccas as coming within the legal definition of a religious charity, thereby broadening and levelling the contribution of religion to social cohesion. In the US the imperative that is the Church/State divide has perhaps licensed a more vigorous and competitive environment for religion, as illustrated by the overspill into the 'culture wars' where proxy religious issues[25] are proving very socially divisive. Again, however, the leavening effect of decisions such as that in *World Vision*[26] expands the status of religious charity across a broader field, thereby providing equal if diluted recognition to the social role of the growing numbers of contemporary religions. This approach which seems to treat religion objectively as just another social activity – like sport or entertainment – that is good in itself but may cause some to be disruptive, is also becoming apparent in the judicial attitude towards secularism. Canadian cases such as *Trinity Western*[27] and *Loyola High School*[28] show the judiciary distancing themselves from any suggestion that the courts should be secularist and instead making a point of treating secularism as they would religion – at arm's length. As the hegemony of the traditional religions in England and Wales, Ireland and other common law countries gives way to the mixed multifaith environment that has for some decades typified the US, as secularism becomes stronger and more challenging, and as militant strands of Islam harden attitudes among some Christians, it seems increasingly important that the judiciary hold the line by maintaining a strict neutrality and insisting upon balance and perspective.

Discrimination

The judicial precedents established in the US, as it continues to work through many issues associated with racial discrimination, have set useful benchmarks for other nations – particularly those responding defensively to the 2015 European migrant crisis[29] – and has served to focus equality jurisprudence on the rights of minorities more generally. Of particular relevance are the lessons to be learned

---

22 See, in particular, *Trinity Western University v The Law Society of Upper Canada*, 2015 ONSC 4250.

23 See, *R (on the application of Hodkin and another) v Registrar General of Births, Deaths and Marriages* [2013] UKSC 77.

24 *McFarlane v Relate Avon Ltd* [2010] IRLR 872.

25 *Burwell v Hobby Lobby* 573 US 134 S. Ct. 2751 (2014).

26 *Spencer v World Vision Inc.* No 08–35532, 2011 WL 208356 (9th Cir 25 January 2011).

27 *Trinity Western University v Nova Scotia Barristers' Society* 2015 NSSC 25.

28 *Loyola High School v Quebec (Attorney General)* 2015 SCC 12.

29 The Slovakian government's initial response that it would not take in migrants because they would be largely Muslim and it wished to protect its Christian culture was criticised as being discriminatory by other European nations – but not by all.

from the fastidious US judicial scrutiny of circumstances in which the State may be complicit in preferencing one group over others, especially in the functioning of social institutions. The transference of principles is now playing out in all the common law jurisdictions studied in the context of education, dress, and a range of culture specific practices. As those nations inevitably follow the US and become evermore multicultural, so also are the 'affirmative action' – or positive discrimination initiatives pioneered in cases such as *Bakke*[30] – now being applied in many different contexts to redress asymmetry in social disadvantage. The balance to be struck in affirming minority cultures while protecting the identity of the majority, and doing so in a way that does not feed a competitive splintering of society, has long exercised the US, and its response to that challenge is again one from which other common law nations are now learning. Unfortunately, such US domestic judicial fastidiousness has to be set against its government's more cavalier international approach towards effecting change in Islamic countries.[31]

Equality

Everyday life in the workplace, schools, public transport, shopping and a range of other social settings provide the mundane context in which most people experience inequality, and it is there where it has proven most resistant to change. However, some promising initiatives in the fields of both charity law and human rights indicate that this will now be more purposefully addressed.

The traditionally privileged treatment of religion within charity law has been shaken by international revelations of decades of child abuse by clergy. This has generated concern that religious bodies should be as amenable to regulatory supervision as any other charitable entity. If the scandal has a redeeming feature, however slight, it may lie in a general awareness that all charity registration should be accompanied by regulary controls. This change in approach can be seen in the regulatory probing that now follows claims from religious entities for exemption from equality legislation when employing staff: there is now an onus on an employer to show why such an issue should not be resolved by reasonable accommodation instead of exemption. Further, in England and Wales, followed by the other three UK jurisdictions, the charity reform processes concluded with the inclusion of the promotion of equality and diversity as a charitable purpose.[32] The fact that the progenitor charity law jurisdiction should make such a commitment will undoubtedly in time convince others to follow suit; the case law

---

30 *Regents of Univ. of Cal. v Bakke*, 438 US 265 (1978). Also, see, *Grutter v Bollinger et al.*, SC 02–241 (2003).
31 A relationship between US-led armed intervention in Islamic countries – Afghanistan, Iraq, Libya, Somalia, Syria – the subsequent Islamic State uprising and the eventual 2015 migrant crisis is difficult to ignore. As also is the absence of US leadership in response to the latter which, it would seem, is to be defined as a problem for Europe.
32 For England and Wales see the Charities Act 2011, s.3(1)(h).

generated in the UK will itself set challenging precedents for judiciary and regulators elsewhere in the common law world. Indeed, the *Pemsel* plus approach adopted in the UK jurisdictions and Ireland, where reform outcomes included a statutory extension of charitable purposes, is arguably a positive development in charity law. Specifically enumerating the socially disadvantaged groups that merit charitable status is not only justifiable but necessary if government is to differentiate between types of social need, recognise that the needs of some are more acute and urgent than others, give equal weighting to the claims of new categories relative to those already granted charitable status, and target resources effectively. This has been reinforced in some jurisdictions by the statutory introduction of new legal structures for charity, to facilitate a developing trend whereby commercial companies opt to establish charitable foundations, funded and staffed from their profits.

The Human Rights Council UPRs steadfastly draw attention to matters such as the gender pay gap, the treatment of women, and access to family planning and abortion services. The existence of a cultural dimension to such inequalities is evident, for example, from the Ireland profile (see, further, Chapter 5). By calling the government of such countries to account, before an international panel of representatives from fellow signatory States, the exposure increases the pressure to move towards compliance.

Conclusion

As suggested in the opening paragraphs of this chapter, the business of charities and human rights is and always has been intimately related to the business of governments. Poverty, manifestation of religious belief, education, civil liberties, and other components of Titmuss's 'universality of need' provide the *raison d'être* for both charities and human rights and are ultimately also political matters. Given their shared history, institutions and contemporary political ethos, the fact that the social policy of the common law nations has not sought to bring these strands into a more complementary, harmonious and ultimately more purposeful relationship is intriguing.

It would seem that the answer at least in part lies in cultural context: the welfare state experience being indicative, whether as cause or effect, of deeper differences that predispose governments and other sectors to forge sustainable partnerships. Such working arrangements are probably a pre-condition for constructing the more participative form of democracy necessary to address the balance between charity and rights and ensure both contribute congruently to the public benefit. It can only be hoped that those jurisdictions which emerged from the charity law reform process with strengthened political partnership arrangements and having made a tentative start at bringing some synthesis to these two bodies of law will eventually return to complete the task.

Conclusion

The provisions of charity law and human rights need to be harmonised. This is necessary in order to clarify their separate terms of reference and allow the respective agencies to address social disadvantage in a focused and complementary fashion. The lack of mutuality in the roles of these two key strands of social democracy in the developed common law nations is evident from the case law history of the jurisdictions profiled in Part II. Intervention by charity and human rights is more likely to impact social disadvantage, in particular the concerns identified by the Human Rights Council, if their roles can be clarified and co-ordinated.

The consequences of the failure to do so are only too graphically displayed in the scale of suffering accompanying the recent migrant crisis in Europe. This resonates with the asylum seeker phenomenon that has long been evident in Australia, the US, the UK and elsewhere. Clearly, the primary onus to respond to these and any other such humanitarian crisis falls on politicians: only executive decision-making by governments can authorise the strategy and command the resources necessary to tackle its causes and effects. Equally clearly, both charities and human rights organisations also have important roles to play. The public benefit principle, underpinning all three modes of intervention, strongly suggests that if each is to be deployed to maximum effect in dealing with social disadvantage, then the first step is for politics to transcend the present confusing dissonance and rationalise the functions of charity law and human rights.

Arguably, any such rationalisation will have to confront the key question – given that politics, charity and human rights all address social disadvantage, and do so from a shared public benefit platform, how then should their respective responsibilities be distributed and co-ordinated? It may be that an answer, or a step in that direction, lies in separating out responsibilities specific to either government or to charities from those entwined in a government/charity nexus.

Government

From at least the time of Magna Carta, reciprocal rights and duties have provided the basis of a civic contract between rulers and citizens: the common law grew from a simple code of judicially enforced rights; citizenship in all the nation states considered in Part II is now rooted in a mutual acceptance of rights owed to and by government. Ultimately, it was the susceptibility of the rights threshold to the vagaries of national politics and to wanton abuse in and by rogue states that gave rise to the introduction of fundamental human rights and justifies the continuing issue of further treaties, conventions and protocols designed to update and copper-fasten citizens' rights. The platform of such rights and the accompanying regulatory machinery is now extensive. The six common law jurisdictions considered in Part II are all signatory nations to most international rights instruments. These binding agreements, voluntarily entered into, are intended to underpin and extend citizens rights. They require government implementation.

Unless it has formally derogated, government will be called to account by the UN Human Rights Council through the UPRs for any implementation failure. The record shows that, in fact, governments are only too regularly so criticised, often for repeated failures in respect of the same rights; the third world treatment of indigenous citizens in first world countries is a particularly stark indictment, but child poverty, gender inequality, privacy rights and discrimination are also included among implementation failures. The case law reveals a concentration on issues involving a clash of rights between citizens or between the latter and institutions, as the judiciary arbitrate and seek to accommodate, while government all too often simply fails to implement and prosecute to enforce basic protections (e.g. the lack of FGM prosecutions in England and Wales).

Government capacity to discharge its primary duty to citizens is, however, shrinking in the face of globalisation. Whether dealing with international economic recession, climate change, pandemics, or political instability in the Caucuses and the Middle East, the exposure and vulnerability of citizens knows no borders, and governments are limited in what they can do. Perhaps in acknowledgement of their protective duty, or as a public relations exercise designed to allay anxiety, governments in all six jurisdictions studied have put in place layers of legislation to tighten security in the face of the current global menace – international terrorism. While it may or may not be an effective response to this particular globalised threat, the legislation constrains the rights of citizens, affects the chanelling of overseas aid and may well also be utilised by government to generally muzzle advocacy charities such as PEN, Amnesty International and Greenpeace.

The primary duty of government is to provide for the safety and welfare of its citizens. This duty vests reciprocal rights in the latter. Non-citizens may also be vested with rights (to claim asylum) in the event of government failure in their country of origin. As governments in all the developed common law countries become more defensive – oriented around economic planning and fiscal management, reliant upon extensive internal surveillance to detect possible terrorist activity and absorbed by the challenges of responding to foreign wars, climate change and the implications of demographic trends – so the dangers of an erosion of the civic contract increases.[1] The 'fire sale' of public utilities in the UK

---

1 Bizarrely illustrated by the recent British drone strike against British citizens in a country with which the British parliament had not sanctioned armed intervention.

and government acquiesence in the conversion of many charities in the US and elsewhere to for-profit commercial entities – notwithstanding that successive generations had paid in taxes and donations for the ongoing public benefit of such services – has served notice of government intent. Diminishing industrial productivity and capacity to provide for the welfare of its own ageing and more disabled population is also increasing government reluctance to enlarge the care burden by accepting responsibility for the lengthening queue of migrants seeking opportunities for a better life – including many from the countries it has helped to destabilise. The incarceration of asylum seekers, tighter immigration controls, quotas and the introduction of citizenship tests all testify to a general government policy of filtering citizenship eligibility and, with it, entitlement to access welfare services.

Charities

For at least the last millenium, charities have played a distinctive role in moderating the civic contract.[2] In circumstances where government was unable to directly provide for the care and welfare of citizens, the burden of doing so was passed to charities, with costs offset by grants and/or tax privileges. Also offset by that delegation was the clarity of government responsibility and accountability, accompanied by an obscuring of citizens rights, in respect of such provision. Although contingent upon the varying degree of their welfare state experience, this arrangement typified the government/charity sharing of responsibilities in all Part II jurisdictions. It has led to the current position of uncertainty as to what government has a duty to do and what a citizen might expect by right or by charity.

There can be no doubt as to the significance of the difference for the recipient. Judt, having made the admittedly incontrovertible point that 'it is cheaper to provide benevolent handouts to the poor than to guarantee them a full range of social services as of right', then goes on to argue that this is not the case if we factor in the cost of the accompanying humiliation experienced by the recipient. Then 'we might conclude that the provision of universal social services, public health insurance, or subsidised public transportation was actually a cost-effective way to achieve our common objectives'.[3] In fact, any such full programme of public benefit provision, exclusively by government, would be extremely controversial and is probably becoming steadily more impractical given the present economic climate and demographic trends. However, his point that humiliation can bring with it a hidden cost in the form of debilitating personal damage, with a consequent dysfunctional impact on families and social groups, is very relevant.

---

2 Records show that many public benefit facilities such as schools and hospitals (e.g. St John's Hospital, Malmesbury which dates from the early 10th century) were founded by religious organisations with support from State taxes (e.g. King Edward's code promulgated at Andover in 963).

3 Judt, T., *When the Facts Change*, Penguin Press, New York, 2015, at p. 334.

In contrast, the social capital bonus that goes with the retention of self-respect when receiving an entitlement delivers a positive net gain to the recipient and their social circle.

For charities, the significance of their assuming a role as proxy government provider also carries a hidden cost. While it may offer a coveted social status, tax privileges and an entree to government policymaking, it also compromises their capacity to represent the interests of the socially disadvantaged. Charities, required by the law of trusts to maintain their independence, have long been expected to mediate between government and those in need: to be accessible to the latter and be able to advocate on their behalf. But charities in the pay of government are unable to effectively champion the cause of those neglected by government. For that reason, if for none other, it seems important that charities should not step into the shoes of government: they can be supplementary or complementary but not a substitute for that which government has a duty to provide and citizens a right to receive.

Arguably, the responsibilities of charity lie in contributing with government (or as aided by tax-exemption privileges) to basic public benefit service provision in less-developed countries and for supplementary domestic services such as community-based support organisations and special interest groups, for research units and piloting new ways of doing things, for maintaining cultural artefacts and heritage, caring for the environment, and for establishing 'added value' public benefit facilities such as parks and sports grounds etc. Involvement in matters such as those listed above as being of concern to the CRC may well compound or obscure government accountability for its failings.

Government/charity

It is trite but true to note that the *Pemsel* classification of charitable purposes, reflecting the social concerns of government in common law countries many centuries ago, no longer fits the spectrum of social disadvantage in what are now among the most-developed countries in the world. While it is not possible to start afresh with the remit of charity – because the bedrock of the nonprofit sector throughout the common law nations consists of charities and charitable institutions established for hundreds of years and destined to continue in perpetuity – it should be possible to clarify and shape its future path.

The division of government/charity responsibilities as embodied in the initial agenda of charitable purposes would not be so distributed today. Given that its core business is the care and protection of citizens, it would now fall squarely upon government to ensure that provision was made for matters fundamental to their wellbeing – such as the relief of poverty and the advancement of education – rather than be left to charitable discretion. Charity should not be the default for the most basic domestic responsibilities of government. An agenda of statutory *Pemsel* plus charitable purposes could be tailored and thereafter adjusted to suit the particular pattern of jurisdictional needs, with care being taken to ensure that charity does not stray into territory that belongs to other sectors (e.g. elite fee-paying schools) and that government retains responsibility for universal provision in respect of certain core services (e.g. drinking water and policing).

Where government and charity are to be conjoined in public benefit provision – as in health and social care services and some public utilities – then this hybrid entity should be distinctly branded, regulated and tax exempted as such. There are few limits on the potential extent of this government/charity category, the content and spread of which will probably vary in accordance with each jurisdiction's past experience of the welfare state and its future development of a government/sector partnership. It may well accommodate nonprofit and for-profit entities that also contribute to the collective public benefit. A specific legal framework would be required to govern and promote the growth of such collaborative ventures, and ensure they do not undermine core government responsibilities and are directed towards furthering civil society rather than just reducing government costs. The distinguishing characteristic of this nexus is that the public benefit provision must not compromise the integrity and independence of charity nor the basic civic contract duties of government.

In conclusion, it can, perhaps, be said that the 2015 European migrant crisis has triggered a more general awareness of what 'citizenship' means, of how vulnerable the status of 'citizen' has become, and of the related responsibilities of government. The challenge to civil society in the developed western nations as to how they should respond to the arrival of non-citizens fleeing countries now rendered dangerous and dysfunctional – due at least in part to the armed intervention of those western nations – will take time to work through, as will its implications for social democracy. The crisis has revealed the overwhelming importance of politics – international and domestic – relative to the wholly subsidiary and supplementary role of charities. It has certainly highlighted the growing importance of the UNHRC as monitor of government responsibilities and of failings that infringe citizens' rights – and the duties owed to non-citizens escaping imminent danger or pervasive dereliction.

Index

For Product Safety Concerns and Information please contact our EU
representative GPSR@taylorandfrancis.com
Taylor & Francis Verlag GmbH, Kaufingerstraße 24, 80331 München, Germany